Democratic Intergovernmental Organizations?

This work posits that, over the past two centuries, democratic norms have spread from domestic politics to intergovernmental organizations (IGOs). Alexandru Grigorescu explores how norms shaped IGO decision-making rules such as those driving state participation, voting, access to information, the role of NGOs, and transnational parliaments. This book emphasizes the role of "normative pressures" (the interaction between norm strength and the degree to which the status quo strays from norm prescriptions). Using primary and secondary sources to assess the plausibility of its arguments across two centuries and two dozen IGOs, the study focuses on developments in the League of Nations, International Labor Organization, United Nations, World Bank, European Union, and World Trade Organization.

Alexandru Grigorescu is an associate professor of political science at Loyola University Chicago. His research has been published in numerous journals such as the *International Studies Quarterly*, *Review of International Organizations*, *Journal of Conflict Resolution*, and *Ethics & International Affairs*. Prior to his academic career, between 1992 and 1997, he served as a diplomat in the Romanian Foreign Ministry and was posted at the Romanian Mission to the United Nations in New York.

D1260752

Democratic Intergovernmental Organizations?

Normative Pressures and Decision-Making Rules

ALEXANDRU GRIGORESCU

Loyola University Chicago

 CAMBRIDGE
UNIVERSITY PRESS

CAMBRIDGE
UNIVERSITY PRESS

32 Avenue of the Americas, New York NY 10013-2473, USA

Cambridge University Press is part of the University of Cambridge.

It furthers the University's mission by disseminating knowledge in the pursuit of
education, learning and research at the highest international levels of excellence.

www.cambridge.org
Information on this title: www.cambridge.org/9781107461864

© Alexandru Grigorescu 2015

First published 2015
First paperback edition 2015

A catalogue record for this publication is available from the British Library

Library of Congress Cataloguing in Publication data
Grigorescu, Alexandru, 1963–
Democratic intergovernmental organizations? : normative pressures and
decision-making rules / Alexandru Grigorescu.
pages   cm
ISBN 978-1-107-08999-0 (hardback)
1. International agencies – Management.   2. International agencies – Decision making.
3. League of Nations.   4. International Labour Organization.   5. United Nations.
6. World Bank.   7. European Union.   8. World Trade Organization.   I. Title.
JZ4850.G75   2015
341.2–dc23   2014047357

ISBN 978-1-107-08999-0 Hardback
ISBN 978-1-107-46186-4 Paperback

Achevé d'imprimer
en février deux mille quatorze, sur les presses
de l'imprimerie Gauvin, Gatineau, Québec

Contents

List of Figures	*page*	vii
List of Tables		ix
Acknowledgments		xi
1	Introduction: "Democratic" Intergovernmental Organizations	1
	The Question Driving This Book	1
	Placing the Study in the Broader International Relations Literature	4
	"Theorists" and "Practitioners"	12
	The Structure of the Book	15
2	Normative Pressures and Strategies for Defusing Them	19
	Existing Answers to the Question	19
	Normative Pressure	22
	Normative Pressure and Change	26
	Strategies for Reducing Normative Pressure	29
	Expectations Based on Arguments	38
	The Plausibility Probes	43
3	Fair State Participation	47
	The Norm	47
	A History of the Application of the Norm to IGOs	51
	Answering the Questions of the Study	75
4	Fair Voting	89
	The Norm	89
	A History of the Application of the Norm to IGOs	93
	Answering the Questions of the Study	118

5   Transparency   130
     The Norm   130
     A History of the Application of the Norm to IGOs   136
     Answering the Questions of the Study   163

6   Participation of Nongovernmental Actors in
     Intergovernmental Organizations   177
     The Norm   177
     A History of the Application of the Norm to IGOs   181
     Answering the Questions of the Study   210

7   Transnational Parliamentary Oversight   222
     The Norm   222
     A History of the Application of the Norm to IGOs   226
     Answering the Questions of the Study   251

8   Conclusions: Summarizing and Interpreting the Main Trends   263
     Summing Up the Answers to the Questions   263
     Plausibility of Hypotheses   267
     Theoretical and Practical Implications of the Findings   273

Works Cited   283
Index   311

Figures

1.1	Variance in the Impact of Normative Pressure on IGO Decision-Making Rules	*page 2*
2.1	Strategies of Challenging, Narrowing, and Broadening Norms and Actions	32
2.2	Variance of the Impact of Normative Pressure on IGO Decision-Making Rules	41
3.1	Average Political Participation Score of All States Across Time	49
3.2	Strength of Fair Participation Norms from 1920 to 2010	80
3.3	Degree to which Participation Rules Depart from Norm Prescriptions	81
3.4	Power Controlled by Permanent Members of League Council and UNSC	86
4.1	Average Franchise Score of All States Across Time	91
4.2	Proportion of World's Material Capabilities and World Bank Votes Controlled by the United States	112
4.3	Strength of Fair Voting Norm	120
4.4	Departure from Norm Prescriptions in World Bank: U.S. Voting Share vs. GDP Share	121
5.1	Proportion of States with Free Press and Freedom of Information Laws	132
5.2	Flow of Information from an IGO to the Public	134
5.3	Proportion (%) of Open League Council Meetings	142
5.4	Proportion (%) of Open UNSC Meetings	152
5.5	Number of Countries and IGOs Formalizing Public Access to Information	157
5.6	Strength of Transparency Norm	165

5.7	Departure from Prescriptions of Transparency Norm in League of Nations and UN	169
5.8	Number of Articles Discussing IGO Scandals	170
6.1	Average Level of "Civil Liberties" Scores of All States	179
6.2	Proportion (%) of NGOs Partnering with the League of Nations	187
6.3	Proportion (%) of International NGOs with Consultative Status in ECOSOC	190
6.4	Transnational Actor Access Index	203
6.5	Independence of Nongovernmental Representatives in ILO	204
6.6	Strength of Pro-NGO Norm	211
6.7	Degree to which League, ILO, and UN Depart from Pro-NGO Norm Prescription	212
6.8	Media Coverage of Anti-IGO Protests	216
7.1	Strength of the Parliamentary Oversight Norm Across Time	223
7.2	Domestic and International Models of Parliamentary Oversight	225
7.3	Original IPU Model of Parliamentary Oversight (before Emergence of IGOs)	229
7.4	Number of IGOs with Parliamentary Assemblies	250
7.5	Average Strength of the Parliamentary Oversight Norm Across All States	253
7.6	Support for Direct Elections of the EP	258

Tables

2.1	Actors' Strategies for Reducing Normative Pressures	*page* 31
2.2	Actors' Strategies for Reducing Normative Pressures and Possible Outcomes	41
3.1	Normative Pressures Involving State Participation in IGO Bodies and Reactions to Pressures	78
4.1	Normative Pressures Involving IGO Voting Procedures and Reactions to Pressures	122
5.1	Normative Pressures for IGO Transparency and Reactions to Pressures	166
6.1	Normative Pressures Involving NGA Participation and Reactions to Pressures	214
7.1	International Parliamentary Assemblies in IGOs	248
7.2	Normative Pressures Involving Parliamentary Bodies and Reactions to Pressures	256
8.1	Distribution of Normative Pressure Across Cases	265
8.2	Distribution of Outcomes Across Cases	266
8.3	Relationship between Strength of Normative Pressures and Outcomes	268
8.4	Relationship between Normative Pressures and Number of Strategies Used	268
8.5	Relationship between Norm Strength and Strategy Choice	269
8.6	Relationship between Departure from Norm Prescription and Strategy Choice	269
8.7	Distribution of Strategies Used at the Norm Level	270
8.8	Distribution of Strategies Used at the Implementation Level	270
8.9	Relationship between Strategies and Outcomes	271

Acknowledgments

I cannot remember when I first began thinking about the topic of this book. As someone who grew up in one of the harshest modern-day dictatorships, I have long been interested in questions of democracy and democratization. With the end of the Cold War, I, and many other East Europeans in my generation, experienced an initial euphoria as we looked to "the West" for solutions to all of our political, economic, and social problems. As we began understanding the complexity of the issues facing us, we realized that our fate was strongly tied to the decisions of international institutions such as the European Union, the World Bank, and, in some cases, the United Nations. For us, many of these organizations were as much "the West" as their more visible member-states. When my career shifted more than twenty years ago from a physics laboratory to the halls of the United Nations and the International Organizations Department of the Romanian Foreign Ministry, my thoughts about these two apparently disparate topics – democracy and intergovernmental decision making – began coming together, continuously changing and adding more questions than answers.

As I later traded a diplomatic career for an academic one in international relations, I became even more interested in understanding how two important post–Cold War processes (the growing role of intergovernmental organizations and the spread of democracy) relate to each other. Initially, my work focused on the effects that one particular democratic change to intergovernmental organizations (increased transparency) had on domestic politics. Later, I became fascinated by many different examples of intergovernmental organizations (IGOs) mimicking domestic democratic mechanisms (such as those involving NGO access or internal oversight). This book slowly grew out of all of these interests, bringing together two topics that stimulated my academic curiosity and simultaneously resonated with my personal experiences. In the end, all of the questions I was asking came together in one overarching question: How have democratic norms shaped IGO decision-making rules? This question drives this book.

As I began conducting the actual research to answer this question, my work led me to the archives and libraries of the organizations discussed here. I am grateful to the several dozen women and men working at the European Commission's Central Library, European Parliament's Library and Archives, Historical Archives of the European Union, International Labor Organization Archives, Joint World Bank–IMF Library, League of Nations Archives, United Nations Library and Archives in Geneva, and United Nations Dag Hammarskjöld Library. I would also like to thank librarians from the Loyola University Library and from the government unit at Northwestern University Library. I am particularly indebted to Phil Wilkin, from the University of Pittsburgh Library, for all of his help.

Various stages of my research and writing were supported through funding from Loyola University Chicago, the Woodrow Wilson Center for Scholars, the European Union Center of Excellence and European Studies Center at the University of Pittsburgh, and the European Union. I am grateful to all of these institutions.

Parts of this project benefited at different stages from the advice and feedback I received from a number of colleagues. I would like to extend my warm gratitude to all of them: Steven Bernstein, Tim Büthe, Klaus Dingwerth, Matthias Ecker-Ehrhardt, Erin Graham, Ian Hurd, Claudio Katz, Mathias Koenig-Archibugi, Ronald Krebs, Tobias Lenz, Molly Melin, Bob Reinalda, Thomas Rixen, Peter Sanchez, Jan Aart Scholte, Susan Sell, Dale M. Smith, Duncan Snidal, Thomas Sommerer, Theresa Squatrito, Jonas Tallberg, Emek Ucarer, Lora Anne Viola, Joel Westra, Michael Zürn, and four anonymous reviewers for Cambridge University Press. I am particularly grateful to Vince Mahler, who through subtle yet incisive advice, helped me truly understand what mentoring means among colleagues. This book (like much of my other research) would have been much poorer without his support and advice throughout the research and writing process.

I benefited greatly from the research assistance of the following graduate students: Jacob Hogan, Kimberly Loontjer, Jessica Mecellem, Natalie Moran, Samantha Seaman, Sarah Solari, Nelson Wainwright, and Andrea Walker. I wish to thank them all for their hard work.

I would also like to thank the editorial team at Cambridge University Press for the support and very efficient professional handling of the book project. I am particularly indebted to Robert Dreesen, who patiently walked me through my first (often overwhelming) book-writing experience.

Most important, I am deeply grateful to my family. This book would never have been possible without them. My parents, Valentina and Dan, instilled in me early on a sometimes annoying curiosity that later was transformed into a more healthy love of research – first in the physical and then in the social sciences. My wife, Arabela, through encouragement, kind words, and her belief in me, and my children, Vlad and Anna, through their contagious idealism (necessary for writing on such a topic), have helped me through the most difficult times of research and writing. I dedicate this book to the five of them.

This book has been produced with the assistance of the European Union. The contents of this book are the sole responsibility of Alexandru Grigorescu and can in no way be taken to reflect the views of the European Union.

Introduction: "Democratic" Intergovernmental Organizations

The Question Driving This Book

There is general agreement that, over the past two centuries, democratic norms[1] have become increasingly powerful. This trend has produced pressures on states to embrace democratic rules and practices domestically. However, national governments are not the only entities affected by democratic norms. Decision-making in organizations and among groups of individuals at all levels involves procedures that we often describe as "democratic." Fair voting procedures, fair representation, and access to information have come to be expected from decisions in forums as diverse as company boards of directors and student organizations. The pressures to adopt such practices are often present even in organizations from countries that are not themselves democratic.

I argue that such pervasive democratic norms have influenced even decision-making at the highest level of human interaction, that of intergovernmental organizations (IGOs), where billions of people are being represented by a small number of decision-makers. The main question driving this study is, *how* have democratic norms shaped IGO decision-making rules?

This book shows that, for democratic norms to influence IGO rules, it is not sufficient for them to be "strong" – that is, to be broadly accepted. In addition, the rules that are in place need to be perceived as departing substantially from the norm prescriptions. When both such conditions

---

[1] Throughout this book I refer to "norms" based on the broad understanding of the term in international relations as "shared expectations about appropriate behavior held by a community of actors" (Finnemore 1996, 22).

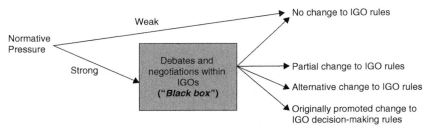

FIGURE 1.1. Variance in the Impact of Normative Pressure on IGO Decision-Making Rules.

are in place, actors are under "normative pressure" to change the rules. Furthermore, as Figure 1.1 illustrates, even when such pressures are strong, there is variance in outcomes. In other words, there have been some instances when strong normative pressures have led to changes to IGO rules but also other instances when they led to only partial changes, alternative changes, or even no changes.

To explain this variance this book proceeds to open up the "black box" of debates and negotiations in IGOs of Figure 1.1. I show that, when IGO member-states are under normative pressure to make rules more similar to democratic models from the domestic realm, it is rare for them to simply accept the proposed changes. In most cases, some states (usually the most powerful ones that want to maintain control of the IGO) seek to alleviate the pressure by attempting to alter (1) the interpretation of the democratic norm itself or (2) its implementation to IGOs. Each of these two broad approaches to reducing normative pressures can be broken down further into three more specific ones: (a) "challenging," (b) "narrowing," (c) "broadening" the interpretation of the norm or its implementation. Together, these approaches generate six possible strategies of defusing normative pressures: challenging the norm (CN), narrowing the norm (NN), broadening the norm (BN), challenging application of norm (CA), narrowing the application of the norm (NA), and broadening the application of the norm (BA).

I find that the choices of strategies are in great part dictated by the strength of the norm and the degree to which the status quo departs from the prescription of the norm. In turn, the strategies chosen to defuse normative pressures greatly determine the outcomes (illustrated on the right side of Figure 1.1). Specifically, they determine whether changes to the rules will be the ones originally proposed by those seeking reforms or whether we will see partial or alternative changes. It is through such indirect processes that democratic norms come to shape IGO rules.

As I will show in Chapter 2, the main question of this book is of great importance for ongoing debates in the broader international relations (IR) literature. Most important, an approach incorporating the role of democratic norms can account for some changes to IGO rules that existing scholarship has difficulties explaining. There are, indeed, other important factors besides norms that shape IGO rules. Previous research has convincingly shown that power considerations (e.g., Mearsheimer 1994) and effectiveness (e.g., Koremenos, Lipson, and Snidal 2004) underlie the design of IGOs. This book asks whether these two approaches can fully account for the establishment and changes of many important IGO rules (Wendt 2001a). For example, such approaches have difficulties explaining the inclusion of non-permanent members in the League Council (after initial plans envisioned the body to include only five permanent members) or even in the United Nations (UN) Security Council. They also offer incomplete explanations for the compromises underlying the voting procedures developed in the World Bank and the International Monetary Fund (IMF) in which each country was originally allotted a number of votes proportional to its quota contributions as well as 250 basic votes. These approaches also have little to say about the changes in access to information rules that followed important crises of legitimacy in some IGOs, such as the resignation of the entire European Commission amid corruption charges or the Seattle protests against the World Trade Organization (WTO), both in 1999. I argue that many such rules can only be understood fully by complementing arguments related to power and effectiveness with those considering the impact of normative pressures deriving from domestic democratic analogies.

The main question of this book also has become increasingly important for practical reasons. Many of the world's biggest problems – from wars to major environmental threats and from economic crises to fast-spreading diseases – can best (and sometimes only) be addressed in global or regional intergovernmental forums. Decisions of IGOs can affect billions of lives and, therefore, need to be done "right." But what does that actually mean? Some may claim that the effectiveness of IGOs' decision-making and their eventual actions and policies is more important than the way such decisions are made. However, most agree that there is no real choice between effectiveness and appropriateness. Both are necessary, being sometimes referred to as the "output" and "input" facets of an organization's legitimacy, respectively (Scharpf 1997; Zürn 2000 and 2004). Decisions that are not perceived to be legitimated by a "fair" decision-making process are less likely to be accepted by those who need to implement them, whether these are states or non-state actors. This is especially true in a world that increasingly expects democratic procedures at all decision-making levels (Woods 1999).

The current ubiquity of the term "democratic deficit" is a reflection of such increased expectations that IGOs adopt decisions in a democratic fashion. Although the term was first coined in the 1970s to characterize, narrowly, the irrelevance of the European Parliament in decisions of the European Economic Community (Mény 2003; Featherstone 1994), it is now applied to express the lack of democratic mechanisms in almost every existing IGO, from the International Whaling Commission (e.g., Kuyper 2013) to the International Monetary Fund (e.g., Nye et al. 2003). By addressing the question of how democratic norms have impacted rules in IGOs, this book will implicitly contribute to the rich literature on the democratic deficit by assessing the changes in the democratic character of international institutions and sparking more research on ways to reduce this deficit.

The most important practical implication of this book derives from its finding that democratic norms indeed can alter IGO rules that, in turn, affect international relations. For example, the use of democratic norms to include small- and medium-sized states such as Belgium and Spain in the influential League of Nations Council exacerbated international tensions in the years leading to World War II. The establishment and later empowerment of the European Parliament by those promoting a more democratic organization spurred European integration over the past half century. Democratic pressures to give labor and employer representatives an independent role in the International Labor Organization (ILO) facilitated important international agreements and constrained the adoption of others. The World Bank and WTO have accepted public information policies under pressures from those invoking democratic norms. These changes, in turn, have empowered some states and nongovernmental groups and weakened others. Currently, regional power struggles are being shaped by the use of democratic norms to promote the admission of countries such as Brazil and India as permanent members in the UN Security Council. In sum, democratic norms matter. They play a significant role in IGOs and, more broadly, in international relations.

Placing the Study in the Broader International Relations Literature

A study of the influence of democratic norms on the functioning of intergovernmental organizations necessarily speaks to at least two broad bodies of IR literature: one on norms and their impact on actions in the international realm and a second on the applicability of democratic principles to international relations. The literature on norms (and the study's connection to it) will be discussed in detail in Chapter 2. Here I only mention the main contribution of the present research to that literature.

Rather than simply discussing how some actors promote norms and others are either convinced of their appropriateness or shamed into action without any "fight" on their part (as much of the early literature on norms has suggested), this book emphasizes actors' multiple possible reactions to normative pressures. I suggest that states have seldom accepted the application of democratic norms to IGOs as originally promoted by those seeking reforms. Conversely, they seldom withstood the normative pressures without taking any actions. In the vast majority of cases, they have reacted to such pressures by attempting to alter the interpretation of the norm or the actions prescribed by the norm. The relative success of these strategies for defusing normative pressures has resulted in different degrees of acceptance of the original norms and, implicitly, of the decision-making rules. The strategies have also led to changes in other IGO rules and/or other organizations as "side-payments" to those responsible for the pressures.

This section primarily focuses on the second body of literature mentioned earlier – global democracy. I consider the arguments of this scholarship here, in an introductory chapter, as it places this book's main question in a broader context. More importantly, I use the following literature to tease out five main types of democratic rules that are considered to be the most significant ones applicable to decision-making in IGOs.

The vast majority of IR literature has taken one of the four following positions regarding the relationship between democracy and IGOs, the topic of this book:

1. It dismissed the question altogether as one that does not merit attention (e.g., Wight 1960).
2. It explained why we should be skeptical of any meaningful relationship between democracy and interactions in the international realm (e.g., Dahl 2001).
3. It sought to identify a set of fairly narrow democratic mechanisms (especially focusing on accountability) that are applicable to IGOs and called for their improved implementation (e.g., Keohane and Nye 2000b; Florini 2003).
4. It discussed IGOs as essential elements in moving toward a comprehensive system of "global democracy" and therefore elaborated

a broad set of democratic expectations for such organizations (e.g., Held 1995; Holden 2000; McGrew 2002; Archibugi, Koenig-Archibugi, and Marchetti 2012).

The last two bodies of literature offer important starting points for the present research and are further discussed in the following sections.

The Literature on IGO Accountability

Most of the IR literature acknowledges the current lack of democratic character of IGOs (often referred to as their "democratic deficit"). However, the third body of literature mentioned earlier suggests that we should not hold international institutions to domestic democratic standards but rather seek the kinds of mechanisms that would make them more legitimate and/or effective (e.g., Woods 1999; Keohane and Nye 2000b). It therefore tends to focus on the decision-making processes in IGOs that are seen as those in which the domestic democratic analogy has the most to offer and leaves out broader discussions involving important aspects of a democratic polity, such as those about human rights.[2]

This third body of literature primarily emphasizes accountability as the key democratic characteristic that is relevant to the functioning of IGOs (e.g., Keohane 2001; Florini 2003; Kahler 2004; Grant and Keohane 2005). It begins from the argument that states have always collectively held IGOs accountable and that such governmental links between IGOs and the general public need to be improved (Keohane 2005; Grant and Keohane 2005). In addition, some scholars have emphasized the role of the European Parliament holding the other European institutions accountable (Caporaso 2003; Moravcsik 2004), and others have sought to extend the parliamentary model of accountability from the European Union (EU) to other international institutions (Nye et al. 2003, 33–46; Slaughter 2004b; Held 1995). Many authors have highlighted the important role that nongovernmental actors (primarily transnational nongovernmental organizations) have played as transmission belts through which the general public can hold IGOs accountable (e.g., Benner, Reinicke, and Witte, 2004; Scholte 2004; Tallberg and Uhlin 2012; Tallberg et al. 2013, 19). Still others have discussed the development of additional mechanisms of "horizontal accountability" such as

---

[2] For an exception, see Caporaso 2003. The reason Caporaso is able to incorporate a discussion of human rights (alongside accountability) into an assessment of IGO democracy is that he focuses on the European Union, one of the only IGOs that has a truly functional judiciary system in which individuals rather than states can file cases.

IGO ethics offices, internal and external oversight bodies, or ombudsmen (Woods and Narlikar 2001; Woods 2003; Grigorescu 2008).

Virtually all of this literature has underscored the importance of IGO transparency for accountability. Transparency – the ability of outside actors to access information about decision-making processes and actions – is generally seen as a precondition for all types of accountability and, more broadly, for the effective functioning of such organizations (e.g., Keohane and Nye 2000b; Florini 2002; Grigorescu 2007). It allows governments, transnational parliamentary assemblies, nongovernmental actors, and even the general public to determine whether IGOs are performing their duties in effective and appropriate ways.

All of these arguments suggest that multiple actors are involved in a struggle for holding IGOs accountable and, implicitly, for controlling such organizations. Such main actors are governments of member states, transnational nongovernmental actors, parliamentary assemblies, and the general public. Their abilities to control IGOs both shape and are shaped by the decision-making rules. Not surprisingly, each of the existing struggles over who holds the IGO accountable corresponds to one or more democratic norms discussed at the domestic and international levels: (1) fair representation in decision-making, (2) fair voting, (3) participation of representatives of civil society in decision-making and implementation of decisions, (4) parliamentary oversight of the executive, and (5) public access to information.

The Global Democracy Literature

The idea of any type of global government is generally perceived as utopian.[3] One of the most common reasons cited for the difficulties in achieving democratic global governance is the lack of a global (or even regional) political community. It is often argued that the heterogeneity of the world's (or even a region's) population makes it difficult to determine the "general good" or common interest of such a polity, something without which democracy simply is not possible (Dahl 2001, 26).

To counter this statement, David Held has argued that political communities have changed over the ages. For centuries, democracy implied the physical gathering of individuals in public spaces. It was only toward the end of the eighteenth century that representative democracy replaced

---

[3] Several surveys among both policy makers and the general public found that more than two-thirds of respondents considered a world government (whether democratic or not) either a bad idea or implausible. See, for example, Chase-Dunn et al. 2008 and Koenig-Archibugi 2011.

the initial paradigm of direct democracy (1995). Held contends that we are currently moving to a form of "cosmopolitan democracy" that associates the political community with not only the national one but also a global one (2001).

Cosmopolitan democracy is not a utopian system for future global governance, according to Held. It is a necessary model – and the only viable one – as the locus of power has shifted from the national level to the regional and global levels and as individuals' lives are increasingly affected by international forces (Held 2000, 26). He argues that such global changes have led to five major "disjunctions" between the formal domain of political authority and the actual practices and structures of the state and economic system (Held 1995, 99). These disjunctions derive, on the one hand, from the continued emphasis of state sovereignty as the main principle of international relations and, on the other hand, from five international trends that are eroding such sovereignty: (1) the development of international law, (2) the increased role of IGOs entrusted with collective policy problems, (3) the ability of great powers and military blocs to impose their will on others, (4) the development of individual loyalties that transcend nation-states, and (5) the globalization of production and financial systems (Held 1995, 99–140).

To resolve these disjunctions, Held proposes a set of short- and long-term objectives that will allow us to attain the cosmopolitan model of democracy. They derive from his broader definition of democracy as "rule by the people" which implies that all individuals need to be represented and involved in decision-making and that rulers need to justify their actions to the ruled (implicitly, to offer information about decisions) and be held responsible for their actions by representatives of the people (Held 1996, 3).

The short-term objectives deriving from such an understanding of democracy are especially relevant for the study of democratic decision-making in IGOs. They include the reform of the UN to alter the veto system and to give smaller states greater representation and voice, the establishment of a UN second chamber modeled after the European Parliament and of more regional parliaments (with a goal to establish a global parliament in the long run), and the establishment of "broad avenues of civic participation in decision-making at regional and global levels" (Held 1996, 353–359).

This cosmopolitan model of democracy stands in contrast to the communitarian one. Although both models take the individual (rather than the state) as a point of departure for understanding democracy, communitarianism emphasizes social ties among individuals. The communities that form on the basis of such ties deserve respect and protection. Communitarians therefore see states (which often, but not always, overlap with such communities) as important entities that need to be represented in a global democracy just as much as individuals need to be represented (Bienen, Rittberger, and Wagner 1998, 301–302).

The two models of democracy are often seen as complementary. Indeed, Held's proposed objectives for the cosmopolitan model do not do away with existing state representation mechanisms in IGOs; they add to them. However, as some of the cases in the following chapters show, when states had different interests in shaping IGO rules (whether they debated fair representation, fair voting, or the role of transnational parliamentary assemblies), their arguments often pitted one democratic model against the other.

We should point out that Held's model also includes other short-term objectives such as the creation of an international human rights court, the establishment of an international military force, "experimentation with different organizational forms in the economy," and provision of resources to those "in the most vulnerable social positions" (1995, 279–280). Yet these innovations involve the establishment of new institutions that have not yet been truly discussed and negotiated by practitioners. Therefore, we have very little indication of the ways in which states interpreted such additional democratic norms and their implementation to alter decision-making rules in ways that benefit them, the topic of this book.

Building on Held's arguments, Mathias Koenig-Archibugi shows that there are even more possible "paths" toward achieving global democracy besides Held's intergovernmental one (which involves changing existing IGOs and establishing new ones). There is also a "global movements" path (involving transnational networks of nongovernmental organizations), a "laborist" path (based on the transnational organization of labor unions), a capitalist path (driven by transnational business interests), a "functionalist" path (involving networks of specialized bureaucracies), and an imperialist path (in which the dominant power takes the initiative to achieve a global democratic system) (2012, 177–178). Yet, Koenig-Archibugi, like virtually all authors writing on the advancement of global democracy, considers the democratization of IGOs a necessary part of this process.

While acknowledging the importance of these additional democratic norms and mechanisms for future developments, the present study nevertheless limits itself only to those within IGOs, the focus of this book. Additionally, I limit my discussion only to norms and mechanisms discussed by Held that have already been applied to IGOs and, more importantly, that have already been shaped by the debates and negotiations in IGOs – that is, within the "black box" of Figure 1.1. The book's approach is therefore primarily an empirical one, seeking to identify past long-term trends. It only derives some brief conclusions regarding possible future developments. Yet, even in such cases, I do not seek to advance a normative agenda (even though I examine norms) by promoting one particular democratic model over another. In fact, one of the main arguments of this book is that the dynamics of rule changes in IGOs have been so complex and interesting precisely because there are multiple plausible understandings of what democratic global governance entails.

How the Book Complements Existing Literature

The aforementioned literature on IGO accountability and global democracy are primarily relevant for this book because they help us identify the specific elements we need to focus on when assessing the evolution of democratic norms in IGOs. Indeed, the concept of democracy, especially as applied to IGOs, is not a self-evident one (Caporaso 2003, 365). The literature has offered many different definitions of democracy and even more conditions for achieving it. In fact, as this book shows, it is precisely because of the complex nature of this concept that actors have been able to alter its interpretations to fit their goals. At best, we can only identify the main components of democracy from existing studies.

Although, as this book shows, some such components sometimes clash with each other, overall, it is generally assumed that they are all important for moving closer to democratic standards. This is especially pertinent as recent literature on democracy at the domestic level has shown that in this third wave of democracy there is a danger that polities become "illiberal democracies" by embracing only elections and a handful of other democratic components and leaving out others such as civil society participation in the political process and access to government-held information (Zakaria 1997).

As mentioned, the IGO accountability literature emphasizes five important democratic norms that need to be applied to such organizations: (1) fair representation in decision-making, (2) fair voting, (3) participation of representatives from civil society in decision-making and in implementation of decisions, (4) parliamentary oversight of the executive, and (5) public access to information. While the global democracy literature also considers the possibility of establishing additional international institutions such as an international human rights court and an international military force, the same five aforementioned principles can be identified among those that need to be applied to current IGOs to move toward a more democratic global system.

These five norms already identified by the existing literature as relevant for IGO accountability and democracy are the main focus of this book. These norms are also chosen because they simultaneously drive and reflect power relations among the most important actors in international relations: governments, transnational parliaments, nongovernmental actors, and the general public. The study of how norms influence IGO decision-making rules is therefore also significant for understanding the direction and degree of the broader changes in relative power among the main actors in the international realm.

While existing scholarship offers a starting point for this study by identifying the main norms that are relevant for an IGO's democratic character, beyond this point, the book departs from this literature. I do not consider the present study to be one of IGO accountability or one of democratic global governance. Rather, the research seeks to complement these bodies of literature in several ways. First, I suggest that existing works tend to discuss the present advances in IGO accountability and democracy (and sometimes possible future advances) in isolation from past developments, considering that the recent trends are specific only to the post–Cold War era (e.g., Florini 2003). Second, even the most complete studies of democratic advances usually discuss the five aforementioned types of democratic changes in IGOs in isolation from each other (e.g., Tallberg et al. 2013). This approach is the result of built-in assumptions that such democratic advances have taken place at the same time.

The present research questions both previous assumptions. It argues that IGOs have struggled with normative and practical aspects of applying democratic norms to their decision-making processes for a long time. It offers evidence that the degree to which democratic rules were applied to IGO decision-making did not advance in a linear fashion across time. Also, it shows that the application of democratic rules to IGOs sometimes did not go hand in hand with their advancement across states (i.e., with the strength of domestic democratic norms). Lastly, the various democratic norms did not advance simultaneously; in fact, at times, when IGOs appeared to advance one democratic dimension, another seemed to erode. These observations lead to important answers to the initial question driving this book regarding the impact of democratic norms on IGO decision-making rules.

This book departs in yet another important way from existing literature on democratic global governance. As I explain, it moves away from some of the broad questions of *whether* we should strive for democratic global governance and *whether* we can actually transform IGOs into democratic entities (that are essential for the normative literature on global democracy). It, rather, seeks to understand *how* IGOs have actually been altered over more than a century in response to calls for greater democracy. The patterns we can discover by taking this approach offer some indication of where IGOs are in fact headed.

"Theorists" and "Practitioners"

Despite the previous emphasis on the study's connections to the scholarly literature, this book also speaks to practitioners of international relations. Indeed, there is a discrepancy between the academic discourse on global democracy and the one among officials who are actually involved in shaping IGO rules and who are responsible for moving such organizations toward more democratic practices. IR theory, on the one hand, has tackled (as well it should) the broader questions regarding the possibility of democratic global governance, focusing on ideal types of governance, the long-term processes that may lead us to such ideals, and possible "mid-range" solutions to improving IGO democracy and/or accountability. Practitioners, on the other hand, tend to emphasize short-term goals, whether these are ones of their country, their organization, or, very often, their own personal preferences. For instance, a foreign minister from a country vying for permanent membership in the UN Security Council (UNSC) would consider that she has been very successful by obtaining support for the country's candidacy for such a position from one or, better yet, two great powers. Most likely, this would increase her political clout back home. Similarly, a small country's ambassador to the UN would be thrilled to initiate a change in rules allowing for increased access to information about certain aspects of the organization's work that would lead to benefits for a number of member-states (and not just for the general public). If the initiative is successful, the individual's chances of being elected for a prestigious (and well paid) position within the organization's secretariat may increase. Both such individuals may use the language of "democracy" and emerge as promoters of democratic norms in negotiations over decision-making rules. Moreover, it is even possible that they believe in the appropriateness of such changes to the IGO rules. However, even in such cases, I suggest that their actions are driven as much (if not more) by their immediate goals as by long-term lofty democratic ones.

IR theorists usually view IGO reforms in a holistic fashion, emphasizing end results, whereas practitioners tend to focus on immediate and very specific proposals for changes that may or may not fit with their broader view of how they would want the organization to eventually function. Examples of such changes are the establishment of a working group to discuss the addition of permanent or non-permanent members to an IGO body, the modification of the calculus used for the weighted voting system, the opening of certain types of meetings or documents to the press and public, the inclusion of some types of nongovernmental organizations (NGOs) in the implementation of IGO programs, or the addition of a specific oversight task to the ones the IGO parliamentary assembly is already entrusted. The debates surrounding such actions are often clothed in the language of democracy, adding to the normative pressure for change. Those opposing such changes seek arguments or actions to defuse the pressures. The changes that eventually take place in IGOs and that may be presented as democratic advances are the result of painstaking negotiations among those who gain and those who lose by adopting them. It is rare that a specific democratic model is accepted by all relevant international actors and then transposed to an IGO identically as in the domestic realm (Grigorescu 2008).

As the following chapters show, there are many instances in which officials used democratic norms based on domestic analogies to promote certain rules in IGOs. One of the most famous examples of democratic language applied to the functioning of an IGO (even if it refers only indirectly to its decision-making rules) is the opening phrase of the UN Charter: "We the Peoples."[4] When the U.S. delegation to the 1945 UN Conference on International Organization proposed that the UN Charter begin with those words (analogous to the first words of the U.S. Constitution), officials from a number of other governments opposed the idea. Representatives of several states (both autocratic and democratic) argued that in their constitutions "authority did not rise from the

---

[4] These words are considered even today to reflect the efforts to make the UN a more democratic IGO. The IGO's Web site notes: "Although the United Nations Charter includes no mention of the word 'democracy,' the opening words of the Charter, 'We the Peoples,' reflect the fundamental principle of democracy, that the will of the people is the source of legitimacy of sovereign states and therefore of the United Nations as a whole" (United Nations 2013).

people but came from above, from the throne" (Schlesinger 2003, 237). The U.S. representatives eventually prevailed. One of them later explained the American position in the following way: "[T]he fact that in many countries of the world the people were not (and still are not) sovereign could not be permitted to disturb the American principle that all authority derives from the people" (Bloom 1948, 278). In the end, the wording remained as the Americans had suggested, but other clarifying legal sections were added to the document.

Other debates at the founding of the UN used democratic normative pressures to promote even more meaningful (if not more symbolic) changes to the draft Charter, such as those involving the number of seats in the UNSC, the use of the veto, or the transparency of future deliberations. As this book shows, such debates surrounding the meaning of democracy and its application to IGOs took place many times in many other organizations over more than a century.

The presence of such pressures, based on domestic analogies, should not surprise us. After all, IGOs are forums in which groups (typically states) are being represented and in which such representatives adopt collective decisions, most often by casting votes that are supposed to reflect their groups' preferences. The votes lead to decisions that all members are then encouraged (and in a few cases, obligated) to accept. Often IGOs also allow representatives of subnational groups (such as ethnic minorities, labor unions, and employers) and supranational interests (transnational nongovernmental organizations or multinational corporations) to take part, and in a few cases even to vote, in the decision-making and decision-implementing processes. In addition, IGO actions are being monitored by the press and by interest groups that publicize the work of such organizations and criticize some of their decisions. In many cases the public uproar with regard to IGO policies and actions, as in the case of the Oil-for-Food scandal in the United Nations (Gordon 2006) or the building of the World Bank's Sardar Sarovar Dam project in India (Udall 1998), have led to changes in the way such IGOs function. In all of these instances, decision-making rules in IGOs (involving participation, voting, or public access to information) seem to mimic democratic ones that have been applied at the state level for some time.[5]

This book combines both the academic and practitioners' perspectives on the application of democratic mechanisms to IGOs. On the one hand, I take a long-term view of developments in such organizations, which

[5] For examples of the application of domestic institutional analogies to IGOs see Reus-Smit 1997 and Burley 1993. For a comprehensive discussion of such analogies to the international realm see Suganami, 1989.

is characteristic of analytical scholarly approaches. On the other hand, the cases I focus on across time are individual moments when practitioners were engaged in debates involving specific changes to rules. The end result of my research is an account of almost two centuries of struggles between the main international actors involved in shaping some of the most important decision-making rules in prominent IGOs. Although the main actors influencing IGO rules were generally member-states, NGOs, domestic and transnational parliaments, and even IGO officials also affected the outcomes. These struggles often involved changes that in fact constituted material, institutional, and normative package deals among those engaged in the negotiations. I suggest that the pressures democratic norms generated contributed significantly to shaping IGO rules over time.

By focusing on what practitioners describe as "democratic" and on how they use democratic norms to promote their interests, the book complements the existing scholarly literature that discusses whether IGOs are democratic and whether they can become more democratic. Conversely, by highlighting existing debates in the scholarly literature discussing the multiple kinds of democratic norms and mechanisms that are applicable to IGOs, I offer an analytical approach identifying important trends that have characterized the changes in actual rules across IGOs and across time. A book meshing the theoretical and practical perspectives on the application of democratic norms to IGOs is relevant both to debates among IR scholars and those among policy-makers.

The Structure of the Book

The following chapter discusses in greater depth the norms literature and how my research and arguments speak to existing scholarship. I show that, when states have been under strong democratic pressures to accept rules that ran counter to their interests, they sought to defuse the pressures. They have done so by attempting to reshape the interpretation of the norms that were at the basis of the actions they were being pressured to take or, directly, to reinterpret the actions that derived from such norms. They did not do so simply by arguing against such norms and rules in IGOs or by seeking to limit the way in which they would be applied. Very often, they simultaneously discussed multiple norms and actions and bargained on the final outcome. Sometimes the end result of such *normative bargaining* was that the norms and rules that were considered very important to states (usually those involving participation and voting procedures) remained unaltered, whereas other norms and rules that were less important (such as transparency and nongovernmental actor participation) were changed. In other cases states allowed for changes to rules in some IGOs (that were less important to them) to alleviate pressures for giving up their advantages in the ones that were of greater importance. Regardless of the strategy used by those opposing the application of democratic norms, in the majority of cases some change to the IGO rules indeed did take place. Even powerful states could not withstand strong democratic pressures for long periods of time without taking some action to defuse them. The changes brought about by the pressures and, more importantly, by the reaction to pressures, could not be understood if one were to focus solely on one single norm (as much of the literature has). One cannot neglect the linkages between the multiple norms that, at the domestic level, we have become so accustomed to bring together under the broader umbrella of "democracy."

My theoretical arguments lead to a series of expectations regarding the conditions under which (1) actors will seek to alter the interpretation of the norm or its application, (2) they will apply one or multiple strategies of defusing normative pressures, (3) they will prefer certain strategies over others, and (4) the normative pressures and strategies of defusing them will lead to different types of changes. Chapters 3 through 7 test the plausibility of these arguments by following developments in IGOs across more than a century. The research is based on primary sources and, when not available, on secondary ones. It seeks to identify in such sources the arguments used in official debates surrounding the reform of IGO decision-making rules.

Each of the empirical chapters focuses on one of the five democratic norms listed earlier and on the history of the application of the rules prescribed by such norms to IGOs: fair state participation (Chapter 3), fair voting (Chapter 4), transparency (Chapter 5), participation of nongovernmental actors in the work of IGOs (Chapter 6), and oversight through international parliamentary assemblies (Chapter 7).

The chapters follow the evolution of these norms (and the rules they shaped) across long periods of time. They do so to show that democratic norms have played an important role well before the most recent democratic wave of the post–Cold War era. Just as important, the long analytical time frame allows me to identify many critical junctures when democratic normative pressures were applied (successfully or not) to adopt or change certain rules. In most chapters, I trace the first signs that such democratic norms influenced rules in the international institutions as far back as the nineteenth century.

Although an ideal test of the arguments would take into account developments in all IGOs, in practice this is not possible. This study therefore selects only a subset of such organizations: the League of Nations, International Labor Organization, United Nations, World Bank, European Union and its precursors, and World Trade Organization and its precursor. The multiple considerations underlying the choice of IGOs are discussed in greater depth in Chapter 2, outlining the main arguments and tests. For now, I simply mention that the six IGOs are relevant for this study because they are among the most prominent ones. It is more compelling to show that democratic norms shaped decision-making rules of even such significant IGOs, in which important national security and economic interests are expected to be the main factors shaping decision-making rules. In addition, the IGOs are selected because they were established at different times. The League and ILO formed immediately after World War I. The UN and World Bank emerged after World War II. The WTO and EU were established after the end of the Cold War (although both had important precursors during the Cold War). The temporal differentiation between the six IGOs is important because one expects variation in the strength of the democratic norms that led to normative pressures at the founding of these IGOs.

The study considers all significant moments when democratic pressures were applied to establish or change each of the five types of decision-making rules in each of the six IGOs. For each such case I seek to answer a similar set of questions that allows me to assess the impact of normative pressures and strategies to defuse them on changes to decision-making rules: What types of decision-making rules were being established or changed? Did actors invoke democratic norms to pressure others in accepting new decision-making rules? How powerful were such pressures? What actions did actors opposing the new rules take under normative pressure? What were the outcomes of the attempts to adopt or change rules? Would outcomes have been the same in absence of normative pressures and reactions to pressures?

Although the seventy-two cases discussed in this book do not allow for rigorous statistical tests of the study's arguments, they do nevertheless allow us to assess their plausibility. These critical junctures, together, hint at a series of important patterns regarding the relationship between normative pressures and change in IGOs. I discuss these patterns and offer several theoretical conclusions in Chapter 8.

In practical terms, the book finds that all five democratic norms have indeed impacted the rules of virtually all IGOs across time. Although one certainly cannot yet characterize IGOs as "democratic" (at least by purely domestic standards), the general trend over more than a century has been one that has taken such IGOs closer to domestic democratic models. I conclude comparing this trend to the one in the domestic realm and suggest several possible directions for future developments in IGOs.

Normative Pressures and Strategies for Defusing Them

Existing Answers to the Question

How do democratic norms come to shape IGO rules? The international relations literature has not yet offered a comprehensive answer to this question. For a long time, it did not even acknowledge any role for such norms. Realism, the dominant theoretical approach to the field for many decades, has explained IGOs and their rules as reflections of the material power structures (Mearsheimer 1994). Other rationalist approaches emphasized the role of additional factors, beyond power, in explaining the rules of such organizations. Some of these explanations were based on a broad understanding of institutional inertia that treated such organizations as having a "life of their own" (e.g., Keohane 1984; Krasner 1983). Others focused on the need for effectiveness in the working of IGOs (e.g., Koremenos, Lispon, and Snidal 2004).

Several other bodies of literature, ranging from international law to economics, have exhibited an interest in the impact of norms on human behavior for some time. In IR, both the English School and Regime Theory emphasized norms as important explanatory factors. With the post–Cold War constructivist turn in IR (Checkel 1998), interest in this subject area increased. Dozens of works that emerged throughout the 1990s showed that norms truly mattered. In other words, they affected behavior of international actors. The main goal of this literature was to offer evidence that actors behaved differently in the presence of a specific norm than in its absence. The cases discussed early on by constructivists were examples of norms constituting actors' identities (and, implicitly, shaping behavior) as well as regulating their behavior, even when the norms were not completely internalized.

In the mid- to late 1990s some of the realist-constructivist debates (Mearsheimer 1994; Wendt 1995) and, just as important, several critiques from constructivists themselves (Checkel 1998; Finnemore and Sikkink 1998; Legro, 1997), led to a second wave of literature that refined the initial arguments, asking a different but related set of questions: When are norms more likely to have an impact on individuals' actions? What types of norms are more likely to have an impact on such actions? Also, very important for the present book, How do norms affect actors' actions?

The first question asked by this new wave of norms literature led to an increased interest in the evolution (Florini 1996) and life cycle (Finnemore and Sikkink 1998) of norms. Those addressing this topic focused on the emergence of norms, their empowerment, and the pathways through which they traveled to reach international actors. The process through which weak norms became more powerful through actions of *norms entrepreneurs* (Finnemore and Sikkink 1998; Risse-Kappen, Ropp, and Sikkink 1999) generated particular interest as it allowed for a focus on not only structures but also agents.

The second question, regarding the types of norms that are more likely to have an impact, led to a particularly strong interest in the explanatory power of a norm's *specificity* or *determinacy* (the degree to which the guidelines for restraint and use are clearly defined) (Legro 1997, 34; Florini 1996, 376), its "concordance" (the degree of intersubjective agreement on the norm among actors) (Legro 1997, 35), and its "resonance" with other norms (the degree to which the norm fits with other existing ones) (Checkel, 1998).[1] This literature has found that the more specific a norm is, the greater concordance there is among actors regarding its relevance, and the more it resonates with other existing norms, the greater its impact will be.

The third question regarding the processes through which norms alter behavior has led to important research on the degree to which they are accepted, institutionalized, and internalized (not necessarily in that order). This research, in turn, led to greater interest in operationalizing the strength of norms, beyond the dichotomous presence-absence approach of the first wave literature (Goertz and Diehl 1992; Legro 1997, 33; Simmons 2009). It also led to a broad body of work on how

---

[1] Similar terms used are *coherence* (e.g., see Florini 1996; Rittberger 2004, 13), *cultural match* (Cortell and Davis 2000), *congruence* (Acharya 2004), or *grafting* (Price 2003).

norms are used in persuading actors to change their actions (Payne 2001; Herrmann and Shannon 2001; Krebs and Jackson 2007).

I draw from this second wave constructivist research to explain the impact of democratic norms on IGO decision-making rules. In line with the literature discussing the life cycle of norms (Finnemore and Sikkink 1998), I argue that the process begins with the export of democratic norms from the domestic level to the international one. However, before a norm is promoted by and through IGOs, it needs to be sufficiently powerful in the states where it originated. Democratic norms based on long-standing domestic models only reach IGOs after they are strong among multiple member-states.

Although democratic norms originate at the domestic level, they do not "float freely" (Risse-Kappen 1994). This book, therefore, identifies the actors promoting the democratic IGO rules. Specifically, as such rules are adopted by member-states, I focus primarily on the battles among states for framing norms and their implementation. I show that nongovernmental organizations, secretariats, members of national and transnational parliaments, and even public opinion have played important roles in promoting the norms. However, the role of such secondary actors has generally been an indirect one, adding support to the cause of one group of states or another involved in a struggle to shape IGO rules.

Drawing from the literature dealing with norm specificity and resonance, I seek to identify multiple democratic norms and assess their varied impact on IGO rules. I also refer to this literature in emphasizing how different democratic norms interacted with each other as well as with other norms, sometimes resonating and other times clashing.

Lastly, I use arguments from the second-wave constructivist literature to explain in greater detail the processes through which norms affect behavior. I posit that the actions of states and other actors involved in shaping IGO rules can be explained, in part, by their propensity to abide by norms and mechanisms involving the logic of appropriateness. I also argue that such norms are often promoted instrumentally on the basis of a logic of expected consequences.[2] The degree to which such actors find a balance between the two logics will depend, in part, on the strength of the

---

[2] I acknowledge that, at times, it is difficult to draw neat lines between the types of norms that affect behavior (regulative vs. constitutive) or, more broadly, between the various types of logics of action. For a more complete discussion of these problems, see e.g., Risse 2000; Sending 2002; Müller 2004. I nevertheless seek to disentangle the various norms and, especially, the various logics to identify the types of arguments used in attempts to alter IGO rules or to defuse normative pressures.

democratic norms in play. Therefore, like the aforementioned literature, I also seek ways of operationalizing the strength of various norms in IGOs across time.

All of the previous factors drawn from existing constructivist literature are nevertheless not sufficient to explain the impact of norms in shaping IGO rules, as illustrated in Figure 1.1. In some cases, strong democratic norms, promoted by a large number of important actors using convincing arguments, led to the adoption or changes of IGO rules, and other times it did not.

The remainder of this chapter offers two additional arguments to explain the variance in the impact of democratic norms on IGO decision-making rules. In the following section I discuss the relevance of normative pressures (rather than simply of norm strength) on actors' actions. Then, I emphasize the role played by opponents of changes to IGO rules. One of the most important arguments of this book is that the way in which the literature has often portrayed actors simply accepting norms and internalizing them without a fight or, alternatively, withstanding norms without taking any actions to meet demands is not accurate. Additionally, I argue that those actors who are promoting the norms and those opposing them negotiate with each other and eventually reach normative bargains that shape such rules. The arguments therefore are intended to complement existing literature by offering an explanation that considers outcomes as being shaped by actors' constantly fluid strategies that are, in turn, adapting to a similarly fluid normative and material environment in a process of mutual constitution between structures and agents (Wendt 1987).

Normative Pressure

The first important argument this book makes is that a major driving force behind changes in IGO rules is the "normative pressure" that develops. Although the term "pressure" is used often in IR writings, its meaning is not adequately explained. I define normative pressure as the interaction between the strength of a norm at a certain point in time (that is, its general acceptance by actors) and the degree to which the status quo departs from the norm prescription in a particular case. This implies that, even if democratic norms are strong at one moment, the pressures for change in a particular case may not be great unless there is a situation that is visibly inappropriate. Conversely, even if a situation is viewed by a handful of actors as highly undemocratic, the normative pressure to alter the status quo is expected to be low if democratic norms are weak – that is, if most actors do not embrace the norms.

The impact of norms on specific cases can only be a diffuse one. They travel across states and levels of governance *because* they are not precise and are applicable to different entities and situations. Pressure, on the other hand, only affects a specific case when it is perceived that something is truly inappropriate in a given situation. For that reason, normative pressure is dictated not only by how powerful the norm is but also by how actors interpret its application to the case at hand.

The distinction between the concepts of strength and pressure follows the analogous one in physics, from which we, social scientists, have borrowed the terms. In physics, pressures are greater when (1) the force that is being applied is strong and (2) the force is concentrated on a very small surface. A force that is distributed across a larger surface does not have as significant effect as the one that is narrowly distributed. In the social realm, one similarly expects that a norm will have a greater impact when its promotion is concentrated toward a specific, flagrant, instance of norm non-compliance rather than toward multiple different instances. The concentration of normative efforts usually takes place when the status quo is seen as departing substantially from what is expected on the basis of the norm.

A pertinent example of the relationship between norm strength and norm pressure is the one surrounding the 1965 addition of four non-permanent seats to the UN Security Council. As Chapter 3 will show, the strength of the fair participation norm was generally constant throughout the UN's first two decades of existence. Yet the normative pressure to expand the Security Council with more non-permanent seats was less in 1954, when 56 countries were vying for 6 non-permanent seats in the Council, than in 1964 when UN membership had almost doubled and 104 countries were coveting the same 6 seats. The increased normative pressure in 1964 was because the norm was being more blatantly violated than it had in 1954. In other words, over those ten years, it was the UN's drift away from the norm's prescription that altered normative pressures and contributed to the 1965 expansion of the UNSC, not the increased strength of the democratic norm of fair representation.

Normative pressures can increase or decrease when the norm strengthens or weakens, respectively. However, such pressures also vary after events that trigger indignation or, conversely, complacency. In IGOs there are therefore two factors that increase the likelihood of democratic norms having an impact on a specific rule: (1) the norm strength and (2) the lack of conformity to the norm in one particular instance.

The focus on normative pressure, rather than norm strength (as in existing literature), already implies a first answer to the question of how democratic norms shape IGO rules. Democratic norms, even when strong, are more likely to have an impact on IGO rules when they are accompanied by strong perceptions that the rule departs considerably from what the norm prescribes.

As mentioned earlier, this book starts out from the assumption that the democratic norms applied to IGOs originated in the domestic realm. Individuals who were socialized within such norms in their domestic environment are more likely to apply them to IGOs than those who were not. This argument does not imply that democratic states are always going to support the application of democratic norms to IGOs. There are other norms that may clash with the democratic ones (such as the sovereignty norm). Moreover, states' material interests may clash with the application of such norms to IGOs. However, all other things being equal, we expect that the more powerful the democratic norms are across member-states, the more likely it is that member-states representatives to IGOs will be socialized in such norms and, implicitly, the more likely it is that the IGO will adopt decision-making rules that are similar to domestic democratic ones.

Therefore, the strength of a democratic norm at the IGO level is considered to be reflected by the aggregate support it receives from its member-states. The measure of "democratic density," calculated as the average Polity democracy score for all members of an IGO, is often used as a gauge of the strength of such democratic norms in that organization (Pevehouse 2005; Grigorescu 2007; Tallberg et al. 2013).

However, as mentioned in Chapter 1, not all democratic norms go hand in hand. Therefore, this book differentiates between multiple types of democratic norms and develops separate measures of participation, voting practices, transparency, strength of civil society, and parliamentary oversight, at the domestic level. I then use these measures to assess the strength of the five norms across time in IGOs. To allow for comparisons between the five norms, I establish a common method for determining their strength. Whenever possible, I consider all values for the strength of each norm across the period between 1920 (after the League of Nations and ILO, the first two major IGOs discussed in this book, were established) and present day. I then scale all such values from 0 to 1, with 0 being the minimum norm strength for the time period and 1 the maximum. I consider values in the top third as reflecting high levels of norm strength (H), those in the middle third as moderate strength (M), and those in the bottom third as low strength (L). Developing these three categories (rather than using scores) makes it easier to compare developments across time and norms. It is also important to note that this gauge, based on domestic levels of democracy, allows me to assess the strength of norms in IGOs independently of the effects attributed to them, as the literature suggests (Legro 1997, 33).

I develop separate measures of the second component of normative pressure, the degree to which the application of the norm departs from the norm's prescription. I do so in a way that also allows it to be independent of its effects. I first identify the interpretation of the norm's application to IGO rules, as presented by those actors promoting reforms. It is such interpretations that are behind the normative pressures for change. For instance, small and medium states have often implied that, the fewer non-permanent seats there are in an executive body and the more IGO members compete for such seats, the less "fair" the system of representation is. Therefore, in the case of fair participation, I gauge the degree to which the application of the norm departs from its prescription in the UN by calculating the number of states vying for each non-permanent seat in a given year. Similarly, I gauge the degree of an IGO's transparency by assessing the proportion of meetings that are open to the public in a given year, as this interpretation is used by states promoting access to information reforms. I then distinguish between times when the degree to which the status quo departed from the norm prescription was high (H), moderate (M), or low (L), using, whenever possible, analogous cutoff points as in the assessment of norm strength.

In addition, I consider moments when new IGOs were established and assess the degree to which the new rules differ from past IGO rules. This is especially important as past practices shape actors' expectations regarding the new institutions. For example, the initial attempt to establish an exclusive League of Nations Council, in which only five powerful states would be represented, was seen as a case of a new rule straying from what the fair participation norm dictated. This was in great part a result of the practices of the previous century when formal IGOs, even if they were technical in nature, were always inclusive. Similarly, in 1945, when the UNSC was established, it was considered to stray substantially from what the norm of fair voting prescribed because all previous IGOs had either accepted equal voting (as in the League and ILO) or weighted voting, but did not accept a differentiated veto system. Such instances of IGOs establishing new rules that differ substantially from those in previous IGOs also are considered cases with high levels of departure from norm prescription.

Normative pressure is then assessed by considering the level of both components: norm strength and departure from norm prescription. When both factors are high (H), normative pressure is considered to be very high (VH). When one component is high (H) and the other is moderate (M), the pressure is high (H). When one component is high (H) and the other is low (L), the pressure is moderate (M). I consider cases in which both components are moderate (M) as cases of moderate pressures (M). Those cases in which one component is moderate (M) and the other is low (L) are of low pressures (L). Lastly, when both the strength of the norm and the departure from its prescriptions are low (L), the pressures are very low (VL).

Although I define pressure as the interaction of two factors, like many other composite variables (including the one of pressure in the physical sciences), it can be observed independently of its two components. One example of changes in the observed normative pressure is discussed in Chapter 7 and focuses on the empowerment of the European Parliament (EP). I show that, although the domestic democratic norms in support for parliamentary oversight were consistently very high among Europeans, the support for the application of the norm to the international level, by empowering the EP, increased only when the European Council was being established and the intergovernmental character of the organization grew substantially. The increase in public support for direct elections for the EP in the late 1970s was therefore a reflection of the (consistently) strong parliamentary oversight norm as well as of the changes in perceptions that the norm was being seriously violated in the European Economic Community. Unfortunately, there are few other opinion polls conducted on IGO rules (especially over time). The following chapters nevertheless suggest other possible direct measures for normative pressures.

Normative Pressure and Change

Normative pressures can increase or decline. As the earlier definition implies, they can become very strong when the norms are themselves empowered. This is usually the result of structural changes, such as the power shifts at the end of the Cold War that translated into the strengthening of democratic norms in the post–Cold War era. Yet, structural changes are not unidirectional. They can also lead to the erosion of certain norms (such as was the case of slavery or colonialism norms). Democratic norms were themselves eroded in the interwar era with the rise of fascism and during the Cold War with the spread of communism. They became powerful again for a short while after World War II and, then again, even more powerful after the fall of the Soviet Union.

Alternatively, normative pressures can become stronger when it is increasingly clear that the rule strays considerably from the norm prescription. This, too, can be triggered by structural factors such as the growth in membership that preceded the 1960s UNSC reform, mentioned earlier. The decline in League membership in the 1930s (and, implicitly, the reduction in the number of states vying for non-permanent seats in the League Council) is an example of how structural factors can also lead to smaller departures from norm prescriptions and, implicitly, to reduced normative pressures, not just increases in such pressures.

Yet another structural change that can increase normative pressures is the spread of a certain type of rule or mechanism across IGOs (such as public information policies or internal oversight offices) that alters understandings about what is truly an appropriate application of such norms. These "horizontal diffusion" mechanisms function both at the domestic and IGO levels (Grigorescu 2010). Once some IGOs embrace certain types of rules, the expectations for their adoption in other IGOs are higher and normative pressures also increase.

The increase in normative pressures can also be the result of individual agents' actions. The corruption scandal that led the European Commission to step down in 1999, the Oil-for-Food scandal in the UN, and the resignation of World Bank President Paul Wolfowitz are examples of agents inadvertently increasing normative pressures very quickly. Because of the relevance of scandals in increasing normative pressures, I take them into account when gauging the degree to which IGO rules are departing from norm prescriptions.

Of course, agents can also act purposefully to increase normative pressures. After all, most reform campaigns in IGOs (or in any organization for that matter) need "norm entrepreneurs" to spearhead the efforts for change (e.g., Sunstein 1996; Finnemore and Sikkink 1998). Lastly, as the following section will show, agents can also act to alleviate such normative pressures when they do not support the actions that are being promoted by those applying the pressures.

Indeed, actors often react to normative pressures because it is difficult to withstand them for long. Most of us have probably been under normative pressure to take one action or another many times. While the international realm is traditionally seen as the locus of power politics and less of actions derived from norms, such pressures are also applied to official state representatives. Government officials are used to keeping a straight face and not divulging that they are under pressure. Nevertheless, that does not mean that they do not feel pressure.[3] In many cases officials can withstand the pressures without taking any actions. But in many others they react by seeking ways to reduce them.

Even by focusing solely on the most important global institutions of each era (such as the League of Nation's Council and the UNSC) and on the two most important decision-making rules for states (state participation in IGO executive bodies and voting procedures), where power politics, not norms, are generally considered to have shaped outcomes, one would notice that over the years there have been many attempts to use democratic norms to pressure great powers into altering the rules. Such norms were successfully invoked, for instance, in 1919 by small states that wanted the addition of non-permanent seats to the newly established League of Nations Council. As mentioned earlier, a similar successful attempt unfolded in the 1960s, when the UNSC decided to add four more non-permanent seats.

Other attempts were partially successful. In the 1930s small states invoked the democratic norms again when attempting twice to increase the size of the League of Nations Council, but the increase was smaller than what they had requested and was only "temporary." Similarly, the strong democratic pressures of the post–Cold War era have not been successful in altering the composition of the UNSC or the veto system but have instead led to greater transparency and informal rules allowing both small states and non-state actors increased access to the decision-making process. Although democratic norms were not involved, arguments related to fairness led even the great powers of the post-Napoleonic era to alter their original plans regarding the composition of the Concert of Europe and the participation rules in other international forums.

---

[3] An example of an official under normative pressure captured on film is that of Ambassador Valerian Zorin, Soviet Permanent Representative to the UN during the Cuban Missile Crisis, in his famous exchange with the then U.S. ambassador Adlai Stevenson. Footage of that UNSC meeting shows a nervous Zorin being hounded by Stevenson to acknowledge that the Soviet Union indeed was placing missiles in Cuba. Zorin refused to give a straight answer to Stevenson's questions but his uneasiness was evident throughout the exchange, especially after the American famously declared that he was willing to wait for a straight answer (thus prolonging the pressure) "until hell freezes over" and that he would present evidence that the missiles were indeed being installed.

There were also many instances of democratic pressures not leading to any changes in IGO rules, such as the ones that promoted direct elections of the European Parliament in the 1950s and 1960s. Pressures also did not lead to any changes in 1979–1980, when they were used to promote an increase in UNSC membership.

There are, of course, many more cases of successful, partially successful, and unsuccessful attempts to use such democratic norms in pressuring states into altering decision-making rules involving participation, voting, nongovernmental actor involvement in IGO work, transparency, and oversight of IGO bodies by parliamentary bodies. The multiple possible outcomes of applying such normative pressures was illustrated in Figure 1.1, which showed that even when normative pressures are strong, debates and negotiations among states (and sometimes nongovernmental actors) can lead to different outcomes involving decision-making rules.

To determine the factors that affect the final outcomes of such debates and negotiations, one needs to move beyond the traditionally static model usually discussed in the norms literature that implies having norm entrepreneurs empowering and promoting norms that, in turn, affect actors who do not defend themselves from such normative pressures in any way (Bob 2009, 12; Checkel 2012). States act strategically by seeking arguments or actions that will alleviate the normative pressure. How do they react? Which reactions will lead to no changes, partial changes, alternative changes, or proposed changes? These additional questions will be discussed in the following section.

In addressing these questions, the book proceeds to open the "black box" of Figure 1.1, which involves the negotiations and debates leading to such decisions and investigates the mechanisms linking normative pressures to actors' actions. By tracing the process through which some actors applied pressures to alter IGO rules and others sought to defuse such pressures, I identify the factors that can explain the variance in outcomes across time and IGOs. In other words, I uncover the intervening variables between the normative pressures and changes of rules.

Strategies for Reducing Normative Pressure

What can state representatives do when they are under normative pressure to take a certain action that they do not want to take? Before answering this question one should, of course, ask whether they need to react in any way. The realist view implies that states, particularly powerful ones, can withstand such pressures indefinitely without having to react to them.

Yet there are many reasons why states, even powerful ones, will not consistently withstand the pressures derived from violating a norm. For example, their ability to gain support for future actions sometimes relies on the soft power (Nye 2004b) that, in part, comes from embracing generally accepted norms.

Also, if the states are members of an IGO, they are likely interested in maintaining the legitimacy and, implicitly, the effectiveness of the organization. It is difficult to maintain such legitimacy while withstanding changes that a large number of actors are seeking to bring about using norms-based approaches. Indeed, there is an important body of literature that shows how states act strategically (often by altering rules) to legitimize organizations that are important to them and how such legitimation is based to a great degree on the IGO's compliance with norms (e.g., Hurd 2005, 2007). This literature nevertheless tends to focus on individual rules, such as those guiding NGO access to IGO work (e.g., Tallberg et al. 2013, 34–40) or transparency (e.g., Grigorescu 2007), overlooking the fact that actors can choose from among multiple types of IGO rules that can be reformed and, moreover, that there are many different ways to reform them. The choices for such reforms need to be better understood.

At the individual level, government officials who can find ways of reducing "pesky" demands for rule changes in IGOs are often rewarded by their superiors. Therefore, in most cases, most actors will do something to alleviate the pressures; they need to find a "pressure valve" (to continue the analogy with the physical sciences).

There are two main strategies to reduce such pressures short from yielding to them and accepting the exact action the actors are being asked to take. They derive from the definition of normative pressures: actors can either attempt to alter the interpretation of the norm or of its implementation – that is, the actions that are seen as deriving from the norm. In the former, they seek to weaken the norm's strength. In the latter, they seek to weaken the degree to which the status quo is seen as departing from norm prescription.

These two broad approaches to reducing the normative pressures can be further broken down into three types of strategies – *challenging*, *narrowing*, and *broadening* – thus generating six possible options. The strategies are illustrated in Table 2.1. The most facile (but not necessarily most common) strategies of "yielding" to pressures (through which actors accept both the norm and the actions being prescribed) or

TABLE 2.1. *Actors' Strategies for Reducing Normative Pressures*

Type of Action	Challenge	Narrow	Broaden
Alter interpretation of norm	1. Challenge appropriateness of norm	2. Limit interpretation of norm	3. Promote additional norms together with original one
Alter interpretation of norm implementation	4. Challenge application of norm	5. Limit application of norm	6. Promote additional actions beyond those for which pressures are exerted

"withstanding" them (which implies that the actor does not take any actions to reduce the normative pressure and does not accept any of the proposed changes) are not captured in the table.

The challenging strategy (the main one discussed in the norms literature) implies a *rejection* of the "appropriateness" of the norm or of the ability to apply it in that particular instance. The narrowing strategy entails accepting either only some interpretations of the norm (but not all of the ones considered by those promoting the norm) or only some of the actions (but not all of the ones being promoted). Broadening implies either promoting other norms (presented as coming under a broader normative umbrella) in addition to the one used to apply normative pressures or promoting other actions in addition to the ones being sought by other actors. This section expands on the earlier definitions of the six strategies, offering examples of each of them. Figure 2.1 helps illustrate the strategies and examples.

A first possible option for an actor faced with pressures to take Action A, which runs counter to the actor's interests, is to challenge Norm X, on which such pressures are based, as illustrated in Figure 2.1. The actor can of course challenge directly the appropriateness of the norm itself. However, more often, when the norm is already strong, the strategy implies invoking other norms that clash with the one being promoted.

Indeed, norms rarely exist in isolation from each other. There are always multiple contested norms that vie for superiority. As some norms

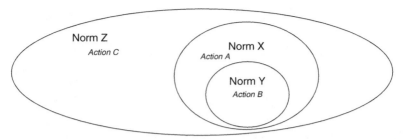

FIGURE 2.1. Strategies of Challenging, Narrowing, and Broadening Norms and Actions.

Eight Possible Reactions to Normative Pressure Deriving from Norm X to Take Action A:

1. *Yielding to pressure* involves accepting Norm X and Action A which are being promoted by others.
2. *Challenging norm* involves arguing against Norm X.
3. *Narrowing norm* involves accepting Norm Y (a *sub-norm* of Norm X) but not Norm X.
4. *Broadening norm* involves promoting Norm Z, which subsumes both Norm X and other norms.
5. *Challenging action* involves arguing against Action A.
6. *Narrowing action* involves supporting Action B, but not action A.
7. *Broadening* action involves accepting Action A but also promoting Action C.
8. *Withstanding pressure* involves not accepting Norm X or Action A and not arguing against them.

rise, others may erode (see e.g., Sandholtz and Stiles 2009). Surprisingly, the literature on the interactions among norms in IR is still underdeveloped (for an exception, see, e.g., Cortell and Davis 2005). In fact, the literature has more often emphasized the clashes between the material and normative implications of actions (sometimes labeled logic of expected consequences vs. logic of appropriateness) rather than the normative clashes.

There are many examples of such clashing norms that are often invoked by competing sides in the international arena. Ideological clashes, such as the ones between the Western and Eastern blocs of the Cold War, often pitted multiple norms against each other. The norm of sovereignty has been used very often to challenge norms such as the ones underlying the promotion of human rights and democratization across states. Sovereignty has also been invoked when challenging the promotion of norms of peace keeping or nuclear non-proliferation. The civilian protection norm has been countered with arguments involving the antiterrorism norm (Replogle 2013).

As the following chapters will show, democratic norms in IGOs have also clashed in multiple instances with the norm of sovereignty. One such example, discussed in Chapter 4, took place in 1919, at the founding of the League of Nations. At that time, small states pushed for the adoption of a majority voting system, invoking democratic norms to boost their case. Powerful states countered this norm, emphasizing the greater relevance of the sovereignty norm and, implicitly, the need to maintain unanimity voting on substantive issues both in the Council and in the Assembly.

When narrowing the norm, actors claim that the proposed understanding of what is appropriate (Norm X) is too loosely defined and, in fact, only a more narrowly understood sub-norm (Y) is truly acceptable. Such a strategy has been used, for example, by those suggesting that only individual (and not group) rights are true human rights. This implied that group rights did not carry the moral strength that the more traditional individual human rights carry (Donnelly 2005). A strategy of narrowing the norm being promoted in an IGO was used, for example, by those opposing greater public access to WTO information. Chapter 5 shows that many developing countries argued that "internal" transparency (involving the flow of information to all member-state representatives) was truly appropriate but that "external" transparency (to the public and, especially, to NGOs) was not. That was because they felt that domestic actors from the developed world would be in a much better position to make use of information releases than those from the developing world and, perhaps, even more than some governments.

The strategy of altering the normative environment through broadening involves an argument that it is not enough to focus on one norm (X) but, as long as certain norms and actions are being contemplated, we also need to consider other norms that fall under the umbrella of a broader norm, Z (in Figure 2.1). This strategy is yet another illustration of the possible interactions among norms mentioned earlier when discussing the challenging strategy. However, in this case, those resisting the normative pressures for change seek norms that resonate (rather than clash) with the main norm being promoted. Indeed, the constructivist literature has discussed such resonance as an important form of norm interaction with a great deal of explanatory power (e.g., Checkel 1997; Risse-Kappen et al. 1999, 272).

An example of the norm-broadening strategy applied in the international realm unfolded in the late 1990s. At that time, the World Bank began developing its anti-corruption programs after it decided to broaden its focus from development to "good governance" (Doornbos 2003). This normative shift was seen by many developing countries as a necessary deal they had to strike with developed states that wanted to use the World Bank to promote political changes along with development aid (Brademas and Heimann 1998).

In the ILO, this strategy was used to broaden the understanding of the participation norm. When developing countries invoked this norm to promote increased state membership in the ILO's Governing Body, powerful states argued for a broader understanding of this norm that also subsumed the norm of nongovernmental actor participation (and that applied to representatives of labor and employers). This allowed them to link the proposed reforms to Governing Body state membership to representation of independent nongovernmental representatives.

Although the strategy of broadening that involves developing *normative package deals* is a very common one, it has not been sufficiently studied. It has two potential benefits for the actor promoting it. First, it can empower a norm that the actor considers useful for its interests by allowing it to piggyback on an already strong norm. The linkages that developed states in the World Bank emphasized between the anti-corruption norm and the already accepted development one allowed them to boost the former (McCoy 2001). If, on the one hand, a proposed package deal is reached by states, the actor at least gets something in return for accepting the action it is pressured to take. If, on the other hand, the package deal is not accepted (but the link between norms remains strong), the actor will have at least shifted some of the normative pressure from itself to other states by having inserted additional normative considerations in the debate.

Of course, a precondition for such a broadening strategy to work is that the multiple norms that the actor wants to bring together need to either resonate sufficiently or to fit under the umbrella of a broader norm, such as the one of sovereignty, human rights, or democracy. In fact, an important conclusion of this book is that the original (facile) framing by small states of participation and voting rules in IGOs as questions of democratic practices and the traditional linkages between multiple democratic norms (plural) have allowed powerful states to adopt on multiple occasions strategies of broadening in the negotiations and debates over decision-making rules. These, in turn, have led to important alternative changes to IGO rules that, in time, have become significant, such as the empowerment of the European Parliament or the increased transparency of the UNSC.

One should distinguish the mechanism of framing norms that I refer to earlier from those based on the logic of communicative action discussed by Risse (2000). The latter logic implies that the actors who come together in negotiations are open to any possible collective solution. It also emphasizes mechanisms through which actors are persuaded of the appropriateness of one specific norm or another. In fact, I join those who are skeptical about the possibility that international actors will actually be persuaded in their interactions with each other (Payne 2001). State representatives almost never concede on a normative argument during negotiations by switching their original position.[4] At most, they may be "maneuvered into a corner" and trapped into accepting an action because of strong arguments for which they cannot find a "socially sustainable rebuttal" (Krebs and Jackson 2007, 36, 42).

The mechanisms that I discuss are, rather, forms of strategic social construction (Saurugger 2010, 472). The main difference between such a process and the ones based on the logic of communicative action is that, while, in the former, persuasion does not take place during the rhetorical exchanges (as in the case of the latter) (Shannon, 2000), it may unfold after it is completed. The result of the normative negotiations will later shape norms and material structures and, implicitly, alter actors' interests. Yet this process in which the actors internalize the norm that has emerged from the lack of counterarguments will not be as immediate as the logic of communicative action implies.

The second broad type of reaction to normative pressures, represented in the bottom row of Table 2.1, is to alter the proposed implementation of the norm. The reasons offered for such changes to implementation are usually of practical (not normative) nature. When actors adopt a challenging strategy for the implementation of a norm (X), they often argue that although they support the norm, the action derived from such a norm is not possible. A well-known example of this approach is the

---

[4] This is especially true of state representatives who are agents of their governments (as opposed to heads of state in summit meetings). They cannot afford to be persuaded by other arguments because they may not be able (or even have the opportunity), in turn, to persuade their superiors or legislators who need to accept the deal they strike in the IGO. The gap between the two separate levels on which domestic and international interactions take place (Putnam 1988), and the long decision-making chains, makes persuasion even more difficult to achieve in the international realm than in the domestic one.

emphasis that Western states placed on the "justiciability" problem of economic and social rights – that is, the problems of protecting them through judicially enforceable obligations in national law. In the years immediately after World War II, the argument led some states to oppose the inclusion of such rights in a binding international treaty (e.g., Whelan and Donnelly 2007). This argument is different than one challenging the norm. In this case, many Western states acknowledged the appropriateness of promoting the norms underlying economic and social rights, but they simply argued that international treaties could not be used to implement them in practice.

In the case of IGOs, such a strategy of challenging the application of a norm often involves arguments suggesting that even though the norm is applied in the domestic realm, things are different in international relations. One example of this strategy is the one used by those opposing direct elections of members of the European Parliament in the 1960s. They argued that the electorate cannot make sufficiently informed and democratic decisions when selecting Europarliamentarians because it is not really aware of the technical aspects that the European bodies dealt with (compared to its knowledge of domestic issues). Therefore, they claimed that indirect selection of the Parliament would lead to a more effective outcome (not necessarily a more appropriate one) than the direct one.

Alternatively, an actor can agree both on the norm and on the kind of action that it dictates, but it can nevertheless decide to only take partial action toward its implementation (conceding only to action B but not to A in Figure 2.1). Sometimes, this decision is explained by the fact that not all actions the actor is asked to take derive from the norm. For example, when the United States was accused of engaging in torture against enemy combatants by using waterboarding, the Bush administration argued that it did not condone the use of torture and that the methods it used did not, in fact, constitute torture. To support this argument it emphasized that methods that did not cause severe physical or mental pain could not be considered torture (U.S. Department of Justice 2002). This limited, of course, the number of actions that would be seen as deriving from the anti-torture norm.

Yet, most often, narrowing strategies invoke the practical problems involving the complete acceptance of the proposed actions. A sobering example of the use of the narrowing strategy is the one in which the South African Constitutional Court ruled that a hospital and the government did not have an obligation to prolong a man's life through renal dialysis (although the case was presented on the basis of the right to life) because "the state's resources are limited" and it "has to manage its limited resources in order to address all such claims" (Constitutional Court of South Africa 1997). The government did not challenge the norm underlying the right to life. Nor did it deny that it should actually allow that individual to use renal dialysis, which could have been seen as a case of challenging the application of the norm. Rather, the issue at stake was the number of times that the treatment should be offered – in other words, the degree to which the government could allow for the costly procedure given the practical considerations related to its material resources.

In IGOs, there were many instances when the promotion of the norm of fair participation clashed with expediency. Chapter 3 will show that this was particularly the case in debates surrounding the increase in the number of members in IGO executive bodies such as the League Council, UNSC, ILO Governing Body, or World Bank Board of Directors when supporters of the status quo argued that large bodies do not allow for effective decision-making.

One category of partial acceptance of actions is the one in which, instead of acquiescing to a formal legal instrument, actors support the rule, but only informally. An instance of such strategy is the U.S. decision to support the Mine Ban Treaty informally by setting a moratorium on the production of land mines. This action reduces the normative pressure on the United States to join the official treaty, yet it allows it to later restart the production of such weapons more easily than if it were bound by the treaty. The following chapters will discuss many such cases in IGOs in which states narrowed the application of an important democratic norm (such as transparency, state participation, or nongovernmental actor participation) by accepting the implementation of informal rather than formal rules.

Lastly, an actor under normative pressure can adopt a strategy of broadening by accepting action A together with additional actions (C) that are included as side payments. Such a strategy is the normative equivalent to ordinary (material) bargaining situations. An example of such a strategy is, once more, that of the U.S. actions with regard to the Mine Ban Treaty. While the United States has not joined the treaty and continues to stockpile antipersonnel mines for future use, it has publicized the fact that it is the single largest donor to mine clearance and victim assistance programs around the world (Human Rights Watch 2011).

In IGOs the strategy of broadening the application of the norm was used fairly often in cases when multiple organizations were being established around the same time. Those opposing the application of the norm in a major IGO brought other international bodies into the conversation. In most cases, this strategy led to the application of the norm in the less significant IGO or in neither of the organizations because the negotiations became too complex. As I will show in Chapter 7, a pertinent example of this broadening strategy was the one used at the time that the Council of Europe and the European Coal and Steel Community were both establishing parliamentary assemblies.

Just as the first set of broadening strategies, used to alter the understanding of the norm itself, should not be understood as ones simply based on the logic of communicative action, the broadening at the level of actions should not be viewed as simple bargains involving only actions based on logic of expected consequences. As suggested earlier, the strategic options that an actor has to reduce the normative pressure are more successful when they are perceived as appropriate, on the basis of that respective norm. The United States will be more successful alleviating normative pressures involving the Mine Ban Treaty by emphasizing that its aid is going specifically toward mine clearance and land mine victim assistance rather than, for instance, building wells or roads (which are also worthwhile causes). The strategy of broadening is more effective if it involves the reshaping of the agenda by adding actions that are seen as deriving from the same norm, or at least from a norm that is seen as sufficiently close to the original one, most often coming under a broad common normative umbrella such as the one of democracy.

Expectations Based on Arguments

The previous arguments (as well as extensions of their logic) lead to a series of expectations. The following chapters will assess their plausibility.

First, I assess the "baseline" hypothesis of this study:

H_1: *Changes to IGO rules are more likely to take place when normative pressures are high.*

Yet, I argue that normative pressures alone cannot account for change because actors can respond to such pressures through various strategies. Therefore, the outcomes are determined by a combination of the strength of norm pressure and the strategies chosen.

How do actors choose strategies to defuse norms? First of all, as suggested, actors can choose to apply one or more strategies. I expect that the greater the normative pressure, the more likely it is that actors will choose more strategies because they are more eager to find at least one that works. This suggests the following:

H_2: *The stronger the normative pressure for change, the more likely it is that actors will seek multiple strategies to defuse them.*

Whether they decide to apply one strategy or more, the first important decision in selecting how to best defuse normative pressure is whether to attempt to alter the interpretation of the norm itself or its application to the specific case. I suggest that this decision is not random. Actors are more likely to attempt reshaping the weaker of the two components of normative pressure. They will seek to reshape the interpretation of the norm when it is weak rather than when it is strong. Also, they are more likely to attempt to reshape the interpretation of its application to a specific case when the norm does not depart too much from norm prescription. When the departure from norm prescription is too great, and the status quo blatantly contradicts standards of appropriateness, it is more difficult to argue against that specific interpretation of norm application.[5] These arguments lead to the following two expectations:

H_3: *When under normative pressure, actors who want to avoid changing IGO rules are more likely to attempt altering the interpretation of the norm when the norm is weak than when it is strong.*

H_4: *When under normative pressure, actors who want to avoid changing IGO rules are more likely to attempt altering the interpretation of how to apply the norm to the IGO when the status quo does not depart much from the norm prescription than when it departs substantially from such prescription.*

Once actors decide on the level of the strategy used to defuse normative pressures (norm or implementation), they will need to select whether to apply a challenging, narrowing, or broadening approach. I suggest that this second decision also is not random. When deciding to alter the norm itself, they will prefer the broadening strategy to the narrowing one and, especially, to the challenging one because the broadening strategy is the safest at this level. It does not contradict existing understandings of the main norm being discussed. It simply adds other normative prescriptions

---

[5] Of course, when normative pressure is high, it is likely that both norm strength and the status quo's departure from norm prescriptions are high. That does not mean, of course, that actors will not seek strategies to defuse the normative pressures, especially considering our expectations on the basis of H_2. Rather, it implies that they will act at the level where they expect the greatest relative success. In other words, even when the departure from the norm's prescription is great, those seeking to defuse normative pressures for change may nevertheless seek to alter the interpretation of the application of the norm if the norm itself is very powerful (as they are less likely to "attack" that norm).

derived from similar norms, usually under the same broad umbrella. Moreover, the broadening strategy generates more complex debates that can lead to a stalemate (no change), which is the preferred outcome of those attempting to block changes to rules.

When deciding to adopt a strategy to alter the application of the norm, actors will prefer the narrowing strategy to the broadening one and to the challenging one because arguments involving the application of norms are more specific than ones about the appropriateness of norms. Therefore, such debates can lead to more fine-tuned solutions. They often involve pitting the norms against practical considerations. It is easier to select strategies calling for intermediary solutions somewhere between what the norm dictates and what effectiveness calls for. These arguments lead to the following two expectations regarding the type of strategy an actor will use within the broader approaches of altering the interpretation of the norm or its application:

H_5: *When under normative pressure to change IGO rules that they do not want to change, actors who attempt to alter the interpretation of a norm will prefer the broadening strategy to the narrowing strategy and to the challenging strategy.*

H_6: *When under normative pressure to change IGO rules that they do not want to change, actors who attempt to alter the interpretation of the application of the norm will prefer the narrowing strategy to the broadening strategy and to the challenging strategy.*

H_3–H_6 refer to strategy choices. Yet such choices are only the intervening variables between normative pressures (that, as suggested, dictate the choices) and outcomes. To offer a complete understanding of when norms shape IGO rules, we need to also consider the arguments connecting the strategy choices to the final outcomes.

Figure 2.2 opens the "black box" of Figure 1.1. It shows that each of the strategies discussed in Table 2.1 is conducive to one type of outcome from Figure 1.1: no change, partial change, alternative change, or the originally promoted change.

The strategies and their likely outcomes are brought together in Table 2.2. This table takes the two rows of Table 2.1 with the possible strategies for reducing normative pressure and adds one more (shaded) row that specifies the likely outcome of each strategy. It shows that challenging strategies, when successful, are likely to stop the proposed changes to the rules. Narrowing strategies are likely to lead to only partial changes to IGO rules. The broadening strategy, whether applied at the level of normative environment or at the one of specific actions, leads

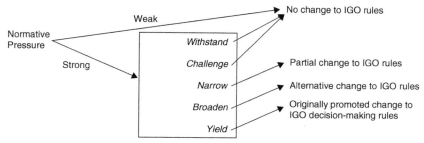

FIGURE 2.2. Variance of the Impact of Normative Pressure on IGO Decision-Making Rules.

TABLE 2.2. *Actors' Strategies for Reducing Normative Pressures and Possible Outcomes*

Type of action	Challenge	Narrow	Broaden
Alter interpretation of norm	1. Challenge appropriateness of norm	2. Limit interpretation of norm	3. Promote additional norms together with original one
Alter interpretation of norm implementation	4. Challenge application of norm	5. Limit application of norm	6. Promote additional actions beyond those for which pressures are exerted
Likely outcomes	No change to IGO rules	Partial changes to IGO rules	Alternative changes to IGO rules

to more complex debates. Depending on actors' abilities to promote their preferred norm or action, the broadening strategy will result in the proposed change as well as an additional change or in an alternative change (without the proposed one). Moreover, when additional norms or actions are included in the conversation, the result may lead to a stalemate, in other words, to no change in the rules.

These arguments lead to the seventh and final expectation:

H_7: *Challenging strategies are likely to lead to no changes in IGO rules; narrowing strategies are likely to lead to partial changes; broadening strategies are likely to lead to additional or alternative changes to such rules.*

Before turning to how I assess the plausibility of the seven expectations, I need to introduce a note of caution accompanying Table 2.2 and the previous discussion. As the following chapters remind us, the real world rarely fits neatly in our typologies. Some of the strategies used by states to defuse normative pressures for changes to IGO rules often can appear to straddle multiple cells of the table. Two clarifications are therefore necessary. First, we need to distinguish between the cases in which actors purposefully select to apply multiple strategies and those when one single strategy can be *interpreted* as falling in more than one cell. Only the latter cases lead to problems of operationalization across both the horizontal and vertical dimensions of the Table 2.2.

Second, we need to distinguish between the strategies used by different actors. Indeed, as the following pages will show, there are many examples of entire debates pitting a group using one strategy against another using a different strategy. The most common cases are those in which one group applies a narrowing strategy while another applies a broadening strategy. One well-known example was mentioned earlier, involving debates between those promoting group rights as an additional form of human rights and those arguing that only individual rights are truly human rights. In such cases of groups applying different strategies, I consider the strategy that is used by actors opposing changes to the status quo because they are the ones seeking to defuse normative pressures for change, which is the focus of this study.

Perhaps even more important, it is often difficult to discern between strategies in which status quo states attempt to alter the interpretation of the norm and those in which they attempt to alter the interpretation of the actions prescribed by the norm. This is primarily because such actors may refer to specific rules, as illustrations of their arguments, even when attempting to alter the normative environment. As a rule of thumb, I consider the cases when an actor attempts to shape the argument on which the norm is built to be at the norm level and those when the actor accepts the norm but attempts to shape only its implications as those that alter actions. Virtually all of the cases in the second category refer to practical problems of applying a democratic norm to IGOs (rather than to the domestic realm where they were originally developed) or the problems of expediency that the application of such norms pose. Therefore, when determining whether an actor's strategy operates at the norm level or at the level of norm application, we need to differentiate between arguments challenging, narrowing, or broadening actions solely on the basis of the problems with the way in which the norm is applied and those that emphasize the problems of the norm itself from which, of course, problems of application *also* derive.

To clarify this distinction even further, those debates explaining *why* one particular action is appropriate relate to strategies in the second row of Table 2.2. Those that discuss *how* to act on the basis of the accepted norm (given existing pragmatic constraints) refer to the third row of Table 2.2.

The Plausibility Probes

The relatively small population of IGOs, the significant functional differences between them (compared to those between states), and the relatively few attempts to adopt or reform decision-making rules do not allow for a rigorous testing of the seven arguments. Each of the following chapters nevertheless offers a series of plausibility probes (Eckstein 1992) for them. I point out in each chapter a few cases illustrating particular arguments from the seven listed in this chapter. I nevertheless refrain from offering a broader discussion of whether the findings are consistent with the hypotheses until Chapter 8, where I bring together all 72 cases and, therefore, can reach more meaningful conclusions.

As mentioned, the following five chapters each focus on one democratic norm: fair state representation (Chapter 3), fair voting (Chapter 4), transparency (Chapter 5), nongovernmental actor participation (Chapter 6), and parliamentary oversight (Chapter 7). They follow the evolution of the application of such norms across time.

I especially focus on developments in six major IGOs: EU and its precursors, League of Nations, ILO, UN, World Bank, and WTO and its precursor. These are particularly relevant because they offer hard cases in which important national security and economic interests are expected to trump democratic norms in shaping IGO rules.

Additionally, they are selected because they offer significant variance with regard to some important factors. They are examples of IGOs established in three major time periods: the League and ILO were established after World War I; the UN and World Bank were established in the aftermath of World War II; the EU and WTO are probably the most prominent IGOs established after the end of the Cold War (even though they both had precursors established after World War II). This is important because, as I show, the differences in strength of democratic norms (and pressures) across these three periods affected the initial IGO rules.

The IGOs also offer a fairly diverse set of experiences with regard to the normative pressures that were exerted on the basis of the five democratic norms. Perhaps most significant, the pressures to establish and then empower a parliamentary assembly in the European institutions have not been paralleled by any similar efforts in the other IGOs. Similarly, the pressures to promote a strong role for nongovernmental actors in the ILO are distinctive from those unfolding in the other IGOs. Nevertheless, the two cases are not unique. The chapters on parliamentary assemblies and on participation of nongovernmental actors consider important developments in all six IGOs.

The six IGOs offer some additional differences such as the number of issues that they deal with. The League, EU, and UN have taken on many different issues, whereas the ILO, World Bank, and WTO are concerned with single issues (albeit fairly broad ones in some cases). The ability in the first group of IGOs to link negotiations across their various bodies dealing with the multiple issues is expected to be much greater than in the second group of IGOs.

There are also differences in terms of the types of issues that the IGOs deal with and their regional versus global character. These forms of variance allow me to ascertain whether the findings can travel across a broad range of IGOs.

Of course, even by narrowing down the selection on the basis of the previous criteria, one could make an argument for choosing several alternative IGOs. For example, the IMF is just as important and was established at the same time as its sister Bretton Woods organization, the World Bank. I included the World Bank in the study because many of the normative pressures for change (such as those promoting greater NGO access or transparency) were first developed in that IGO. When similar pressures developed in the IMF and the regional development banks, the bargains that were forged in the World Bank were often accepted unaltered in those other IGOs. It is important therefore that we focus on the IGO where such debates first took place because we can access the full range of arguments used by those involved in negotiations.

Similarly, the study could have included another important UN specialized agency instead of the ILO, such as the World Health Organization (WHO) or the UN Educational Scientific and Cultural Organization (UNESCO). However, although both of these alternative organizations can trace their roots to institutions within the League, the ILO is the only IGO to have withstood World War II and continued to function for almost an entire century. The broad time frame offered by the ILO allows for a more complete assessment of the changes in rules discussed in this book.

It should nevertheless be noted that virtually all of these aforementioned alternative IGOs (such as the IMF, UNESCO, and WHO) are also discussed in this book, even if much more briefly than the six main ones. In fact, the arguments offered earlier make it necessary to discuss developments in other IGOs. This is to show that indeed the models established in older IGOs influenced expectations in more recent ones. In addition, one of this study's main arguments is that, to reduce normative pressures in major IGOs, states sometimes utilized broadening strategies that led to changes in organizations that they perceived to be less important. Therefore, I also consider examples from many other IGOs, especially those that were established (or were under pressure to adopt important changes to their rules) around the same time as the aforementioned principal ones. Examples of such secondary IGOs are the Central Commission for Navigation of the Rhine, many of the UN specialized agencies, and the Council of Europe. I also discuss developments in the Inter-Parliamentary Union (IPU), an institution that *chose* to not become intergovernmental in nature, and, consequently, contributed to later decisions involving the application of the parliamentary oversight norm in IGOs.

All five empirical chapters will consider the critical junctures when decision-making rules were first adopted in such IGOs or when there were significant pressures to change them. In most instances, even the establishment of a new IGO, will be treated as cases of changes to rules because, with very few exceptions (such as the Concert of Europe or Central Commission for Navigation on the Rhine), the rules that were being established for the new organizations in fact used as starting points rules from similar previous IGOs.

I introduce multiple gauges of such normative pressures to assess the plausibility of the first hypothesis. The gauges reflect the conceptualization of normative pressure discussed earlier in this chapter. The chapters also assess the types of strategies used by actors opposing the implementation of the democratic norms to IGO rules. By adopting similar ways of gauging normative pressure and a common understanding of the various strategies, I allow for comparisons across developments involving all five norms. Furthermore, it allows me to bring together all the cases of the five chapters and observe broader trends. I do so in the concluding chapter where I assess the plausibility of the 7 hypotheses across all 72 cases.

In testing the plausibility of these hypotheses, the chapters ascertain whether actors used arguments to promote a norm, alter its meaning, or alter the interpretation of its implementation. In other words, they seek to identify the strategies that actors used.

The analysis adopts complementary methods that have been used increasingly in the study of norms (Lupovic 2009). I apply process-tracing, a method that allows the researcher to identify the "intervening causal process" between the independent variable and the outcome (George and Bennett 2005, 206). The method is therefore appropriate for identifying not just the actions states took to respond to normative pressures but also the causal chain linking the use of strategies to outcomes, illustrated in Figure 2.2.

I also assess counterfactual arguments. To do so, I consider cases when democratic pressures led to different outcomes across more than a century. The variance across the dependent variable (the outcomes) allows me to assess the impact of the respective strategies. Moreover, I discuss the likelihood that the adoption or change of rules would have taken place *in the absence* of democratic pressures and the reactions to such pressures (Checkel 2012).

Additionally, although the lack of sufficient primary sources for all 72 cases does not permit the rigorous application of discourse analysis as a methodology, I nevertheless rely as much as possible on such sources to uncover actual wording used by actors promoting norms and those seeking to defuse normative pressures. This is important because in many cases it allows me to uncover a "trail of communication" that can offer evidence (albeit an indirect one) of the presence and strength of norms (Finnemore and Sikkink 1998). I complement such primary sources with secondary ones.

As I focus on critical junctures where actors attempted to change relevant decision-making rules, I seek to answer the same set of questions in all chapters:

- What types of decision-making rules were being established or changed?
- Did actors invoke democratic norms to pressure others in accepting new decision-making rules?
- How powerful were such pressures?
- What actions did actors opposing the new rules take under normative pressure?
- What were the outcomes of the attempts to adopt or change rules?
- Would outcomes have been the same in absence of normative pressures and reactions to pressures?

3

Fair State Participation

The Norm

Decision-making procedures among any group of actors, whether at the national, subnational, or international levels, elicit two basic questions: Who decides? How do they decide? This chapter will begin with the first of these two questions. Although later chapters will discuss how decision-making in intergovernmental organizations (IGOs) can also involve representatives of international nongovernmental organizations, labor and employers' representatives, members of parliamentary assemblies, and, to some degree, even the general public, governments and their official representatives have traditionally been considered the main actors involved in international decisions.

This chapter and Chapter 4 will focus on the degree to which IGOs promote equality among states. As I show, the norms of state equality have two different sources: (1) domestic democratic analogies and (2) the international norm of sovereign equality. While this book is primarily interested in the former source, it also recognizes that norms do not exist in isolation from each other. Therefore, I discuss briefly the evolution of the norm of sovereign equality and the way it interacted with domestic democratic norms in shaping decision-making rules in IGOs. I show that, in the case of fair participation, the domestic democratic norm and the international sovereign equality norm usually reinforced each other. In the case of fair voting, discussed in Chapter 4, the domestic norm and the international one based on sovereignty often clashed.

Fair Participation as a Domestic Democratic Norm

In the domestic realm, the issue of fair participation has long been seen as a necessary condition of democratic decision-making (e.g., Rawls 1971). Without participation in decisions, all other rules, such as the ones involving voting, access to information, or parliamentary checks on the executive, discussed in the following chapters, become irrelevant. It is perhaps because of their basic significance that, historically, the rules involving participation were often the first to be hotly debated at the domestic as well as at the international level.

As democratic norms began shaping domestic politics in the seventeenth and eighteenth centuries, participation rules at the state level reflected complicated mixtures of egalitarian and exclusionary tendencies. When free elections began spreading across states with the first wave of democracy (Huntington 1991), starting in the early nineteenth century, various rules based on gender, ethnicity, race, and wealth kept large groups of individuals outside the political processes. Even today democratic states seek ways to encourage larger numbers of women or ethnic and racial minorities to take part in politics at the same time as various material incentives and cultural factors continue to establish important imbalances.

To gauge the degree to which there has been a global movement toward more egalitarian national political participation rules and practices (a reflection of the strength of domestic norms of fair participation), I calculated the average of two components of the Polity measure of democracy that speak directly to issues that are relevant for political participation: PARREG (regulation of participation) and PARCOMP (competition of participation).[1] Together, these two components offer a useful reflection of the degree to which participation in politics is open or closed. Figure 3.1 illustrates that the norm of fair political participation has become stronger across time, even though it has experienced declines during several periods, most clearly in the interwar era and during the Cold War.

The Sovereign Equality Norm in the International Realm

As the feudalist system declined, state sovereignty became the most powerful principle of international relations (Ninčić 1970, 1). It initially implied that all sovereign princes had supreme authority domestically and were not responsible to anyone externally. In time, the concept of

---

[1] Each component is operationalized on a scale of 1 to 5 (from least to most participation).

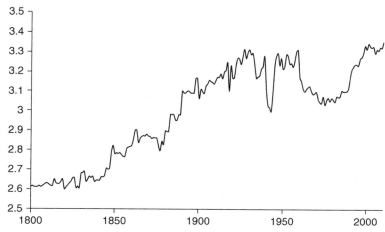

FIGURE 3.1. Average Political Participation Score of All States Across Time. For codebook and data, see the Polity IV Web site at http://www.systemicpeace .org/polity/polity4.htm

sovereignty shifted its application from the individual leaders of states to the states themselves (Klein 1974, 7).

The idea that state sovereignty implies equality among states can be traced at least as far back as the seventeenth century and the writings of Emer de Vattel. Vattel applied the principles of natural law to relations among states, arguing that state equality is just as inalienable a right as equality among individuals within society. He thus famously argued that "a dwarf is just as much a man as a giant: a small republic is no less sovereign than the most powerful of kingdoms" (1916, 7). Later proponents of sovereign equality did not necessarily emphasize the domestic-international analogy as Vattel had. Rather, they argued in legal terms that, if all states are sovereign in relations with each other, no state, whether large or small, can be legally bound against its will by other states. They are implicitly legally equal (e.g., Ninčić 1970, 37).

The great power primacy perspective developed as an alternative to the idea of state equality. This view saw state equality as a legal myth running counter to a political reality (e.g., Fenwick 1948; Broms 1959). Great power primacy proponents distinguished between the "legal" (formal) equality of states and "actual" equality (e.g., Kelsen 1944). The distinction was perhaps best summarized by James Lorimer who argued that "all states are equally entitled to be recognized as states, on the simple ground that they are all states; but all states are *not* entitled to be recognized as *equal* states, simply because they are not equal states" (1884, 260).

The tension between sovereign equality and great power primacy intensified at the founding of the Concert of Europe. The main argument of great power primacy advocates at the time was that not all states had equal obligations to resolve international issues. It was only fair, therefore, for powerful states to have a greater say in international relations than the smaller ones because they were the ones who contributed more to resolving such issues (Klein 1974, 10, 73; Kelsen 1944). Since those first clashes between equality and great power primacy arguments at the beginning of the nineteenth century, the strength of the sovereign equality norm slowly increased. It became more powerful in the second half of the nineteenth century when the United States often promoted equality among states from the Western Hemisphere in the new inter-American conferences. Some of the Latin American states later found themselves leading other small states in the promotion of this norm in the Second Hague Peace Conference of 1907 (Klein 1974). By 1945, the norm was sufficiently powerful to allow sovereign equality to be mentioned in the second article of the UN Charter as a founding principle of the new organization. Today most international jurists consider sovereign equality to be so deeply enshrined in international law that the structure of the UNSC or the Non-Proliferation Treaty, which give great powers clear advantages, are generally seen as "anomalies" in the international system rather than the standard practice (Kingsbury 1998, 600).

The fair participation norm in IGOs was sometimes promoted through a domestic democratic analogy and other times by emphasizing the importance of sovereign equality. Despite this distinction, starting with the argument of Vattel, the domestic and international sources of the fair participation norm often appear to have gone hand in hand. Moreover, in some cases, even when the argument for increased state participation invoked the sovereign equality principle, it was presented using the language of democracy. The following sections will seek nevertheless to disentangle, as much as possible, the two types of arguments. This allows me to show that, while the fair participation norm appears to have been initially based mainly on sovereign equality, in time, as the domestic democratic norms became stronger, those promoting more open participation rules in IGOs increasingly used domestic democratic analogies.

In some cases, especially in regional IGOs, the use of fair participation norms was intended to establish normative pressures for broadening membership of the IGOs (as was the case of NATO and the EU in the 1990s). Yet, more often, they were used to increase the number of seats in some of the smaller executive IGO bodies (such as the League Council, the ILO Governing Body, or the UNSC). The rest of this chapter will primarily discuss this latter set of attempts to change IGO rules and the role that normative pressures played in such reform efforts. The clashes took place mostly between powerful states that wanted to maintain exclusive executive IGO bodies that they could control and small states that applied pressures to have greater representation and influence in such forums.

A History of the Application of the Norm to IGOs

Developments before World War II

The first significant multilateral intergovernmental decision-making processes are generally considered to be the ones of the Concert of Europe and of the system of international congresses and conferences of the nineteenth century. The system was initiated in 1815 with the Congress of Vienna. This congress was seen as path-breaking because, unlike past meetings that took place in the aftermath of great wars that simply dealt with the peace process and division of spoils among victors of the conflict at hand, the Congress of Vienna also sought to find ways of avoiding future conflicts (Craig and George 1995, 29). This implied developing a system of semi-regular meetings between states – in other words, of institutionalizing the process of intergovernmental decision-making.

The main promoters of the idea to move toward such regular meetings are generally considered to be the British, particularly Robert Stewart Castlereagh, foreign secretary at that time. Although the emergence of such an institutionalized system can be understood as simply a natural development in the evolution of international relations, one cannot overlook the powerful impact on this process of Napoleon's brief return to power from his exile in Elba, starting March 20, 1815, when the Congress of Vienna was still unfolding. This fairly brief reminder (over a period of 100 days) of the continuous nature of threats on the continent strengthened the appeal of the British proposal and contributed to the forging of a consensus for periodic meetings between great powers, even in times of peace. The Second Peace of Paris, signed in November 1815, consequently stipulated in Article VI that the great powers would meet at fixed periods to discuss measures "most salutary for the repose and prosperity of nations and the maintenance of the peace of Europe" (Nicolson 1946, 238–239).

Although some have warned against exaggerating the role of the Concert system on the subsequent emergence and development of intergovernmental organizations (e.g., Claude 1964, 28), the literature has increasingly emphasized the usefulness of considering the institutional character of the nineteenth-century congresses and conferences, as it allows for a better understanding of long-standing patterns of cooperation in international relations (e.g., Holsti 1992, 39; Richardson 1999, 49). There is indeed a fairly broad literature analyzing the rules, norms, and decision-making procedures that gave the Concert system an institutional character (e.g., Elrod 1976, 163–167; Lauren 1983, 31–64).

One key change brought about by the Concert of Europe was that, for the first time, there was a clear and formal differentiation in the decision-making process between great powers and all other states. Until the Congress of Vienna, the dichotomous distinction between great and small powers had simply not existed (Ikenberry 2001, 102). Starting with the Peace of Westphalia, international meetings and agreements had previously worked under the assumption that states were all equal and sovereign (Nicolson 1946, 142; Klein 1974, 10). This novel and essential differentiation was reflected primarily in the decision to limit participation in the most important meetings of the Congress of Vienna to only five great powers.[2]

The differentiation between great powers and lesser ones was evident even months before state leaders came together in Vienna. Although Portugal, Spain, and Sweden had been part of the 1814 Peace of Paris that ended the war with France, the four major victors of the wars (Austria, the United Kingdom, Prussia, and Russia) introduced a secret article in the peace agreement stipulating that they would be the only ones to decide on territorial issues throughout the peace process.

When the Congress of Vienna opened, the first meetings took place solely between the four victorious great powers. As the defeated party, the French had to be informed of the secret article during the postwar negotiations. When Talleyrand arrived in Vienna to head the French delegation, he quickly became the self-appointed champion of all states who

---

[2] The distinction between the five most powerful states and all others appears to have influenced the structure and rules of intergovernmental organizations to this day. Many of the major global IGOs of the twentieth century, such as the League, UN, World Bank, and IMF also started out by defining a special role for the five most powerful countries of that time. Although the specific powers have not always been the same across the various IGOs and across time, the "magic" (and somewhat arbitrary) number was the same as in the original Concert system.

were left out of the decision-making process. He met with the Portuguese, Spanish, and Swedish representatives and then conveyed to the four great powers the consternation of being treated as second-order partners. He argued that such exclusion was not built on any "legal, contractual, logical or moral basis," that it lacked "legitimacy" and called for all signatories of the peace process (including France) to have equal voices in future decision-making (Nicolson 1946, 142).[3] Not surprisingly, once it was allowed to join the Concert as the fifth great power of this new exclusive system, France never raised the issue of the formal differentiation among states on the basis of power again. One of Talleyrand's biographers compared the French representative's actions to someone who succeeded in "getting his foot into the European Council Chamber" but who afterwards, to the satisfaction of the other four great powers, "shut the door behind him, leaving his former partners in the passage" (Cooper 1967, 252). Indeed, when Spain argued for its inclusion in the Concert as a sixth great power, the five existing members of the Concert refused, suggesting that Spain was not sufficiently powerful to warrant its inclusion in this elite group (Klein 1974, 25).

The decision of the four great powers to include France in the Concert showed that the great power primacy norm was sufficiently important to them to warrant even the inclusion of the defeated party in the international collective decision-making process. At the same time, by excluding smaller states, even those that had been on their side in the war, they indicated that they did not accept the fair representation norm (or the sovereign equality norm on which fair representation was being promoted). In other words, France was accepted as an equal partner by the four powerful victors of the Napoleonic Wars to make clear the distinction between great and small powers and, by doing so, to justify the exclusion of all other states.

Talleyrand's intervention nevertheless signaled to all great powers the problems they may be confronted with by imposing such an exclusive system on the lesser powers. They all therefore considered various options for their future discussions with other states. As in the establishment

---

[3] Unlike later meetings that led to the founding of major international institutions (such as the ones in 1919 Paris that established the League and the ones of 1945 in San Francisco that launched the United Nations) where we have fairly complete minutes of the discussions, we do not have as detailed records of the meetings of 1815. Fortunately, there are multiple comprehensive sources that offer important details of the proceedings of the Congress of Vienna. The most complete collection of such sources is that of Nicolson (1946), cited throughout this section.

of most other international institutional frameworks that followed the Congress of Vienna, to our day, great powers adopted a compromise between what was later referred to as the "democratic" option and the "authoritarian" one (Nicolson 1946, 138). They divided the work of the Congress of Vienna into ten different committees. The composition of the committees varied between very exclusive (where only the five great powers participated) and very inclusive (where virtually all states took part). The most exclusive ones tended to be the committees in which territorial issues were being discussed. The inclusive ones dealt with more technical issues such as the international rivers committee or the committee dealing with slave trade. It is telling that of the fifty meetings held as part of the Congress of Vienna, forty-one were exclusive, allowing only the five great powers to take part in the proceedings, while nine were also open to other states present at the Congress. This decision can be interpreted as a strategy of narrowing the actions prescribed by the fair participation norm (to only some international bodies).

The exclusive participation rules introduced in the Congress of Vienna became institutionalized in future peace congresses and conferences of the nineteenth century (Ikenberry 2001, 102, 104). Only the five great powers would take part in such meetings. In yet another possible example of the narrowing strategy in the application of the norm of fair participation, small states sometimes would be invited, especially if their sovereignty or territorial integrity were at stake. Even in such rare cases, their representatives would have access only to some of the discussions and did not take part in the actual decision-making process.

Toward the middle of the nineteenth century, the very strong exclusive system of the Concert slowly began eroding (Reinalda 2009). As Figure 3.1 shows, this took place around the same time that the strength of domestic democratic participatory norms experienced a substantial increase at the global level. The 1830 London Conference allowed Belgium to attend. In the 1840 conference (also in London) the Ottoman Empire was represented and by 1856 virtually became a permanent participant in all peace conferences alongside the other great powers. Romania, Serbia, and Greece were invited to attend the 1878 Berlin Conference (once more, without any formal decision-making power) (Sédouy 2009, 19). Also, starting with the 1878 conference, Italy emerged as an almost equal partner of the other five great powers (Richardson 1999, 69). However, overall, the international peace conferences continued to remain fairly exclusive forums for the entire nineteenth century.

Although small states would have liked to be represented at the peace conferences and to be part of the decision-making process, they were not able to alter the exclusive character of the Concert system through normative pressures as they did later, after World War I. Throughout the nineteenth century, although domestic egalitarian norms were becoming stronger, they were nevertheless relatively weak compared to the levels of the twentieth century, as Figure 3.1 suggests.

An interesting example of the weakness of democratic egalitarian norms and of the problems small states had in opposing the exclusionary system of the Concert unfolded soon after its establishment. In 1823 the king of Württemberg wrote to several heads of state arguing that the decision of the great powers to keep small states out of the Verona conference was unacceptable because the results of those meetings affected all of Europe. His argument was based on the sovereign equality norm. Interestingly, when Metternich, the Austrian chancellor, responded to the king's letter, he treated it, scornfully, as one stemming from a democratic understanding of international relations. He asked sarcastically whether the king wanted a system of representative diplomacy that would meet in an assembly and decide by majority voting. The king of Württemberg immediately backed down with a retraction of his previous criticism in the Gazette de Stuttgart (Klein 1974, 35–36). He, like the vast majority of state leaders at that time, was not in a position to promote the norm of fair participation on the basis of domestic democratic analogies when he himself was not the product of a truly egalitarian democratic system. Moreover, although his initial argument was based on the sovereign equality norm rather than on democratic analogies, he did not point out that distinction to Metternich.

The few normative arguments used by small states when seeking participation in international decision-making in the first half of the nineteenth century seem to have always been based on the norm of sovereign equality rather than on domestic democratic analogies. Such arguments implied, as the king of Württemberg had, that one state, even a powerful one, should not decide the fate of another state in exclusive international conferences (Nicolson 1946, 137).

Another important reason for the lack of support for egalitarian norms in international relations at that time was the extremely skewed distribution of power among European states. In 1816, according to a widely accepted measure of national power (Singer, Bremer, and Stuckey 1972), the five states of the Concert of Europe controlled more than three quarters of the material capabilities of the entire world and almost 90 percent of such capabilities in Europe. It was difficult to argue for the implementation of the norm of fair participation when, in practice, collective decisions truly only needed the power of a handful of states to be enforced.

The exclusiveness of the peace conferences contrasted with the very inclusive nature of the dozens of technical intergovernmental conferences that emerged in the second half of the nineteenth and early twentieth centuries. These latter conferences dealt with such diverse issues as the regulation of postal services (1863); fisheries (1882 and 1890); slave trade (1889, 1904, and 1910); health (twelve times between 1851 and 1911); railways (1878, 1881, and 1886); industrial and literary property (1880, 1884, and 1885), and statistics (1853).[4]

The rapid spread of technical conferences is generally considered to be the result of the advances of the industrial revolution and the ensuing international collective action problems that necessitated common international solutions (Lyons 1963, 15; Murphy 1994, 48). The industrialization of transportation, in particular, allowed for increased interaction among governmental and nongovernmental groups. The spread of transnational steamships starting in the 1830s, transnational railways from around the 1840s, and telegraphic connections in the 1860s (after the first transatlantic cable was set in place) led to a general confidence in the ability to overcome obstacles of distance (Osterhammel and Petersson 2005, 67, 82–83).

The increase in the number of international conferences also appears to have been a result of an apparent fad among states seeking greater prestige by embracing specific causes. In fact, some note a certain "division of labor" between states vying to sponsor international conferences. Belgium was generally the country to organize all trade conferences. Russia hosted seismology conferences. Switzerland sponsored conferences dealing with railways (Murphy 1994, 49).

In an age of monarchies and nobility, the national support for organizing such conferences was often difficult to distinguish from the specific interest of an individual. Queen Victoria's consort, Prince Albert, who had studied art history in his youth, organized a conference to discuss exchanging plaster casts, photographs, and other reproductions of artworks. Baron de Coubertin organized the Olympic movement. Prince Albert of Monaco sponsored the first conference on international crime.

---

[4] For a comprehensive list of such conferences, see Murphy 1994, 57–59.

The invitations sent out for such conferences, even when issued by royalty or nobility, were considered official and were treated as being sent by the governments, not the individuals (Murphy 1994, 60, 76).

While in the peace conferences of the nineteenth century, major powers were selfishly guarding their narrow security and territorial interests by keeping the decision-making process exclusive, in the more technical conferences they sought to include as many states as possible to avoid free-rider problems inherent in such collective decisions. The number of states participating in the international conferences dealing with fairly technical issues was impressive considering that, despite the advances mentioned earlier, there were still lingering difficulties associated with the speed and costs of international travel and communication at that time. For instance, twenty-two countries were present at the Postal Conference of 1874. Twenty took part in the international weights and measures conference of 1875 (Reinsch 1911, 23).

The inclusiveness of international forums slowly became the standard even in conferences outside the narrow technical realms. At the 1899 and 1907 Hague conferences, which led to the establishment of the International Court for Arbitration, twenty-six and forty-six countries, respectively, were represented (Sédouy 2009, 15). In fact, by the 1907 Hague Peace Conference, it was clear that the norm of fair participation had gained much ground. When the question of establishing a court for the pacific settlement of disputes came up, small states sought to have equal representation of their judges while great powers fought to have special representation privileges. Ruy Barbosa of Brazil took the lead among the officials supporting equal participation. He argued that "Civil rights are the same for men everywhere. Political rights are the same for all citizens. Lord Kelvin or Mr. John Morley have the same vote in electing the august and sovereign Parliament of Great Britain as the ordinary workman dulled by work and misery.... We have demanded equality of right for the peoples." He continued by arguing that in this context it is a terrible mistake "teaching the peoples that rank between the States must be measured in accordance with their military situation" (Klein 1974, 57). None of the great powers argued against Barbosa's democratic analogy. In the end, the disagreement between the two groups of states simply blocked the establishment of a permanent arbitral court of justice (Kingsbury 1998, 603).

The practices allowing for broad state participation in international institutions during the nineteenth century were reflected in the rules of what is often considered to be the first intergovernmental organization, the Central Commission for the Navigation of the Rhine (CCNR). The CCNR was established in 1815 by one of the most inclusive committees of the Congress of Vienna, mentioned earlier. All seven states that held Rhine territory – Baden, Bavaria, Hessen-Darmstadt, Nassau, Prussia, France, and the Netherlands – became full members of the CCNR and were represented in all of its bodies. Throughout the long history of this organization, none of the riparian states were ever excluded from participation.[5]

The intergovernmental organizations established in the second half of the nineteenth century (often referred to as "public international unions"), such as the International Telegraph Union, Universal Postal Union, International Railway Congress Association, or Central Office of the International Railway Transport founded in 1865, 1874, 1884, and 1890, respectively, continued to embrace a very inclusive approach. These IGOs had virtually no restrictions on membership, just as there had not been any restrictions on participation in the conferences that preceded their establishment (Murphy 1994, 47).

The increasingly broad membership of the technical international conferences and IGOs created a dilemma for powerful states. On the one hand, they were the ones who had opened up such forums to all states when it appeared to be in their interest to do so. On the other hand, as membership increased, so did their difficulties in controlling outcomes in such organizations in the same way that they had become accustomed to in the security conferences.

One solution to this dilemma was to move much of the relevant work in conferences and organizations from the inclusive forums to smaller committees where they could more easily shape decisions just as they had done at the Congress of Vienna. IGOs established toward the end of the nineteenth century and in the first two decades of the twentieth century indeed developed such committees. Yet the norm of open participation had become so deeply entrenched in intergovernmental conferences and organizations that up to the end of World War I even such smaller IGO bodies remained very inclusive, allowing all member-states to take part in all meetings (Reinsch 1911, 153–154). In cases where small states did not participate in all committees, it was usually because of their inability to

---

[5] Conversely, it must be mentioned that Great Britain and the United States, countries that obviously did not control any Rhine territory, were included as members of the Commission in the aftermath of World War I and II, respectively. They both stepped down from the organization in 1964.

meet the high costs of sending sufficient delegates rather than to official rules excluding them from these forums (Lyons 1963, 23).[6]

When the League of Nations was established in 1919, on the one hand, nothing much had changed over the past century in the exclusive nature of international conferences dealing with security issues. On the other hand, the highly inclusive technical conferences and organizations of the previous decades raised expectations for an IGO with very open participation rules, especially one that was intended to establish institutions that were to deal with many issues outside the security realm. The tension between these two trends became evident in the process leading to the adoption of the League's Covenant.

As in cases of other important international decisions following major wars, powerful countries sought to monopolize the process of designing the emerging international institutions after World War I. The initial plan, negotiated in the Supreme Council and the Council of Four (only between France, Italy, the United Kingdom, and the United States) while World War I was still being fought, was to leave all control of the new IGO in the hands of great powers, in the League's Council. The Assembly, where all League members would have a say, was intended to be a very weak organ meeting sporadically, perhaps once every few years (Marks 1995, 191).

Even after the end of the war, as Woodrow Wilson was adamant about making the League Covenant part of the 1919 Paris Peace Conference Agreement, the first detailed conversations involving the future IGO continued to take place only among the victorious great powers. These discussions led to the selection of a joint American-British draft for the Covenant from the dozens of drafts that had been circulated in academic and government circles before and after the war. This draft was then used as the starting point for deliberations with other states.

---

[6] An interesting exception to the inclusive rules within the new intergovernmental organizations of the late nineteenth century was the Commercial Bureau of the American Republics (CBAR), a precursor to the Organization of American States. Soon after it was founded in 1889, the CBAR simply worked under the supervision of the U.S. Secretary of State and submitted its annual reports to the U.S. Congress (Manger 1961, 33). As a result of this arrangement, the United States insisted that the executive committee include only foreign diplomats serving in Washington. This, of course, implied that countries without diplomatic relations with the United States (such as Mexico) were left out of the committee. It was only in 1923 that these exclusive rules were changed to allow for representation of all American states in the committee, regardless of its relations with the United States and that allowed for any state to chair the committee. Although there is no evidence that such changes were considered "democratic" at that time, academics have since labeled them as such (e.g., Stoetzer 1965, 29).

The Cecil-Miller draft (named for its two authors) envisaged an extremely strong role for great powers in the League. It sought a weak assembly where all states would be represented and a powerful council composed only of the five major victorious powers: the United Kingdom, France, Italy, Japan, and the United States (Miller 1928, 131–41). The proposed council appeared so much a step back from the more inclusive late nineteenth century unions to the early exclusive model of the Concert system, that small states were in "almost open revolt"(Miller 1928, 84)[7] and became very vocal in their criticism of the draft as soon as they had access to it. Belgian and Serbian officials openly drew analogies between the plans for the League and the international arrangements of the post-Napoleonic era. In one of the first meetings between representatives of powerful and small states, Belgium's Paul Hymans declared, "What you propose is a revival of Holy Alliance of unhallowed memory" (Bonsal 1944, 26).[8] Others used similar arguments to point out the dangers of establishing a League of Nations where small powers would be excluded from decision-making (Miller 1928, 162).

Small states were especially appalled by the fact that the initial discussions and drafts of the League had only been among a handful of great powers in a very exclusive and, at times, secretive manner. This contrasted with the ideals of inclusiveness and openness that had been highly touted by Wilson in his Fourteen Point Speech as well as by other great power leaders while the war was still being waged and when allied unity was essential.

Wilson's initial plan at the Paris Peace Conference was to form a small drafting committee for the League Covenant, made up of ten representatives, two from each of the five major powers. However, the "violent discussions" and the "vigorous language" (Miller 1928, 84) of the first meetings with small states led to the addition of five more representatives

---

[7] The most detailed account of the discussions leading to the League Covenant (in the initial exchanges among great powers, later in the drafting committee, and in the final stages of negotiations), often in the form of verbatim records, is offered by David Hunter Miller. Miller was a legal adviser attached to the U.S. peace delegation who co-authored the Covenant draft that was eventually used as a basis for negotiations.

[8] It is probably not by chance that the Belgian representative used the analogy of the Holy Alliance rather than the one of the Concert of Europe. As negotiations were underway to design a League that would include only democratic or at least quasi-democratic states, the reference to the Holy Alliance played on the poor reputation of nineteenth century Austria, Prussia, and Russia. Moreover, by alluding to the three great powers that were not present at the negotiations, the representative avoided any hard feelings from Britain and France, the other two great powers of the Concert that were indeed present in Paris at the drafting of the League Covenant.

to the drafting committee, all from small countries. During the first few sessions of this committee, small-state pressures led to a vote resulting in yet another increase in the size of the committee to four more representatives of small states. This second increase in the size of the committee came despite opposition from both the United States and the United Kingdom. One of the American delegates present at the meetings noted that "the exclusion of Belgium and all other Small Powers from the drafting of the Covenant was an impossibility and a reluctant acceptance of the facts by Wilson" (Miller 1928, 84–85). Such partial concessions on the part of great powers can be understood as examples of narrowing the application of the fair participation norm to defuse the strong normative pressures for fair participation.

As soon as small powers were included in the drafting committee, they began demanding seats in the Council alongside the great powers. The main counterargument of great powers to the proposed enlargement of the Council was of practical nature: it would be impossible to adopt decisions in such a large forum because of the unanimity voting rules envisaged for this body (Miller 1928, 147).

This initial strategy of challenging the application of the norm was soon followed with a narrowing one. Indeed, when confronted with continued pressures to increase the size of the League Council, powerful states first accepted the addition of two seats for small states. However, this proposal was quickly brushed aside as inappropriate by the small states. In the end, their insistence led to a League Council composed of the five great powers and of four small states, an interesting balance between the acceptance of the norm of fair participation and the tradition and perceived effectiveness of exclusive great power decision-making. The United States and United Kingdom made it clear that they could not accept a League Council where great powers would be outnumbered or even equaled by small states. Nevertheless, small states were assured that further enlargement of the League Council with non-permanent seats would be considered at a later date, especially if and when other great powers (such as Germany and the Soviet Union) would join the League (Miller 1928, 140).

One of the factors contributing to small powers' success in the negotiations was the strength of domestic democratic norms in the immediate post-war era (as reflected in Figure 3.1), considered to be the peak of the first wave of democracy (Huntington 1991). Such norms were especially relevant in a time when Woodrow Wilson as well as other leaders of the victorious alliance had called for a League of Nations that would consist only of democratic states and emphasized the importance of having public support in setting up postwar institutions.

Wilson's arguments were taken further and applied directly to the proposed functioning of the IGO by his secretary of state, Robert Lansing. Lansing declared openly that he was opposed to the establishment of "an international oligarchy to direct and control world affairs." He sought an organization on the basis of equality of states and "international democracy," not one reflecting an "international aristocracy" (Lansing 1921, 58). Despite his initial statements during the war, Wilson was not prepared to go as far as his secretary of state in allowing for equality among states in the League. He argued that, although "no one asks or expects anything more than an equality of rights," great powers nevertheless needed to have a greater say in the founding and running of the new organization because the burden of responding to international threats was greater for them than for small states (Miller 1928, 97–98). In the end, his position seemed to favor great power primacy over equal participation. The disagreement between the secretary of state and the president on this issue contributed to Lansing's resignation in 1920. Many other similar clashes took place among individuals and states supporting one of these two main positions. Each side used multiple types of arguments at this time, when normative pressures were high.

The question of state equality in the League was often portrayed as one based on appropriateness. One representative argued during the negotiations involving the composition of the League Council that "the chief point is to impress the world by the fairness of the Covenant" (Miller 1928, 160). Several other representatives, including those from great powers, mentioned the need for the Covenant's "favorable acceptance by public opinion" (Miller 1928, 149). Speakers made references to "the moral perspective," "ideas of right," or "moral impressions" (Miller 1928, 151). Yet, the words "democracy" or "democratic" were not used very often in the international debates immediately preceding the founding of the League. They had not yet become common for practitioners of international relations. Indeed, Lansing's aforementioned reference to the democratic analogy was the exception rather than the rule. In fact, the word democracy was rarely used by international representatives even when referring to qualities of states that were intended to be members of the League. Speakers would refer to the need for including only "liberal" states in the League and to a "liberal solution" for the drafting of the Covenant (e.g., Miller 1928, 151).[9] Nevertheless, in the end,

---

[9] Academics, on the other hand, often referred to the need for "democratic international institutions" in the aftermath of World War I. (e.g., Mater 1920, 70).

the arguments for the appropriateness of an inclusive League, whether on the basis of domestic analogies or sovereign equality, contributed to the acceptance by great powers of considerable small-state representation in the League's Council, despite counterarguments related to effectiveness of the organization and great power primacy.

Once the draft of the Covenant was accepted by the members of the drafting committee, negotiations were opened with all other potential League members (Miller 1928, 306–307). Although such discussions involved additional requests to increase the Council with several more non-permanent members, great powers did not make any more concessions on this point and, in the end, maintained their slight majority in the League Council. Yet the negotiations in the committee, as well as later ones with all other states, eventually led to some concessions on the part of great powers that increased the prerogatives of the League Assembly and the frequency of its meetings. This suggests that a strategy of broadening the application of the norm (in addition to those of challenging the norm, challenging its application, and narrowing its application, already mentioned) was used by great powers to include arrangements involving both the League Council and the League Assembly in negotiations.

Soon after the League began functioning, two important developments shifted the majority in its Council from powerful states to small ones. The first was that the United States never joined the League. Second, the unanimity system that gave both great and small powers de facto veto power in all IGO organs allowed the latter group to bargain for three more seats in the League Council a few years later, when Germany joined the League and sought permanent membership to this body.

A similar struggle for balance between great and small powers appears to have shaped the ILO. The ILO was considered one of the most intrusive IGOs at the time it was established. The labor legislation it dealt with was perceived by some, even as late as 1911, as too difficult to resolve through international agreements (Reinsch 1911, 42). In a similar process as the one in the League, which involved normative pressures to allow greater representation for small states, the drafting of the ILO's constitution eventually led to the establishment of the Governing Body with twelve members representing governments, of which eight were nominated by states of "chief industrial importance." This, of course, originally gave powerful states greater representation in this forum than small states. In 1922, states already reached an agreement to add four more non-permanent seats, thus allowing for equal number of seats for small and great powers. Yet only in 1935 did the reform actually enter into force because many states, especially some of the powerful ones, were slow to ratify the changes to the rules. Later reforms of the Governing Body membership, after World War II, tipped the majority in favor of small states.

The aforementioned developments in the League and ILO suggest that, even in such IGOs that initially allowed for obvious unequal representation in the IGOs' key organs, member-states were able to periodically adjust the balance between applying the norm of fair participation and offering at least some advantages to great powers. Only two years after the founding of the League, when membership had grown by about 25 percent (from 42 to 51), discussions to expand the League Council were already underway. By 1923 the League agreed to increase Council membership from eight to ten. Specifically, the number of non-permanent seats increased from four to six, while the number of permanent ones remained at four. The discussions of reform in the 1920s and 1930s revealed a great degree of agreement among states on the "appropriateness" and "democratic nature" (e.g., Motta 1926, 34) of matching the increase in League membership with a proportional increase in its Council (Bourgeouis and Balfour 1922, Annex 422). In these debates, the fair representation norm does not appear to have been promoted any more by invoking the sovereign equality argument.

The most intriguing debates took place in 1926, when Brazil and Spain, which both had vied for permanent seats in the League Council, vetoed the allocation of a permanent seat to Germany. When it became clear that Brazil would not be granted such a privileged position, it withdrew from the League. Spain stayed on after it was promised a "semi-permanent" seat (*Time* 1926). In the end, the negotiations of 1926 allowed Germany to gain a permanent seat in the League Council and raised the number of non-permanent seats from six to nine. In addition, they allowed for three of the nine non-permanent seats to be eligible for reelection, making them semi-permanent. In 1933 the League Council added one more temporary seat and in 1936 yet another, bringing the total of non-permanent seats to eleven. The simultaneous discussions of the addition of one permanent seat for a powerful state and of several more seats for less powerful and of making the seats semi-permanent offer an interesting example of a broadening strategy as applied to the implementation of the fair participation norm. Moreover, the decision to not expand the number of permanent seats further (and to only allow for semi-permanent ones) offers an example of a narrowing strategy used by powerful states under normative pressure.

In deliberations surrounding changes to League Council membership rules, in the 1920s and 1930s, many of the speakers framed their support for the increase in the number of non-permanent seats as a reflection of their "democratic" principles (rather than "liberal ones" generally used in the debates leading to the adoption of the Covenant in 1919) (e.g., League of Nations 1922b, 220–222). Those wanting to maintain the status quo challenged, yet again, the application of the norm through increases in the size of the Council by arguing that an even larger body would adversely affect efficiency, slowing down the deliberative process. Interestingly, even when making such arguments, they sometimes responded to the normative pressures with their own analogies based on democratic domestic systems. One official argued:

In order to justify the proposed increase the democratic principle has been invoked, and, in my opinion, wrongly invoked, for the Assembly is, so to speak, the popular organ of the League in which all its Members are represented. The Council, by its very nature, should be based upon the principle of selection. If the democratic principle means that everybody should govern everybody, I reply, in the words of Jean Jacques Rousseau: "There never has been and there never will be any real democracy." (Struycken 1922, 223)

Overall, the composition of the League's Council was altered four times over its two-decade-long existence by allotting more non-permanent seats for the growing number of smaller states. The League Council also accepted several additional great powers such as Germany and the Soviet Union among its permanent members as soon as they joined the IGO. This contrasts with the slow process that only allowed the "enemy states" of Japan, Italy, and Germany (both the Federal Republic and the Democratic Republic) to join the UN ten or more years after its founding. Moreover, Germany and Japan have not been included in the UNSC as permanent members even to this day, although, during the founding negotiations of the UN, most states took their future permanent member status for granted, following the model of the League.

The changes to League membership would have been even greater had those opposing it not used a broadening strategy bringing together the application of the fair participation and transparency norms. This strategy and the dynamics involving it will be discussed in depth in Chapter 5.

As mentioned, the ILO also altered the composition of the Governing Body during the interwar era. In an apparent nod to the great power primacy norm, it also introduced from the start a system that allowed members to decide periodically which states were of "chief industrial importance." For example, in 1935, Belgium and Canada were replaced by the United States and the Soviet Union, both new members (Riches 1940, 100–101).

Interestingly, in the interwar era, whereas the League and its affiliated institutions, such as the ILO, moved almost constantly toward greater inclusion of states in its executive bodies, several other IGOs appear to have moved toward greater exclusiveness. For instance, the Bank for International Settlements (BIS), founded in 1930, originally included only representatives of the central banks of Belgium, France, Germany, the United Kingdom, Italy, and Japan, as well as three American private banks. Similarly, the International Commission for Air Navigation established in 1919 was set up with rules allowing for exclusive practices (Erler 1970, 647). In addition, in other organizations that had been established prior to World War I, although membership remained inclusive, much of the work increasingly moved to smaller committees where, contrary to the nineteenth-century practices, powerful states were now more likely to be represented than small ones (Reinsch 1911, 153–154; Lyons 1963, 23). This trend toward greater exclusion in the interwar era appears to mirror the erosion of the democratic norm of fair participation at the global level, as depicted in Figure 3.1. It also appears to mirror the trend toward increased contestation of the sovereign equality norm in international law. Treaties published at that time increasingly emphasized the distinction between "legal equality" of states and "equality of their rights and duties" (Ninčić 1970, 40). This distinction appeared to be even more important now that major IGOs had been established and the principle of state equality was being used by small states to gain greater political influence. James Brierly argued that the idea of state equality was "innocuous as long as there existed practically no corporative management of affairs of general international interest," but it would be "indefensible and unjust in principle" in an actual international organization (1942, 91–92).

Despite this effort to erode the norm of fair participation, the presentation of the World War II efforts as anti-fascist and pro-democratic made it difficult to promote the great power primacy doctrine wholeheartedly during and immediately after the war. This was reflected, for example, in the important decision to include in the 1943 Moscow Declaration of the United Kingdom, the United States, and the Soviet Union that the three major powers recognized "the necessity of establishing at the earliest practicable date a general international organization, based on the principle of sovereign equality" (Kelsen 1944, 207). The principle eventually came to be introduced in the UN Charter's second article.

Developments after World War II and during the Cold War

In contrast to the initially exclusive great power plans for the League Council, the original blueprint for the UN did allow for some small states to participate in the UNSC even from the start. In fact, this was partly because of the expectations that came after two decades of more inclusive practices in the League and other IGOs.

In the post–World War II system, as in the League, great powers combined, in their initial plans, elements giving them advantages in key institutions with those based on the appropriateness derived from the fair representation norm. They initially suggested including in the new UNSC six non-permanent members – one more than the permanent ones. This number was higher than what the League Council started off with in 1919 but two seats fewer than in the late 1930s.

During the United Nations Conference on International Organization in San Francisco, some small states called for an increase in the number of the non-permanent members originally proposed for the UNSC. Yet such calls did not garner much support and appear to have been made only as part of the broader bargaining process that surrounded the all-important veto issue, which will be discussed in Chapter 4.

The first decade of the UN's history also saw very few discussions of possible increases in the size of the UNSC. Most of the organization's members had joined one of the two already clearly delineated sides of the Cold War and resigned themselves to only secondary roles in IGOs. Yet, by 1955, UN membership had already grown to seventy-six, representing approximately a 50-percent increase from the number of countries that had signed the Charter in 1945. Moreover, the vast majority of the new members were from Asia and Africa, two regions grossly underrepresented in the UNSC.

The first calls to increase the size of the UNSC came in 1955, a decade after the establishment of the organization. Formal proposals for reform were made in 1956. Such proposals stayed on the General Assembly's agenda for several years but never even came to a vote (Hiscocks 1974, 98). The debates surrounding the increase of the Security Council in the UN's first two decades of existence made references to the lack of democratic character of the organization. The powerful states that were permanent members of the UNSC (often referred to as the P5) responded to such arguments by questioning the applicability of domestic norms to international relations. The U.S. Senate, where some debates surrounding this proposal took place, was among the most critical of the reforms and of using domestic democratic analogies to promote them (e.g., U.S. Senate

1955, 1358). For a while, such strategies of challenging the application of the fair representation norm appeared to be sufficient to stave off the impetus for reform.

Yet, by 1961, when UN membership increased to more than twice the original 1945 numbers, the pressure to reform the UNSC became too powerful to neglect. The 1960s reform efforts were framed once more in terms of making the organization more "democratic" and of reducing "injustice" and "inequity" (Luck 2003, 50).

In 1963 the General Assembly adopted Resolution 1991(XVIII) recommending the expansion of the UNSC from eleven to fifteen members by adding four non-permanent seats. France and the Soviet Union voted against the GA resolution while the United States and United Kingdom abstained. China was the only P5 country to support it. Yet, before the resolution reached the UNSC for a vote, there was a bandwagon process that eventually led all five of the permanent UNSC members (that technically could have each blocked the adoption of this reform) to support the change and to ratify the new plan very quickly. None of them appeared to be prepared to stem the tide of reform.

It is noteworthy that, when the U.S. Senate considered the ratification of the changes to the Charter allowing for an increase in the number of UNSC non-permanent seats, even Dean Rusk, the U.S. secretary of state, used the democratic domestic analogy in calling for the ratification of the Charter amendments. He argued: "[O]ur world is a better and more democratic world because [the new non-permanent members] have taken their rightful places in the councils of our times ... this is the last nation on the face of the earth to shun diversity, or to reject the open forum, or to fear the growth of democratic practices" (U.S. Senate 1965, 13). A senate that, as mentioned, just a decade earlier had questioned the need to introduce democratic rules in the UN accepted this argument and ratified the increase in size of the UNSC.

At the founding of the UN, great powers were also given permanent representation in the other main organs through a series of both formal and informal arrangements. For instance, Article 86 of the Charter stipulated that all UNSC permanent members, even those not administering trust territories, were to be represented in the fairly exclusive Trusteeship Council. The ability of great powers to veto any nomination for the International Court of Justice (ICJ), together with the important rule incorporated in Article 9 of the ICJ Statute requiring that its judges represent the "principal legal systems of the world," has led the permanent members of the UNSC to consistently have nationals sitting as judges on the World Court.

The five great powers have also had de facto permanent representation in the Economic and Social Council (ECOSOC) even though formal rules do not offer them that advantage. In fact, the lack of official great power advantages in ECOSOC has often been interpreted as a reflection of their initial lack of interest in dealing with economic issues through the UN in the immediate post–World War II era (Kennedy 2006, 115).

Another possible interpretation of this differentiation between the UNSC and ECOSOC (as well as the General Assembly and other UN bodies) is that, to defuse the normative pressures applied by small states at its founding, powerful states used a broadening strategy to simultaneously discuss the application of the norm of fair state participation in multiple UN bodies. In the end, the negotiations led to rules allowing for broader member-state participation in some (less important) organs and to a fairly exclusive UNSC.

The more egalitarian rules of ECOSOC also allowed for multiple membership reforms in this body throughout the years. When the UN was established in 1945, ECOSOC consisted of eighteen members. In 1965, the same year that the UNSC was expanded to fifteen members, ECOSOC membership increased to twenty-seven. In 1973 ECOSOC doubled its membership to fifty-four.

Attempts to continue increasing the size of the UNSC in the 1970s and 1980s were not successful. Perhaps the most obvious such attempt took place in 1979 when UN membership had tripled from its original fifty-one members of 1945. That year, ten small states introduced a draft resolution (A/34/L.57) to increase the number of non-permanent seats to sixteen, thus allowing for the UNSC to grow at approximately the same pace as UN membership. The resolution did not garner sufficient support. There appears to have been somewhat more support for a United Nations General Assembly (UNGA) resolution also supporting UNSC expansion in 1980 (Winkelmann 1997, 40–41). However, that second attempt for reform fell short as well.

The rapid growth in the number of states in the international system led to pressures for changes in participation rules in other IGOs during the Cold War era. They were certainly present in the ILO, discussed earlier. In 1951, Germany and Japan were admitted to the ILO and joined the Governing Body as states of chief industrial importance. That same year smaller countries began calling for increases in non-permanent seats in the Governing Body. By 1954 two more non-permanent seats for member states and two others for deputy employer and worker representatives were added to this body. In the 1960s, as a result of decolonization, membership in the ILO grew rapidly, just as it did in all global IGOs. This led to the addition of four more non-permanent seats to the Governing Body in 1964. In 1976, the number of non-permanent members was raised yet again by four.

Small states' efforts to increase the number of seats in the ILO Governing Body was met with several strategies of defusing normative pressures. For instance, in the early 1960s powerful states applied a strategy of challenging the norm of fair participation as presented by small states. In a speech particularly reflective of this strategy a representative of Italy (a state of chief industrial importance) argued:

The justification of the principle of a balance between members as of right and elective members was precisely that it was a principle of true rather than formal democracy. Formal democracy would claim that everyone had an equal right to sit on such a body whereas true democracy would seek to ensure the presence of States with the largest labor force. (International Labor Organization 1961, 40)

The argument operated at the norm level as it challenged the appropriateness of giving all states equal representation, not the practical difficulties of applying it. It conflated in an interesting manner the norm of great power primacy with a "cosmopolitan" interpretation of democracy. Specifically, the Italian representative argued that great powers deserved to be represented more often (through permanent seats) because as a result of their large work forces, they have more at stake than smaller states. This was similar to Wilson's argument that powerful states needed permanent representation in the League Council because the burden of responding to international threats was greater for them than for small states. Yet, at the same time, the argument in the ILO also implied that great powers deserved a special status because they had larger populations and therefore represented more people. This argument used a "cosmopolitan" interpretation of democracy, in which individuals are the basic units for democratic procedures in the international realm, to challenge a "communitarian" one, in which states are the main units (Bienen et al. 1998).[10]

Yet, the most important strategy used for defusing the pressures for increased state representation in the ILO Governing Body was one of

---

[10] I am grateful to an anonymous reviewer for pointing out this distinction between the two democratic models and norms.

broadening the norm of fair participation. This strategy brought together both questions of state participation and those of nongovernmental actors' participation. It will be discussed in greater detail in Chapter 6.

Other organizations established at the end of World War II also struggled with the question of fair participation in their decision-making bodies. The World Bank and the IMF combined inclusive boards of governors, in which all members would participate, with more exclusive boards of directors in which powerful countries were individually represented (a form of "permanent membership"), while groups of smaller states would be represented by a single common director (a virtual "non-permanent membership"). Later, as the number of states in the international system increased, these IGOs were also under pressure to allow for broader representation in their executive bodies.

In the case of the World Bank, the original Articles of Agreement stipulated that the Board of Directors be made up of twelve directors, five of which represented individual (powerful) states. As in the case of the ILO, where it was recognized that changes in economic power should lead to changes in Governing Body membership, the World Bank allowed in its rules for a flexible system of altering the number of representatives in its executive body. Specifically, even though the Articles of Agreement (still) stipulate that there be twelve executive directors, and even though the Articles can only be altered through complete processes of ratification, early on in the history of the IGO it was decided that small changes in the composition of the Board of Directors would simply require a decision of the Boards of Governors by an 80 percent majority of the total voting power. This procedure has allowed the World Bank to alter the number of executive directors nine times over its seven-decade existence. The increases came in 1951, 1952, 1953, 1959, 1963, 1981, 1987, 1992, and 2010.[11] The changes were incremental, leading to additions of only one or two more seats each time (and three more in 1992, after the changes in East Europe and the dissolution of the Soviet Union). Unfortunately, because of the secret nature of debates within the World Bank, whether they took place in the Board of Directors or in the Board of Governors, it is difficult to determine the degree to which democratic norms were invoked in pressuring powerful states to accept participation rules and whether any challenging, narrowing, or broadening strategies

---

[11] The information is based on the listings of executive directors included in the summary proceedings of the annual meetings of the Boards of Governors available on the World Bank Web site, at http://documents.worldbank.org/curated/en/home.

were used by those opposing such changes. Nevertheless, even though the number of executive directors did not keep pace with the increase in the number of World Bank members, the changes in the Board of Directors were smoother (especially during the rapid growth in membership of the decolonization era) than those in the other IGO bodies discussed here.

The participation rules of the European Coal and Steel Community (ECSC), and later, the European Economic Community (EEC), were very inclusive. This is, of course, typical of most regional organizations (starting with the Central Commission for the Navigation of the Rhine) where the reduced number of members does not necessitate the establishment of smaller and more exclusive executive bodies. As a reminder, the ECSC and later EEC, had only six members until the first enlargement of 1973, when membership rose to nine. Membership later increased to ten in 1981, twelve in 1986, and fifteen in 1995. The enlargement of the European institutions throughout the Cold War did not lead to any changes in the inclusiveness of any of its bodies.

Developments in the Post–Cold War Era
The Cold War era saw changes in membership in virtually all global IGO executive bodies. They were spurred by the decolonization processes that had led to extraordinary increases in the number of states and in the pressures to make IGOs somewhat more inclusive. These inclusive trends have continued to some degree in the post–Cold War era. Many of the debates surrounding IGO participation in this period have been triggered by the breakup of the Soviet Union and the changes in East Europe. Perhaps most important, these changes led to pressures for IGOs that had previously only been open to the West, such as the Council of Europe, the European Union, and NATO, to accept former Communist states.

Indeed, the addition of ten more members in 2004, two more in 2007, and yet another in 2013 led to a European Union with more than twice as many members as the one at the end of the Cold War. The decision for enlargement was not an easy one. The potential economic and political problems that would come with such a growth in membership were, at best, unclear in the early 1990s, as many of the political and economic reforms in East and Central European countries were moving very slowly. To reduce such uncertainty, the EU members decided at the 1993 Copenhagen Council to establish a set of fairly specific economic and political criteria that these countries needed to meet before they could be considered for membership. The vast literature on the eastern enlargement generally agrees that normative pressures were essential in opening up the West European IGOs to East European states (e.g., Schimmelfennig 2003, 4–5).

Post–Cold War pressures toward greater inclusiveness surfaced even with regard to the UNSC. In the early 1990s, several countries such as Germany and Japan increased their efforts to gain permanent seats in this organ. Moreover, as the end of the Cold War led to the emergence of a large number of new states, UN membership once more increased, leading to calls for a more balanced participation of all states in the UNSC and an increase in both permanent and non-permanent seats. In 1991 alone thirteen new states joined the UN, which was the largest number since the end of the decolonization period.

At the first ever UNSC summit meeting, in early 1992, powerful countries vying for new permanent seats, such as Japan, called for reform. Later that year the Non-Aligned Movement members also added their voices to such calls in their summit meeting. The P5, of course, attempted to delay the discussions of reform, but the pressures were too great (Fassbender 2003, 187–188). By November 1992, the General Assembly took on the issue of UNSC reform.

Not surprisingly, as the debates took place at the peak of democratization's third wave, the rhetoric that surrounded discussions of reform framed the issue as one of democratization of the organization. In fact, this rhetoric had been foreshadowed by Boutros Boutros-Ghali's June 1992 *Agenda for Peace*, where the secretary-general argued: "[D]emocracy within the family of nations means the application of its principles within the world organization itself. This requires the fullest consultation, participation and engagement of all States, large and small, in the work of the Organization" (Boutros-Ghali 1992).

States involved in reform debates used the domestic democratic analogy even in the early 1990s, when most proposals for UNSC enlargement referred only to the addition of two permanent seats for Germany and Japan. Yet, as soon as the more populous countries of India and Brazil, representing the Global South, became strong candidates for permanent seats, the use of the analogy appeared to increase substantially. For instance, in 2005, when the four aspiring permanent members (dubbed the G4) introduced a resolution for UNSC enlargement, the majority of state representatives taking the floor referred to the need for change by using the words democratic or democracy. Virtually all others at least referred to equality and fairness (hardly ever invoking the sovereign equality principle to make the argument for reform), without mentioning the "D-word" directly (United Nations General Assembly 2005).

A useful gauge of the increased pressures to reform the UNSC is the frequency with which heads of states and governments mention the topic in their annual speeches at the opening of the General Assembly, often viewed as one of the best summaries of countries' foreign policy priorities. For instance, in 2009, even after some considered that the process of UNSC reform had already ended in failure (e.g., Fassbender 2003), more than 100 of the 172 state representatives who took the floor at the opening of the Sixty-Fourth Session called for reform of the UNSC. Almost all of them mentioned the need for an increase in membership. More than twenty of those speeches made at least some references to the need for a more "democratic" organization. In contrast, only one speaker referred to the principle of sovereign equality (United Nations, 2009).

The aforementioned pressures are expected considering that state participation in the UNSC had reached its lowest point, with almost 190 countries vying for ten non-permanent seats. It is perhaps noteworthy that, even if the UNSC would be reformed according to one of the most popular proposals that would add six permanent members and three non-permanent members, the UNSC would not allow for the same degree of participation as the League Council during years when it was at its lowest level (as reflected in Figure 3.3).

The pressures to reform UNSC membership in the 1990s were at best partially successful as a result of a strategy of narrowing the application of the fair representation norm. Whereas the formal participation rules did not change, several informal initiatives slightly improved participation in this exclusive forum. For example, the "Arria" formula allowed for informal consultations of states from outside the UNSC (and even of nongovernmental representatives), especially in discussions of sanctions and peace-keeping operations (Weiss 2003, 154).

Pressures for more inclusive IGOs have also been applied in the past few decades to other UN organs and agencies as well as to IGOs outside the UN system. Even the International Court of Justice – one of the organs in which states are only represented symbolically – through nationals that are supposed to act in their own individual capacity, has experienced pressures to reform the way judges are selected. In the past decade, states, IGOs, nongovernmental organizations, and academics have offered dozens of different reform proposals, almost all involving an increase in the number of judges sitting on the court (e.g., Karl 2006).

In several IGOs the pressures for wider state participation have already led to important changes. In the World Bank, as mentioned, the Executive Board added three more seats in 1992, in great part because of the inclusion of former Soviet Republics and satellite states. This increase was the largest one in the history of the Board.

While formal IGO rules appear to be moving toward greater inclusiveness, in some cases informal ones are leading to more exclusiveness. For example, the WTO, one of the few IGOs to be established in the post–Cold War era, allows for participation of all states in all of its major bodies. Nevertheless, informal rules have led the WTO to be criticized for its exclusiveness. In particular, the "Green Room" consultations system has often been considered the "Security Council of the WTO" (e.g., Monbiot 2004, 206). Although such exclusive consultation practices can be traced as far back as 1957 in the General Agreement on Tariffs and Trade (GATT) (Blackhurst 1998, 33, 35) – when the United States began its discussions of new proposals in consultation with the then newly formed European Economic Community – current procedures have become more institutionalized and have developed a semi-formal character (Jones 2010, 22, 352). Whereas Green Room consultations in the 1970s typically included about eight countries, the normative pressures to make the forum more inclusive led similar consultations in the WTO to now allow representatives from approximately twenty-five states – a substantial increase. As the Green Room system became more inclusive, powerful states developed yet another, more exclusive, system of consultations among the "Quad" (Canada, Japan, the United States, and the EU). By 2005, the Quad consultations expanded to include Brazil, India, and Australia (World Trade Organization 2012). As pressures to open up these informal forums have increased, Chapter 5 shows that those under normative pressure used a broadening strategy to include discussions of transparency at the same time with those of participation.

Answering the Questions of the Study

What Types of Decision-Making Rules Were Being Established or Changed?

All IGOs need to decide what states will be granted membership. The global IGOs discussed in this chapter adopted very inclusive membership practices after the perceived failure of the Concert of Europe experiment. Most regional IGOs have also been fairly inclusive in terms of their membership. After a short period of uncertainty, the EU, as well as other European organizations, decided to adopt an open membership policy after the end of the Cold War, on the basis of a set of fairly precise criteria.

As the number of states increased in the international system, the main rules that are relevant for true state participation in IGO decision-making are the ones that establish who can take part in the smaller executive bodies. Most IGOs have special arrangements for powerful states, assuring such countries of permanent representation in virtually all IGO bodies. The decision-making rules that have been discussed in this chapter refer to (1) the degree to which such rules offer permanent representation to such states, (2) the number of permanent members in IGO executive bodies, and, especially, (3) the number of non-permanent members.

Table 3.1 considers all cases discussed in this chapter when there were attempts to alter participation rules in the League of Nations, ILO, UN, WTO, and World Bank. The European institutions are not included in the table because, as a result of their open participation rules, throughout their existence there were no significant attempts to restrict member-state participation in smaller forums.

In several instances, other rules were included in the debates surrounding membership in such bodies, as a result of the adoption of broadening strategies. The power of other IGO bodies, participation and independence of nongovernmental representatives in the executive bodies, and transparency of the executive bodies became part of the debates. All of these issues are mentioned briefly in the second row of Table 3.1. They are discussed in greater depth in the chapters discussing the respective norms and rules.

Did Actors Invoke Democratic Norms to Pressure Others in Accepting New Decision-Making Rules?

Democratic norms were invoked on many occasions in the debates surrounding increased membership in IGO executive bodies. While the debates involving the Concert of Europe and even some of the early ones at the founding of the League invoked the sovereign equality principle, the domestic democratic analogy appears to have been by far the main source of legitimation of the fair participation norm over the past century. Since the League was established, even when the sovereign equality principle was mentioned (most notably in the UN Charter), it was usually presented as an argument closely connected to the democratic fair participation norm.

The democratic analogy was used by small states at the founding of the League, usually by using the word "liberal" rather than "democracy." Starting in the early 1920s, the "D word" became common in discussions of League Council membership reforms. Such normative pressures were also applied in debates in the ILO (both during the interwar era and during the Cold War), and in the UN (during the Cold War and in the post–Cold War era). Small states used the democratic analogies to argue that they needed more seats in IGO executive bodies as the status quo had strayed too far from what the fair participation norm dictated.

How Powerful Were Such Pressures?

Figure 3.2 is similar to 3.1 but offers a representation of the evolution of the norm of fair participation worldwide only during the period from 1920, after the League and ILO were established, until present day. It is scaled from 0 (lowest level of norm strength over this period) to 1 (highest level of norm strength over this period).

This allows us to distinguish between moments when the strength of the norm is high (for values in the top third of the graph), moderate (the middle third), and low (bottom third), as discussed in Chapter 2. The values of norm strength for each case of actors applying normative pressure to change IGO participation rules are included in the third row of Table 3.1.

Yet, this study suggests that the strength of a norm, alone, does not allow us to understand when such a norm has an impact on developments. The degree to which the status quo departs from the norm prescription as presented by those seeking reform also needs to be taken into account. Indeed, small states often used the argument that the greater the number of members vying for a seat in an executive body, the less fair IGO participation rules are. Figure 3.3 therefore illustrates the evolution of this variable by tracking the number of states vying for a "non-permanent" seat in the executive bodies of the League of Nations, United Nations, ILO, and World Bank. All variables are scaled from 0 (minimum value for IGO throughout its history[12]) to 1 (maximum value for IGO throughout its history). It is important to note that the measure is based, as discussed in Chapter 2, on the interpretation of the fair representation norm used by those promoting reforms, not by the opponents of reform or by outside observers. As this ratio increased, and the status quo departed further from what the fair representation norm prescribed, so did the normative pressure to add more seats to these bodies. When reforms led to increases in the number of seats within IGO executive bodies, the ratio (and implicitly the pressure) declined.

---

[12] Because the UN and League of Nations struggled with the same fair representation questions, they are placed on the same 0–1 scale.

TABLE 3.1. *Normative Pressures Involving State Participation in IGO Bodies and Reactions to Pressures*

IGO/Moment Rule involves	League/1919 –Number of non-permanent seats in Council –Unanimity in Council & power of Assembly	ILO/1919 Number of non-permanent seats in Governing Body	League/early 1920s –Number of permanent and non-permanent seats in Council –Access to Council information –Semi-permanent seats in Council	League/late 1920s –Number of non-permanent seats in Council –Access to Council information	League/early 1930s Number of non-permanent seats in Council	ILO/mid-1930s –Number of non-permanent seats in Governing Body –Independence of nongovernmental actors	World Bank/1944 Number of executive directors
Norm strength	M	M	M	H	M	M	L
Departure from norm prescription	H	H	M	L	L	H	L
Normative pressure	H	H	M	M	L	H	V L
Strategy	NA; BA; CA; CN	NA	NA; BA; CA	BA; NA; CA; BN	BA; NA; CA	BN; NA	NA
Outcome	PC; AC	PC	PC	PC; AC	PC	C; AC	PC

Note: CN = challenging norm; NN = narrowing norm; BN = broadening norm; CA = challenging application of norm; NA = narrowing application of norm; BA = broadening application of norm; Y = yielding; W = withstanding; C = originally promoted change; NC = no change; PC = partial change; AC = alternative change.

Period	Indicators					
UN/1945	–Number of non-permanent seats in UNSC –State representation in other UN bodies	M	L	L	BA	AC
UN /early 1950s	Number of non-permanent seats in UNSC	M	M	M	CA	NC
ILO/1950s	–Number of non-permanent seats in Governing Body –Independence of nongovernmental actors	M	L	L	BA; BN	PC; AC
World Bank/1950s and early 1960s	Number of executive directors	M	M	M	NA	PC
UN/early 1960s	Number of non-permanent seats in UNSC	L	H	M	Y	C
ILO /early 1960s	–Number of non-permanent seats in Governing Body –Independence of nongovernmental actors	L	H	M	CN; BN	C
UN/1970s	Number of non-permanent seats in UNSC	L	M	L	BN	NC
ILO/1970s–1980s	–Number of non-permanent seats in Governing Body –Independence of nongovernmental actors	L	M	L	BA; BN	AC
UN/1980s	Number of non-permanent seats in UNSC	L	H	M	W	NC
World Bank late 1980s–early1990s	Number of executive directors	M	H	H	NA	C
UN/1990s	–Number of non-permanent seats in UNSC –Access to UNSC information and number of permanent members	H	H	VH	BN; BA; NA	AC
WTO late 1990s and 2000s	–State participation in informal forums such as the Green Room –Transparency of informal forums	H	M	H	NA; BA	C; AC

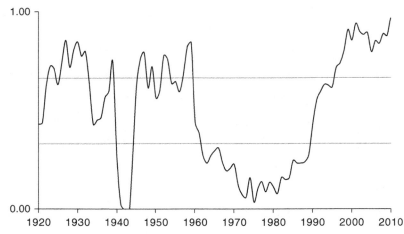

FIGURE 3.2. Strength of Fair Participation Norms from 1920 to 2010.

The degrees to which the membership rules departed from the norm prescription were considered high if they were in the top third of the graph in Figure 3.3; they were moderate if they fell within the middle third of the graph; they were low if they fell in the lower third of the graph. In addition, as mentioned in Chapter 2, I consider that in 1919, at the founding of the League, the variable was high (rather than moderate, as the figure suggests) because the organization was established at a time when virtually all previous IGOs had allowed for full participation of all members in all bodies.

Figure 3.3 suggests that there were times when this ratio increased dramatically. Such sudden increases were visible in the League, in the first few years after it was established, in the ILO after it was established and in the 1950s and 1960s, in the UN in the 1950s and early 1960s, and in the World Bank in the late 1940s and throughout most of the Cold War. At such times when there was a sudden decline in the ability of small states to take part in executive bodies, and when norms were strong, the normative pressure to enact reforms was great. In the WTO I consider that the application of the norm only departed moderately from the prescriptions because the rules that limited participation in the Green Room and other forums were informal ones. The values of the variable reflecting the departure from norm prescriptions are included in the fourth row of Table 3.1.

Table 3.1 also includes an assessment of the normative pressure at each of the critical junctures in the evolution of participation rules within

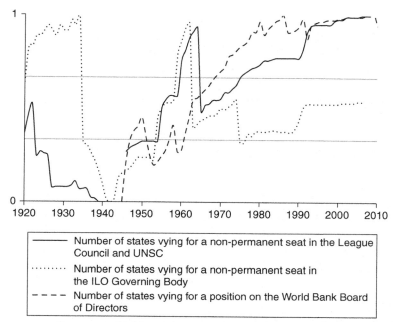

FIGURE 3.3. Degree to which Participation Rules Depart from Norm Prescriptions.

IGOs. It is based on the interaction between norm strength and degree to which the status quo departs from the norm prescription. As mentioned in the discussion of normative pressure in Chapter 2, the pressure is considered very high when the norm strength is high and the number of states vying for a non-permanent seat is high. This was the case in the UN in the 1990s. When one of the two factors is moderate and the other is high (as at the founding of the League and ILO as well as in the ILO in the 1930s or the World Bank in the 1990s), the pressure is high.

When one factor is high and the other is low, the pressure is moderate. This was the case in the UN in the 1960s, at the peak of the decolonization era. At that time, even though the norm of participation appears to have eroded worldwide, the number of states kept out of the UNSC was so high that the normative pressure for reform was nevertheless significant.

When both factors are moderate, the pressure is moderate. When one factor is low and the other moderate, the pressure is low. When they are both low, the pressure is very low.

As a reminder, although the operationalization of normative pressure in Table 3.1 follows the definition of this concept, as an interaction of two separate variables, such pressures can also be observed independently. The preceding narrative of developments surrounding the attempts to reform the executive bodies of the League, ILO, and UN has suggested that, indeed, the frequency with which democratic norms were invoked was greater at moments when the pressures were high or very high (such as the founding of the League and ILO or in the post–Cold War era in the UN).

What Actions Did Actors Opposing the New Rules Take under Normative Pressure?

Table 3.1 also includes the reactions of status quo states to the normative pressures applied at the main critical junctures. In virtually all cases, it was the powerful states with permanent representation in IGO executive bodies that sought to maintain the status quo and that were behind the strategies for alleviating normative pressures. The ones seeking reform were less powerful states that did not hold permanent seats in these bodies. Table 3.1 suggests that there were few instances when there was no reaction on the part of great powers, even if the normative pressures were moderate or low. Moreover, in many cases powerful states simultaneously adopted multiple strategies. This reflects their interest in defusing normative pressures and, more broadly, in maintaining small and effective executive bodies that they could more easily control.

For example, at the founding of the League of Nations, when normative pressures were high, powerful states used multiple strategies to defuse the strong normative pressures (as we should expect on the basis of H_2). Some of them challenged the fair representation norm by emphasizing great power primacy and arguing that the most powerful states had greater obligations and therefore needed to have a greater say in the IGO. They also challenged the application of the norm by arguing for a smaller and, implicitly, more effective League Council (made up only of great powers). As this strategy did not quiet representatives of small states, they also included other somewhat related institutional issues in negotiations (especially those referring to the power and frequency of meetings of the League Assembly, the body with universal participation) in a strategy of broadening the application of the fair participation norm. They also narrowed the application of the actions demanded by those using the normative pressures by accepting some non-permanent seats, but not as many as small states had demanded. Although small states wanted six seats in the League Council, great powers first accepted only two and, later, four.

An even more successful narrowing strategy was used in the negotiations leading to the establishment of the ILO. There, although small states wanted to have at least eight non-permanent seats in the Governing Body to balance the eight permanent ones (for states of "chief industrial importance"), they were only given four such seats.

As small states did not get the number of non-permanent seats they had requested at the founding of the League and ILO, they continued to pressure for additional increases in the size of the League Council and Governing Body, respectively. Powerful states used, once more, multiple strategies to defuse such pressures. They narrowed the application of the actions deriving from the norm by limiting the number of non-permanent members they would accept. In the 1930s, states in the League used this strategy by introducing temporary additional seats, which they planned to eliminate after some time. At the same time, powerful states adopted strategies of broadening the actions that derived from the norm by including other issues in the negotiations. In the 1920s, for example, they linked the question of small state representation in the Council to the addition of more permanent seats and to the establishment of "semi-permanent seats." They also used arguments of expediency to challenge the application of the norm.

In the ILO even though members accepted an increase in the size of the Governing Body as early as 1922, great powers dragged on the ratification processes for more than a decade. Therefore, throughout the late 1920s and early 1930s, while normative pressure for change continued to be high, the debates involved an instance of challenging the participation norm based on the communitarian model with one based on the cosmopolitan model. Powerful states also adopted a strategy of broadening the norm of participation to include the issues of participation and independence of nongovernmental representatives, not just governmental ones. This important strategy was used virtually throughout the entire history of the ILO but was especially obvious in the late 1970s. Lastly, in the late 1920s, in the League Council and in the 1970s and 1990s in the UNSC, the strategy of broadening the norm of participation was applied by including in the debates questions related to IGO transparency. These broadening strategies offer a first illustration of the need to discuss multiple democratic norms simultaneously to understand their advancement across IGOs. The linkages between norms of state participation on the one hand and transparency and nongovernmental actor participation on the other are discussed in greater depth in Chapters 5 and 6, respectively.

When the UN was established, there were some pressures for including more non-permanent members in the UNSC. However, the strength of such pressures was low, especially compared to the high normative pressures for eliminating the proposed veto in the UNSC. Chapter 4 shows that, in this case, powerful states broadened the discussion of fair voting, showing that they were willing to include more non-permanent members in the UNSC than they had originally included in the League but were not willing to give up their veto. Moreover, they added questions related to the rules of the UNGA as well as other organs to the one involving UNSC membership. While they were willing to concede on the rules in the other UN bodies, they stood firm in the ones concerning the UNSC. In the 1950s, when the first attempt to enlarge the UNSC took place, status quo states sometimes challenged the application of the norm to the UN arguing for the need to have a more efficient body.

In the 1990s, powerful states utilized multiple strategies (successfully) to defuse pressures. They adopted strategies of narrowing the actions deriving from the norm by allowing states informal access to some of the body's meetings. In addition, as mentioned, they used the broadening strategy to include both the norm of transparency and the one of participation on the reform agenda. Lastly, they broadened the application of the norm by including issues related both to the number of permanent and non-permanent members, making any agreement more difficult to reach.

It is noteworthy that on two occasions (both in the UN) powerful states did not use any of the six strategies to defuse normative pressures, although the pressures were moderate. In the early 1960s they yielded to such pressures and allowed for an increase in the membership of the UNSC, and in 1979–1980 they were able to withstand the pressure without taking any relevant actions.

In the World Bank, the strategy of narrowing the application of the norm was used on several occasions to defuse normative pressures for increasing the number of executive directors. At the founding of the World Bank, powerful states allowed a number of executive directors to represent multiple smaller states, while they themselves were represented by only one such director. That implied that all states were technically represented on the Board of Directors although, in most cases, only indirectly. Throughout the history of the organization they also allowed for increases in participation but, when doing so, they only accepted part of the demands for reform of small states. The one exception may be the increase in 1992 when they accepted three new directors just as the small states proposed.

The normative pressures to increase member-state participation in the WTO's Green Room have been met with two strategies. First, status quo states sought to maintain the participation rules informal, in a narrowing strategy. Second, they included the issue of the body's transparency in debates, pursuing a strategy of broadening the actions that derive from the norm of fair participation.

What Were the Outcomes of the Attempts to Adopt or Change Rules?

Figure 3.2 suggests that powerful states had varied success in maintaining fairly exclusive IGO executive bodies. They were less successful in the World Bank as well as throughout most of the history of the League of Nations. They have been more successful in the UN (especially since 1965) and in the ILO up to 1935, in the late 1950s, and in the early 1960s.

Overall, the cases discussed in this chapter appear to exhibit considerable variance with regard to the outcomes. There were five instances when the originally promoted changes took place. As H_1 suggests, three of these took place in cases when the normative pressures were high or very high and two of them when the normative pressures were moderate. In eight more cases only partial changes took place. There were also eight cases in which alternative changes to rules took place. In only three cases (all in the UN), the reform efforts did not lead to any changes.

Would Outcomes Have Been the Same in the Absence of Normative Pressures and Reactions to Pressures?

Traditional realist approaches to international relations emphasize that IGOs reflect the power distribution among states (Mearsheimer 1994). On the basis of this argument, we would expect IGOs to be more inclusive when powerful states control a smaller proportion of the total power. In other words, when there is a need for a large number of states to accept and enforce IGO decisions, participation in executive bodies should increase.

Figure 3.4 illustrates the proportion between the combined power of the major states within the IGO and the total power of all states within that specific year. It is based on measures of power from the National Material Capabilities data set (Singer et al. 1972). I considered major powers the permanent members of the League's Council for the period 1919–1944 and the permanent members of the UNSC after 1945. The measure takes into account the comings and goings of various major powers in the League Council as well as the change from China to

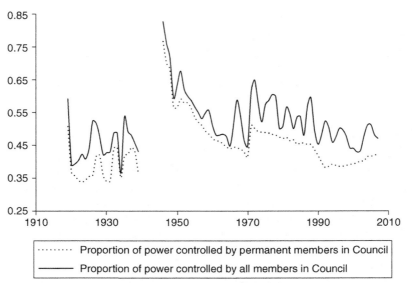

FIGURE 3.4. Power Controlled by Permanent Members of League Council and UNSC.

Taiwan and then to the People's Republic of China in the UNSC. In addition, for 1919 (but not later), I included the United States because, during the important negotiations that led to the establishment of the League, there was a general assumption that the United States would join the organization. Moreover, it played an important role in the planning of the IGO.

There is strong support for the preceding realist argument throughout the nineteenth century (not included in Figure 3.4), when the majority of the world's power (and more than 80 percent of Europe's power) was controlled by only five states. At that time, great powers indeed decided to exclude all other states from the Concert of Europe system because they knew that when they all supported a decision they could easily impose it on all the other states. It is noteworthy, however, that, even in the Concert system, power considerations alone cannot explain membership decisions. In 1815 and through the first half of the nineteenth century, Austria, Britain, Prussia, and Russia together controlled more than half of the world's power and did not truly need to include France in the Concert. Yet, as mentioned earlier in this chapter, arguments on the basis of "appropriateness" (derived from the great power primacy principle) led them to include France in the system.

With the rise in power of the United States and the destruction of World War I on the European continent, there was a shift in global power distribution. The five original great powers of the post–World War I era controlled well over half of the world's material capabilities. If participation rules would have been solely on the basis of power considerations, the League Council indeed did not have to include any small states.

Because the United States never joined the League, the permanent members of the League Council represented a relatively small proportion of the world's power (varying from around 30 percent in some years to a little more than 40 percent in others). This may explain the relative inclusiveness of the League Council.

After World War II, the five major powers that established the UN also controlled a majority of the power of the international system. Once more, even a smaller set of great powers (the Soviet Union, United Kingdom, and United States) controlled more than half of the total world's material capabilities. The P5 collectively continued to have a greater share of the power than all other states put together even after the Chinese Civil War that led to the People's Republic of China's de facto exclusion from the global forum. The increase in UNSC membership in 1965 could also potentially be explained by great powers' need for a more powerful UNSC at that time, when the overall power of the P5 had declined to less than 50 percent.

Yet, in most cases, realist arguments need to be complemented with additional ones to explain the acceptance of non-permanent members throughout time. Figure 3.4 shows that the expansion of non-permanent membership in 1923 and 1926 in the League Council and in 1965 in the UNSC did indeed bring about some changes to the overall power of the countries in these bodies. Yet the annual fluctuations because of the temporary inclusion of some non-permanent members and the departure of others appear to be greater than the overall changes to the relative power of the countries in these bodies that accompanied the reforms of membership rules. In many cases, the increase in aggregate power of the Council members that came after the reforms was followed the very next year by a decline in power. Moreover, the power distribution immediately after World War I and, especially, after World War II does not explain the need to include any non-permanent members, as the five great powers controlled more than 50 percent of all the world power both times. This argument is especially relevant for the design of the UNSC. The great amount of power controlled by the P5 in 1945 does not explain why they allowed six non-permanent members in the UNSC. Because they held a greater proportion of the world's power than the League, the P5 could have established even more control over the UNSC than they had over the League Council.

Overall, the figures suggest that the inclusiveness of IGOs is not simply a reflection of the power distribution. At times, IGOs could in fact have been even more exclusive (with regard to non-permanent members) based simply on power considerations and would have needed to be more inclusive (with regard to permanent members) at other times. The power-based explanations need to be combined with a broader understanding of the role of norms and normative pressures as well as the strategies that were used to defuse such pressures.

Similarly, arguments emphasizing effectiveness of IGOs would find it difficult to explain the growth in size of the formal executive bodies in the League, ILO, UN, World Bank, and, the informal one in the WTO. With such increases came greater difficulties in reaching decisions.

4

Fair Voting

The Norm

After discussing in Chapter 3 a first important question involving decision-making in intergovernmental organizations – the one of "who decides" – this chapter turns to the question of "how they decide." It shows, as expected, that the answers to the two questions are related and therefore lead to other explanations for the variance in the application of the fair participation norm in IGOs, in addition to the ones discussed earlier.

While equal voting is one of the most important democratic norms at the domestic level, it also appears to be the one that has the greatest difficulties in being transposed to the international realm. As this chapter will show, there has always been a tension between the egalitarian norm of one-country-one-vote and the norm (arguably even more "democratic" in nature) that dictates more votes for more populous states. It is perhaps because of this tension that the rules for fair vote distribution among states appear to have triggered more heated debates regarding the "democratic" character of IGOs than any other rules.

Yet this dilemma, related to the choice for equal or differentiated voting in IGOs, is accompanied by a second one, between majority and unanimous voting. On the one hand, majority decision-making has often been associated with democracy in the domestic realm. In fact, democracy has sometimes been defined as a system that needs to have periodic losers (not just winners), something that unanimity voting systems do not allow (Przeworski 1991, 10). On the other hand, state sovereignty, traditionally the most important principle of international law, implies that collective decisions in the international realm can never be imposed on states. This, of course, suggests that unanimity needs to be used in seeking such decisions. The inherent tension between prescriptions based on democratic analogies and those based on state sovereignty has contributed to shaping voting rules in IGOs.

As this chapter shows, states have experimented with a multitude of IGO voting rules. They used systems of unanimity, supermajorities, simple majority, or weighted voting. They have adopted rules that indirectly favor some types of states, such as the colonial powers in the nineteenth-century public international unions, the "founder members" of the Organization of the Petroleum Exporting Countries, or the major victors of World War II in the UN. They have also embraced informal rules altering the formal ones. Yet, in the end, virtually all IGOs have come to seek ways of balancing equal voting rules with mechanisms for enticing powerful states to be part of international decision-making by adopting formulas through which such actors could at least block major decisions that they oppose and, in some cases, also adopt ones they favor.

Compared to other rules discussed in this study that allow for gradualist approaches, voting rules may, at first sight, imply a very discrete set of solutions. In other words, although states can easily tinker with the degree of inclusiveness of the organization or its executive body by adding one or several more members, with the degree of transparency by opening up one or several more meetings to the public (of the hundreds that they hold each year), or with the degree of nongovernmental actor participation by allowing one or more types of such actors to take part in IGO proceedings, it appears to be more difficult to adopt an incremental approach to voting systems. IGOs have nevertheless been able to develop fairly complex and gradualist voting formulas. Thus, while some decisions in IGOs require unanimous support of all members, others, such as the UNSC, only require unanimous support of some states. Moreover, IGOs that adopted weighted voting systems have often tinkered with the relative weights of states' votes over time. Lastly, the kinds of decisions that require unanimity, majority, or supermajority also vary across IGOs and across time. These gradualist approaches allow for sufficient variance to assess the impact of democratic norms on voting rules in IGOs.

Fair Voting as a Domestic Democratic Norm

As in the case of the fair participation norm, the fair voting norm in IGOs has two sources: the analogy to the one-person-one-vote domestic systems and the international norm of sovereignty. In domestic systems "fair

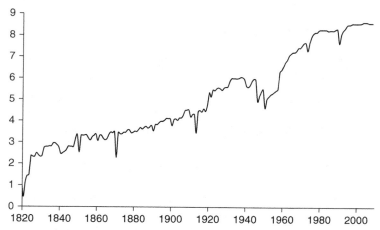

FIGURE 4.1. Average Franchise Score of All States Across Time.

voting" probably equated to "equal voting" much more easily than "fair participation" equated with "equal participation." That is because, as polities grew from the ancient city-states to modern nation-states, the gathering of all citizens to conduct politics in a forum became impossible and direct democracy was replaced by representative democracy where individuals were only indirectly represented (Held 1995). Voting, on the other hand, could still include all individuals in a direct fashion. Over time, the norm of equal voting at the domestic level has become one of the strongest, if not the strongest, domestic democratic norm. In fact, the history of democracy within states can often be portrayed as a continuous fight to include in electoral processes previously excluded groups. Such exclusions have been based, at various times and in various countries, on ethnicity, religion, literacy, wealth, social status, and gender (Przeworski et al. 2013).

Figure 4.1 reflects the strength of the equal voting norm at the domestic level. It is based on the "Franchise" measure (representing "qualifications for the right to vote in national elections") of the Political Institutions and Political Events (PIPE) dataset (Przeworski et al. 2013).[1]

---

[1] A country's annual "franchise" score is made up of two digits. The first digit is scaled from 1 (most restrictive) to 7 (most inclusive). The measure's second digit distinguishes between political systems where women cannot vote (0), those where women are qualified to vote on a narrower basis than males (1), and those where women are qualified on an equal basis as males (2). The measure used for Figure 4.1 is the sum of the two digits and can take values from 0 (a country with many restrictions on suffrage) to 9 (a country with hardly any restrictions on suffrage). I am grateful to an anonymous reviewer for suggesting this dataset for assessing fair voting norms.

Like Figure 3.1 (reflecting the evolution of the average political participation score of all states across time), Figure 4.1 shows, as expected, that at the global level, over the past two centuries, democratic norms have become stronger. Indeed, the average franchise score increased from less than 1 in the early nineteenth century to an almost perfect 9 by the end of the twentieth century. Moreover, both Figures 3.1 and 4.1 show that although, from afar, the average scores have increased almost consistently since the beginning of the nineteenth century, there have been shorter or longer periods of time when the world experienced declines in fair participation and fair voting, respectively. In the case of the fair voting norm, the most serious declines appear to have taken place during World War I and II as well as immediately after World War II. The decolonization era that was characterized by a decline in the fair participation norm appears to have been a period of rapid increase in fair voting across the world. Also, although the immediate post–Cold War era showed a very brief decline in fair voting (perhaps as a result of the outbreak of a number of civil wars around the world and the emergence of a number of new states), over the past two decades, the vast majority of countries in the world have eliminated virtually all restrictions on voting rights.

The Sovereignty Norm in the International Realm

The international norm of sovereignty and the fluctuations in its strength discussed in Chapter 3 also impacted voting rules in IGOs. In fact, this norm may have had a more direct and stronger effect on voting rules than on participation rules.

As far back as the Concert of Europe, the first intergovernmental forums adopted all of their major decisions by unanimity. The unanimity rule was essential because the strong legal principle of sovereignty dictated that outsiders could not impose a decision on any state. Throughout the nineteenth century, when representation in international conferences took place at a very high level (because of the inherent problems of communication with states' capitals) and when travel to meetings was costly and time-consuming (Richardson 1999, 54–55), states had to be induced to participate in such conferences. They simply would not take part in international forums if they knew that these could lead to decisions they would later be forced to accept. Conferences that did not adopt the rule of unanimity beforehand were generally considered "a waste of time" by those who considered attending them (Riches 1940, 8, 13).

Yet, as permanent IGOs emerged and as expectations for their effectiveness in adopting minor day-to-day decisions were raised, the unanimity decision-making systems of the first international forums began being replaced with majority voting systems. It is at that point that the major debates surrounding fair voting arose. In unanimity systems, the number of votes a country had was not consequential as each state could veto a decision. In majority systems, the number of votes allotted to each state, or the type of differentiated veto systems in place, mattered. As I show, the vigorous debates surrounding the differentiated allocation of votes often led to clashes between various interpretations of what "fair" voting implied in the international realm. Most important, the norms based on the communitarian model and those based on the cosmopolitan model clashed. Whereas the former dictated equal votes to all states, the latter implied that larger (more populous) states deserved voting advantages.

The following sections follow the evolution of voting rules in IGOs. They show how the domestic democratic norm of fair voting impacted developments in IGOs. They will also discuss how the international sovereignty norm supporting unanimity voting often clashed with the democratic norm to shape IGO rules.

A History of the Application of the Norm to IGOs

Developments before World War II

On the one hand, as discussed in Chapter 3, the Congress of Vienna introduced the "great power principle" in the participation rules of international peace congresses and conferences of the nineteenth century. On the other hand, it maintained the most important principle of international decision-making, the one of unanimity. The question of "voting rules" was not even discussed in Vienna as it appeared to be obvious to all that decisions could not be reached in any way other than through consensus (Lyons 1963, 24).

Because of the very strong norm of state sovereignty, with very few exceptions, the rule of unanimity was used in all of the intergovernmental meetings and intergovernmental organizations of the first half of the nineteenth century. In fact, some argue that even as late as the 1920s, the rule had been established for so long in the international realm that it acquired the status of customary law for decision-making among states (Lyons 1963, 22–23).

Yet, even in the Concert of Europe system, strict unanimity had to be somewhat softened. As the peace conferences of the early nineteenth century took on a more multilateral and institutionalized approach to decision-making than previous international forums, it became obvious that great powers needed to find ways of reaching agreements even in cases in which one of them did not support the action of others. A quasi-abstention option therefore developed as an alternative to supporting or opposing the common position of all other states (Holsti 1992). This became apparent in at least two important cases, when Britain did not support the decision of the other four great powers in repressing liberal revolutions. In 1821, at the Congress of Laibach, Austria sought to receive approval from the Concert of Europe to intervene against a revolt in Naples. The British foreign secretary did not attend the meeting, writing: "[T]he principle of one state interfering by force in the internal affairs of another, in order to enforce obedience to the governing authority, is always a question of the greatest possible moral as well as political delicacy" (Temperley and Penson 1966). Britain was represented in the Congress only by its ambassador in Vienna. He was instructed to simply attend the meetings and to ensure that the outcome would not violate any of the existing treaties. Despite pressures from the other four great powers, the British representative refused to either offer his country's support for the actions or, more importantly, to officially oppose it (Butterworths 1891). Britain took a similar "observer" position, at the Congress of Verona, of 1822, where France sought great power support for its intervention in Spain. In both cases the decision of the majority of great powers was carried out despite the British quasi-abstention.

For some, the two aforementioned conferences reflected the lack of consensus that led there and then to the end of the Concert of Europe system (Claude 1964; Nicolson 1946). Yet, for many others the Concert system is considered to have lasted until the end of the nineteenth century or even up to World War I (Holsti 1992). If one takes the latter view, then the possibility of having states take such quasi-abstention positions may in fact have given the system the needed resilience to withstand great power disagreements. It is likely that without the possibility of opting out of the unanimous decision-making process, the five great powers would have ended the consultation processes that preceded their decisions. It was essential for all sides to understand whether a state attached sufficient importance to a specific issue so as to act unilaterally or to oppose all others' actions through use of force. For instance, in the two aforementioned cases Britain understood that Austria and France, respectively, considered their military interventions essential for their interests and that the two would not back down from their decisions, regardless of the British position. Conversely, the other great powers understood that although Britain did not support their actions, it was not sufficiently opposed to them to take military or other strong actions to stop them (Richardson 1999, 59).

The preceding discussion suggests the problems that the Concert had in reaching unanimous decisions even among five participants. It is perhaps a result of the decision to institutionalize consultations among the great powers that the exclusivity of the Concert of Europe emerged as a necessary condition for its functioning. In an age when decisions needed to be unanimous, the great powers understood the difficulties of agreement in even larger forums. This may therefore be the main reason Austria, Britain, Prussia, and Russia excluded Spain, Sweden, and Portugal, as well as other small powers, from the Concert systems and initially also wanted to exclude France, as discussed in Chapter 3. This argument reminds us of important links between participation and voting rules and how considering one separate from the other can only offer an incomplete understanding of their evolution.

The long-held custom of adopting decisions by consensus in international forums did not only apply to security conferences. The acceptance of unanimity was so powerful at that time that even the Congress of Vienna's committees dealing with technical issues functioned through rules of unanimity. It was also the main decision-making rule of the first intergovernmental organization, the CCNR, established in 1815. Yet, it quickly became apparent that in a permanent institution such as the CCNR, to allow for the day-to-day work of the permanent secretariat, some decisions in the organization would have to be taken by majority vote. While international meetings used majority voting for at least some of the procedural matters, the kinds of questions that were seen as being procedural early on were very narrow (Riches 1940, 18).

The shift (1) from security-related issues to other less salient ones and (2) from ad hoc meetings where participants needed to be enticed to join conferences to the permanent IGOs (where the effectiveness of decision-making began playing a greater role) created powerful pressures to move toward majority voting in the international realm. Yet the move from unanimity to majority voting was slow and gradual. As two observers who were deeply involved with the establishment of some of the early twentieth century IGOs noted in 1944: "[I]nstitutionally, the struggle to organize international society has been a struggle to shake off 'the rule of unanimity'" (Sweetser and Sharp 1944, 2).

The tension between the powerful rule of unanimity and the need to develop a system that would allow breaking potential deadlocks in a permanent organization is evident even in the wording of the treaty establishing the CCNR. Article 17 of Annex 16-B of the Treaty of Vienna establishing the CCNR stipulated that each state would be represented by one commissioner and that decisions would be adopted by a simple majority of such commissioners. However, the article went on to state that the decisions adopted through a majority would not be compulsory for the states whose commissioners opposed the decision, a provision that illustrated the strength of the sovereignty norm. The treaty and the original rules of procedure made no distinction between substantive and procedural decisions. The founders of this first IGO with permanent secretariat apparently had not foreseen the types of problems arising from the day-to-day work and the decisions necessary to make such an institution work. The commissioners were left to determine such distinctions on their own. They quickly discovered that the best way to deal with the cumbersome official rules while making sure that the organization functioned was to develop informal rules. Therefore, in cases that they jointly considered to be procedural matters, they informally made their decisions by simple majority vote and then agreed to formally present them as being adopted by unanimity so that they would be binding to all parties. In all other matters, they used the formal system of unanimity, and in the cases in which one or more members opposed a decision, it would indeed only apply to the countries that had supported it (Walther 1965, 813).

Yet, in time, the apparent camaraderie of these commissioners who were dealing with fairly technical issues in an organization far away from their capitals led the organization to slip into the adoption of increasingly substantive decisions through the majority system previously described. In 1868, the Treaty of Mannheim made several important changes to the CCNR's original statute. The most important one was intended to curtail the independence of the commissioners. The new treaty stipulated that none of the CCNR decisions would be mandatory for a state whose *government* opposed it (rather than its *commissioner* as in the Treaty of Vienna). This led commissioners to avoid taking important decisions without first gaining approval from their own governments. Of course, the solution made decision-making more cumbersome, as in a time of slow communications it was often difficult for the commissioners to seek their government's consent for every issue that came up in discussions.[2]

---

[2] This problem, compounded with the need to adopt solutions by unanimity, was not solved until the rules of procedure of the CCNR were changed in 1963. At that point members adopted an innovative procedure through which decisions made by commissioners would not be final until thirty days after their vote. In those thirty days, governments

Virtually all of the public international unions established in the second half of the nineteenth century, such as the International Telegraph Union (established in 1865) and the Universal Postal Union (established in 1874), also struggled to find ways of combining the all-important rule of unanimity with the need to have some questions resolved by majority vote (Riches 1940, 63). One of the solutions such organizations adopted was to introduce a mechanism, somewhat similar to the one of the CCNR, through which smaller subsets of states from within the organization could adopt decisions that would only apply to them and not to all members of the IGO. The Union for the Protection of Industrial and Literary and Artistic Property and the Institute of Agriculture, for example, allowed for "restricted unions" that consisted of groups of states within the larger unions that committed themselves to more (or fewer) agreements than the other members (Lyons 1963, 24).

By the beginning of the twentieth century, the increasingly cumbersome unanimity decision-making processes in IGOs led to an obvious need to introduce more majority voting. Soon, majority voting was officially accepted even for substantive decisions in several of the new intergovernmental organizations. Some of the first organizations to introduce majority voting rules in substantive decisions were the ones in the realm of international arbitration and adjudication. For example, the Convention that set up the Permanent Court of Arbitration, in 1907 stipulated in Article 78 that all court questions were to be decided by a majority of judges present at hearing.

As the unanimity rule began eroding, and as membership in IGOs grew, powerful states became increasingly hesitant to accept decision-making systems in which they had little influence over outcomes. They therefore sought ways of introducing voting rules that would give them a greater say. That was difficult to achieve in a world in which virtually all international decisions were adopted by the one-country-one-vote system. After all, as Chapter 3 showed, the principle of sovereign equality among states had become increasingly accepted by the end of the nineteenth century, and, moreover, it resonated strongly with the one-person-one-vote democratic norm that at that time had become very powerful in the domestic realm. Indeed, the sovereignty norm and domestic democratic analogies did not clash as long as the unanimity rule was maintained. Once

could officially reverse the vote of their commissioners. This has, in practice, led to an increased number of decisions being adopted unanimously by the members of the CCNR (Doerflinger 1987).

majority decision-making rules emerged, the two norms could potentially clash, depending on one's interpretation of the domestic analogy.

Powerful states sought to change the system of simple majority rule in decision-making almost as soon as it began being applied in IGOs. For example, as it quickly became apparent that majority voting would play an important role in decision-making in the CCNR, Prussia tried to replace the simple majority voting system stipulated in the founding documents by a weighted majority system. Its case was bolstered by the stipulation in Article 13 of the Vienna Treaty of an interesting formula for the election of the organization's chief inspector. In such an election (and only in such a case), the votes of the CCNR states were to be weighted proportionally to the length of the Rhine River that each member controlled. It is difficult to ascertain whether this first example of weighted majority voting in an IGO was the result of a very strong great power primacy norm or simply one reflecting the fairness of a system in which the length of the Rhine in each country was intended to play at least a token role in decision-making. Indeed, in this case the great power also happened to control the longest section of the Rhine.

Regardless of the reason behind the adoption of this rule, Prussia, which benefited from such a weighted vote formula, pushed for its use in other decisions, beyond the narrow one in which it was originally intended to be used. When the other states refused to use the system, Prussia revealed the problems inherent in the unusual decision-making procedures of the CCNR. It blocked simple procedural decisions (such as those related to the IGO's personnel), claiming that, according to the CCNR's formal agreement, even such decisions could not be imposed on any of its members. This practice led to a crippling of the organization's work. Because even this tactic did not lead to the changes it wanted, Prussia left the Commission for four years, from 1825 to 1829. During that time, the CCNR felt the financial burden that came with the loss of Prussia's substantial share of dues (Van Eysinga 1935). Negotiations with the other members eventually induced Prussia to return to the CCNR but there was no change to the formal decision-making rules. The incident nevertheless reminded all members of the influence Prussia had in the IGO and led smaller states, whenever possible, to informally make some concessions to meet Prussian demands.

It was only after World War I when a weighted voting system was put in place that powerful states in the CCNR were able to gain the advantages that Prussia had initially sought. The new decision-making system combined objective criteria such as the need to have voting power proportional to the length of the Rhine territory in each country, with other arbitrary ones intended to give the victorious powers of World War I additional control in the Commission (Riches 1940). In the end, this compromise was formalized in Article 355 of the Versailles Treaty that gave France five votes, Germany four, Netherlands three, and Switzerland, Belgium, Italy, and the United Kingdom two each.[3] In the International Commission of the Elbe (formally established in 1924) a similar compromise led to a system giving Germany four votes, Czechoslovakia two, and the United Kingdom, France, and Italy one each (Riches 1940). These formulas seem to reflect a compromise between those seeking to give great powers important advantages in the IGO and egalitarian voting norms.

Yet, even in the second half of the nineteenth century, great powers were somewhat successful in introducing stipulations giving them some voting advantages within the IGOs that were being established at that time. While norms of equality among states continued to be too powerful to allow for formal mechanisms of differentiated voting, the United Kingdom, France, and some of the other major powers were able to introduce rules through which their colonies would be given voting rights to some IGOs. For instance, in the Universal Postal Union (UPU), established in 1874 and often considered the model for the League's egalitarian one-country-one-vote system, some colonies and protectorates were also allotted votes. That meant, for example, that the British Empire controlled six of the approximately sixty votes in the UPU (Codding 1964, 34–39, 80–83). Colonial empires had similar advantages in the International Telecommunications Union and the Metric Union established soon after the UPU (Riches 1940, 249).

The International Institute of Agriculture (established in 1908) and the International Office of Public Health (established in 1909) were the first IGOs to adopt formal weighted voting systems based on the scale of financial contributions (Sweetser and Sharp 1944, 6). This implied, of course, that larger and wealthier countries had greater voting power than smaller ones (Riches 1940, 250–252).

After World War I, similar voting rules as those used for the first IGOs of the late nineteenth century and early twentieth century were applied to the new League of Nations. Alfred Zimmern, a close observer of the IGO, had in fact argued: "[T]he League of Nations was never intended to be, nor is it, a revolutionary organization .... It is not even revolutionary

---

[3] It is noteworthy that in the aftermath of World War II the egalitarian system of voting once more replaced the one of weighted voting (Walther 1965).

in the more limited sense of revolutionizing the methods for carrying on interstate business. It does not supersede the older methods. It merely supplements them" (1936, 4). The League required unanimity in the vast majority of substantive decisions, both in the Assembly and the Council, and allowed for majority voting only in procedural decisions.

In the debates leading to the drafting of the Covenant there were some disagreements among states with regard to the decisions in which majority voting could be used rather than unanimity. In virtually all such cases small states appear to have championed the cause of majority votes while powerful ones promoted the use of unanimity. This was true, for example, in the debates surrounding the mandatory effect of the decisions that a majority of the Council recommended (Miller 1928, 180) or the ones involving the process of amending the Covenant (Miller 1928, 204–205). One could interpret small states' willingness to accept majority voting as a reflection of their long-held understanding that, despite the formal existence of the sovereignty principle, their fate had always been dependent on great powers' interests. Conversely, great powers felt that their responsibilities in the international system and their specific interests were different than those of other states, and, therefore, they were not willing to accept a system in which the many small states could impose their will on them (Miller 1928, 97–98).

Small states' support for majority voting appeared to pay off in certain instances as the final draft of the Covenant and subsequent rules of procedures allowed for majority decisions in several cases, even beyond the usual procedural ones. First, new members were elected with two-thirds of the Assembly votes. This implied that the most powerful states could not block such admissions, as was later the case in the UN. Second, although the League Council could not act without a unanimous decision, it could adopt reports regarding disputes between states with a simple majority vote.

Most important, in disputes between states, all League Council decisions required only unanimous approval of states not involved in the dispute. This rule, of course, implied that even powerful states could not block all League Council decisions. For example, in 1935 the League Council adopted a report condemning Italy's attack on Abyssinia despite the fact that Italy, a permanent member of the Council, voted against the report. The report later led to the adoption of economic sanctions against Italy (Grigorescu 2005). This provision of the League Covenant was the most important departure from the unanimity rule as it took away for the first time a great power's ability to veto decisions that ran counter to its basic interests. In fact, this rule was at the center of some of the most intense deliberations when the victors of World War II drafted the UN Charter.

What is significant is that although powerful states were given an advantage through permanent representation in the executive bodies of the League and its satellite organizations, such as the ILO, they did not have any advantages in the number of votes that were allocated. Interestingly, during that same period, weighted voting systems permeated many of the other organizations that were established and that did not deal with security matters. As a reminder, in the CCNR the new rules of 1921 introduced a differentiated system of voting. The International Commission for Air Navigation, established in 1919, gave more votes to the United States, the United Kingdom, France, Italy, and Japan and fewer votes to small states (Sweetser and Sharp 1944, 7). In other IGOs founded in the interwar era, such as the International Wine Office and the International Office of Chemistry (both established in 1928), weighted voting systems were also put in place. Organizations that were established at that time to deal with the trade of certain important commodities gave more votes to large importing countries than to the much smaller exporting ones. For example, in the Council of the International Sugar Regime (established in 1937) the United States and the United Kingdom each had seventeen votes while small states such as Cuba, Peru, and Haiti, had ten, three, and one votes, respectively (Riches 1940, 252, 253).

Developments after World War II and during the Cold War
Of the IGOs established in the interwar era, perhaps the most influential model for post–World War II organizations was the Bank for International Settlements (BIS). BIS, the first major intergovernmental organization to deal primarily with economic issues, was established in 1930. It adopted a voting system weighted proportionally to members' financial contributions to the organization and, implicitly, to their economic power (Bank for International Settlements 1930). The BIS model was later used as a starting point for the voting system of the World Bank and the IMF (Mason and Asher 1973, 15).

It is perhaps noteworthy that, whereas the unequal status of great and small powers in the UNSC was challenged and debated with great passion in San Francisco, the unequal votes in the World Bank and the IMF appear to have been more easily accepted by small states at the Bretton Woods conference. In fact, most of the disagreements regarding organizational issues of the World Bank and IMF seemed to be between the United

Kingdom and the United States rather than between these powerful states and small ones (Mason and Asher 1973, 30–31; de Vries 1986, 12).

It was the United States that pushed for the introduction of a number of "basic votes" for each member-state, in addition to the number of votes that were supposed to be allocated on the basis of the quota contribution – in other words, proportionally to the country's wealth (Gianaris 1990). The British did not see the value of such a system and argued that the international financial institutions needed to function just like all other banks and commercial institutions, with votes proportional to each shareholder's contribution. The American side, especially the press, hinted at domestic democratic analogies when promoting this more egalitarian system of voting. During the negotiations John Maynard Keynes wrote in a letter to a British Treasury official in Washington responding to such analogies: "It is depressing that so much attention has been concentrated on voting. It never crossed my mind that we were under an accusation of having tried to rig this.... Some of the American press comments dealing with this as a branch of power politics is, in its way, an extraordinary exhibition of vulgarity" (Gold 1972, 27). This exchange was one of the first examples of democratic norms being used to promote greater equality in IGO voting rules and of a challenging strategy (on the part of the UK) arguing that such norms should not be applied to banklike entities.

Interestingly, because of practical considerations, small states did not emerge as strong promoters of the democratic analogy and of the equal voting norms. These stem from the fact that the voting system in the World Bank was supposed to be connected to the one in the IMF. However, there were different incentives built into the two decision-making systems. In the IMF, on the one hand, drawing rights were based on quota. This, of course, established the incentive for states to have larger quotas. In the World Bank, on the other hand, the amount a country could borrow was independent of its contribution. This led to a weak incentive to have large quotas in the World Bank and, implicitly, to have a large number of votes. In the end, the compromise between the United States and the United Kingdom (and other states) led to a system both in the World Bank and the IMF in which member-states each had 250 basic votes plus one additional vote for each $100,000 subscribed (Gianaris 1990).

In addition to the previously mentioned argument, there are several other reasons why smaller countries did not object too strongly to the unequal voting system that the United States and the United Kingdom established. First, as mentioned earlier, the weighted voting systems had been slowly introduced in a number of IGOs in the interwar era. The great power primacy principle of the interwar era had made it a common practice that organizations dealing with technical issues would allow wealthier states a greater say in decision-making. Weighted voting became common practice in organizations that relied on substantial funding (and, implicitly, differentiated state contributions) to fulfill their tasks, as in the case of the BIS. Therefore, the World Bank and IMF voting rules were not interpreted initially even by small states as departing too much from what fair voting norms of the times dictated.

Moreover, at the end of World War II, when the United States controlled an extraordinary share of the global wealth (perhaps more easily measurable than the share of military power that the UNSC permanent members controlled in 1945), it became obvious that it also had to carry a large proportion of the financial burden of the new Bretton Woods institutions. This prominent role translated into a generally accepted voting system that gave the United States a sizeable degree of control over the new organizations.

An additional possible reason for the general acceptance of the unequal voting system in the World Bank and the IMF (compared to the tensions brought about by the proposal for the voting advantages of great powers in the UNSC) is the fact that the Bretton Woods meetings took place in July 1944 while the war was still being fought and when there was a greater degree of uncertainty with regard to the future of international relations than during the June 1945 San Francisco meetings. It is likely that small states took more conciliatory positions in Bretton Woods while great powers were leading the still ongoing war than later, when the war had already ended in Europe.

Lastly, the Bretton Woods institutions were, in fact, able to adopt a more balanced solution to the tension between the norm of state equality and the need to give great powers greater control over outcomes by finding a formula that included both basic votes and votes proportional to their quota contributions (Caliari and Schroeder 2002, 2). The decision to avoid a pure weighted system by introducing some degree of equality in the voting formula can be interpreted as a deliberate choice to narrow the application of the fair voting norm to defuse potential normative pressures from small states, once they regained their voice, in the aftermath of the war. As a reminder, H_4 and H_6 together indeed suggest that when the status quo is not perceived to depart too much from the norm's prescriptions, actors who want to defuse normative pressures for reforms will use such a strategy of narrowing the application of the norm. In the end, the Bretton Woods voting formula contrasted with the less gradualist differentiation of votes in the soon to be established UNSC, where states either had or did not have a veto.

The search for a balance between voting equality and maintaining power in the hands of the most influential states became especially obvious in the drafting of the UN Charter in 1945. By that time, the founders of the UN benefited from the existence of a multitude of decision-making systems in inclusive IGOs. In fact, in early 1944, when the United States was already considering various models for the design of the new UN, a confidential document, titled "The Differential Participation of States in International Organizations," was produced for limited circulation among American officials. One of the two authors, Arthur Sweetser, had been deeply involved in the establishment of the League and even in its work before it became obvious that the United States would not join the organization. It is noteworthy that, although the document clearly advocated the use of differentiated systems of voting in the new organizations of the post–World War II era, it also made great efforts to convince readers of the appropriateness of such mechanisms by pointing out that unequal voting power in an IGO is not inconsistent with principles of legal equality among states (Sweetser and Sharp 1944, 2). The document offered the examples of many of the aforementioned IGOs that had been established with weighted voting systems. While listing the possibilities of introducing elements of differentiated voting between the powerful and smaller states, the document concluded with a sentence suggesting that democratic norms based on domestic analogies were fairly powerful among those involved in the drafting of the UN Charter (albeit, more with regard to representation than voting): "It goes without saying that equality of representation for all states, great and small, will continue to have its place in the deliberative and general policy-making councils, assemblies and conferences which are an essential feature of any democratic system of international cooperation" (Sweetser and Sharp 1944, 11). This document illustrated the growing tension between the great power primacy norm, on the one hand, and the sovereign equality and equal voting norms, on the other.

The same two major powers that had shaped the League Covenant, the United States and the United Kingdom, also initiated the drafting of the UN Charter. They then discussed their initial plans with the Soviet Union and China in 1944 at Dumbarton Oaks, and later with France. After incorporating some of the changes demanded by the Soviets, the three main great powers came from their Yalta conference with a common position on the structure of the United Nations.

The "Yalta formula" for the UNSC voting system was a combination of important features that had been present in the League and new ones that were intended to make the UN a more efficient organization. This was the result of a general understanding among all states, great and small, that although the League of Nations had failed to meet expectations, any plan for a new global organization still had to begin from the League (Goodrich 1947; Lee 1947, 36).

The Yalta Charter draft allowed for five permanent seats in the new Security Council, the same number as in the original plans for the League Council. The seats were allotted to the main victors of World War II: China, France, the Soviet Union, the United Kingdom, and the United States. As in the case of the League, the founders of the UN decided to make all substantive decisions in the Council require unanimous backing of the five great powers. The draft Charter also allowed for six non-permanent seats for other states. As a reminder, the League Council included four non-permanent seats in the original formula of 1919 but later increased this number to six in 1923, nine in 1926, ten in 1933, and eleven in 1936.

However, there were several important breaks from the League voting rules. First, in the UNSC great powers eliminated the important rule of the League Council in which a state involved in a conflict was not allowed to cast its vote, the most important exception to the powerful unanimity principle in the League voting rules. Because of powerful Soviet insistence, in the UN, this exception was to apply only to votes involving the peaceful settlement of disputes (US Department of State 1945, 326, 658). In all decisions that did not involve peaceful settlement of disputes the UN allowed the five great powers to vote (and veto) even when they were directly involved in the conflict. In the San Francisco conference it quickly became obvious that the five great powers were adamant about their ability to use the veto for virtually all future decisions of the UNSC. At one point, the subcommittee that dealt with the veto issue presented a questionnaire to China, the Soviet Union, the United Kingdom, and the United States seeking clarifications with regard to their interpretation of the possible use of the veto in cases of pacific settlement. After long disagreements among themselves, these four great powers eventually responded to the questionnaire through a document that was later referred to informally as "the Statement." The document did not answer most of the questions that had been included in the original questionnaire. However, it did respond to the one regarding the types of issues in which the veto could not be used. It indicated that none of the veto holders could prevent the consideration or discussion of a dispute or situation brought to the UNSC's attention. They also could not block the hearing of disputants or of any "reminders of their obligations." Yet, beyond these specific cases, they indicated that even decisions that referred to peaceful settlement of disputes could be vetoed because they otherwise may have "major political consequences" as a result of the chains of events that they might trigger. Therefore, even decisions to investigate disputes or to call on or recommend to the parties to settle their disputes peacefully could be vetoed as they could lead to such major political consequences (Lee 1947, 40).

More important for this chapter, the UNSC voting system differed from that of the League Council as it did not allow for small powers that were on the UNSC to single-handedly block resolutions; the change essentially took away the veto from such small powers, and, by doing so, it eliminated equal voting among states in the most important organ of the most important IGO of the post–World War II era. No doubt, great powers remembered how Spain and Brazil had been able to block German membership in the League (and permanent membership in the Council) in the debates of the mid-1920s, despite British and French strong support for admitting Germany. The proposed Yalta formula of voting in the UNSC therefore eventually combined a unanimous decision-making system for great powers with majority voting for the entire body.[4]

In discussions of the draft Charter at the San Francisco conference, the issue of the great power veto involved the longest and most contentious debates. The new rules that differentiated between states that had a veto and all others that did not were met with bitter criticism from small states. They were similar to the critiques that ensued after the great power victors of World War I had suggested a differentiation in participation in the League Council. The strong feelings of the small states led to discussions on the contentious issue of the veto that lasted almost throughout the entire two months of the conference. Seventeen different delegations (of the forty-five represented in San Francisco) proposed amendments to the veto rule. Small states also sought dozens of other amendments that tried to redistribute power from the UNSC to the General Assembly or to introduce a clear definition of the kind of "acts of aggression" that the UNSC would deal with (Wilcox 1945, 946).

---

[4] Another interesting (yet rare) case of such differentiated veto power can be found in the Organization of Petroleum Exporting Countries in which the five "founder members" (Iran, Iraq, Kuwait, Saudi Arabia, and Venezuela) are the only countries to have a veto in some of the important collective decisions.

In the long deliberations of the 1945 San Francisco Conference, the domestic analogy to democratic institutions was used much more often than in the debates that took place in Paris in 1919 that led to the establishment of the League. Most of the heated discussions involving the structure and procedures of the UNSC took place in the first of twelve technical committees that dealt with issues related to the UNSC. A close reading of the minutes of debates within that Committee reveals that the words democracy or democratic appear dozens of times both criticizing and defending the veto system. For example, the representative of the Philippines claimed that a majority voting system, even one based on weighted voting in the UNSC, was preferable as it was "more democratic" than one in which the veto is given to a limited number of states (United Nations Conference on International Organizations 1945, 1914). The Cuban representative argued that the right of veto was contrary to the fundamental principles of democracy and would become a source of future problems. He continued by saying: "[O]ne of the democratic ideas for which the United Nations had been courageously fighting is that of government by the majority. This would be completely destroyed by permitting the will of one nation to dominate the will of the rest of the world" (United Nations Conference on International Organizations 1945, 1914–1915).

The British representative responded to such arguments by challenging the interpretation of the fair voting norm presented by small states. He suggested that it was not undemocratic to give the five great powers an advantage in the UNSC because they represented more than half of the world's population (United Nations Conference on International Organizations 1945, 1837–1844). This argument was also used in academic circles that defended the veto system (Wilcox 1945, 947). The strategy was similar to the one discussed in Chapter 3 used by an Italian representative to challenge the norm of fair representation in the ILO, as presented by small states. In both cases great powers suggested that because they have larger populations, democratic norms dictate that they have advantages in decision-making: permanent representation in the case of the ILO and a veto in the case of the UNSC. This perspective emphasized a cosmopolitan understanding of democracy that operated at the level of individuals and therefore considered differences based on populations of states (albeit not rigorously) over the communitarian one that operated at the state level and that implied that all states should have equal votes.

The United States applied the strategy of challenging the fair voting norm in a different way. In the debates of the committee discussing the future UNSC, American delegates made multiple references to the words of President Roosevelt who had passed away shortly before the San Francisco conference had gotten underway. Roosevelt indeed was considered the "father" of the new United Nations by virtually all representatives present in San Francisco, and, therefore, his words carried a great deal of weight. One particular passage from a speech Roosevelt had delivered just months before the San Francisco conference, and soon before his death, was quoted several times by American officials: "We cannot deny that power is a factor in world politics any more than we can deny its existence as a factor in national politics. But in a democratic world, as in a democratic nation, power must be linked with responsibility, and obliged to defend and justify itself within the framework of the general good" (United Nations Conference on International Organization 1945, 5333–5336). This excerpt was used by U.S. officials to convince small states that giving certain advantages to powerful states in the UNSC was not necessarily "undemocratic" as long as such advantages were used to defend the "general good." By adopting this argument, veiled in the language of democracy, the U.S. delegation, in fact, challenged the norm of equal voting by invoking the appropriateness of additional obligations (and roles) for great power, deriving from the great power primacy norm.

In the end, although great powers did not make any concessions on the question of the veto in the San Francisco conference, they appear to have been sufficiently successful in defusing the normative pressures of equal voting to garner the necessary two-thirds majority for introducing the differentiated veto system in the Charter. One of their most powerful arguments throughout the debates was that they simply would not be willing to accept a charter without a clear stipulation granting them (and only them) such a veto. In what was one of the most dramatic moments of the conference, U.S. Senator Tom Connally tore up a copy of the Charter declaring: "You may if you wish go home from this Conference and say that you have defeated the veto. But what will be your answer when you are asked: 'Where is the Charter?'" (Wilcox 1945, 954). This threat was a powerful one as the U.S. decision to not be part of the League of Nations was fresh in everyone's mind.

Great powers were also able to maintain other proposed rules involving the use of the veto that gave them important advantages in the organization. For example, they could veto the admission of new members to the organization, something that, as mentioned earlier, had not been possible under the League system. They could individually stop amendments to the Charter. They could also use their veto to block the election of judges in the International Court of Justice.

At the same time, the broadening strategies involving simultaneous discussions of voting rules in multiple UN bodies led to egalitarian systems in the other principal UN organs. In the General Assembly, the Economic and Social Council, and the Trusteeship Council, great power votes were equal to those of all other members. Virtually all of the UN agencies, such as WHO or UNESCO, also gave all states equal votes. Older IGOs, whether under the new UN umbrella or outside it, continued their egalitarian practices, as in the case of the ILO, or increased them as in the CCNR or the UPU, which eliminated both the formal and informal post–World War I voting advantages of great powers, mentioned earlier.

In time, the equal voting rights of states in many of the IGOs not dealing with security issues led to instances in which great powers felt that their interests were not reflected in the decisions being adopted. In extreme cases, such as the one of the United States in the ILO and both the United States and the United Kingdom in UNESCO, great powers used "exit strategies" (Tobin 1999) in attempting to induce other member-states to accept their demands; in a similar fashion Prussia had used this strategy to flex its muscles in the CCNR in the nineteenth century.

Organizations with regional or limited membership outside of the UN system – whether using primarily majority voting, as in the case of the Organisation for Economic Co-operation and Development (established in 1960), or unanimity, as in the case of the Council of Europe (established in 1959) and the Organization of American States (established in 1947) – also used egalitarian rules in their decision-making procedures. One of the few exceptions to this trend was, interestingly, the ECSC, the precursor of the European Union, in which France, Germany, and Italy originally had twice the number of votes than did the other three founding members: Belgium, Luxembourg, and the Netherlands. This decision is perhaps not that surprising if we consider that the original purpose of the IGO was to deal with industries in which output in the six states was very unequal. In the ECSC state inequality was also reflected in the nascent Common Assembly, in which France, Germany, and Italy each had eighteen representatives, Belgium and the Netherlands each had ten, and Luxembourg had four (Wells 2007, 13). This formula seems to balance the sovereign equality norm (that would have given all states equal representatives and votes), great power primacy (that would have given only powerful states voting power), and democratic norms (that would have emphasized the distribution of votes based on states' population).[5]

Such weighted voting systems continued to function in the European Economic Community and, later, in the EU. The system that was put in place in the Council allowed for qualified majority voting in a few policy areas even from the start. In time, important treaties have allowed for an increasing number of policy areas to be decided by qualified majority voting rather than unanimity. The most important shifts took place after each membership enlargement (starting with the one of 1973); after the Treaty of Nice, when a direct population-dependent condition was introduced; and after the Treaty of Lisbon, when individual country votes were abandoned in favor of a "double majority," depending only on the number of states and the population represented (Hosli 2000). This suggests that, as the European institutions moved away from unanimity voting to qualified majority voting, the system shifted to an increasingly more representative one based not just on the size of a country's economy (as in the case of the World Bank and IMF) but also on its population. These changes in voting rules have generally been considered by observers as examples of an advancement of the European institutions toward more democratic systems (e.g., Micossi 2008). Just as important, the changes have been accompanied by important shifts in the balance between the Council and the Parliament, as Chapter 7 shows.

The move toward greater voting equality in IGOs during the Cold War is also reflected in regional development banks such as the Inter-American Development Bank (established in 1959) and the African Development Bank (established in 1964). In both of these IGOs, the voting rules made sure that borrower (developing) countries together had more votes than creditor (developed) countries. This formula differed considerably from the ones the World Bank and IMF established at the end of World War II that allowed a handful of powerful economies to control virtually all decisions.

Yet another reflection of the more egalitarian trends of the Cold War era is the fact that in the other World Bank institutions that were created well after the Bretton Woods negotiations such as the International Development Association (IDA), established in 1960, or the Multilateral

---

[5] In 1952, the first year of the ECSC's existence, Germany had a population of approximately 69 million, Italy of 48 million, France of 43 million, Netherlands about 10 million, Belgium about 9 million, and Luxembourg 0.3 million (see http://www.geoba.se). Therefore, the preceding numbers of seats reflected a compromise between a strictly one-country-one-vote system and one based purely on population considerations.

Investment Guarantee Agency (MIGA), established in 1985, the voting formulas gave developing countries much greater influence. In IDA, originally each member had 500 basic votes plus one additional vote for each US$5,000 subscription. Moreover, while developing countries can make additional subscriptions to avoid a reduction in their voting power, developed countries only receive additional votes after a set contribution. In the case of MIGA, the original rules stipulated that, during the first three years of the agency's existence, developing countries could receive additional votes to make sure that, together, they reach a minimum of 40 percent of all votes. All of these decisions, whether in the World Bank institutions or in the regional development banks, can be interpreted as the result of a strategy of narrowing the application of the fair voting norm.

Lastly, it should be noted that throughout its almost seven decades of existence the World Bank has altered voting weights. The changes came as a result of the increase in the number of states and fluctuations in their economic strength. For example, throughout the Cold War, the United States' percentage of total votes shifted from 35.07 percent in 1946 to 24.99 percent in 1951, 29.25 percent in 1961, 23.82 percent in 1971, 20.84 percent in 1981, and 17.22 percent in 1990 (Gianaris 1990). As I discuss in the following section, yet another voting reform took place in the post–Cold War era, in 2010, when U.S. voting weight moved from 15.5 percent of total votes to 14.99 percent (Bretton Woods Project 2010). These changes followed, to some degree, the relative economic power (measured as the U.S. proportion of the world's GDP[6]) and relative overall power (based on data from the National Material Capabilities dataset) of the United States, as illustrated in Figure 4.2.

The adjustments in voting weights in the World Bank, IMF, and the regional development banks were nevertheless exceptions to the general trends in IGOs. During the stagnant Cold War era there were no major changes in the voting rules of any other global IGOs.

The Post–Cold War Era

The proliferation of IGOs with egalitarian voting rules and the growing number of states in the international system throughout the Cold War led to increased pressures to eliminate the veto (or, at least limit its use) in the UNSC. Whether it was the end of the Cold War that triggered a greater

---

[6] U.S. overall GDP and proportion of world GDP are based on World Bank country data (http://data.worldbank.org).

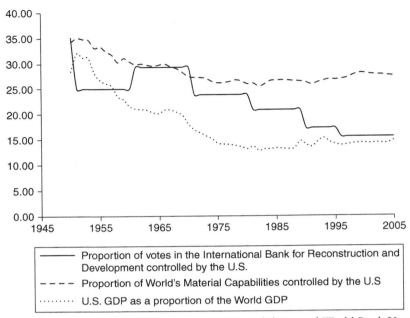

FIGURE 4.2. Proportion of World's Material Capabilities and World Bank Votes Controlled by the United States.

interest in the now potentially functional UNSC or the looming fiftieth anniversary of the United Nations in 1995 that reminded everyone how UN rules had hardly been altered since its inception, although the world had witnessed important changes, the pressures for UNSC reform became even stronger in the early 1990s. As mentioned in Chapter 3, small and medium powers that had been left outside of the UNSC stepped up their efforts to increase membership of this organ. In addition, some states also pushed for changes to the veto.

Post–Cold War efforts to reform the UNSC have included proposals to completely eliminate the veto altogether. Other proposals simply seek the introduction of new rules that would reduce its use. These include provisions that permanent members should at least be obligated to explain their reasons for using the veto and that would not allow for the use of veto in cases of genocide or crimes against humanity. Yet others have suggested that new rules should allow the veto to be overturned by an absolute majority of the General Assembly or by a vote of two-thirds of the UNSC itself (proposals clearly based, yet again, on domestic analogies) (Center for UN Reform 2009).

So far the P5 countries have repeatedly expressed their opposition to all proposals to do away with the veto or even to reduce its use. The fact that any change to the UNSC voting system must be accepted by all five permanent members suggests that even if this UN organ will experience reform of its membership, it is unlikely to alter its veto rules.

Interestingly, it has not been the great powers that have placed reforms to both the UNSC voting system and its membership simultaneously on the agenda. If this is indeed a broadening strategy, it appears to be applied by smaller states. It is possible that small states decided to tackle both such issues in the hope that the P5 will apply a strategy of narrowing and accept at least part of the proposals on the table. As Chapter 5 shows, powerful states, indeed, applied a broadening strategy to reduce the normative pressures for membership reforms in the UNSC in the 1990s. Yet it was one that linked state participation in this exclusive organ to greater transparency, rather than to the all-important veto.

The World Bank and IMF have also experienced pressures for reforming their voting systems. Most proposals for such reforms do not attempt to do away entirely with differentiated voting. Nevertheless they do seek a better balance or even equality in the representation of the interests of borrower and creditor countries as in the aforementioned cases of the Inter-American Development Bank and the African Development Bank. To achieve such a balance, proponents of reform suggest, for instance, that the allocation of basic votes and total votes return at least to the ratio of 1944. The argument is based on the observation that even though the total number of basic votes (250 for each country) has increased only about four times since the founding of these organizations, at the same rate as the increase in membership, the IMF quotas and World Bank shareholdings have increased almost forty times. This has led to a relative decline in the voting power of small states that rely more on basic votes than on their votes deriving from quotas and shares (Paloni and Zanardi 2006, 34–35).

There have also been proposals to bring about more meaningful changes to the voting system of the World Bank and IMF. In the World Bank, there have been increased calls to change the supermajority required for the amendment of World Bank articles, for capital increases, or for the selection of the World Bank president. The supermajority has allowed the United States, the only country that has had (until recently) control of more than 15 percent of all votes, to have de facto veto power in such important cases requiring 85 percent of all votes (Pincus and Winters 2002, 58; Caliari and Schroeder 2002, 4).

The pressures for such reforms in the Bretton Woods institutions have come both from developing countries and from nongovernmental organizations. Although the former group has promoted voting reforms by emphasizing issues of "fairness," it rarely used the democratic analogy. Many NGOs and academics, on the other hand, have indeed discussed the need for such changes by invoking democratic domestic analogies (e.g., Bretton Woods Project 2010; BBC 2005; Peet 2009).

At first glance, the pressures for reform appear to have been fairly successful. In 2010, in great part as a response to the economic crisis of 2008, the World Bank was able to obtain $86 billion capital increase. With this increase came some changes to the voting power of states. Developed countries' share of the vote fell from 66.59 to 60.52 percent, while developing and transition countries' shares rose from 33.41 to 39.48 percent. The World Bank touted these changes as important ones that allowed it to move toward greater equity (Bretton Woods Project 2010). The World Bank president Robert Zoellick hailed the reforms by explaining them in the following way: "We're moving towards a multipolar framework and institutions need to adapt to these changes. We can no longer resolve big international issues without the support of developing countries" (Parliamentary Network on the World Bank 2010).

Yet critics argue that the increase in developing countries' voting power was far smaller than original reform proposals called for (implying that a strategy of narrowing the application of the norm was applied). Moreover, they show that, if one looks closely, the changes are in fact very small as the numbers that the Bank uses are deceiving. For example, several NGOs pointed out that the category of transition countries used by the Bank, in fact, includes sixteen high-income economies (that together hold more than 5 percent of the vote), such as Saudi Arabia and Hungary. The seventy-eight countries actually eligible to borrow from the Bank remain with slightly more than one-third the voting power (34.1 percent) rather than 39.48 percent, as the Bank declares (Beattie 2010).

It is also important to point out that the Bank has presented the voting changes of 2010 as only one part of the broader reform agenda that also includes a new Access to Information Policy, an Open Data Initiative for developing countries, investment lending reforms, and strengthened governance and anti-corruption efforts (World Bank 2010). It is perhaps because of this broadening strategy that the changes in voting structure took longer and were smaller than expected. As a result of the complexity of such negotiations, powerful states also appeared to have obtained a reprieve of five years (and probably, in practice, much more) for any other future voting reforms. Critics argue that, at this slow rate of change, it will be decades before developing countries will reach the same number of votes as developed ones (Bretton Woods Project, 2010).

Parallel to these pressures for more egalitarian IGO formal voting rules, in the post–Cold War era there has been an interesting move from majoritarian practices to informal and even formal unanimity rules (often referred to as "consensus seeking" procedures). For instance, in the General Assembly, member states have increasingly sought to adopt resolutions by consensus. In the fiftieth UNGA session (of 1995–1996), 73 percent of all General Assembly resolutions were adopted by consensus, whereas only 46 percent were adopted by consensus in the thirtieth session (of 1965–1966). This trend is partly a result of the lingering euphoria that came with the end of the Cold War and that led to what is often described as the "age of consensus" in this universal body. It is also because of the fact that unanimous decisions are seen to offer UNGA resolutions greater legitimacy. This is important for a body whose resolutions rely on the power derived from such legitimacy rather than on formal legal power (as in the case of the UNSC). Overall, the number of resolutions adopted in the UNGA without a vote has risen considerably in the past two decades.

The trend toward seeking unanimous decisions is especially visible in the UNGA Budget Committee that, since the late 1980s, has informally adopted its resolutions through consensus. In this case, the change was primarily a result of U.S. pressures to institute a system allowing it to block unwanted spending in an organization to which it contributes close to a quarter of all funds.

The emphasis on unanimity is also reflected in the rules adopted in the newest major intergovernmental organization, the World Trade Organization, established in 1995. When the General Agreement on Tariffs and Trade was established in 1947, the rules of procedure stipulated that each country would have one vote and that decisions would be adopted by two-thirds majority (1947). Yet, starting in the late 1960s the majority voting in GATT began being replaced informally by unanimity (Steger and Shpilkovskaya 2010, 134; Steinberg 2002). There is no indication whether powerful states, that were behind this initiative, used democratic normative pressures to promote the change. Not surprisingly, the shift toward informal unanimous voting came around the same time that the developing countries in GATT began outnumbering the developed ones.

At the founding of the WTO, in 1995, powerful states pushed to have the informal unanimity rule from GATT play a more important role, if possible a formal one. They succeeded in having the rule mentioned in the WTO's founding documents. Article IX of the Marrakesh Agreement stipulated: "[T]he WTO shall continue the *practice* [emphasis added] of decision-making by consensus followed under GATT" (World Trade Organization 1994, 13). Yet, the article continued by noting that if a decision cannot be reached by consensus, it should nevertheless be decided by a vote (World Trade Organization 1994, 13). Since the inception of the organization there have been very few cases in which the organization actually had to replace the consensus procedure with three-quarters majority voting. As in the case of the UNGA Budget Committee, discussed previously, the unanimity decision-making process in the WTO has generally been viewed as giving advantages to great powers (especially the Quad) that would likely be outvoted in most decisions necessitating majority voting (Jacobs 2002, 4).

Not surprisingly, some of the greatest pressures to introduce a formal unanimity rule in the WTO came from the United States. When in 1994 the Senate held hearings on the WTO, outspoken critics of the new IGO, such as Ralph Nader and Jesse Helms, all made references to the majority voting system and argued that this would be the first major international forum in which the United States would lack either a veto or at least a large number of votes (Barfield 1994). Such opponents of the WTO presented the organization as "undemocratic" for two reasons. First, it was argued that it imposed policies on states bypassing democratic domestic political systems (an argument that conflated the democratic source of the pro-unanimity norm with the one based on the principle of sovereignty). Senator Richard Shelby expressed this argument when stating: "[T]he thought of an under-developed and undemocratic nation passing judgment on the laws of the largest free market and most democratic nation in the world is simply offensive to most Americans" (Hardy 1994).

Second, it was argued that many of the dispute settlement cases that would impact U.S. interests in the WTO took place in secrecy. Such critics presented both of these features of the new organization as "completely alien to [U.S.] democratic traditions" (Nader 1994). In the WTO negotiations with other states, the Clinton administration used some of these critiques to pressure others into accepting at least the practice of unanimity, if not the formal rule (Denniston 1994). The aforementioned wording in the Marrakesh Agreement was a result of great power normative and material pressures and other states' strategies of defusing such pressures.

Now the WTO appears to pride itself in the use of the unanimity procedure. On its Web site, in a presentation of the "Ten Common Misunderstandings about the WTO," the organization claims that its decision-making procedure by consensus is "even more democratic" than those by majority rule "because no decision is taken until everyone agrees" (World Trade Organization 1999).

There are two additional observations that need to be mentioned to allow for a better understanding of the impact of democratic norms on IGO rules in the aforementioned cases. First, one should note that powerful states are the ones that generally seem to have pushed for such unanimity. In doing so, they have based their arguments on domestic democratic analogies much more than on great power primacy norms (as they certainly could have in the case of the UNGA Budget Committee) or even on sovereignty norms. Second, while great powers have promoted unanimity decision-making rules in IGOs where equal votes are allotted to all members, of course, they have not sought similar changes in IGOs with differentiated system in place (as in the IMF, World Bank, or UNSC).

Despite these differences in the positions of small and great powers, the move toward unanimity decision-making has affected even IGOs where it is more difficult to identify great power interests. For instance, the Constitutive Act of the African Union (AU) stipulates in Article 11 that the Executive Council first seeks decisions by consensus and, only if it fails to reach such consensus, does it adopt decisions by simple majority vote (African Union 2000).

Similarly the International Renewable Energy Agency (IRENA), formally established in 2011 (and like the WTO and the AU, one of the few IGOs established after the end of the Cold War), adopts decisions in its council by consensus. Nevertheless, IRENA's statute stipulates that "consensus shall be considered achieved if no more than 2 Members object."[7] It is perhaps important to point out the similarity between this "near-consensus" decision-making formula in one of the most recent IGOs and the ones in the first international forums such as the Concert of Europe and the CCRC, discussed earlier in this chapter.

---

[7] See http://www.irena.org/documents/uploadDocuments/Statute/IRENA_FC_Statute_signed_in_Bonn_26_01_2009_incl_declaration_on_further_authentic_versions.pdf

Answering the Questions of the Study

What Types of Decision-Making Rules Were Being Established or Changed?

IGOs have adopted several types of voting procedures. A first broad distinction is the one between unanimity and majority. Within the majoritarian procedure they have further developed systems that give all member-states equal votes or that give some states an advantage. This advantage, in turn, can be in the form of a differentiated veto (as in the UNSC) or of weighted votes (as in the multilateral development banks).

One of the most interesting developments across the past 200 years is the shift from unanimity voting (which assured all states that IGO decisions will respect members' sovereignty) to majority voting (which leads to decisions running counter to some state interests) and, to some degree, back to unanimity. Majority voting was first introduced in IGO bodies that dealt with the less significant, day-to-day, operational decisions. The most important IGO bodies, in which substantive decisions were adopted, maintained unanimity systems. Yet, in time, as IGOs became more complex and included more states, they increasingly moved toward majority voting to be more effective. The League of Nations maintained unanimity voting in the Council and in the Assembly for major decisions. The ILO embraced majority voting systems in its bodies but, because of the need to have all of its major treaties ratified by its members, it assured all states that their sovereignty would be protected.

It is only after the shift toward majoritarian voting that democratic analogies appeared in the debates surrounding the adoption or changes in decision-making procedures. The first major IGOs to adopt majoritarian systems with weighted votes emerged in the interwar era. The World Bank, IMF, and ECSC (followed later by the EEC and EU) later adopted such models. Voting in the UNSC can simply be understood as a combination between a unanimity system, as in the League Council (but one that only applied here to five powerful states), and a majority one (which applied to all other states). There appears to be a shift once more to unanimity voting systems in the post–Cold War era.

In most cases the voting systems that were originally set in place remained the same throughout the existence of IGOs. The exceptions are generally those in which increases in the number of members led to the adoption of informal rules alongside the formal ones (as in GATT) or those in which shifts in the IGO's resources altered voting weights (as in the World Bank). The European institutions have experienced the most frequent changes in voting rules, moving toward an increasing number of decisions with qualified majority voting and, also, altering the weight of such votes. Although there have been strong pressures to change voting rules, there have not been any such reforms in other IGOs (such as the UN).

Did Actors Invoke Democratic Norms to Pressure Others in Accepting Decision-Making Rules?

Democratic analogies and norms were rarely invoked before World War II when strong sovereignty norms maintained unanimity systems in virtually all major IGOs. It was only after the emergence of majoritarian differentiated voting procedures that they began being used in debates. There were some normative pressures at the establishment of the World Bank and IMF, but for a variety of reasons, they did not appear to match the powerful ones that emerged just one year later when the UNSC was established with only five veto holders.

Democratic norms were invoked a great deal in debates surrounding the UNSC veto in 1945 and more recently in the post–Cold War era, but not during the Cold War. They were also not used in the debates surrounding World Bank voting during the Cold War but were once more present in those after the Cold War ended.[8] Democratic analogies were also adopted to emphasize the fairness of the unanimity system in the WTO in the post–Cold War era.

How Powerful were Such Pressures?

Figure 4.1 illustrated the evolution of the fair voting norm across all states since the beginning of the nineteenth century. Figure 4.3 follows this measure only since 1920 after the first major IGOs were established. Also, as in other chapters, it scales the measure from 0 (minimum strength of norm over entire period) to 1 (maximum strength of norm over entire period). As for all five democratic norms, I consider the strength of the fair voting norm to be high for levels in the top third of the graph (as was the case since the late 1960s), it is moderate when it is in the middle third (as it was, barely, throughout most of the 1930s, immediately after World War II, and, more clearly, in the second decade of the Cold War), and it is low when it is in the bottom third (in the 1920s and during the first

---

[8] Records of important World Bank meetings, such as those discussing changes in voting, are not sufficiently detailed to allow us to identify whether such norms were in fact invoked. The previously made argument is based solely on secondary sources.

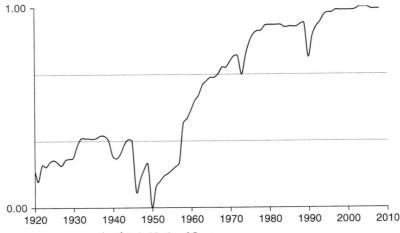

FIGURE 4.3. Strength of Fair Voting Norm.

decade of the Cold War). By comparison to the global norm, the strength of the norm in member-states of the European institutions was strong since the 1950s. The values of norm strength are represented in the third row of Table 4.1.

Normative pressure is based both on norm strength and on the degree to which the status quo departs from the norm. Therefore, even though norm strength was high on multiple occasions, the voting arrangements in IGOs were often not seen as departing from such norm prescriptions and, norm pressures were not significant. For instance, at the founding of the League (in which unanimity decision-making was based on equal votes) as well as at the founding of the ILO and GATT (in which equal majoritarian rules were in place), decision-making was seen as reflecting the norm's prescriptions, and therefore, normative pressures to change such rules were low.

When the World Bank was founded, on the one hand, its unequal voting system was seen as departing from models of other global IGOs but not from the more limited membership ones that dealt with economic issues (such as BIS), and therefore, the perceptions that they were deviating from the norm's prescriptions could be considered moderate. This assessment is supported by another, more objective, gauge of the degree to which the voting rules in the Bank departed from norm prescriptions, which is illustrated in Figure 4.4.

Figure 4.4 follows the evolution of the ratio between U.S. relative voting power in the World Bank and its share of the world's GDP.

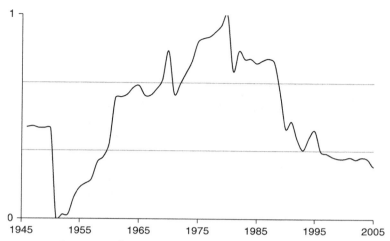

FIGURE 4.4. Departure from Norm Prescriptions in World Bank: U.S. Voting Share vs. GDP Share.

Although many of the critiques of those who wanted to reform the voting system referred to the proportion of weights allotted to all developed countries (compared to the developing ones), most often they would point to the extraordinary power of the United States, the one country that, for a long time, could block major initiatives within the IGO. As a reminder, the vast majority of such states rarely questioned the need for differentiated voting. They did argue, however, against the tendency to allot even more votes to powerful states than economic power dictated.

Indeed, Figure 4.4 shows that the ratio between the proportion of votes allotted to the United States in the World Bank and the proportion of the U.S. relative economic power fluctuated throughout the history of the World Bank. In 1951, the ratio was at its minimum (coded 0 in Figure 4.4), when the U.S. voting share represented only about 78 percent of its relative economic power (based on proportion of global GDP). In 1980, the ratio reached a maximum (coded 1 in Figure 4.4) when the United States had 1.81 times as many votes in the Bank as the proportion of GDP would dictate. The perceived departure from the application of the norm was high throughout the 1970s and 1980s when the United States (and other powerful states) received more votes than one would expect based on its relative wealth. In the 1950s and since 1995 the departure from norm prescriptions was low, when the United States actually controlled fewer votes than one would expect based on GDP

TABLE 4.1. *Normative Pressures Involving IGO Voting Procedures and Reactions to Pressures*

IGO/Moment Rule involves	League/1919 Unanimity in Council and Assembly (and participation in Council)	ILO/1919 Equal majority voting	World Bank/1944 Weighted voting	UN/1945 Vetoes in UNSC (and voting in other UN bodies).	World Bank/1950s Voting weights
Norm strength	L	L	M	M	L
Departure from norm prescription	L	L	M	H	L
Normative pressure	VL	VL	M	H	L
Strategy	CN; BA*	NA	CA; NA	BA; CN	NA
Outcome	NC	PC	PC	AC	PC

Note: CN = challenging norm; NN = narrowing norm; BN = broadening norm; CA = challenging application of norm; NA = narrowing application of norm; BA = broadening application of norm; Y = yielding; W = withstanding; C = originally promoted change; NC = no change; PC = partial change; AC = alternative change.

* Strategy used to defuse normative pressure from other norm.

	ECSC/1951	World Bank/1960s	GATT/early 960s	UN/early 1960s	EEC/1960s through 1980s	World Bank/1970s and 1980s	World Bank/early 1990s	WTO/1995	UN/late 1990s and 2000s	World Bank/late 1990s and 2000s	EU/1990s and early 2000s
	Weighted voting	Voting weights	Unanimity vs. majority	Elimination of veto	–Qualified majority voting –Role for EP	Voting weights	Voting weights	Unanimity voting	–Change veto system in UNSC –Transparency of UNSC	Voting weights	–Qualified majority voting –Role of EP
	H	M	M	M	H	H	H	H	H	H	H
	L	M	L	H	L	H	M	L	H	L	L
	M	M	V L	M	M	VH	H	M	V H	M	M
	NA	NA	NA	W	BA	NA	NA	NA	BN	NA	BA; NA
	NC	PC	PC	NC	AC	PC	PC	PC	AC	PC	PC

alone. At all other times the departure from the application of the voting norm was moderate, including at the founding of the organization, as the preceding qualitative assessment suggested.

Compared to other IGO voting systems, the ones in the European institutions did not depart much from norm prescriptions. At the founding of the ECSC, its weighted voting system, based on economic power, was balanced, with considerations of population, perhaps the most democratic criteria for differentiating among states in a voting system. Other IGOs established before the ECSC to deal with economic issues did not take population into account in their voting formulas. Population considerations were especially prevalent in the European Parliament (EP), even from its inception. As the independence and prerogatives of the EP have increased over time so has the relevance of "fairness" in the overall voting system. When the Treaty of Nice and the Treaty of Lisbon, introduced in 2003 and 2009, respectively, direct population-dependent conditions in the qualified majority system of voting in the Council (and not just in the Parliament), one can argue that the status quo moved even closer to fair voting norm prescriptions. Therefore, even though there has been some interesting variance regarding the departure from the fair voting norm prescription in the European institutions, I consider such departure to have been consistently low compared to developments in other IGOs.

Perhaps the most flagrant case of rules departing from the fair voting norm (from the perspective of those seeking change) was the one in 1945, at the introduction of the veto system in the UN. The new rules were seen as departing substantially from past practices and, implicitly, from what the norm of fair voting prescribed. This perception remained strong throughout the Cold War and in the post–Cold War era as the proportion of countries holding a veto was even smaller than in 1945. This gauge of departure from norm prescription is captured in the fourth line of Table 4.1.

The fifth line of Table 4.1 represents the strength of the normative pressures for change. It is calculated, as in other chapters, as the interaction between norm strength and degree to which status quo departs from norm. The operationalization suggests that the normative pressure was high in the UN in 1945, at the introduction of the veto system and very high in the post–Cold War era. It was also very high in the World Bank in the second half of the Cold War and high at the beginning of the post–Cold War era. In all other cases discussed in this chapter the pressures were moderate, low, or very low. The cases in which normative pressures were high or very high were also the ones in which states invoked democratic norms more frequently in the debates surrounding reform.

What Actions Did Actors Opposing the Rules Take under Normative Pressure?

Almost all types of strategies for alleviating normative pressures discussed in Chapter 2 were used at one time or another to defuse pressures for changes to IGO voting rules. When the League of Nations was established, powerful states did not give in to small states' pressures to adopt majority voting rules because they wanted to avoid situations where they would be obligated to accept actions that they opposed. Therefore they used the sovereignty norm to challenge the democratic majoritarian norm. Also, as discussed in Chapter 3, they promoted the use of the unanimity rule in a strategy of broadening the application of the norm that linked such rules to the need for small IGO bodies. The unanimity rules allowed them to make the case for a small, exclusive League Council (which they could more easily control).

In the ILO, states accepted majority decision-making rules during a time when many other technical IGOs had embraced such practices. Yet, they managed to broaden the application of this norm by allowing all states to accept or reject the IGO's decision through important ratification processes that maintained the all-important sovereignty principle intact. As was shown in Chapter 3, the cumbersome ratification processes have played a very important role in maintaining permanent membership in the Governing Body.

At the founding of the World Bank, although the use of weighted voting had become customary in organizations that dealt with economic tasks, there were nevertheless some pressures to soften the degree to which powerful states controlled the voting in the IGO. Some great powers reacted to such pressures by challenging the application of fair voting norms by emphasizing the similarities between the IGO and private banks, rather than those to public institutions. They did not question the application of the norm to other governmental institutions. However, they did question its applicability to this organization because of its "bank" character. Just as important, they narrowed the application of the norm by accepting a compromise between a pure system of weighted voting and a system giving all states equal votes. Throughout its history, as more pressures built to alter the relative weight of great power votes, powerful developed states did give in but virtually always, through yet other narrowing strategies, by conceding only to smaller changes than those proposed by developing states.

As expected based on H_2, the high normative pressures to do away with the veto system proposed in the UN in 1945 were met with multiple strategies to defuse them. The United States challenged the norm of sovereign equality among states with arguments based on the norm of great power primacy (by emphasizing that power considerations needed to drive the rules of the IGO to defend "the general good"). Britain also challenged the norm of equal voting based on the communitarian (one-state-one-vote) understanding of democracy by invoking (in a subtle manner) the cosmopolitan model of democracy. The latter model was based on the one-person-one-vote principle and, implicitly, on countries' populations. Lastly, great powers broadened the debates and offered multiple concessions in other UN organs to defuse the pressures in the UNSC.

Maintaining the veto in the UNSC has been so important for the P5 that they have withstood the pressures for any change to this rule throughout the Cold War even though they accepted the addition of non-permanent members in the 1960s. In the 1990s they refused any limitations to the veto proposed by other UN members. In the post–Cold War era, when such pressures were very high, the P5 did nevertheless attempt to broaden the normative debates involving fair voting (as expected based on H_5). As Chapter 5 shows, they did so by placing on the reform agenda questions related to other "democratic" aspects of decision-making in the UN, especially those involving the organization's transparency.

The egalitarian voting rules in GATT did not lead to significant normative pressures for change. When the WTO was established, small states wanted to maintain the formal one-country-one-vote majority rules in the IGO.

Yet, even during the Cold War, great powers had pushed to introduce a unanimity voting system. This was a rare example of great powers promoting a change to IGO rules through normative pressures rather than small states. The normative pressures for adopting formal unanimity decision-making were defused by the promoters of the majority rule by accepting informal unanimity procedures, a narrowing strategy (as expected based on H_6). Such pressures reemerged at the establishment of the WTO. At that time, U.S. domestic actors were among the most active promoters of such pressures for change. Their arguments conflated, in an interesting way, prescriptions based on the sovereignty norm (suggesting that WTO decisions should not bypass domestic politics) with those based on democratic norms (arguing that in the case of the United

States, domestic decision-making is truly democratic and implying that IGO decisions are not). Their view is also reflected in the WTO statement that decision-making by consensus is more democratic than decisions by majority. Once more, a strategy of narrowing the application of the norm was adopted by the status quo states (which, in this case, were the developing countries) by accepting informal unanimity rules as a practice while maintaining formal majority voting ones for cases when such practices failed.

In the case of the European institutions, in which votes were not allotted equally, powerful states also used multiple strategies to defuse the normative pressures that smaller states applied for more egalitarian voting rules. At the founding of the ECSC, when the difference in economic power between France, Germany, and Italy, on the one hand, and Belgium, Luxembourg, and the Netherlands, on the other, was so great, the three larger countries accepted a voting formula that gave them some advantage but not one proportional to the size of their economies (or population). Later, in the EEC and EU, some states used a broadening strategy (which brought together both issues of voting and those of European Parliament prerogatives) intended to defuse normative pressures derived from the parliamentary oversight norm. Just as important, when normative pressures were used to promote qualified majority voting, powerful states opposing such procedures were able to narrow the application of the norm by limiting the number of policy areas where such procedures could be used.

What Were the Outcomes of the Attempts to Adopt or Change Rules?

Voting rules in IGOs appear to be even more important to powerful states than participation rules. This was especially true in the debates surrounding the veto in the UNSC. Whether the P5 used strategies to defuse normative pressures, or they simply withstood the pressures, they have been successful in maintaining the status quo for seventy years. At most, they accepted alternative changes in rules within other UN organs or to other types of rules.

In most of the other IGOs, great powers made more concessions. They did not receive any advantages in voting in the League of Nations and the ILO. It is perhaps for this reason that some great powers never joined the League, or they decided to leave it.

In the World Bank great powers have slowly allowed for more votes for developing states. They have also given up their ability to control important decisions within the European institutions by allowing for the use of qualified majority voting rather than unanimity. More importantly, they have given up their ability to block decisions in the WTO by accepting formal (albeit not informal) majority voting decision-making rules. Overall, one can argue that, even when it comes to the all-important voting rules, normative pressures appear to have had an important impact on outcomes.

Would Outcomes Have Been the Same in the Absence of Normative Pressures and Reactions to Pressures?

One cannot truly assess states' decisions to adopt certain voting rules in absence of their prior decision of who they should allow to be part of IGOs and their bodies. In the first exclusive international institutions, such as the Concert of Europe and the League Council (especially in its original proposed composition of just five permanent members and no non-permanent members), one can understand the acceptance of unanimity voting. However, as IGOs became more inclusive and were given more tasks, it became impossible to maintain such a cumbersome system. Once majoritarian systems were put in place, states were faced with a dilemma between choosing systems in which powerful states would be given an advantage or ones in which all states would be equal. It is difficult to explain the variance of voting rules across IGOs and across time solely on basis of the need for efficiency and, implicitly, for exclusive IGO bodies. There are examples of small IGOs, such as the ECSC, that did not use unanimity voting and others of large IGOs, such as the WTO, that emphasized unanimity.

One could also argue that if voting systems were only based on power considerations, all IGOs would offer voting advantages to the most powerful states. The fact that they do not suggests that great powers "pick and choose" their battles. The great number of IGOs with one-country-one-vote systems cannot be explained through theories emphasizing only such power considerations. It is true that powerful states can still use an "exit strategy" to get their way in such IGOs. Yet this makes the puzzle even more intriguing: Why have powerful states accepted to be part of IGOs that they need to leave to get their way? Would a veto rule or a weighted vote help them avoid this situation and all disruptions that come with it? The simple fact that small states were able to promote egalitarian voting and that powerful states usually accepted such systems suggests that the international realm has indeed accepted powerful equal voting norms.

Moreover, if democratic fair voting norms had not been powerful, we would not have seen states trying to reinterpret the best way of applying them to IGOs. For example, the United Kingdom would not have had to make the case that powerful states "deserved" the veto because they were more populous. Similarly, great powers would not have used the argument that unanimity in the WTO is the most democratic form of decision-making.

Some may suggest that rhetoric is meaningless. For example, powerful states got what they wanted in the UN, regardless of the arguments that they or others used. Nevertheless, it is worth pointing out that states felt the need to use such wording to defuse normative pressures for eliminating the veto, implicitly offering evidence that the fair voting norm was relevant to them. In addition, it should be noted that powerful states did not get a formal unanimity system in the WTO, having to settle for informal unanimity. This is a fairly obvious example of how power considerations alone cannot explain voting rules.

Lastly, this chapter has suggested that the many cases of compromises in voting systems, such as the interesting mixes of equality and weighted voting systems in the post–World War II international financial institutions, could not be accounted for by pure power or norms explanations. They reflect a constant battle between those applying normative pressures and those attempting to narrow their application. Moreover, the multiple cases of simultaneous changes in voting rules and in the European Parliament's power within the EEC and EU could not be explained without taking into account normative pressures and the efforts to defuse them, as Chapter 7 shows in greater depth.

5

Transparency

The Norm

The study of international relations has long been interested in the relationship between information flows and power (e.g., Haas 1990). With the advent of electronic communications, online databases, digitization of documents, and other technological changes of the recent turn of the century, the literature has come to investigate even more closely this relationship (e.g., Nye 2004a).

The renewed interest in information flows has made "transparency" become a buzzword second only to "globalization" in its recent prominence and has led many to tout it "as the solution to everything from financial volatility to environmental degradation to corruption" (Florini 2003, 198–199). Indeed, in international relations there has been a great interest in transparency in research on conflict (e.g., Fearon 1995; Schultz 1999; Finel and Lord 2000) and international regimes (e.g., Krasner 1983; Mitchell 1998), as well as global governance (Keohane and Nye 2000a; Florini 2003), to name just a few.

To discern between the various meanings of the term used in such bodies of literature and to clarify the exact type of transparency discussed in this chapter, it is useful to begin by defining A's transparency to B as "the ability of B to receive information from A" (Grigorescu 2003, 646). This understanding of information flow reflects its relational character. In other words, just as power should not be defined in absolute terms but, rather, specified with regard to who exerts power and whom it is exerted on (Dahl 1957, 203), any discussion of information flow needs to specify the actor offering the information and the one receiving it. The conflict literature generally focuses on information flow between states, the international regimes literature refers primarily to information sent by states to international institutions, and the global governance literature tends to discuss information flows from international institutions to the public. As I show, although only this third type of information flow, from institutions to the public, appears to be directly associated with democracy, international actors have interpreted the transparency norm and its application to various IGOs in ways that benefited them and, therefore, have extended debates of democracy to discussions of other information flows.

The Transparency Norm at the State Level

In the domestic realm, democratic theory literature considers public access to information essential and necessary (but not sufficient) for government accountability and responsiveness and, implicitly, for the working of a truly democratic polity (March and Olsen 1994). The relevance of information in this literature derives from the broader understanding of democracy as a deliberative space (Bohman and Rehg 1997). The public must have access to information to assess the quality of governance and hold leaders accountable. Moreover, increased transparency leads to greater public trust in government and in democratic systems, therefore, facilitating democratic consolidation (Almond and Verba 1963).

At the domestic level, governments have become increasingly open to their publics through institutions and practices. The increased transparency of the first democracies of the eighteenth and nineteenth centuries primarily took place through improvements in press freedom. Independent journalists emerged as important intermediaries between governments and their publics. However, even with a free press, domestic flow of information is incomplete without clear rules regarding the kind of information that the government is obligated to offer.[1] The more recent movement toward greater government transparency has therefore been strongly associated with the emergence and improvement of freedom of information (FOI) laws across states (e.g., Martin and Feldman 1998; Florini 2003; Mock 1999). With the exception of Sweden, which adopted a first such law in the eighteenth century, states have only begun introducing access to information legislation after World War II. The number

---

[1] Hence, the emphasis on the information that B can receive rather than the information that A offers (including propaganda) in the aforementioned definition. For an emphasis on this distinction, see, e.g., Rodan 2004.

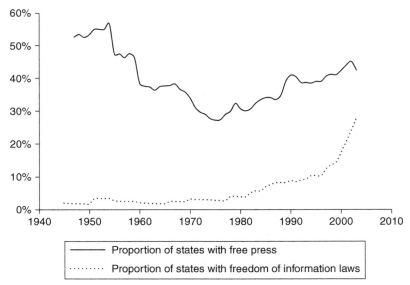

FIGURE 5.1. Proportion of States with Free Press and Freedom of Information Laws.

of countries with legislation pertaining to citizens' access to information has increased almost six times since 1990. This spectacular recent trend has been cited as proof of the empowerment of the transparency norm and of its eventual "cascade" at the domestic level (Florini 2000).

There are no comprehensive measures of press freedom and freedom of information legislation going back before World War II. It is generally believed that press freedom slowly improved worldwide throughout the nineteenth century. Anecdotal evidence further suggests that such freedom was curtailed in the interwar era (e.g., Hampton 2004, 139).

Figure 5.1 uses some of the few existing datasets dealing with press freedom and freedom of information to illustrate the evolution of government transparency in the post–World War II era.[2] The two measures represent the proportion of countries with a free press and with freedom of information legislation. Figure 5.1 shows that, at the global level, freedom of the press increased slightly in the first decade after World War II and then again after 1975. It was eroded between the mid-1950s and mid-1970s. The proportion of countries adopting freedom of information

---

[2] The measure of press freedom uses data from Van Belle 2000 and Freedom House (at http://www.freedomhouse.org/report-types/freedom-press). Data on access to information legislation are based on two surveys: Vleugles (2012) and Right2INFO.org (2012).

laws increased slowly after World War II. In the late 1990s it began growing dramatically, thus supporting the general argument in the literature that we have entered an "age of transparency" (Finel and Lord, 2000).

The Transparency Norm at the International Level

This chapter shows that intergovernmental organizations (IGOs) have also begun adopting policies of public access to information since the early 1990s at a similarly rapid pace. This trend has been cited as further proof of the empowerment of the global transparency norm (Nelson 2000; Florini 2000; Grigorescu 2002). The IGO transparency that this literature refers to characterizes the flow of information from such organizations to the public. It is not the same type of transparency as the one discussed earlier by the international regimes literature reflecting the flow of information from states to IGOs. It also needs to be distinguished from the transparency of IGOs to states or even from the one of IGOs to nongovernmental organizations. Most important, as this chapter shows, IGO transparency toward the public is very different from transparency reflecting the ability of some IGO member-states to access information from a handful of countries that are members of exclusive IGO forums such as the UNSC or the WTO Green Room.

Figure 5.2 illustrates these various flows of information. The distinction between these several types of transparency is salient because various actors have conflated them, sometimes willfully, to gain support for rules governing the information that was of interest to them. Although not all forms of transparency are truly linked to democracy, those promoting increased information flows for themselves (via T_2, T_3 or T_6) have implied that their proposed rules are indeed democratic ones.

The various information flows represented by arrows in Figure 5.2 do not always go hand in hand. For instance, states that seek World Bank funding may offer a great deal of fairly sensitive information to the IGO (T_1). However, that does not necessarily mean that the Bank staff will release such information to the public (T_0), to NGOs (T_3), or even to other member-states (T_2) (Udall 1998). Moreover, even if the Bank does offer such information to member-state representatives, it may decide not to release it to NGOs (T_3) or the public (T_0). Of course, the information can be released solely to the executive directors (who come from a limited number of member-states). The executive directors may not necessarily share all of his information with the other states (T_6) even though they technically represent them. Similarly, the World Bank staff may decide to offer important information discreetly to state representatives (T_2)

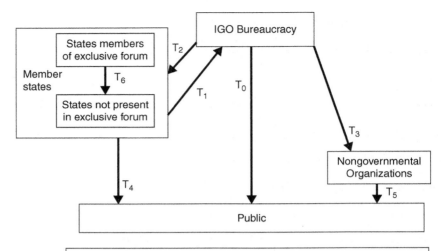

FIGURE 5.2. Flow of Information from an IGO to the Public.

and to some partner NGOs (T_3) but not make it public (T_0). In all such cases, actors may call for transparency invoking democratic norms, yet they are referring to different information flows that are serving different interests and that are often only vaguely connected to actual democratic mechanisms.

Figure 5.2 suggests that, unless governments and nongovernmental organizations are themselves transparent to the public (T_4 and T_5), one cannot take for granted that any other form of IGO transparency (T_2 to governments and T_3 to NGOs) implies that the public will actually have access to the information. Governments and NGOs have often taken on the role of privileged gatekeepers to IGOs, refusing to release to the public information they themselves receive (Florini 2003; Grigorescu 2007). Because of such problems with the transparency of these intermediaries (T_4 and T_5), any form of information flow other than the direct one from IGOs to the public (T_0) may not necessarily be considered as enhancing the IGO's democratic character.

Indeed, transparency of IGOs to the public has come to be touted by many as the most important condition for holding such organizations accountable (e.g., Nye et al. 2003; Stiglitz 2006). In turn, such accountability is seen as essential to democracy in IGOs.

Keohane and Nye offer the following example and argument to illustrate the relevance of transparency for the democratic character of IGOs:

> It is not inherently any more undemocratic for the US president to delegate authority to the US Trade Representative to negotiate at the WTO than for the president to delegate authority to the attorney general to deal with organized crime. As long as the public knows what actions the delegated agent took, it can reward or punish the president and his party for its deeds. The key is transparency. (2002, 235)

One implication of emphasizing this direct link between IGOs and the public is that national legislatures, which articulate public interests more directly than executive representatives in IGOs (and are more vulnerable to the public's discontent), will play a greater role in the struggle for IGO transparency than they do in those for fair participation or voting rules discussed in the previous chapters. Indeed, as the following pages show, legislators played an especially prominent role in the struggle over transparency in several organizations such as the World Bank, IMF, and WTO.

The current interest in IGO transparency should not suggest that the struggle to open IGOs to the public is only a recent one. The idea that international relations can be improved through the involvement of the general public can be traced as far back as the writings of Immanuel Kant (2005). Idealists such as Woodrow Wilson built on those arguments when designing IGOs such as the League of Nations and the ILO. Such organizations were revolutionary in the degree of access they offered to journalists. However, just as in the case of domestic transparency, the simple presence of a free press is not sufficient for achieving true IGO accountability as long as officials do not have an obligation to release sensitive information. The battles for press access of the interwar era, and even after World War II, were therefore complemented starting in the late 1980s by additional ones for adopting clear rules delineating the kind of information that IGOs need to make accessible to the public. The following sections discuss how IGOs have struggled for more than a century to balance the pressures of the transparency norm and the need to conduct confidential intergovernmental negotiations about sensitive issues.

A History of the Application of the Norm to IGOs

Developments before World War II

For many centuries prior to World War I, there was a powerful belief that international relations should be the business solely of government officials and that the public should not be involved in the sensitive issues of diplomacy. In his classic sixteenth-century book *The Perfect Ambassador*, de Vera y Figueroa argued, for example, that diplomacy without secrecy was simply impossible (2004, 91).

The culture of secrecy deeply pervaded diplomatic bureaucracy for centuries. Even after many began blaming secret diplomacy for the outbreak of World War I, in the 1920s, treaties of diplomacy continued to glorify secrecy. For instance, Jules Cambon, a French signatory of the Versailles Treaty, together with Christopher Rede Turner, published an influential book in 1925, *The Diplomatist*, that argued: "It is obvious to any one who has been in charge of the interests of his country abroad that the day secrecy is abolished negotiations of any kind will become impossible" (1931, 30).

The lack of a true international press corps was another barrier to the free flow of information in the international realm. The cost of having international correspondents placed for long periods of time in other countries made it virtually impossible for all but a handful of newspapers to afford such a luxury (de Franch 1926). Moreover, the cost of intercontinental (and even continental) communications was very high. Some, in fact, argue that the League never acquired the necessary domestic support in the United States precisely because of the paucity of information coming from the Paris negotiations, which, in turn, was the direct result of the very high price of transatlantic cables (Sweetser 1920, 201).

Even when the press did play a role in the international institutions of the nineteenth century, it was rarely an independent role. During the highly secretive Concert of Europe, state representatives involved in the Concert's proceedings sometimes used the press to promote their own perspective to the publics of the other states. Their targets were primarily elites within such states, rather than the general public, because foreign affairs were not open to broad-based discussions. For example, the Russian ambassador in London was instructed to push for the publication in British journals of stories about Lord Castlereagh's opposition to the tsar's proposal for an independent Poland. The Russians hoped that such news would serve as ammunition for members of the opposition in the British Parliament. Other Concert officials would use their personal connections with the press in their own countries to leak unflattering gossip about their foreign counterparts (Nicolson 1946, 201–202). However, for the most part, meaningful information about Concert of Europe negotiations hardly ever reached the public.

The technical nature of many of the international conferences and, later, of the public international unions of the nineteenth century, led to opaque practices even within such non-political forums. In fact, in the vast majority of cases, as a result of costs, states did not appoint permanent representatives to such unions. Instead, the ambassador who was closest to the headquarters of the organization (often hundreds of miles away) was responsible for overseeing its work. Their lack of pertinent expertise and the physical distance often led such officials to hardly ever be involved in the work of the unions, leaving most of the decisions to the IGO officials and thus allowing for secretive decision-making (Murphy 1994, 107).

World War I substantially eroded the elitist view that only government officials should have a say in international relations. The broad understanding that secret negotiations and pacts dragged the world in a terrible conflict occupied a central role in the international relations immediately after the war. The attack on secrecy was foreshadowed by the very first of the fourteen points of Woodrow Wilson's famous speech.[3] The speech was followed by more U.S. efforts to promote the principle of "publicity" in the international realm.

When Wilson and the other main promoters of the "open covenants of peace, openly arrived at" returned to their capitals, they left medium-level officials with the task of adopting the specific decision-making rules of the new League. While there was little opposition to opening the League Assembly, controversy surrounded the transparency of the League Council.

The British, who had been the most active in the League's design, after the Americans, took a strong position against opening up the League Council proceedings to the public. This position was voiced by Maurice Hankey, secretary of the British Cabinet. Hankey rose to the ministerial office from the British civil service, an institution famed for valuing discretion and secrecy (Vincent 1998). He carried an intense correspondence

---

[3] Wilson emphasized that "diplomacy shall proceed always frankly and in the public view." See http://avalon.law.yale.edu/20th_century/wilson14.asp. The emphasis on publicity was also captured in the preamble of the League's Covenant that prescribed "*open*, just and honourable relations between nations" (emphasis added). See League Covenant at http://avalon.law.yale.edu/20th_century/leagcov.asp (August 1, 2013).

in the summer of 1919 with Eric Drummond, a British diplomat who at the time had just been appointed the first secretary-general of the League. Hankey made a strong case against opening the proceedings of the League Council to the press (stating that he was "dead against" it). He argued: "By all means have all the publicity you want in the case of the Assembly, – just as they have it in Parliament or in the United States Senate ... but believe me, your league of nations is doomed from the first if you have Press representatives present at the Council" (Hankey 1919). He noted that "the Council would rather resemble a Cabinet or Board of Directors, and I never yet heard of any Cabinet in any nation or any Board of Directors which allowed the Press to be present at its Meetings, and I still believe that this would be ruinous" (Hankey 1919).

The main support for League Council transparency came from two Americans who were affiliated with the League. Arthur Sweetser, a journalist and member of the American Peace Commission that Woodrow Wilson established, participated in the Paris meetings that led to the founding of the League. He was then assigned to the provisional secretariat of the League and worked in the League's Public Information Section for about two years, until it became clear that the United States would not join the League and, therefore, Americans could not be part of the new organization's secretariat. In 1920 Sweetser wrote a book on the workings of the League in which he dedicated an entire chapter to "open diplomacy," writing that this topic is "of all the questions before the League ... far and away the greatest" (p. 187). Perhaps more important for our understanding of the domestic-international analogy, the chapter mentioned that "publicity has for a long time been considered as a source of moral strength in the administration of National Law. It should equally strengthen the laws and engagements which exist between nations" (Sweetser 1920, 191). Sweetser wrote to Drummond pleading the secretary general to support the opening of all League meetings to the press. He argued that the "public in America is strongly against secret meetings of the Council" and that if the American people "feel they are again to be denied, they will turn against the League in bitterness" (Sweetser 1919).

Another American who lobbied Drummond for League Council transparency was Raymond B. Fosdick. During the War, Fosdick served as a special representative of the War Department in France and as a civilian aide to General Pershing during the Paris Peace Conference. In 1919, he was appointed under secretary-general for the League of Nations, becoming the highest ranking American in the new organization's secretariat.

Fosdick sent half a dozen letters to Drummond, each time bringing counterarguments to the points Hankey had made. Perhaps the most important such argument was that "the American people – the people of all democracies – are instinctively suspicious of public business conducted behind closed doors" (Fosdick 1919).

These normative pressures led Drummond and the top League diplomats to eventually accept the rules allowing the public and press access to virtually all League Council meetings. They did so, in great part, in the hope that this would increase the chances of bringing the United States into the League. The initial League rules therefore specified that both the Assembly and the League Council should generally conduct their meetings in public (League of Nations Information Section 1935, 221). Yet, Article 5 of the League Council's Rules of Procedure stipulated that *"unless the Council decides to the contrary* [emphasis added], the reading of reports presented by the reporters, the final discussions and the voting on the resolution that have been proposed, shall take place at public meetings" (League of Nations 1920, 273). Such wording, of course, gave Council members a great deal of discretion in deciding when they would allow their meetings to be public and when they would hold them behind closed doors.

Without an American delegation present to push for the implementation of transparency rules that had been formally adopted, the British perspective dominated the initial practices of the Council. In the first meeting of the Council in February 1920, Lord Balfour, then president of the Council, argued that while supporting the principle of publicity, he believed that "the details of our work cannot with advantage take place in an open assembly" (League of Nations 1920, 30). In 1920 only one-quarter of the League Council meetings were public.

The League Council's lack of transparency was quickly criticized in a resolution adopted in November 1920 by the League Assembly. Most of these critiques came from states that were not members of the League Council (League of Nations 1920, 58–64). British and French officials argued that the League Council was sufficiently open to the public and the press and did not have to move any further in the direction of publicity (League of Nations 1921a, 57). Nevertheless, because in great part to the overwhelming criticism, the number of private League Council meetings was greatly reduced in the following years. By 1924 about 90 percent of League Council meetings were public.

The first half decade of the League's existence was characterized by a culture of openness. Officials suspected of conducting "hotel diplomacy" – that is, negotiating outside official League meetings and public view – were criticized by their colleagues from other states (Zimmern 1936, 296).[4]

The press was given extraordinary access to League meetings. By 1926, despite the high costs of travel, 333 newspapers and 28 agencies received press accreditations to the League Assembly. Overall, in the first seven years of the League's existence about 1,400 journalists representing more than 1,000 newspapers and periodicals from 51 countries attended at least one of the League's meetings (League of Nations Information Section 1935, 33–39). It is noteworthy perhaps that, during those years, the press did not have access to many of the parliamentary assemblies of countries that were League members.

Journalists had seats reserved for them on a permanent basis in the League Assembly. As the Council room was smaller than the Assembly room, journalists initially had to "compete" for the few available seats with the general public (Pelt 1944, 62). In time, more seats in the Council room were reserved for the press. Another concession made to publicity was replacing the League Council's initial horseshoe seating with a rather awkward one in which state-representatives were all placed facing the public, rather than each other (Zimmern 1936).

Journalists received all documents that were circulated to national delegations at the same time as the diplomats. Moreover, in the League Council, they often had access to the documents before representatives of countries that were not members of the body, suggesting a rare case of an IGO being technically more transparent to the public (T_0) than to states not included in an IGO body (T_6) (League of Nations Information Section 1928).

This depiction of the role of the press needs to be balanced with some considerations regarding the independence (or, rather, lack thereof) of journalists during the interwar era. Indeed, in the 1920s, the relationship between the journalists and foreign ministries was often very close (Pew 1925). For example, Felix Pacheco, the foreign minister of Brazil was also the owner of the *Journal de Commerce*, the largest and most influential newspaper in that country (Wood 1926). Moreover, some countries in the League had very strong censorship systems. Many of the stories that came from the League could therefore be questioned for their bias.

---

[4] It must be noted, however, that, in time, although criticized, such hotel diplomacy became an increasingly common occurrence (Marks 1995).

These foreign correspondents accredited to the League formed an association in 1921. By 1928 the association counted more than 150 members (League of Nations Information Section 1928, 40).[5] It became a force to be reckoned with. For example, in 1922, the League gave journalists access to the very sensitive meetings of the "B Mandates" (involving the fate of the former German territories in West and Central Africa) as a direct response to demands from this association (League of Nations 1922a, 791, 846).

The League established an information section early on to deal with the public's and journalists' access to meetings and to respond to requests for information. Virtually all staff members of the section were former journalists (Pelt 1944). In 1920, the section was the largest one in the League, with a staff of twelve. In 1930, it remained the largest with a staff of nineteen. These numbers do not reflect the staff for the ILO that had a separate information section. Similarly, the Permanent Court of International Justice had its own information section that was considered more forthcoming with information than many domestic courts at that time (Hudson 1943). Moreover, if one were also to consider the staff that was involved in the League's publications department and in the library, as well as those in branch offices that were primarily intended to offer information to government officials and media from the country where they were stationed, the total number of staff working directly or indirectly for achieving greater "publicity" of the League's work reaches to about 50 – of the approximately 500 working for the League in 1927 (League of Nations 1927; also Ranshofen-Wertheimer 1945, 208).

The information section offered about 200 communiqués every year. It published dozens of journals and books about the League's work. As mentioned, it also ran a very large library with League documents and opened ten branch offices in major cities around the world. In 1932 it launched a radio station providing information about the League's work and, in a few cases, even offered live transmissions of meetings (Pelt 1944).

Over the course of 1927 close to two million copied pages (57,000 pages of documents) were made available to the press and public (Ranshofen-Wertheimer 1945, 220). This was a time when all documents had to be typewritten and mimeographed, taking considerably more time and effort than those involving current document multiplication and

---

[5] It is noteworthy that the present day UN Correspondents Association has fewer than 200 members (see http://www.unca.com/about.htm).

FIGURE 5.3. Proportion (%) of Open League Council Meetings.

distribution methods. The costs of such documentation were, of course, considerable. Printing costs alone rose from one-quarter million Swiss Francs in 1921 to more than one million by 1926, representing about 5 percent of the entire League's budget (Webster and Herbert 1933, 105). This led the League Assembly to adopt that year a resolution requesting that the costs of publishing be reduced (League of Nations 1926). The minutes of all League meetings became shorter and vaguer in the 1930s compared to the 1920s (Zimmern 1936). Starting in 1932, the printing of minutes of committees was almost completely discontinued. The number of pages published by the League was reduced from more than 60,000 in 1930 to about 45,000 in 1933 (Ranshofen-Wertheimer 1945).

The return to more secretive practices was reflected even in decisions that did not involve financial costs. Figure 5.3, depicting the proportion of meetings of the League Council that were open to the public,[6] suggests that, after an increase in transparency in its first years, the executive organ became less open to the public by the mid-to-late 1920s. This development is somewhat expected as the work of the League became increasingly complicated and involved more sensitive negotiations. The erosion of Wilson's publicity principle was, therefore, to some degree, a natural reaction of those facing the reality of working within such a complex organization.

---

[6] The data are based on minutes of all League Council meetings from 1920 to 1939.

What is surprising in Figure 5.3 is the renewed increase in transparency of the League Council in the early 1930s (followed, once more, by a reduction in the late 1930s). The proportion of closed League Council meetings declined from about 15 percent in 1924 to more than 30 percent in the mid-1920s only to decline again to 20 percent in 1932 and then continuously rise until the end of the League's existence.

How can one explain the League's second spurt of transparency that occurred in the early 1930s? Part of the explanation is that publicity was used as part of a broadening strategy intended to defuse the normative pressure for increased state participation in the League Council (discussed in Chapter 3). Indeed small states almost continuously applied such pressures for increased representation in the League Council throughout the history of the IGO.

In the 1921–1922 debates on League Council enlargement status quo states returned to the argument used at the founding of the League that a large forum was an ineffective one. Some representatives suggested that participation in the League Council was not crucial as non-members retained information and influence through like-minded states that were represented in this organ. Increasing the League Council's openness was therefore as important as increasing its size (League of Nations 1921a, 57). This argument, linking transparency and participation in a practical way (rather than placing the two norms under the broader umbrella of democracy, as was done in the UN in the 1990s), may partially explain why the 1923 increase in League Council membership only added two more members. The accompanying increase in the transparency of the organization (reflected in Figure 5.3) was used as a way to defuse pressure for even greater increases in membership.

After transparency of the League Council increased in the mid-1920s, it was more difficult to use a similar broadening strategy during the 1923–1925 debates surrounding the second League Council enlargement. Therefore, status quo states were not able to defuse normative pressures for increased state participation as well as they had in the early 1920s. The 1926 reforms added three non-permanent members and one permanent member to the League Council.

As new normative pressures for a larger League Council emerged in the early 1930s, member-states used the broadening strategy yet again, linking the question of the body's membership to transparency (e.g., League of Nations 1931). Figure 5.3 reflects this increase in transparency. The strategy appears to have been successful as no more members were added to the League Council until 1933, when one more "temporary" member was added to the forum.

There were few reasons for League Council members to maintain transparency in the mid- and late 1930s, as normative pressures toward increased membership had diminished. Pre-World War II tensions led to increasingly sensitive meetings. The flow of information from the League Council continued to be eroded during those years (Webster and Herbert 1933). In addition to the categories of "open" and "private" meetings envisaged in the initial rules of procedure, toward the late 1930s the League Council minutes began referring to a third category termed "secret."[7] By 1939, the last year in which the League Council actually functioned, only about one-third of its meetings were public.

The fluctuations in transparency were also evident in the ILO. Because the United States could join the ILO even if it were not to join the League, and, as many saw U.S. membership in this organization as a first step in enticing it to join the rest of the League, ILO officials made great concessions to the United States, including the new organization's publicity. The ILO's first annual conference that was held in October-November 1919 in Washington, DC, was open to the public. It was one of the most important such conferences ever held by the ILO, leading to the adoption of six major international conventions. Sweetser wrote about the transparent nature of this conference: "The International Labor Conference was held almost on the open street.... Casual sightseers to the Pan-American Building dropped in for a few moments to the big hall where the labor experts of forty world states were busily, and at time heatedly, ironing out their differences" (1920, 196). On paper, both the ILO's Conference and its Governing Body appear to have embraced the principle of publicity. They adopted rules of procedure that allowed for only very few circumstances in which it could hold closed meetings. However, also as in the case of the League, states left loopholes giving them discretion over the transparency of these bodies.

The greatest battles for transparency in the ILO involved the executive forum of the IGO, the Governing Body. Similar to the League's Council, the ILO Governing Body was at first closed to outsiders. In fact, in its first two years, it did not allow for any open meetings. By 1924, however, under normative pressure, the Governing Body opened all of its

---

[7] A survey of official League documents suggests that some of the secret meetings involved election of judges of the Permanent Court of International Justice. However, the lack of minutes for such meetings makes it difficult to determine whether any other topics were also discussed during such sessions.

meetings to the public and press. It only began experiencing a decline in transparency in 1930, when it abruptly closed the vast majority of its meetings to outsiders. Throughout the 1930s only about one-third of ILO Governing Body meetings were open.[8] When comparing the two IGOs, it is relevant to note that the main difference in the patterns of transparency is that the ILO lacked the additional spurt experienced by the League Council in the early 1930s. The difference can be explained by the fact that, in the ILO, normative pressures for greater state participation in the Governing Body were alleviated using a different broadening strategy, one that tried to offset increased state participation by emphasizing greater independence of nongovernmental representatives from labor and employers (as is discussed in Chapter 6), not by improving transparency.

After World War II, transparency of the Governing Body increased and has remained fairly high. Starting around 1950, the proportion of open Governing Body meetings grew to the very high levels of the 1920s and, since then, have continued to hover between 80 and 100 percent.

Developments after World War II and during the Cold War

The first negotiations leading to the UN system began as early as May 1943, when the United States hosted the United Nations Food Conference at Hot Springs, Virginia. Because it took place during the war, the conference was organized in great secrecy. The Roosevelt administration barred journalists from attending the conference arguing that "any news that Dr. Goebbels can get on disputes between delegations and the compromises all will have to accept will be used for Axis ends to the limit that is possible" (Krock 1943). The secrecy was met with protests from the press and even from U.S. Senate members.

Journalists' strong criticism of the secretive discussions in Hot Springs (*New York Times* 1943; *Los Angeles Times* 1943) led to somewhat less secret deliberations in Bretton Woods in July 1944. Yet, even Bretton Woods was an exercise in caution. The remote setting was chosen because of security concerns. The grounds at the conference were patrolled by military police and participants were ushered by Army buses. Although the press was admitted to Bretton Woods, they stayed at a hotel five miles away from the conference (Crider 1944). They were allowed to mingle with officials but were barred from meetings (*New York Times* 1944).

---

[8] The data are based on minutes of all ILO Governing Body meetings between 1920 and 1940.

The Dumbarton Oaks Conference of August-October 1944, which shaped the core plans for the UN, was also closed to outsiders.

By the time the San Francisco conference began discussing the future UN Charter in June 1945, most of the important negotiations between powerful states had already unfolded. Nevertheless, the U.S. administration now needed to open the debates to the public to make sure that the new organization would garner the domestic support that the League had lacked. It therefore moved, once more, toward greater transparency in the conference proceedings, opening the door to the press and to hundreds of NGO representatives.

The great secrecy of intergovernmental negotiations tolerated during the war appeared to give way once more to the transparency of the League years. In fact, many of the mid-level government representatives involved in the establishment of the UN came from the League system. Most of those occupying important positions on the Preparatory Commission and its Executive Commission that adopted the UN's rules of procedure were former League officials (Luard 1982). Overall, at its birth, the UN inherited many of the initial rules and practices of the League. There was great pressure to adopt rules providing transparency in an organization "still under the spell of Woodrow Wilson's covenants of peace openly arrived at" (UN official cited in Feuerle 1985, 274).

Major powers nevertheless wanted to change some of the rules they felt had doomed the League, including those on the publicity of the League Council. The initial rules of procedure discussed during the San Francisco negotiations therefore allowed for a substantial number of private meetings in the UNSC. Small states such as Syria, Cuba, Australia, and Norway spoke out very critically against this provision. Although some of these states were not democratic, they used the language of democracy and transparency to promote their goals in the UN. Such states were aware they were unlikely to receive non-permanent seats often and, therefore, they depended on information about proceedings to have any influence on decisions in this forum. Their representatives cited the example of the League and requested that the UN remain just as open to outsiders (Bailey and Dawes 2005, 10–11, 17, 40–41).

The San Francisco negotiations eventually led to formal stipulations that both the UN General Assembly (UNGA) and the UNSC work on the presumption of openness. The rules of procedure adopted for the UNGA indeed specified that all meetings be open. In the UNSC private meetings were left as an option when draft reports to the UNGA were being discussed and in the election of a new secretary-general.[9] Yet, in addition to these explicit exceptions, the rules implicitly left loopholes allowing for discretion in deciding when UNSC meetings would be closed to outsiders.

In February 1946, the UNSC held its first "private" meeting offering only a very brief communiqué explaining that it had "considered the procedure to be followed in dealing with items at present on its agenda" (United Nations 1946b, 173). In October 1956, there were three private meetings dealing with the Suez crisis. In the early 1970s the UNSC held multiple private meetings discussing the Middle East, Cyprus, and Western Sahara.[10] Other than these few exceptions, it functioned in a fairly open manner in its first two and a half decades of existence. There were therefore very few calls for increased transparency at that time.

The first pressures for increased UNSC openness became visible in the late 1970s. Not surprisingly, these came when UN membership had tripled from the original (1945) number and when more than 100 states were being left outside the UNSC with little information about the actual debates within the exclusive forum. Although the UNSC had added four more non-permanent members in 1965 (when UN membership had doubled), as discussed in Chapter 3, small states applied normative pressures once more to gain even more seats throughout the 1970s. In 1979, they introduced a draft resolution (A/34/L.57) to increase the number of non-permanent seats from ten to sixteen to keep the number of states vying for such seats about the same as right after the 1965 reforms (Winkelmann 1997).

To bolster their case for a larger UNSC, those promoting membership reform emphasized their problems with accessing information about UNSC debates. Indeed, although in the 1970s the UNSC held very few official private meetings, it met for many "consultations" that gradually had become semi-formalized private meetings. These consultations had been spurred by the beginning of détente, when the two sides of the Cold War sought opportunities to communicate more frankly with each other, including ones in such private or semi-private forums. The institutionalization of secret consultations led to the construction in 1975 of a room

---

[9] See rule no. 48, Repertoire of the Rules of the UN Security Council, Introduction: Provisional Rules of Procedure of the Security Council, at http://www.un.org/en/sc/repertoire/

[10] Repertoire of the Rules of the UN Security Council, Introduction: Provisional Rules of Procedure of the Security Council, part VIII: Publicity of Meetings, Records (Rules 48–57), various years, at http://www.un.org/en/sc/repertoire/

specifically designated for UNSC closed-door meetings. By 1980, the UNSC held many more informal private meetings than open formal ones (Feuerle 1985, 280).

There is no direct evidence that in the 1970s and 1980s powerful states used their negotiations with those pushing for UNSC membership reform to promise greater transparency as part of a broadening strategy to defuse the normative pressures for more serious changes. Nevertheless, after 1980, formal efforts to add new non-permanent members to the UNSC stopped for more than a decade while, simultaneously, the proportion of UNSC open meetings increased substantially. From 1981 to 1986, the ratio between the number of public meetings and the total number of UNSC meetings (formal and informal) increased from a historical low of about 25 to 50 percent. This observation is consistent with expectations based on the broadening strategy placing participation reforms simultaneously on the agenda with improvements in transparency.

There were many other IGOs that also struggled with the application of the transparency norm throughout the Cold War. The World Bank and IMF developed from their inception a culture of secrecy, allowing only very little information to reach outsiders.

Although transparency was essential to GATT very early on, the flows of information promoted at that time were, as in the case of the IMF, the ones from states to international institutions (T_1 in Figure 5.2) and from such institutions to the other states (T_2) – not transparency to the public (T_0). Indeed, GATT required that member-states publish all domestic legislation and interstate agreements involving trade. Nevertheless, the level of transparency of workings of GATT itself (T_0) were very low.

The European institutions also experienced a long struggle in applying transparency rules. In fact, of the major IGOs discussed in this study, the precursors of the EU, the ECSC, and the European Community seem to have been among the most secretive as hardly any information was released from meetings of their executive forums. This is not surprising as the original European institutions were elite-driven mechanisms of cooperation that were not intended to reveal signs of internal dissent to outsiders (Westlake 1998). Discretion was a necessary condition for the functioning of the ECSC in its early years because, unlike the UN, it needed to immediately bring together both victorious and defeated powers of the war. In fact, some referred to the plans for establishing the IGO as a "conspiracy of the initiators" (Brinkhorst 1999, S128). The institutions were intended to have little input from the publics that still harbored strong animosities toward their former enemies. The highly technical character of the ECSC was both a result of such an elite-driven design and a further cause of the culture of secrecy in this organization.

The culture transferred to the EEC when this organization was established in 1957. Official documents, especially from the EEC's Council, were rarely made public (Bunyan 1999). The lack of transparency of the decision-making process in the EEC was so acute that one member of the European Parliament (MEP) likened the organization to a "totalitarian regime … comparable to Burma and Cuba" (Curtin 1999, 233). Much of the IGO's work took place in committees and subcommittees set up informally with unclear information rules and that generally worked in secret.

While secrecy was, as in the case of all IGOs, a powerful trend in the intergovernmental deliberations in the EEC Council, it was just as pervasive in the EEC Commission where the "collegiate nature" of the institution generated a tight-lipped bureaucracy (Brinkhorst 1999). Moreover, the culture of secrecy, perhaps unexpectedly, often spilled over even to the European Parliament. For instance, as late as 1975, when the EP was calling for a more "democratic" organization (with directly elected members and greater oversight role over the EEC's Commission and Council), MEPs protested the presence of radio and television in their forum (European Community 1975, 59). In fact, it may be because of the long struggle for the empowerment of the EP (discussed in Chapter 7), which monopolized debates on the "democratic deficit" of these institutions, that transparency was not an important issue on the EEC's reform agenda.

Some of the information from more important intergovernmental EEC meetings managed to trickle down to the public through national officials or MEPs. Moreover, the small press corps in Brussels "cultivated" top European officials and, in turn, "was cultivated" by them (Bunyan 1999, 15). Much of the information states and bureaucrats wanted to make public would be leaked through such journalists. This modus vivendi maintained the culture of secrecy in the EEC throughout its existence.

The culture of secrecy was in great part a result of the intergovernmental nature of the European institutions (Brinkhorst 1999). Indeed, the least transparent of institutions has traditionally been the EEC (and later the EU) Council, where intergovernmental negotiations take place. Yet there were other reasons for the lack of transparency. For instance, although the countries that were part of the EEC were democratic, they were not among the most transparent democracies. In fact, none of the original six countries forming the ECSC had freedom of information legislation before 1978. Denmark, which like other Nordic countries had a tradition of openness, adopted its freedom of information law in 1970. Once it joined the EEC that year, it became the principal advocate for transparency. Sweden and Finland (the two states with the world's oldest FOI laws) joined Denmark in the promotion of transparency after becoming members in 1995. On the other hand, Germany only adopted its FOI law at the federal level in 2005 and the United Kingdom adopted such legislation in 2000 (many years after other established democracies and even later than some of the new democracies such as Hungary and Thailand adopted FOI laws). It may not be surprising therefore that Germany and the United Kingdom were two of the main opponents of greater transparency in the EEC (Bunyan 1999, xii).

The Post–Cold War Era

The debates involving UNSC enlargement resurfaced in 1992. Those pushing for changes in the UNSC invoked democratic norms often, as the debates were taking place soon after dozens of countries had just embraced democracy. The negotiations for reform therefore involved multiple demands for democratic changes to the UNSC. Some portrayed the addition of new permanent members as democratic. India, for instance, emphasized a cosmopolitan model of democracy, implying that populous democratic states needed to be represented in the UNSC (United Nations 1993a, 47–48). The Organization of African Unity, on the other hand, invoked a communitarian model of democracy, arguing that Africa needed at least two permanent seats on the UNSC (more than other regions) because there were fifty-three UN members from this continent (Organization of African Unity 1994). As shown earlier, others discussed the elimination of the veto using the language of democracy (Bourantonis 2005). Most importantly, many delegations that proposed increased participation in the UNSC through new non-permanent seats also called for greater transparency of the body (United Nations 1993b, 13, 15, 16, 29, 63). Indeed, after the proportion of UNSC open meetings had increased in early 1980 to about 50 percent, it declined again in the following decade, reaching a low of 27 percent by 1991.

When permanent members eventually joined the debates on UNSC reform in 1993, they cautioned against changes to UNSC membership and instead emphasized the relevance of transparency as a key democratic element of reform (United Nations 1993b, 18, 82, 90, 91). This action was seen as a way for the P5 to buy time in the hope that others would express opposition to membership reform and to alleviate the pressure for substantive changes to the UNSC (Bourantonis 2005, 52). The 1993 debates led to the adoption of Resolution 48/26 establishing an "Open-ended Working Group to consider all aspects of the question of an increase in the membership of the Security Council *and other matters related to the Council*" (emphasis added).

The split title of the Working Group and, implicitly, the discussions of two separate "clusters" of reforms reflected the differences between medium-range states and the P5. The former group primarily wanted changes in UNSC membership rules. The latter group was only willing to tinker with the working methods of the UNSC. A significant group of small states such as Costa Rica, Jordan, Liechtenstein, and Singapore joined the P5 in pushing for increased access to UNSC information (Hansen 2011). Such minor states did not see their chances of formally participating in the UNSC seriously increasing through changes in membership. By improving access to information about deliberations, however, they would at least know more about what was being discussed in this all-important forum (Von Freiesleben 2008).

A reflection of the importance of UNSC information is the ever-present crowd of UN delegates (from non-UNSC members) waiting outside the consultations room to hear from their colleagues about discussions in the informal forum. Such information is often treated as a quasi-commodity. For instance, representatives from non-permanent members in the UNSC expect the colleagues with which they share such important information to reciprocate with other information or with support for their initiatives and/or candidacy for UN secretariat positions.

Since the Working Group was established in 1994, the discussions on the first reform cluster that deals with UNSC membership have not really advanced. In contrast, the second cluster, focusing on working methods, has led to several significant changes. The UNSC's work program is now made public. The UNSC's president began holding briefings of informal consultations to non-members. The UNSC reports to the UNGA have become more detailed. There is greater inclusion of state and non-state representatives in deliberations of sanctions and peace-keeping operations. The new "Arria" formula permits the UNSC to hold informal meetings with independent experts and civil society representatives (Weiss 2003). The UNSC also began holding regular (yet informal) meetings with peace-keeping contributing countries. From 1991, when UNSC reform debates resurfaced, to 2004 the proportion of UNSC open meetings almost doubled from 26 to 50 percent.

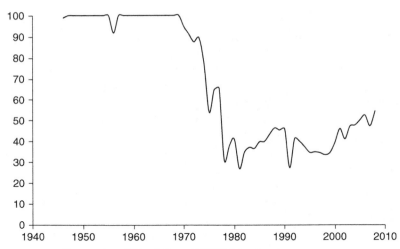

FIGURE 5.4. Proportion (%) of Open UNSC Meetings.

These improvements in the transparency of the UNSC have been ad hoc, however, as the P5 have continued to be successful in avoiding the adoption of formal rules for access to UNSC information. The provisional character of the organ's rules of procedure has led many UN officials to question the endurance of improvements in UNSC transparency and has triggered calls for the adoption of formal (and permanent) rules. Small states fear that once the pressure for membership reform is reduced, the UNSC will go back to its more secretive practices (Global Policy Forum 1997). They have therefore tried to separate the issue of UNSC transparency from the one of membership reform, while status quo states have struggled to maintain them simultaneously on the reform agenda, under the broader democratic umbrella. For now, the battle between those promoting these narrowing and broadening strategies appears to have been won by the P5 as most observers agree that the pressures for UNSC membership reform of the early 1990s have been substantially alleviated (Von Freiesleben 2008; Fassbender 2003; Hurd 1997).

Figure 5.4 illustrates the ups and downs of UNSC transparency. It tracks the proportion of open meetings that this executive organ has held since it was established in 1945.[11] The fluctuations of the UNSC's degree of transparency are a direct result of the discretion that UNSC members

[11] The figure is based on data collected from the UN Journal and from two studies of informal UNSC meetings (Feuerle 1985; http://www.globalpolicy.org/security-council/32941.html).

are given to hold private (formal or informal) meetings. It is noteworthy that, even today, the UN has not established a comprehensive public access to information policy.

In the meantime, many other IGOs have adopted such policies. Some, such as UNESCO, accepted formal information policies as far back as the 1970s. However, in most cases, the push for formalizing greater IGO transparency came a few decades later.

Most IGO adoptions of public access to information policies came as part of a wave that began with developments in the World Bank in the 1980s. Around that time there was a tremendous increase in NGO protests sparked by the Bank's financing of questionable projects. Civil society groups attempting to assess the negative environmental and social consequences of these projects discovered that the Bank had withheld important information from affected communities (Rich 1994). One prominent example was a 1982 World Bank–funded road project in Brazil that led to the deaths of thousands of indigenous people, massive resettlements, and serious environmental damages. Moreover, the half-billion dollar project never led to the benefits that the Bank and Brazilian government anticipated. The cleared rainforest lands that were now accessible through the newly built road system only produced crops for one year. Afterward, the resettled populations had to abandon their new lands (Wade 2011).

Because the principal NGOs involved in initial efforts to uncover the truth about these Bank projects were headquartered in Washington, it was not long until U.S. lawmakers also began pressuring the IGO to review its environmental, social, and, more importantly for this study, information policies. In 1985, Senator Robert Kasten cautioned the Bank president that the organization needed to respond to NGO demands or risk losing congressional funding (Roberts 2006). A congressional directive advised the U.S. executive director at the Bank to encourage borrowing countries to offer more information to those directly affected by projects (Bowles and Kormos 1995). These initial pressures led that year to the adoption of a set of vague internal information disclosure instructions for Bank staff (Saul 2002).

Soon after these events, the Bank was rocked by a series of even greater scandals involving some of its major projects, the most visible being the Sardar Sarovar Dam in India. Initial environmental and resettlement concerns were brushed aside as insignificant both by Indian and World Bank officials. The more than 150 thousand locals who were to be forcibly displaced received very little information about their imminent resettlement.

Local communities organized themselves and began requesting access to resettlement plans, timetables for resettlements, environmental studies, and project appraisals. Neither Indian nor World Bank officials released such information. The information made public through leaks slowly revealed a series of serious violations of World Bank policies throughout the decision-making and implementation stages of the project. The original demands for information were soon accompanied by an increasing number of calls for the complete scrapping of the project and even for broader Bank reforms (Udall 1998, 394–395).

The pressures for Bank reforms from the NGO community were yet again accompanied by those of major donor-states, especially the United States. In 1989, Congress passed the Pelosi Amendment requiring U.S. representatives at the World Bank to vote against loans for which environmental assessments had not been completed and made public (Nelson 2000). Other executive directors at the Bank, such as the ones from the Netherlands and Japan, also began pushing for greater transparency. They felt that the Bank staff was not even sufficiently open with them, let alone with NGOs and the general public (Udall 1998).

The World Bank tried to defuse such pressures through a series of small changes to the project that had triggered the scandal and, more importantly, through the adoption in 1989 of a more formal directive on information disclosure. Moreover, the pressures led to an independent review of the Sardar Sarovar project. The result of the review was embarrassing for the World Bank and exacerbated tensions between those pushing for greater transparency and those supporting confidentiality in decision-making. The main opponents of transparency were major borrower countries (especially India and Brazil) and most of the Bank staff (Nelson 2000). These actors argued that, as a financial institution, the Bank is required to maintain "sound financial management practices, including discretion" and that member-states offer the Bank such information with the understanding that it will remain confidential (World Bank 1994, 14). These arguments challenge the applicability of the transparency norm to the IGO. They imply that the institution needs to be treated primarily as a "bank," accountable only to its board and clients (i.e., governments) rather than a public institution that needs to also be accountable to the publics of member-states.

The main actors promoting transparency of the World Bank were a broad coalition of NGOs, several donor states, and even some of the World Bank staff. These groups took advantage of the fact that the tenth replenishment of the International Development Association (IDA

10) was coming up (Udall 1998). In the U.S. Congress there were calls to not authorize the U.S. contribution (of $3.7 billion) to the replenishment until the Bank offered a written proposal for increased transparency. Senator Patrick Leahy cautioned the World Bank president of lawmakers' "waning tolerance for a public institution supported with public funds that denies the public access to relevant information" (Roberts 2006, 186). After many hours of hearings (in which representatives of NGOs and of the U.S. Treasury testified), Congress accepted only a two-year renewal of IDA (not three as in the past). Moreover, it cut the original pledge to IDA by $200 million. These relatively small changes nevertheless sent strong signals to the World Bank. Top IGO officials scrambled to put together an information policy that was acceptable to all members. In January 1994 the first official World Bank Policy on Disclosure of Information was adopted. The document reflected both sides of the struggle for transparency. Although it formalized to a greater extent the release of information to the public, it nevertheless made clear that there were important reasons to maintain confidentiality in many Bank decisions and allowed for exceptions to the release of information (1994).

This strategy of narrowing the application of the transparency norm, as a response to the normative (and material) pressures for change, has continued to be used in the World Bank for the past two decades. Pressures in the late 1990s led to the adoption of an improved information policy in 2002 that allowed for the first time the release of documents involving structural adjustment loans (only after their approval) as well as information involving the Board of Executive Directors' calendar (Bank Information Center 2013). In 2005, the Bank once more improved transparency by finally allowing for the release of (abridged) minutes of Board of Directors meetings. That same year pressures from the U.S. Congress and NGOs led to the World Bank's adoption of a first set of protections for whistleblowers, an essential tool for the free flow of information from any bureaucracy (Government Accountability Project 2007). Yet another information policy, improving on previous ones, was adopted in 2010. Overall, over the past two decades, the Bank has gradually expanded the kind of information it makes available and its timeliness (Saul 2002), while, at the same time, it has sought to maintain as much control over information as possible. Virtually each time it did so, it only met part of the demands of those pushing for greater access to information.

The regional development banks soon followed the lead of the World Bank (Nelson 2001). Formal information policies were adopted by the Inter-American Development Bank (1994), Asian Development

Bank (1994), African Development Bank (1997), European Bank for Reconstruction and Development (1997), and Caribbean Development Bank (2004).

A decade-long process similar to the incremental one experienced by the Bank unfolded in the International Monetary Fund. As in the case of the Bank, NGOs were the main promoters of transparency in the IMF (Dawson and Bhatt 2002). Also as in the case of the Bank, the U.S. Congress supported NGO-led efforts. In 1998, Congress' IMF Transparency and Efficiency Act warned the IMF that it would limit financial support if it did not adopt rules for publishing board minutes and releasing more documents (House of Representatives 1998). Much of the IMF staff resisted the normative pressures for transparency by emphasizing the intergovernmental character of their organization and, implicitly, their obligation to be accountable solely to governments and not to others (see e.g., IMF Managing Director Horst Köhler, cited in Roberts 2006, 191).

Despite such opposition to change, the IMF began releasing public information notices following the vast majority of its Article IV consultations with states. It also started publishing letters of intent related to IMF programs (Woods and Narlikar 2001). Many board documents, internal and external evaluations, became publicly available (Dawson and Bhatt 2002). Moreover, it began encouraging states to offer accurate and timely financial information through its new "Dissemination Standards Bulletin Board" Web site and its "General Data Dissemination System" Web site.[12] The IMF adopted a first formal public information policy in 2001.

Dozens of other IGOs – as diverse as the Food and Agriculture Organization (1996), Organization of American States (2002), and Interpol (2002) – have also adopted such information policies in the past two decades. Overall, Figure 5.5 illustrates that since the end of the Cold War the number of IGOs that adopted formal information policies followed a similar trend to the one of adoption of freedom of information laws at the domestic level.

The increase in transparency policies and practices in IGOs has taken place despite the resistance of many IGO officials and government representatives. As expected, the tug-of-war between those promoting greater information flows and those opposing them has played out differently across various organizations. Previous work has found that one of the main factors accounting for the differences in transparency in IGOs is

---

[12] See http://dsbb.imf.org/; also http://dsbb.imf.org/Pages/GDDS/Home.aspx

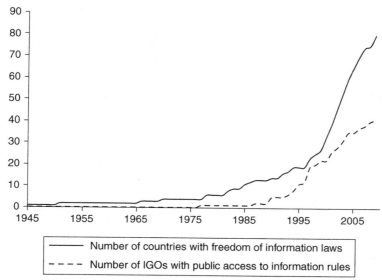

FIGURE 5.5. Number of Countries and IGOs Formalizing Public Access to Information
The graph is based on data from Grigorescu 2007.

the existence of visible scandals involving the organizations (Grigorescu 2007). There have been more than a dozen scandals that led to the adoption of public access to information laws in IGOs. Such scandals are followed by rapid erosion of the organization's perceived legitimacy and of the public's trust in its policies. A common method to regain such trust is for the IGO to indicate that, in the future, it will be more forthcoming with information, especially by adopting an official information policy (rather than the ad hoc release of information) (Grigorescu 2003).

There are many examples at the domestic level of governments sending transparency signals after serious delegitimizing scandals (that generally involved illegal actions followed by attempts to cover them up). In the United States, the Freedom of Information Act was improved substantially after the Watergate scandal. Scandals involving official "entertainment" expenses and HIV contamination of the blood supply triggered the adoption of such a law in Japan (Blanton 2002).

In IGOs, similar scandals led to the adoption of public access to information policies. For example, in 2003, after the World Meteorological Organization announced that one of its officials embezzled $3 million, it adopted an "action plan for management reform" that called for enhanced transparency. One year later it introduced a public access to information policy (Miller 2005). Other IGO scandals such as the one involving the UN Oil-for-Food Program or the Shaha Riza scandal leading World Bank President Paul Wolfowitz to resign were followed by improvements to existing official information policies.[13]

One can couch this mechanism of signaling transparency in the broader argument of this study. Indeed, scandals can be interpreted as discrete events raising public perceptions that the status quo has departed substantially from what norms dictate. While the international norms driving such perceptions (for instance, the transparency or anti-corruption norms) may be just as strong before and after the scandal, normative pressures for changes to rules in that specific IGO increase abruptly.

Both the WTO and the EU were among the IGOs experiencing embarrassing scandals in the post–Cold War Era. The scandals following the riots in Seattle and the resignation of the European Commission, respectively, increased pressures for transparency in the two IGOs. The fact that it took such major events to shake up their information policies is a reflection of their resistance to change in the 1990s, during a period when virtually all IGOs had made some concessions to transparency under normative pressure.

The EU and the WTO may seem to be surprising examples of such resistance to transparency. Even though they are the successors of institutions established immediately after World War II, their current embodiment is the result of post–Cold War material and normative factors. They emerged in 1992 and 1995, respectively, when the norm of transparency was becoming powerful both domestically and internationally.

The pressures for a more transparent WTO emerged during the establishment of the organization. The lack of transparency in its decision-making, especially in its tribunals, was criticized in U.S. Senate hearings prior to the ratification of accession to the WTO by liberals and conservatives alike (Nader, 1994; Hardy 1994). In great part because of these early critiques and pressures, the WTO adopted a set of "procedures for the circulation and derestriction of WTO documents" as early as 1996. At first glance, these rules appeared to follow the general trend toward greater IGO transparency of the 1990s. However, in practice, they proved to be very weak. First, they applied only to documents circulated

---

[13] The relevance of such scandals was underscored in an interview with a government representative from a state that promotes transparency in the UNSC. When asked whether he believed that the UNSC would improve its access to information rules, my interlocutor responded that "we are waiting for the next scandal to move ahead." Personal interview with government official at the UN, June 2009.

among member-states, not to those prepared by the secretariat (Roberts 2006). Second, and more important, as the title of the procedures suggested, the rules only referred to official *documents*, not to general information circulated in the WTO.

The focus on documents was deliberate since most of the IGO's work takes place in informal meetings with few paper trails. The emphasis on informal forums in GATT and the WTO have been a direct result of the move from a majority to a unanimity decision-making system (Jones 2010). As discussed in Chapter 3, the most important of these informal consultations take place between the key players in the Green Room. These meetings are criticized for their informal and, implicitly, secretive nature (Woods and Narlikar 2001).

The WTO's "open-ended meetings," "restricted sessions," "confessionals," and meetings outside of Geneva where states negotiate in private on important matters also take place in informal settings (Bohne 2010). Most of these meetings are not announced to all members and official minutes are not available. The problem is especially acute in the General Council, where "informal heads of delegations meetings" began replacing the few formal meetings, especially before Ministerial Conferences (Third World Network et al. 2003). Even when such informal forums have begun releasing brief minutes and a modicum of information about their proceedings, it is still difficult for outsiders to assess what really goes on in the debates. Keohane and Nye describe this problem in the following fashion: "Negotiators know how to 'wink' – to signal when they are only going through the motions or wish to use a demand as a bargaining chip for something else. If outsiders cannot see the winks, they have a hard time judging how well they were represented in the process" (2002, 229).

As the broad pressures to improve the WTOs transparency increased, developing states adopted a strategy of narrowing the interpretation of the norm. They claimed that the only transparency that really mattered was the "internal" one, referring to their access to information from such informal forums (T_6 in Figure 5.2). They countered the broader Western promotion of transparency (including that toward NGOs and the public, as reflected by T_3 and T_0 in Figure 5.2) with two arguments. First, they felt that opening official records to outsiders would lead to even greater incentives for the powerful states to hold informal meetings and, implicitly, to greater difficulties for smaller states to have access to information (T_6 in Figure 5.2). The second argument was that Western interest groups would gain power through such access to information to the detriment of far poorer and less astute groups from developing states (Roberts 2006). Therefore, according to such countries, only internal transparency (involving information flows toward them) needed to be improved.

Up until 1999, the two sides were faced with a "conceptual divide" (Raghavan 2000). As WTO decisions require consensus, this division between member-states did not allow for any real changes to the WTO's transparency throughout the 1990s.

The 1999 Seattle riots altered the normative structure by increasing pressures to bring about reforms to the WTO's external transparency. The protesters may have disagreed on many of the changes they wanted to see in the IGO. Yet it appears that virtually all groups were critical of the secretive decision-making processes in the organization. One journalist noted in the immediate aftermath of the riots: "Other, more open alliances such as the United Nations or the G-7, the Group of Seven major industrialized nations, make at least a token effort to listen to advice and comments from non-governmental advocates.... The WTO's 135 members hold most of their debates behind closed doors and tell the activists to go stuff it" (Page 1999).

The protesters' calls for greater WTO transparency were quickly picked up by developed states. When President Clinton traveled to Seattle right after the riots, he argued that "it is imperative to make the World Trade Organization more open and accessible" and called for the organization to "open the meetings, open the records and let people file their opinions" (Connelly 1999). Japanese officials also called for reforms that would lead to more transparency (Kyodo News Service, 1999).

The powerful normative pressures empowered "external" transparency. This became apparent in 2002 when Supachai Panitchpakdi of Thailand became the first director-general of the WTO from a developing country. He quickly proceeded to broaden the traditional view of transparency held by developing states to include external transparency, not just internal transparency. The most important change to internal transparency and to state participation in WTO forums came out of the work of the newly established Trade Negotiations Committee. The committee sought to alter the system through which meetings were scheduled so that smaller states (with fewer representatives) would not be at a disadvantage when several meetings took place simultaneously. It also pushed for greater information sharing among states participating in WTO forums and those that could not participate. A newly established advisory board for dialog with civil society also promoted greater access to information for NGOs (an important aspect of external transparency). Both initiatives were considered successful at the time (Williams 2011), but, as they were not formalized through official rules (yet another case of narrowing the application of the norm), they were short-lived. Transparency is generally considered to have eroded once more beginning in 2005 (Van Den Bossche 2010).

The demands for transparency of the European institutions began as far back as the late 1970s and early 1980s, when the increasingly intrusive policies enacted by the EEC started to affect more directly the lives of citizens in the member-states (Driessen 2012). Pressures for greater transparency emerged at that time primarily in the environmental and consumer protection issue areas, where strong nongovernmental actors were increasingly aware of the IGO's impact (Brinkhorst 1999).

The first real step the EEC took toward greater transparency came in the environmental realm. In 1990, Council Directive No. 90/313 on the "freedom of access to information on the environment" specified that member states must adopt legislation ensuring freedom of access to, and dissemination of, information on the environment held by public authorities. This initiative at the domestic level paved the way toward greater access to community documents in this realm.

The most substantive push for transparency, beyond the narrow environmental realm, came after the emergence of the EU. Article 1(2) of the Maastricht Treaty mentioned in passing that decisions should be taken "as openly as possible."[14] Many did not initially expect that such bland wording would have any real impact on the organization (Augustyn and Monda 2011). Moreover, just two weeks after the treaty was signed, the Commission's Security Office submitted a draft regulation that actually limited public access to documents. The regulation was likened to the British Official Secrets Act, one of only two such acts in EU member-states (Bunyan 1999). The Commission's proposal was stopped in the Parliament's Legal Affairs Committee. Yet, the intergovernmental debates that ensued on public access to information carried over to debates within states, especially in Denmark, where the issue influenced the outcome of the 1992 Danish referendum rejecting the Maastricht Treaty.

After this rejection (and the weak French approval), both national and EU officials scurried to deal with what they perceived to be an alienation of the European public (Curtin 1999). Among the issues placed quickly

---

[14] http://europa.eu/eu-law/decision-making/treaties/pdf/consolidated_versions_of_the_treaty_on_european_union_2012/consolidated_versions_of_the_treaty_on_european_union_2012_en.pdf

on the EU's agenda was the one of access to information. Just one month after the Danish referendum, Declaration No. 17 on the Right of Access to Information was attached to the treaty to strengthen the "democratic nature of the EU institutions and the public's confidence in the administration" (*Official Journal* 1992, 1).

By December 1993, the EU's Commission and Council built on Declaration No. 17 by adopting a Code of Conduct on Access to Documents, pledging to provide "the widest possible access to documents" (*Official Journal* 1993, 41–42). The code did not apply, however, to many of the EU's specialized organizations such as the European Central Bank, European Investment Bank, or European Investment Agency (Roberts 2006).

In 1993, 1994, and 1997 the EU's Council (Decision 93/731/EC on public access to Council documents), Commission (Decision 94/90/ECSC, EC, Euratom on public access to Commission documents), and Parliament (Decision 97/632/EC, on public access to European Parliament documents), respectively, adopted more specific rules stipulating exact procedures guiding public access to information. Nevertheless, all three decisions left loopholes for those intent on withholding information. The Commission used such loopholes, for example, when arguing that comitology committees were not obligated to make their minutes public (Neyer 2000).

Of the three decisions, as expected, the one referring to the EU's Council was the weakest and received most criticism. In fact, Denmark and the Netherlands voted against this decision because they felt its wording was too weak. The inadequate implementation of this decision led to numerous challenges. Perhaps most reflective of the continuing culture of secrecy in the EU was the Council's response to a 1995 request from the Union of Swedish journalists for twenty documents. The Union requested an identical list of EU Council documents from the Swedish government and, directly, from the EU Council. While Swedish officials released eighteen of the twenty documents, the EU Council only released two (and later two more) of the twenty documents explaining that it needed to maintain the confidentiality of its proceedings (Bunyan 1999).

Just as embarrassing for the EU Council as the Swedish journalists' test were several protracted battles it fought (and lost) over the right to refuse documents to individual journalists and NGOs. The European Court's 1995 decision in the Guardian case and the 1997 European Ombudsman's efforts in the Statewatch case helped tip the balance in favor of transparency and set up precedents for future information requests.

The results of these hard-fought battles and ensuing incremental steps toward improved practices of transparency of the first half decade of the

EU's existence were institutionalized in the 1997 Treaty of Amsterdam. The treaty contained specific wording acknowledging for the first time in the EU (and in any IGO) a right to access documents (*Official Journal* 1997). Article 151 (3) of the treaty also required for the first time that the Council of the European Union publish the results of votes, explanation of votes, statements, and minutes of meetings. Even such basic requirements (that had been met decades earlier in other IGOs) were seen as a tremendous victory for those promoting EU transparency (Brinkhorst 1999).

Public access to information (rather than just to documents as previous regulations had stipulated) became even more a reality after the 1999 corruption scandal involving the EU Commission. After the scandal, states acted to reestablish the organization's credibility through a series of important measures such as the creation of an anti-fraud office and the adoption of the first comprehensive public-information policy (Commission of the European Communities, 2003). In 2000, the EU also adopted a charter of fundamental rights that included a right to documents extended to all bodies of the Union. Moreover, Article I-50 of the Constitutional Treaty introduced for the first time a requirement that the EU Council meet in pubic when considering and voting on a legislative act (Driessen 2012).

In 2001, the EU's Council and the Parliament adopted Regulation No 1049/2001 on public access to information that applied to all three major EU bodies: Parliament, Council, and Commission. While this step forward was partly a reaction to the 1999 corruption scandal (Grigorescu 2003), the policy may not have passed in its fairly progressive form had Sweden (the country with the oldest tradition of transparency) not held the presidency of the EU's Council at that time (Bengtsson, Elgström, and Tallberg 2004). The policy quickly became viewed as the central instrument for achieving EU transparency (Augustyn and Monda 2011, 1), capping almost a decade of incremental advances in promoting public access to information in the European institutions.

Answering the Questions of the Study

What Types of Decision-Making Rules Were Being Established or Changed?

The rules discussed here regulate several different types of information flows in IGOs. The first debates surrounded public and, especially, press access to League and ILO meetings. Later, the main battles for transparency revolved around rules stipulating the ability of states that were not members of exclusive IGO bodies (such as the League Council, ILO Governing Body, or UNSC) to know what was being discussed by states represented in these forums. In the EU, the main rules that were being challenged involved public access to information from the Commission and, especially, from the Council. In the World Bank, the changes in rules being promoted were those involving NGO and public access to information from the Bank staff. In the WTO, the efforts to make intergovernmental deliberations more open to the public were at times accompanied by calls to improve only the narrower "internal" transparency of the organization. There were other, less visible, "battles" for information in each IGO, such as the efforts to make the World Bank Board of Directors more transparent to governments that were not directly represented there as well as to NGOs and the public or the ones to grant the European Parliament more access to information about deliberations in the EU's Council.

Did Actors Invoke Democratic Norms to Pressure Others in Accepting Decision-Making Rules?

Whether actors promoting greater flows of information emphasized the need for "publicity" (immediately after World War I) or "transparency" (in the post–Cold War era), they all framed such concepts, at least indirectly, as democratic norms. By doing so, they often clothed their self-interested demands for information in language that helped them apply normative pressures for the changes they were promoting.

Although the link between democratic mechanisms and transparency implies that the public is, ultimately, the recipient of information, many actors that were not necessarily themselves transparent (such as member-states or NGOs) often used such tactics as a way to achieve greater access to information for themselves rather than for the public. This was the case in the debates in the League of Nations, in the UN, and in the WTO where smaller states craved more information from proceedings in the more exclusive forums. To some degree, it also appears to have been the case in the World Bank and, again, in the WTO, where NGOs sought more information from the IGOs. Often times in such instances, when actors promoting transparency to the public were co-opted by powerful actors through the adoption of formal or informal rules giving them more access to information (such as the Arria formula in the UNSC), they appear to have ended their quests for broader forms of transparency.

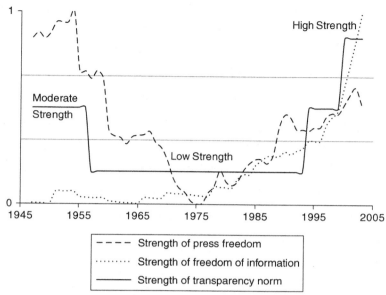

FIGURE 5.6. Strength of Transparency Norm.

How Powerful Were Such Pressures?

The manifestations of the domestic norm of transparency have been discussed both in terms of press freedom and freedom of information. It was emphasized that both elements are important for a free flow of information to societies. I therefore consider a composite measure of the transparency norm's strength based on the proportions of states with free press and freedom of information legislation that are members of an IGO at a given moment in time. The strength of the transparency norm is considered high when both freedom of the press and freedom of information are strong or when one component is strong and the other is moderate. The norm strength is low when both components are weak or when one is weak and the other moderate. All other cases are of moderate norm strength. The operationalization is based on the measures already depicted in Figure 5.1 but scaled, like all other measures of norm strength, from 0 (lowest strength) to 1 (highest strength) in Figure 5.6.

Figure 5.6 also includes a line representing the category of overall norm strength (low, moderate, or high). It shows that the norm was weak from the late 1950s to the early 1990s. It was of moderate strength in the first years after World War II and from the early 1990s to 2000. Since around 2000, norm strength has been high. Table 5.1 includes the

TABLE 5.1. *Normative Pressures for IGO Transparency and Reactions to Pressures*

IGO/moment	League /1919	ILO /1919	League/early 1920s	ILO/1920s	League/early 1930s	UN/1945
Rule involves	Public/press access to Council information	Public/press access to Council information	–Member-states' access to Council information –Council membership	Public/press access to Governing Body information	–States' access to Council information –Council membership	States' access to UNSC information
Press freedom	M	M	M	M	M	H
Freedom of information	L	L	L	L	L	L
Transparency norm strength	L	L	L	L	L	M
Departure from norm prescription	H	H	H	H	L	L
Normative pressure	M	M	M	M	VL	L
Strategy	NA; CA	NA	BA*	Y	BA*	NA
Outcome	C	C	PC	C	AC	PC

Note: CN = challenging norm; NN = narrowing norm; BN = broadening norm; CA = challenging application of norm; NA = narrowing application of norm; BA = broadening application of norm; Y = yielding; W = withstanding; C = originally promoted change; NC = no change; PC = partial change; AC = alternative change.

* Strategy used to defuse normative pressure from other norm.

UN/1970s	World Bank/early 1990s	UN/mid-1990s	WTO/late 1990s	EU/mid-1990s	EU/1999–2000	WTO/early 2000s
–States' access to UNSC information –UNSC Membership	–Access to Bank information –NGO participation in Bank work	–States' access to UNSC information –UNSC membership	Public access to WTO information	Public access to EU Council and Commission information	Public access to EU Council and Commission information	–Public access to WTO information –State participation in informal meetings
L	M	M	M	H	H	M
L	L	M	M	H	H	H
L	L	M	M	H	H	H
H	H	H	H	H	H	H
M	M	H	H	VH	VH	VH
BA*	CA; NA; BA*	BN*; NA	NA; NN	NA	Y	BA*; NN; NA
PC	PC	AC; C	NC	PC	C	PC

two components of norm strength and the overall measure. In addition, I consider the norm strength to be low in the interwar era when press freedom was moderate and freedom of information was low.[15]

There were important differences across time and IGOs in the perceptions that rules and practices were departing from the prescriptions of the transparency norm, the second component of normative pressure. Such perceptions were very strong in the immediate aftermath of World War I, when the public and influential officials believed that the culture of secrecy in international relations had been partly to blame for the outbreak of the war. The fact that these perceptions were especially powerful in the United States, the country everyone wanted to persuade in joining the League, added to the pressures for transparency. Even though the League adopted fairly progressive rules for public access to IGO information, in the first few years of the IGO they did not put them in practice. The actors promoting change to the League emphasized the lack of open Council meetings to show that the status quo was departing from what the norm of publicity demanded. The same indicator was mentioned by those seeking greater transparency at several critical junctures in the history of the UN.

Figure 5.7 represents the proportion of Council and Security Council meetings closed to the press and public on a scale from 0 (year with smallest proportion of closed meetings) to 1 (year with greatest proportion of closed meetings, about 75 percent). It shows that departure from the transparency norm prescription in the League was high in the early 1920s. Then, as transparency practices improved, the departure from norm prescription declined considerably in the mid-1920s only to increase again in the late 1920s and then decline yet again in the early 1930s. Starting around 1933 the League's transparency practices consistently eroded until the IGO ceased to function with the outbreak of World War II. A similar pattern was followed in the ILO, in which initially meetings were closed, despite the progressive rules. Throughout the mid- and late 1920s almost all ILO Governing Body meetings were open only to abruptly close around 1930.

When the UN was established, it picked up the strong original transparency rules from the League and quickly put them in practice. As

---

[15] There are no gauges of press freedom before 1945. I consider this component to be moderate in the 1920s and weak in the 1930s on the basis of qualitative studies of press freedom. As only Sweden had adopted an FOI law before World War II, freedom of information in the world is considered weak in both periods (and even up to the late 1990s). The overall strength of the norm for the interwar era is therefore low.

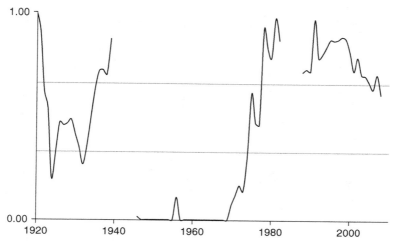

FIGURE 5.7. Departure from Prescriptions of Transparency Norm in League of Nations and UN.

Figure 5.7 indicates, there were only very few closed meeting of the UNSC until around 1970s. Yet, in just a few years, in the early 1970s the proportion of open meetings was reduced considerably, and, by the end of that decade, the executive organ of the UN reached an all-time high with regard to the departure from what the transparency norm prescribed. Figure 5.7 shows that in the late 1970s there were several relatively rapid improvements in transparency followed by similarly rapid reversals to secrecy. The UNSC remained very closed throughout the Cold War and in the first decade of the post–Cold War era. As many other IGOs began adopting rules for greater transparency in the 1990s, the UN's departure from norm prescriptions became even more noticeable at that time. Only around 2000 did the practices in the UNSC improve, to some degree, when they departed moderately from norm prescription, compared to previous decades.

There are no similar comprehensive measures of the practices of transparency for the World Bank, WTO, and EU. Yet, as all three IGOs have always had meetings of their most important bodies behind closed doors, with few and incomplete available minutes, I consider their departures from norm prescriptions as high throughout their history (with the exception of the EU after it adopted its policy on access to information in 2001), compared to developments in the other three main IGO executive bodies discussed in this study.

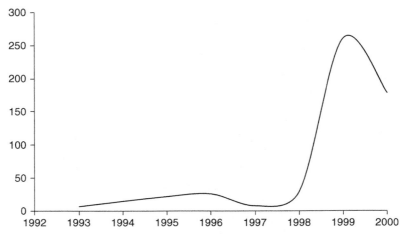

FIGURE 5.8. Number of Articles Discussing IGO Scandals.

Table 5.1 includes the values for departure from norm prescription. It also includes, in a separate row, the values of normative pressure, defined as the interaction between the two. Table 5.1 shows that such pressures have increased from moderate in the interwar and Cold War eras to high in the immediate post–Cold War era to very high starting in the mid-1990s.

Although for sake of comparability across norms and cases the gauge of normative pressures used in this book is only a categorical one, there are ways of assessing the more subtle changes in such pressures. For example Figure 5.8 tracks the measure "Scandal" used in previous works to assess the visibility in the press of scandals involving IGOs. It represents the number of articles discussing IGO-related scandals in Lexis-Nexis and World News Connection between 1993 and 2000.[16] Figure 5.8 shows that although IGOs had experienced some scandals in the mid-1990s, these did not compare to the intensity of the ones affecting the WTO and EU in 1999 (as, indeed, about 80 percent of all articles captured in Figure 5.8 referred to these two IGOs), reflected in the rapid increase in that year and in 2000 in Figure 5.8.

[16] The measure considers approximately seventy-five IGOs. It begins from all articles in Lexis-Nexis and World News Connection mentioning the word "scandal," as well as other words such as "corrupt," "embarrass," "disgrace," "trust," and "legitimacy," with the name or acronym of each IGO. Close reading of this larger pool of articles then allowed for the extraction of only those articles that actually did discuss a scandal involving IGOs. For a full description of the measure, see Grigorescu 2007.

The intensity of such (negative) press coverage can be considered an alternative gauge for the overall normative pressures for changes to transparency in IGOs, as suggested earlier in the discussion of the relevance of such scandals in domestic and international realms. Many governments and IGOs have felt that they needed to react to scandals by adopting or improving information policies. Indeed, while the WTO and EU had been under great pressures to alter their rules with regard to information access even before 1999, the Seattle riots and the resignation of the European Commission in that year added to such pressures considerably. Of course, such subtle and rapid changes cannot be captured with categorical variables such as those used in Table 5.1.

What Actions Did Actors Opposing the New Rules Take under Normative Pressure?

The most common strategy used by those opposing increased transparency appears to have been the one of narrowing the application of the norm, as H$_6$ suggests we should generally expect when actors attempt to alter the application of a norm. It was used very often in the World Bank, the WTO, and the EU in the post–Cold War era by limiting the types of information that should be released, the timing of its release (after rather than before decisions were taken), and, in several cases in the EU, even the number of documents it was willing to release at one time (Bunyan 1999). Moreover, the fact that these IGO policies often referred to "access to documents" (rather than, more broadly, to all information held by the organizations) was a restriction on transparency.

The decision to allow IGO bodies such as the League Council, ILO Governing Body, and UNSC to decide on an ad hoc basis when they should hold open meetings and when they would hold them behind closed doors (without adopting specific formal policies) was also a narrowing strategy as a response to normative pressures for transparency. The adoption of informal rules in the UNSC, such as the existence to this day of "provisional" rules of procedure or the adoption of the Arria formula for some meetings, are perhaps the most obvious examples of such an informal approach to transparency in IGOs. These rules have given members of executive bodies a great deal of control over information, as illustrated through the variance of transparency levels in Figures 5.3 and 5.4.

The acceptance of rules allowing for greater access to information from some IGO bodies and less from others is a reflection of yet another narrowing strategy. Virtually all IGOs have allowed for more transparency in their broader and less influential forums while maintaining greater secrecy in their executive forums. Such decisions were sometimes explained using domestic analogies as was the case at the founding of the League of Nations when the British sought to limit transparency to the League's Assembly, maintaining secrecy in the Council.

While the previous are all examples of actors narrowing the actions prescribed by the norm of transparency, there are also several instances of strategies used to narrow the norm itself. In the WTO, for example, the norm of transparency was narrowed by representatives of developing countries who argued that although the IGO indeed needed to be transparent, the transparency (like its accountability) should be directed solely toward the governments that it serves (T_2), not to outsiders (T_0 or T_3).

Domestic analogies were used in the World Bank to challenge (rather than just narrow) the application of the transparency norm. There it was argued that the organization was more similar to a bank than to a public institution accountable to those affected by its policies. That implied that the World Bank, unlike other IGOs, had an obligation to maintain sensitive economic information out of public view.

One would have expected actors to challenge the application of the norm of transparency more on the basis of the argument that negotiations were more effective if conducted in secrecy. Surprisingly, this position was only expressed publicly in the first years of the publicity debates in the League of Nations. It is possible that the argument was not used later because of the transparency norm becoming more powerful.

Lastly, in the League Council, UNSC, and, to some degree, even in the WTO, actors who opposed pressures for increases in membership of the executive bodies introduced the issue of transparency on the reform agendas in a broadening strategy. When they explicitly linked the two issues, presenting them both as facets of more democratic practices (as in the UN in the 1990s), the strategy brought the two norms together. In cases when this link was not made explicit but rather took the form of a "deal" involving solely the implementation of the transparency norm (as in the League in the early 1920s and early 1930s, in the UN in the 1970s, and in the WTO in the 2000s), the broadening strategy was at the level of actions, rather than norms. Broadening, at both levels, was relatively effective because of the natural linkage between participation and access to information. Indeed, greater transparency reduces the costs of lack of participation for those who are not members of these IGO bodies. Of course, the strategy was only used when both the application of the participation and transparency norms in the IGOs departed considerably from what the norms dictated. It was not used, for example, in the UN in the 1960s, when such transparency could not be improved much further. It is noteworthy that once such increases in transparency served their immediate purpose by defusing pressures for membership reform, the ad hoc nature of the rules governing access to information usually allowed for quick reversals toward greater secrecy (as Figures 5.3 and 5.4 suggest). Although in some cases (such as in the UN in the 1990s and in the WTO in 2000) the states supporting improved participation rules were aware of the potentially negative effects the strategy of broadening would have for them and tried de-linking the issue of transparency from the one of participation, they were not successful.

The emphasis on such broadening strategies reminds us, yet again, that democratic reforms in IGOs need to be studied simultaneously as they often affect each other. In other words, if one were to focus solely on efforts to make the League Council and UNSC more inclusive, it is difficult to understand, as Chapter 3 suggested, when and how changes in membership rules actually took place. Conversely, a discussion focusing solely on the evolution of rules and practices of access to information would miss some of the factors accounting for changes in transparency were it not to consider the parallel evolution of participation rules.

What Were the Outcomes of the Attempts to Adopt or Change Rules?

The strategy of challenging the application of the transparency norm in IGOs was, at best, temporary. Immediately after World War I, the strong pressures to avoid state negotiations behind closed doors led to the opening of all League and ILO bodies to at least some degree of public scrutiny. The World Bank and the other multilateral development banks were not able to sustain the argument that the technical issues they dealt with required greater secrecy. In the 1990s, their status as intergovernmental organizations with accountability requirements appears to have superseded their status as "banks."

In the WTO developing states narrowed the norm of transparency to refer only to information flows toward member-states not included in the exclusive IGO forums (T_6) and not toward outsiders (T_0 or T_3). This has led to a "conceptual" split that has yet to be resolved and that has so far led to only small (partial) changes to the IGO's rules.

As H_7 suggests, the many instances of using the narrowing strategies has led to incremental changes in rules for access to information in many IGOs. Such small changes to information policies have often increased the type of information and speed with which it was offered. In many cases, the narrowing strategy involved the adoption of provisional or informal rules (as in the case of the UNSC at the founding of the IGO in 1945 and, later, in the 1990s, respectively). Powerful states that had the discretion to apply such "loose" rules were later able to increase and reduce transparency when and where they chose. This strategy led to outcomes that sometimes have been described as "one step forward two back" (Bunyan 1999, 2).

The ad hoc nature of some of the access to information rules was especially useful to powerful states when applying the strategy of broadening. They were able to avoid increases in membership in IGO executive bodies by increasing transparency. After such major changes were averted, and when the pressures for membership changes were alleviated, transparency once more declined. At times when transparency was already high, the broadening strategy could not be used and, in some cases, powerful states gave in to the pressure for increases in executive body membership.

Overall, one should note that there appear to be more changes (even if only small and temporary ones) in IGO transparency rules and practices than in rules involving state participation and voting, discussed in Chapters 3 and 4. This could be interpreted as reflecting that the latter issues are more important for states and that it takes more normative pressure to bring about desired changes.

Would Outcomes Have Been the Same in the Absence of Normative Pressures and Reactions to Pressures?

The steady increases in transparency of IGOs over the past century are difficult to explain using solely logic of expected consequences arguments. The strong relationship between information and power, mentioned in the introduction of this chapter, suggests that in the absence of normative pressures, actors should not give up their control over such an important commodity. Indeed, that is why the most important of all organs and IGOs (such as the UNSC, the Council of the European Union, the WTO, and the World Bank Board of Directors) appear to have been the least affected by normative pressures. Powerful states that control the work of such institutions have been willing to allow for greater transparency in other IGO organs in the hope that such concessions would defuse normative pressures to bring about change to the most important forums for them. Yet, virtually all IGOs and IGO organs have opened up to the public, at least to some degree, over the past century. The secret deliberations of the Concert of Europe seem impossible to replicate in any IGO in this day and age. Even compared to the practices of the 1980s, IGOs such as the World Bank and EU have made tremendous strides. Moreover, the rapid adoption of public information rules in IGOs starting in the late 1990s is difficult to explain without taking into account the empowerment of transparency norms at the domestic level, as reflected in the spread of freedom of information laws across states.

All of these changes have taken place despite the fact that, in most (but not all) cases, the most powerful states were the ones opposing transparency. This is expected as they are the ones that are virtually always represented in the most exclusive forums. It is noteworthy that such powerful states have sometimes led the efforts for greater external transparency. In the case of the UN in the 1990s and 2000s, this can be explained through the strategy of broadening. Specifically, great powers alleviated more dangerous normative pressures for them (those intended to bring about membership reform) by accepting greater transparency.

In the World Bank, IMF, and WTO, the United States, in fact, took the lead in promoting greater transparency. One should note, however, that it was the legislative branch in the United States that spearheaded such changes, not the executive branch represented in the IGO.

This observation leads to an alternative explanation for the increases in IGO transparency of the past two decades, beyond those involving normative pressures. The explanation draws from an analogy to the domestic realm in which freedom of information laws have been adopted in great part as a way for legislatures to erode the monopoly over information of executives (Blanton 2002). Similarly, IGO public information policies can be seen, in part, as the result of national legislatures' efforts to gain more control over decisions in the international realm. This has been a natural reaction of legislators when such international institutions began having increasing impact on domestic affairs after the end of the Cold War. Indeed, U.S. legislators played an important role in promoting transparency in the World Bank and IMF. Similarly, the initial debates in the U.S. Senate surrounding the establishment of the WTO revealed much opposition to a secretive IGO. Even the U.S. decision to stay out of the League of Nations was, in part, a result of American legislators' concerns that the executive could not offer sufficient information about the workings and decisions of the IGO. Last, but not least, in the case of the EU, some of the major decisions to open up the organization were because of efforts of members of national parliaments and of the European Parliament who wanted to gain greater control over the information held by the Council of the EU and, implicitly, over the joint decisions of representatives of the executive branches of government. They were helped by independent actors, such as the European Court of Justice and the European Ombudsman, which acted as additional checks on the power of these bodies.

Yet, in all such cases, this additional explanation for increased transparency simply suggests that domestic actors had interests in promoting transparency in IGOs and, in some cases, had the ability to use material incentives to bring about changes (as was evidenced in the case of the World Bank). The preceding argument therefore accounts for the existence of a tug-of-war over information but not for the eventual outcome of this tug-of-war. While the U.S. Congress threatened to use (and in some cases even used) the "power of the purse" on some IGOs, it is difficult to understand why it promoted transparency when it did without considering the empowerment of norms and the increase in normative pressures. These norms were much more powerful in the post–Cold War era than in the past and allowed actors to apply strong normative pressures leading to changes.

Moreover, an explanation based solely on the material interests of legislators to open up IGOs could not explain which states led the reform efforts. For example, of all great powers it was the United States, a country with one of the oldest traditions of transparency, not the United Kingdom (with a long tradition of secrecy), that spearheaded such reforms in the World Bank and even in the WTO. Similarly, Sweden, Finland, and Denmark, with deep-rooted institutions and norms of transparency, were the main countries involved in the promotion of EU transparency. In all such cases, one needs to consider the export of domestic norms to the international realm to understand the differences in various states' positions in the battle over information and, implicitly, to understand the outcomes.

6

Participation of Nongovernmental Actors in Intergovernmental Organizations

The Norm

Participation of nongovernmental actors in IGOs is often associated with the democratic character of the international decision-making process. Yet, the link between democracy and nongovernmental actor activities is not automatic. It implies that such actors are both representative of society and independent of the governmental structures that they are intended to hold accountable. Moreover, it implies that they do not just carry out the policies of governments and IGOs, but they also contribute to shaping them and help hold governmental actors accountable for decisions.

The preceding arguments are an extension of those from the rich literature on the role of "civil society" in domestic politics. Although this term has been used for centuries in many different ways, civil society is generally understood as describing the public sphere that is set outside of the official governmental sphere or the business sphere. By and large, there is a general agreement in the literature that the more such nongovernmental actors are able to participate freely in the political process, the more democratic the system is (Almond and Verba 1963).

Even in contemporary usage, civil society can be interpreted (1) more broadly, as a diffuse deliberative space (e.g., Habermas 1974); (2) somewhat more narrowly, encompassing virtually all associational life outside government (e.g., Putnam 2000); or (3) even more narrowly, as the sum of all formally organized nongovernmental organizations (e.g., Salamon 1999). This chapter begins from the second understanding of civil society, referring to the role of nongovernmental actors. However, as virtually all IGO rules relevant for this topic refer solely to formal NGOs (in great part because it is easier to establish formal relations with them), most of the following pages focus on such transnational NGOs. The exception is the discussion of developments within the International Labor Organization, where representatives of labor and employer groups contribute not only to deliberations but also to the actual decision-making process through direct votes. In this latter case, I use the term "nongovernmental actors" (NGAs).

The "Pro-NGO Norm" in the Domestic Realm

NGAs such as religious or professional groups have acted as useful partners or nagging counterweights to governments virtually as long as political systems have existed. Their number and the degree to which they were allowed to participate have improved throughout time. By the mid-nineteenth century, NGAs had taken an active political role both in domestic and international politics. However, their existence only began being linked to democracy with the enactment of the first laws protecting the right to assembly, association, and expression in the late eighteenth century. Through these laws, the independence and representative character of such actors increased, not just their numbers. The laws were both effects and causes of the increasingly powerful democratic norm that made it appropriate for NGAs to participate in the political processes.

Although the emergence of a global "pro-NGO norm" within states can be traced back to the nineteenth century (Boli and Thomas 1999), and although this norm became more powerful throughout the first half of the twentieth century, the literature suggests that a true "global associational revolution" only took place in the late 1970s or early 1980s (Salamon 1999, 4). Multiple country-level observations based on the increase in number and independence of NGOs support this claim. Most of this literature emphasizes the empowerment of the NGO sector in the consolidated democracies of Western Europe and North America (Salamon, 1994). Yet, similar trends in Africa led the 1980s to be coined as the "NGO Decade" (Sandberg 1994). The mushrooming of NGOs in East and Central Europe, where such associations hardly existed before the end of the Cold War, is an even more obvious example of the norm's empowerment (Opoku-Mensah 2001).

The global trend is also illustrated by the rapid improvement in the Freedom House measure of "civil liberties"[1] across states (in Figure 6.1).

---

[1] The civil liberties (CL) scores of Freedom House vary from 1 (a country with the greatest degree of freedom in a specific year) to 7 (a country with the least degree of freedom in

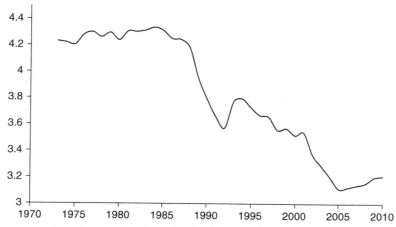

FIGURE 6.1. Average Level of "Civil Liberties" Scores of All States.
For data, see http://www.freedomhouse.org/report-types/freedom-world.

The measure reflects the average worldwide degree of freedom of expression, assembly, association, education, and religion mentioned earlier as essential elements for an independent civil society. Figure 6.1 shows that, starting around 1985, there has been a substantial improvement in civil liberties around the world, although there were setbacks in the mid-1990s and again in the late 2000s. The overall trend can be seen as yet another reflection of the rapid empowerment of the global pro-NGO norm since the mid-1980s.

Government willingness to allow nongovernmental groups to form, assemble, and express their positions is not the only necessary condition for the functioning of a truly vibrant civil society associated with democracy. These groups need to be truly independent of governmental institutions. Also, if such NGAs are to be given a role in decision-making and in keeping governments accountable, they need to be representative of domestic groups. Perceptions regarding the lack of such independence and representativeness have plagued many domestic NGOs and, as I show, many international ones. This, in turn, has led to tensions between the pro-NGO norm and democratic norms of accountability and fair representation.

a specific year). Therefore, the decline in the average CL score in Figure 6.1 reflects the improvement of civil liberties across states over time.

The "Pro-NGO Norm" in the International Realm

The following sections show that NGOs have been playing a role in the international realm for almost two centuries. Yet, the pro-NGO norm that emerged in the international realm appears to have been somewhat different from the one in the domestic realm. In the international realm, the norm seems to have derived less from a perceived link between NGO participation and democracy. It was more likely to be based on the usefulness of such organizations for resolving collective actions and, in time, on the tradition of including them in IGO work. This was in part a result of the fact that international NGOs generally preceded IGOs and, therefore, brought important expertise to the tasks of their newer intergovernmental partners.

In addition, the problems in linking NGO participation in the international realm to democratic principles derived from several factors that differed from the domestic realm, beyond the two of independence and representativeness, mentioned earlier (which are common to both realms). First, in international relations, there was more than just one government that needed to be checked by NGAs. Therefore, the domestic argument that NGOs need to act as important checks on one homogenous all-powerful government that controls virtually all decisions does not really find a strong analogy in the international realm. Indeed, in world politics the multiple governments have competing goals. This implies that, when international NGOs act against one government's interests, they are often supporting another government.[2]

A second important difference between the international realm and the domestic one is that the tremendous power disparities in international relations can lead some NGOs to become (considerably) more powerful than some governments. This problem can be exacerbated by NGO lack of independence, one of the traditional issues that plague the relationship between NGO participation and democracy.

Together, these four potential problems (the lack of independence and representativeness that applies to domestic and international NGOs alike, the likelihood that NGOs will take sides with some governments against others, and their ability to have a greater influence than some governments) have often led to clashes between those promoting the pro-NGO norm and those opposing it. Indeed, by accusing NGOs of lack of

---

[2] Although such problems are also present in the domestic realm (especially in cases of divided government), we do not expect them to be as great as in the international realm where almost 200 sovereign states interact.

independence and representativeness, opponents of the pro-NGO norm can challenge the link between democracy and NGO participation in the international realm. Alternatively, by arguing that international NGOs are imposing external interests on domestic systems, such opponents use the norm of sovereignty to challenge the pro-NGO norm. Lastly, when they point out that domestic decisions (which NGOs may oppose) have been reached democratically, they challenge the pro-NGO norm by stripping it of democratic character. The following sections show that these problems in connecting NGO participation to democratic norms indeed have led to important challenging (as well as narrowing and broadening) strategies on the part of those opposing increased NGO participation in IGO work.

A History of the Application of the Norm to IGOs

Developments before World War II

The initial relevance of NGAs on the world stage is associated with the unsuccessful revolutions of 1848 and with the demand for international contacts between the peoples that had taken part in them (Lador-Lederer 1962, 61). By the beginning of the twentieth century there were approximately 130 transnational NGOs. Examples of such early organizations are the British and Foreign Anti-Slavery Society, the World Alliance of YMCA, the Alliance Israelite Universelle, the International Committee for Relief of Wounded Soldiers (which later became the International Committee of the Red Cross), and the International Peace Bureau. Governments gave NGAs important roles in intergovernmental meetings and in the first intergovernmental organizations of the nineteenth century. For example, at the first International Sanitary Conference of 1851–1852, states were each represented by two delegates: one diplomat and one physician. Delegates voted individually, not as a country group. Several international NGOs participated in the 1889 intergovernmental conference on the Repression of African Slave Trade. Dozens of NGOs were involved in the First and Second Hague Peace Conferences (in 1899 and 1907) (Charnovitz 1997, 5).

Many of the early intergovernmental organizations (IGOs) such as the International Bureau of Education, the Institute of Refrigeration, the International Sugar Regime, and the International Tin Committee actually began as forums for NGAs and only later took on an intergovernmental character (White 1951, 245–246). In many other cases, such nongovernmental entities often set up their own forums parallel to those of existing IGOs (such as those dealing with telegraphy, postal services, weights and measures, customs, and agriculture) to collaborate and influence decisions within the IGOs (Chiang 1981, 21–22). In fact, by the beginning of World War I most international interactions did not distinguish clearly between the international intergovernmental and nongovernmental initiatives and forums (Pickard 1956, 24).

Several NGAs were involved directly in the establishment of the League of Nations and the World Court. The International Foundation of Trade Unions contributed to the establishment of the Nansen International Office of Refugees. International peace NGOs helped form the Institute of Intellectual Cooperation. Perhaps most importantly, labor organizations played a crucial role in the establishment of the ILO (White 1951, 247–248). This led to the unique decision of allowing labor and employer representatives to participate and even vote in ILO decisions, offering the most powerful example of the relevance of NGAs in an IGO.

As the League was established in an era of strong nongovernmental activity, its founders initially sought a prominent role for NGOs. Article 24 of the Covenant stipulated that "international bureaux" should be placed under the "direction" of the League. The murky concept of an international bureau reflected the great overlap between nongovernmental and intergovernmental organizations at the time the Covenant was being drafted. It was intended to allow all types of international organizations to work under the League. They could be intergovernmental, such as the Universal Postal Union, or nongovernmental, such as Save the Children. After this very inclusive approach was formalized in the Covenant, League officials struggled to clarify which organizations could be considered bureaux and which could not. The word "direction" was also long debated by those adopting and, especially, those later interpreting the Covenant. The original word had been "control" but then seemed to be too strong and was replaced (League of Nations Legal Section 1921).

The justification for this official relationship between NGOs and the League never touched on the democratic contribution that the inclusion of NGOs was making to the IGO's character. For example, when the League's Bureaux Section grappled with how to interpret Article 24, it provided four reasons for establishing a relationship between the League and NGOs: to prevent overlap between other international organizations and the League, to promote cooperation between organizations, to prevent a member-state taking over a bureau, and to encourage efficiency (League of Nations 1921b, 1).

Although NGO participation in the League was not presented as a democratic development at that time, there was nevertheless a strong understanding that allowing NGOs to take part in the League was "appropriate." Yet, this pro-NGO norm of the early twentieth century appears to have had a utilitarian origin based on three factors: (1) international nongovernmental organizations had contributed a great deal to the goals of the League well before the Covenant was drafted, (2) international work throughout the late nineteenth century and early twentieth century had often blurred the lines between governmental and nongovernmental initiatives and, more importantly, (3) officials had become used to having NGO representatives taking part in major international meetings (including in the negotiations that led to the establishment of the League). In other words, the origin of this early form of a pro-NGO norm was based on past usefulness of nongovernmental groups and, in time, on what Kratochwil (1984) has described as the "habits and traditions" that shape a norm.

The lack of internalization of the norm is illustrated by the stark difference between the public pro-NGO rhetoric tone of the League and the paternalistic and often half-mocking one used privately by League officials. For example, when explaining in an internal document the third of four reasons given to establish League-NGO relations, Inazo Nitobe, undersecretary general of the League, and director of the International Bureaux Section, argued: "As in states the minorities have access to the League of Nations for protection, so in international associations the League should see to it that the weaker brethren get their share." Therefore, he felt that "some disinterested third party" (i.e., the League) "should keep watch over the different international organisations in order to prevent waste of energy." He also mentioned that such organizations were "in general ridiculously sensitive bodies" and, therefore, one had to be particularly careful in interactions with their representatives (League of Nations 1921b, 3–5).

Despite this underlying condescending attitude, the League did open up to NGOs and attempted to walk a fine line in its relations with them. For example, if an NGO wanted to collaborate with the League, the IGO technically established a right to audit the organization (League of Nations Legal Section 1921). If the NGO did not consent to this relationship, the League's secretariat could still "collect and distribute all relevant information" to the NGO and "render any other assistance which may be necessary or desirable" (League of Nations 1919).

The League's Council initially gave Article 24 of the Covenant a broad interpretation, making it possible for the League to support NGOs and not just IGOs (League of Nations Secretariat 1922, i). The International Bureaux Section that was set up to coordinate collaborations with such organizations developed strong collaborative relations with about 200 NGOs throughout its history.[3] Moreover, because of the stipulation in the article that "the Council may include as part of the expenses of the Secretariat those of any bureau or commission which is placed under the direction of the League" (League of Nations 1919), the IGO initially supported some NGOs financially, offering its facilities for their meetings and covering publishing costs of NGO documents that were relevant for its own work (Inter-parliamentary Union 1921b, 1; White 1951, 251).

However, a quick survey of the section's archives shows that the majority of such collaborations were geared toward the work of a single NGO: the Federation of the League of Nations Societies. The Federation had been set up through grassroots movements across the world before the League was established. After the League began functioning, the NGO saw its role as one of primarily influencing public opinion in favor of the IGO (International Union of League of Nations Associations 1921). Many of the League's public relations efforts were therefore channeled through the Federation (e.g., MacDonald 1934). Even if the IGO would have wanted to tone down its relations with other NGOs, it was difficult to do so while maintaining strong ties with an organization it was working with to improve its public image.

Unlike the ILO, the League did not, of course, allow nongovernmental actors to vote in decision-making bodies. However, it initially attributed to representatives of transnational NGOs a status considered equal to those of IGOs (and, in some cases, even to those of member-states) and that has been described as one of "participation without a vote" (Pickard 1956, 25–26, 54; Seary 1996, 23). The League instituted early on the position of "assessor" for some NGOs. Such assessors were allowed to propose resolutions and amendments and to initiate discussions (League of Nations 1922c, i). However, the League did not specify the criteria and process that allowed some organizations to be considered assessors and others to be left outside of the advisory process.

---

[3] See League of Nations Archives of Section of International Bureaux and Intellectual Cooperation (various years).

The presidents of the League's Assembly and Council consulted regularly with a broad spectrum of NGOs (League of Nations 1923, i). They also called on representatives from virtually all NGOs with which they had relations to offer their views in forums that were often attended by member-state representatives. Some NGOs were invited to submit reports to the League, as was the case for the World Alliance of YMCAs' report on work against narcotic drugs (White 1951, 250). On multiple occasions NGOs were also responsible for proposals that later materialized in intergovernmental treaties and agreements. For example, the proposal for a Declaration of the Rights of the Child, put forth by Save the Children, was adopted by the League in 1924.

In the 1920s, some NGOs were also invited to send representatives to League committees and conferences. For instance, at the League's International Finance Conferences in 1920, the International Chamber of Commerce was permitted to send a delegation made up of four members. After the 1927 Conference on the Abolition of Import and Export Restrictions, the League established a Consultative Committee that included NGO representatives to monitor the implementation of the conference recommendations. Eight NGOs took part in the Communications and Transit Committee of the League. The Committee on Social Questions had about twenty NGO "corresponding members." NGOs dealing with women's issues were given "permanent" (reserved) seats in the Commission on Traffic of Women (White 1951, 249).

In other IGOs established soon after the founding of the League, collaboration with NGOs appears to have been even closer. The International Institute for Intellectual Cooperation (IIIC), established in 1923, provided secretariat services for several NGOs. This model of close collaboration was reflected later in UNESCO (the successor of the IIIC) in which the original (post–World War II) draft constitution gave NGOs actual membership (Seary 1996, 24).

Ironically, the strong role played by labor and employer groups in the ILO (discussed later in this chapter) is generally seen as having led to a smaller role for NGOs in this organization (Thomann 2008). During the interwar era, the ILO followed the League's example and did not establish formal rules for its relationship with NGOs.

In the first years of the League's existence, NGOs appeared to have been very useful for the IGO. They had years of experience that generated significant expertise and institutional networks. This was a very valuable asset for the newly established League that lacked expertise and networks. In several cases, the League requested (and received) NGO assistance when it found that its structures were not yet prepared to deal with some tasks. For example, several weeks after its founding, the global organization turned to the International Committee of the Red Cross and the League of Red Cross Societies to undertake relief efforts for a serious famine and health crisis in Central Europe. As it did not yet have the personnel or funds to deal with the crisis, the League confined itself to a secondary role in this effort and simply urged "support for the activities of these organizations by all countries" (Pickard 1956, 56). In the early 1920s, the League's support for the Red Cross was very strong, even leading to some financial contributions to the NGO. Yet, by the late 1920s, this collaboration eroded as the League did not feel that the Red Cross Societies had "lived up to expectations" (Red Cross 1989, 8).

The mid-1920s are generally considered the "high water mark" of NGO involvement in League activities (Charnovitz 1997, 13; White 1951, 259). The initially inclusive approach that allowed NGOs to participate and be heard in League conferences and committees was replaced by a more lukewarm attitude toward them. By 1925 the League had already reversed its initial decision to interpret the Covenant in a way that allowed for the inclusion of NGOs among the international bureaus with which it would establish formal relations (Seary 1996, 22). In the 1930s NGOs were rarely allowed in League conferences. The Economic Consultative Committee, which included NGO representatives, ceased to function in the early 1930s (Charnovitz 1997). The Committee on Social Questions was reorganized in 1936, becoming entirely governmental (Seary 1996, 23). The use of assessors became increasingly infrequent during that period (Chiang 1981, 38), reflecting the weakly institutionalized nature of League-NGO relations. The last assessors, in the committees on women and children, had their participation rights withdrawn in 1937 (Charnovitz 1997, 21).

It is important to point out that neither the opening up of the League to NGOs in the 1920s nor its closing in the 1930s were debated in any of the IGO's open meetings. This can be interpreted either as a sign that the decisions were driven solely by the secretariat of the IGO or that there were no serious disagreements among states with regard to this relationship.

Figure 6.2 offers an illustration of the relationship between the League and transnational NGOs. It represents the ratio between the number of international NGOs that had a working relationship with the League (as "assessors" or "corresponding members"), and the total number of international NGOs in existence in that year. The data are based on information from the League's *Bulletins of Information on*

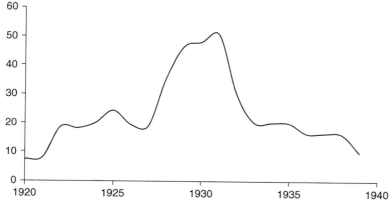

FIGURE 6.2. Proportion (%) of NGOs Partnering with the League of Nations.

Work of International Organizations and the *Yearbook of International Organizations*, respectively.

Developments after World War II and during the Cold War

NGOs played an important role in international conferences immediately after World War II, just as they had after World War I. In fact, more than 1,000 NGOs took part in the process leading to the drafting of the UN Charter. A core group of such organizations dealing with education, agriculture, business, and labor formed around James Shotwell, an important contributor to the ILO's founding in 1919 (Seary 1996, 26). Yet, the most active NGOs were those in the human rights realm. One observer commented that, as the UN was being established, "NGOs conducted a lobby in favor of human rights for which there is no parallel in the history of international relations" (cited in Humphrey 1984, 13).

The important role granted to NGOs in the founding of the UN was in part spurred by U.S. interests in gaining public support for the new global organization. The lessons from the U.S. decision to remain outside the League played an important role in the Roosevelt administration's close relationship with NGOs just prior to the UN's establishment (Charnovitz 1997, 22). In fact, because of the travel costs from Europe to San Francisco, American NGOs played a much greater role in the founding of the UN than NGOs from other states with strong traditions of nongovernmental activism (Seary 1996, 26).

Nevertheless, the U.S. administration was very careful in drawing a line between NGO involvement in the establishment of the UN and their subsequent formal role in the IGO. In fact, the American delegation in San Francisco initially opposed giving NGOs any official role in the UN. It later acquiesced to include them in the work of ECOSOC but made it clear that it would not accept them in the future General Assembly and UNSC (using a strategy of narrowing). Moreover, it only gave in after the wording in the Charter was changed to "consultation" rather than the original "participation without a vote" (Pickard 1956).

In the end, the Charter formalized "consultative" roles for such organizations. Article 71 of the Charter specifically mentioned that ECOSOC should make "suitable arrangements" for consultations with NGOs. The League's Covenant did not include a similar formal stipulation. However, as one observer who was directly involved in IGO-NGO relations both in the League and the UN noted, the formal role given through the UN Charter to NGOs hides the fact that, in practice, they were less influential in the UN in the first few decades of the IGO than they had been in the League in the 1920s (Pickard 1956, 72). In the first place, the UN Charter did not go beyond the economic and social realm of ECOSOC in promoting collaborations with NGOs. By comparison, in the League, NGOs had been active in virtually all issues, including the more political ones of disarmament and mandates. Also, whereas the UN Charter called simply for "consultations" with NGOs, in the League representatives of such organizations could also propose resolutions and amendments (Chiang 1981, 35). The status of "participants without a vote" was given in the UN only to specialized agencies, not to NGOs.

One factor leading to increased NGO access in the League compared to the UN is the strong nongovernmental tradition of the late nineteenth and early twentieth centuries. World War II led to a more governmental approach to international relations. Regardless of such differences, it is noteworthy that in the debates surrounding NGO access to the UN, just as in those to the League, there are no references to the "democratic" need for such organizations in IGO work.

As in the case of the League, NGOs became involved in the work of the UN soon after the IGO was established. In the 1950s thirty NGOs participated in the UN conference that drafted the Convention of Refugees. In 1955 several dozen NGOs took part in an ECOSOC-organized conference on eradication of prejudice and discrimination. The UN Commission on Human Rights began accepting comments from NGOs in 1964.

In some cases, the UN bodies delegated some of their tasks to NGOs. Just as the League had requested that the Red Cross virtually single-handedly deal with the relief efforts in Central Europe in 1920, the UNSC requested in 1950 that the task of providing aid to Korean refugees be handled solely by NGOs (Charnovitz 1997). The number of NGOs with consultative status in ECOSOC grew in the UN's first two decades, from 40 in 1948 to 180 by 1968 (Global Policy Forum 2011).

Many other UN agencies relied on the work of NGOs early on. The 1951 UN High Commissioner for Refugees statute provided that its assistance for refugees be channeled through NGOs. Immediately after they were established, the UN Population Fund, UNESCO, and UNICEF also used NGOs intensely in their programs (Reimann 2006, 49). Even the ILO that, as mentioned, was initially less acceptant of NGOs, starting December 1947, like all UN specialized agencies, formalized its relations with NGOs. In fact, it went further than the UN itself by allowing for formal relations between the Governing Body, its executive body, and NGOs. Nevertheless, the NGOs that benefited from these relations were few and represented the broad interests of labor and employer federations, such as the World Federation of Trade Unions, specifically mentioned in the 1947 Governing Body decision to allow for such relations (International Labor Organization 1948, 322). The vast majority of NGOs never received a similar status. Presently only six NGOs have general consultative status with the ILO (International Labor Organization 2013).

Just as in the case of the League, the initial "honeymoon" between the UN and its nongovernmental partners was soon followed by a cooler relationship. One of the reasons for this reversal in the UN was the realization that Cold War tensions had led both superpowers to use NGOs for their own purposes. In 1967, for example, just before ECOSOC's NGO Committee met, the *New York Times* revealed that the CIA had financed anti-communist NGOs, including some with consultative status in the UN (Willetts 2000, 41). The uproar among the Communist bloc and developing countries represented in the NGO Committee led to pressures for reviewing the system through which NGOs were given access to the IGO.

That same year ECOSOC Resolution 1296 increased the power of the Committee on NGOs to control and limit NGO participation in UN activities. Interestingly, it was not just the Communist bloc and developing countries supporting this resolution, several Western states did so as well. One observer characterized the changes in the attitude toward NGOs as ones that went beyond Cold War rivalries and, rather, reflected "that both government delegates and Secretariat officials welcome those NGOs which contribute technical expertise and knowledge, implement UN programs and disseminate information about the UN, but not those

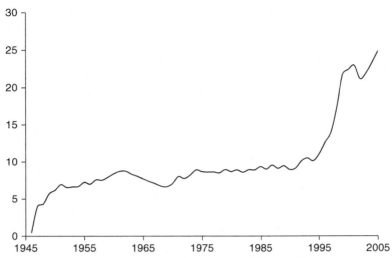

FIGURE 6.3. Proportion (%) of International NGOs with Consultative Status in ECOSOC.
The number of existing NGOs is taken from the *Yearbook of International Organizations*. The number of NGOs with consultative status is based on information from the UN Department of Economic and Social Affairs (see http://csonet.org/; also www.globalolicy.org/component/content/article/176-general/32 119-ngos-in-consultative-status-with-ecosoc-by-category.html).

NGOs that would want to intervene in formulation of UN policies or to criticize the policies and actions of the UN or its member states" (Chiang 1981, 161).

Resolution 1296 introduced the periodic review of NGOs holding consultative status. A first review was conducted in 1968–1969. A second one came in 1978, soon after NGOs were accused by some of the members of the Human Rights Commission of "unfounded and slanderous accusations against states."[4] Although none of the NGOs lost consultative status following these reviews, the late 1960s and 1970s nevertheless were characterized by a slight decline, or at least stagnation, of NGO access and influence in the UN. While the number of NGOs having consultative status at the UN continued to rise even after the aforementioned events, the proportion of NGOs (compared to the total number of international NGOs in existence) declined slightly, as Figure 6.3 illustrates.

[4] This came soon after a 1975 ECOSOC resolution adopted a resolution (initiated by Iran and Egypt in the Human Rights Commission) that threatened to take away the consultative status of NGOs (Chiang 1981, 1).

More importantly, this small decline appears to be a continuation of the one that had begun in the late 1950s. Therefore, one should not consider the scandal of 1967 as the sole reason for such trends. Nevertheless, what the scandal confirmed was that some NGOs in the UN were not as nongovernmental as had been previously portrayed. This realization weakened the pro-NGO normative pressures.

Several other IGOs experienced similar reversals in their relations with NGAs. The Food and Agriculture Organization (FAO) launched in 1957 the Freedom from Hunger Campaign that gave an important role to NGOs. In 1966 it began hosting the Industry Cooperative Program with about 100 transnational companies. Criticism from developing countries (as well as from FAO secretariat) led to a termination of both programs in the 1970s (Liese 2010).

While most of the discussion of developments in the European Union and its precursors focus on the post–Cold War era, it is important to also offer a few observations. Perhaps most important, we should point out that NGOs were not very involved in the work of the European Coal and Steel Community or the European Economic Community. This lack of involvement is reflected in (or a result of) the fact that the European institutions did not establish a similar system of accreditation as the one of the UN. In fact, some observers pointed out that, although producer interest groups were important to the ECSC and were involved in consultation processes even from the founding of the organization (and were even given access to the European Court of Justice starting in 1970), it took two decades for citizens' interest groups to be acknowledged (Greenwood 2009, 95). The EEC's first real consultations with NGOs took place in the environmental realm soon after the organization established its environmental bureau in 1974 (Friedrich 2008, 153; Greenwood 2009).

As in the case of other IGOs prior to the end of the Cold War, it is generally considered that NGOs were accepted in the European institutions more as a way to bolster IGO effectiveness. The increased role of NGOs as a way to improve the democratic character of the European institutions only became relevant starting in the early 1990s (Friedrich 2008).

Developments in the Post–Cold War Era
The domestic empowerment of the pro-NGO norm, discussed in the first section of this chapter, appears to have also affected developments in the international realm. Indeed, the 1980s saw a new interest in opening IGO work to NGOs. The first major IGO to experience the impact of a strong pro-NGO norm around that time was the World Bank. The Bank,

like its sister organization, the IMF, initially kept virtually all NGOs out of its work. This strong intergovernmental attitude can be traced back to the founding Bretton Woods conference, in which NGOs (and most press representatives) were not granted access.

The lack of NGO participation in the World Bank and IMF was, of course, not only the result of their exclusion from the initial Bretton Woods meetings. The highly technical nature of the two organizations was the primary reason for their lukewarm relations with NGOs. Yet, even when the World Bank was aware of NGOs that were conducting relevant work (such as the Rockefeller and Ford foundations), it did not bother to reach out to them until the late 1960s (Shihata, Stevens, and Schlemmer-Schulte 1991, 617).

The World Bank's government-centered practices were evident in other instances. Article V, Section 6 of the World Bank Charter provides for an advisory council to include "representatives of banking, commercial, industrial, labor and agricultural interests." Although a council was selected soon after the World Bank's inception, it never truly functioned (Mason and Asher 1973, 32) – yet another example of narrowing the application of a norm to an IGO.

The World Bank began improving relations with NGOs in the 1980s. This was a natural extension of the dramatic increase of bilateral international aid flowing through NGOs in the 1960s and, especially, the 1970s (Smith 1990). The main reason for including NGOs in aid work was, once again, their perceived usefulness. NGOs were found to be more efficient and cost-effective in supplying aid than governments and IGOs. Moreover, they were seen as useful intermediaries when donor or recipient governments wanted to avoid visible interactions with each other because of potential domestic political costs. Perhaps more important for this study, NGOs were also more effective in forging ties with grassroots organizations in recipient countries than their governmental and intergovernmental partners. This, in turn, empowered such domestic groups in developing (and often authoritarian) countries. Interestingly, this latter benefit, the only one truly connecting NGO participation to democratic norms, was only perceived as truly relevant beginning in the 1970s (Smith 1990).

In the 1980s and 1990s, in an effort to find more effective forms of aid, the World Bank began including more NGOs in its work, presenting them as "partners in development" and promoters of "good governance" (Cernea 1988; Brown and Korten 1991). In time, the NGO channel for aid began to be preferred over the state-centered one (Reimann 2006, 5).

It should not be surprising that the World Bank was among the first IGOs to vigorously promote NGO involvement in its work. NGOs were renowned for their expertise and efficiency in development-related issues. In addition, the Western promotion of the pro-NGO norm had a greater impact on the World Bank, where Western states had more influence than in the UN system, for example.

In 1981 the World Bank took a first real step toward institutionalizing its relations with NGOs by producing a "Central Projects Note" spelling out the conditions for collaboration with such organizations in preparation and implementation of projects (World Bank 1981). The document had a functional tone, never mentioning the "democratic" aspects of NGO involvement in international work. The Bank, as always, wanted to be perceived as apolitical and therefore could not be seen promoting democratic (Western) norms, even if that had been one of its goals.[5]

Yet the World Bank's support for NGOs was evident. In the mid-1980s, it urged several Asian countries to alter regulations hindering NGO development (Beckmann 1991). By 1982 an NGO-World Bank Committee, which included representatives from twenty-six major NGOs, was established (O'Brien, Goetz, Scholte, and Williams 2000, 89). In 1988, a Bank Discussion Paper emphasized the organizational capacity and social mobilization that NGOs can offer (Cernea, 1988). By the 1990s one observer noted that, if in the past you could get sacked for talking to an NGO representative, now you could get sacked for not talking to an NGO representative (cited in Clark 2002, 114).

Starting in the late 1980s there was nevertheless a shift in World Bank-NGO relations. Whereas before such organizations were primarily seen as facilitating World Bank work, a new group of NGOs emerged as harsh critics of the IGO. Around 1985, broad grassroots movements began protesting the lack of information and ability to influence plans for World Bank projects, as discussed in Chapter 5. The protests sparked by such events led to several unprecedented changes in World Bank policies toward NGAs (not just to its public information policies discussed earlier), such as the establishment of an inspection panel allowing individual citizens to file claims against the World Bank and the World Commission on Dams, a body that included both representatives of government and nongovernmental organizations. The changes of the 1990s were also

---

[5] A similar stance characterized the World Bank's long silence on questions related to corruption as a result of the perceptions that any anti-corruption rhetoric was a reflection of a very "Western" view (Brademas and Heimann 1998).

spurred by the approaching fiftieth anniversary of the World Bank (Clark 2002, 117). Street protests unfolded for several years before that anniversary and continued well after it.

By the late 1990s many executive directors, primarily from developing countries, felt that the World Bank had reached the point where it listened more to NGOs than to governments, especially as consultation with NGOs often took place before the Board of Governors would take up the same issue (Nelson 1995; Fox and Brown 1998). This dampened the new World Bank approach toward civil society groups (Clark 2002, 114; World Bank 1998a). The 1998 *World Bank Operational Manual* set off to clarify the guidelines for NGO involvement. The document, once more, did not include any wording regarding the democratic nature of such a process, only referring to its effectiveness. It also mentioned the need to have NGOs (not IGOs or states) more open to "participatory methodologies," implying in a not-so-subtle manner that such organizations needed to be more representative of those they claimed to represent (World Bank 1998b). While NGO influence was considered somewhat acceptable in the implementation of World Bank projects, it was also made clear that it should not erode the decision-making monopoly of governments in the IGO. NGOs have been, of course, kept out of the World Bank's Board of Governors (Ebrahim and Herz 2011).

Although throughout the 1980s developing states appeared to have been the main opponents of NGO involvement in the World Bank, by the 1990s they altered their views to some degree, seeing NGOs as important allies in their fight to tone down the emphasis on structural adjustment programs and free market approach of the Bretton Woods institutions. Indeed, many of the NGOs that had initially been supported by Western states and World Bank staff in the 1970s and 1980s were criticizing the IGO's policies by the early 1990s.

In the late 1990s NGOs advocated for changes not only to the World Bank programs but also to the decision-making rules of the organization. Many promoted reforms of the World Bank voting system that would give an increased number of votes to developing countries. The linkage between reforms involving NGO access and those involving voting changes were now facilitated by the ability to fit both under the broader umbrella of "democratization" of the Bretton Woods institutions (e.g., Global Policy Forum 2006).

Some of the patterns in World Bank-NGO relations can be found in other IGOs, about five to ten years later. In the early 1990s NGOs also began playing a greater role in the UN. For example, in 1990 the International

Committee of the Red Cross became the first NGO to gain observer status (a role hitherto reserved only to states) in the General Assembly. In the next few years two more NGOs (the Sovereign Order of Malta and the International Federation of Red Cross and Red Crescent Societies) also received this status (Willetts 2000, 197). The end of the Cold War also saw an increase in the number of UN-sponsored conferences. NGOs participated and often played important roles in such conferences dealing with environment (1992), development (1992), human rights (1993), population and development (1994), and social development (1995) (Friedman, Hochstetler, and Clark 2005; Martens 2011). The 1990s trend toward a greater NGO role in the UN culminated in an oft cited speech of UN Secretary General Kofi Annan arguing: "The United Nations once dealt with governments. By now we know that peace and prosperity cannot be achieved without partnerships involving governments, international organizations, the business community, and civil society" (1998).

Yet, by the mid-1990s member-states began reversing (or, at least slowing down) the movement toward greater NGO access in the UN. The tension between the need to enhance the role of NGOs in the UN, on the one hand, and the strong intergovernmental character of the organization, on the other, became more obvious starting with the 1993–1996 review of ECOSOC's arrangements for consultation with NGOs. The review discussed three major changes. First, it considered extending the eligibility of national and subregional NGOs for UN consultative status (and not just the global NGOs). It also discussed giving national affiliates of international NGOs such consultative status. Some portrayed these measures as providing "balance without a quota" in NGO representation from the North and South (Global Policy Forum 1996). This was because NGOs from developing countries often were not international in nature. In hindsight, it is not clear if this measure had the anticipated equalizing effect. Moreover, by including more (but smaller) NGOs, the UN in fact diluted the role of the major (and often more critical) ones and even opened the door to some government-sponsored NGOs. The decision indeed led to a tremendous increase in the number of NGOs to be granted consultative status, more than doubling this number over the two decades that followed its adoption.

A second issue discussed in the review involved the development of a common standard procedure for NGO participation in UN conferences. In the past, at each conference, NGOs had to renegotiate such rules. After 1996, their participation in conferences started from a basic accepted level, emulating an "American style" lobbying format (Friedman et al. 2005, 63).

The third topic discussed in the review of NGO consultation arrangements involved extending official relations with NGOs beyond ECOSOC, to the work of the UNGA and even to other UN institutions. The main countries supporting this change were the Scandinavian ones, Canada, Costa Rica, Ireland, Mexico, and New Zealand. Its greatest opponents were China, India and, especially, the United States. China felt that NGOs would bring the issue of Tibet to the UNGA floor. India wanted to avoid having NGOs opening up debates about Kashmir.

Yet it was the United States that led the efforts to block further expansion of the number of NGOs with observer status in the UNGA (United Nations 1994). For the Americans, the greatest problem was that, once the UNGA opened up to NGOs, there would be demands to also include them in the UNSC. One observer noted that, had the United States fear for such potential demands of opening the UNSC not been so great, undoubtedly it would have accepted changing the rules for NGO participation in the UNGA (a possible reflection of the fear of normative pressures that were building).[6]

The United States eventually managed to get its way by having the debates over NGO relations with the UN moved from ECOSOC into the Open-Ended Working Group on UN Reform, where they would be negotiated together with broader questions of reform (Willetts 2000, 198). This can be interpreted as a strategy of broadening from one issue (NGO access) to more issues.

The inclusion of the question of NGO participation in the UNGA was only accepted by the United States after specific wording citing Article 10 of the UN Charter was added to the text of the ECOSOC resolution. That wording emphasized that, even if NGOs were eventually allowed greater access to the UNGA, such access would never spill over into the realm of security, peace keeping, arms control and, more importantly, the fiefdom of the all-important UNSC. Just as important, through a strategy of narrowing the application of the pro-NGO norm, the United States opposed wording introduced by developing countries that would have allowed NGOs to participate more in the "UN system" and, therefore, would have given them a say in virtually all issues, including those of finance and trade. Developing states had tried to introduce such wording to give greater influence to the increasing number of Global South-friendly NGOs in the World Bank and IMF (Willetts 2000, 199).

---

[6] Personal interview with official involved in the aforementioned ECOSOC Working Group, March 16, 2013.

In the end, ECOSOC Resolution 1996/31 was a compromise between those supporting a greater role for NGOs in the UN system and those opposing it. On the one hand, the resolution outlined clear responsibilities of the secretariat in supporting the relationship with NGOs. Most importantly, it emphasized that NGOs would have increased access to information through the secretariat. It also allowed many more NGOs to gain consultative status in ECOSOC and streamlined NGO participation in UN conferences. On the other hand, the resolution fell short of extending NGOs' role outside ECOSOC and UN conferences, although it recommended the inclusion of the issue in the Open-Ended Working Group on UN reform (Economic and Social Council 1996, article 26).

It is noteworthy that the wording of ECOSOC Resolution 1996/31 only included two references to "democracy." In the resolution, as in the 1998 *World Bank Operational Manual,* all such references discussed the obligations NGOs had (rather than states or the UN itself) to be organized and to reach decisions in a democratic fashion. The two conditions were seen as requirements for NGO access to the UN (Economic and Social Council 1996). This can be interpreted as a challenging strategy used to defuse the pressures created by the pro-NGO norm by recalling the problems in linking NGOs to democratic decision-making. The wording implied that NGO participation in IGOs cannot be based on democratic principles unless such organizations are representative of broader public interests.

Around the time that the ECOSOC resolution was being drafted, a number of small yet noticeable measures led to reduced physical access of NGOs to the UN and to member-state representatives. NGO access to the UN building became limited to the visitors' entrance (keeping them out of the 42nd Street entrance, which in the past they could use). Their access to the delegates' lounge, where they could mingle with representatives of states, was also severely restricted. In other words, this period was characterized not only by a lack of advancement in developing formal comprehensive rules for NGO participation in the UN but also by one of eroding practices of such participation. Although the official explanation for reduced NGO physical access was based on security concerns, it was interpreted by many, as in the case of the World Bank, as a backlash from states that were becoming increasingly annoyed with the lobbying persistence of some NGO representatives.[7]

---

[7] Personal interview with UN official, March 16, 2013.

By 1998, when the Open-Ended Working Group on UN Reform completed its work, it was not able to reach any agreement on furthering NGO participation in the UNGA or in other parts of the UN. The lengthy (and fairly unsuccessful) negotiations were characterized by Razali Ismail, then General Assembly president, as a "political football" as he argued that the lack of advancement on this issue "plays into the hands of governments who don't want anything to happen with NGOs."[8] Indeed, as suggested in Chapter 2, such broadening strategies bringing together multiple reform proposals are often adopted precisely because the greater number of issues on the agenda makes agreements difficult to reach, leading to the increased likelihood of preserving the status quo.

Of the six major IGOs discussed in this book, the one that appears to have shown the greatest resistance to including NGOs in its work is the WTO (Steffek and Ehling 2008, 110). The tradition of keeping NGOs outside the organization can be traced to the beginnings of its predecessor, the GATT, although, interestingly, not necessarily to the International Trade Organization (ITO), the IGO that never materialized in the aftermath of World War II. The ITO's draft charter clearly specified in Article 71 that the organization could make arrangements for consultation and cooperation with NGOs (United Nations 1946a).

As the ITO's GATT component (the only part that could be salvaged) was fairly narrow and intergovernmental in nature, it never ended up offering any real role for NGOs. The first relevant pressures to open GATT to NGOs emerged in the late 1980s and early 1990s, during the Uruguay Round of trade negotiations. At that time NGOs focusing on agriculture, development, and food safety complained that they were not able to offer any input in the talks at several ministerial conferences, most notably, the one in Brussels in 1990 (Charnovitz 2000, 175).

To some degree, governments gave in to such pressures and allowed for increased NGO access to information soon after the WTO was established. While the 1996 WTO guidelines for relations with NGOs allowed for a proactive role of the secretariat to engage NGOs (Williams 2011, 115), they also stated that "there is currently a broadly held view that it would not be possible for NGOs to be directly involved in the work of the WTO or its meetings" (World Trade Organization 1996). To this day, the guidelines stand unaltered. They stipulate that NGOs are

---

[8] See http://www.greenstone.org/greenstone3/nzdl;jsessionid=20CBE76965722C3A8AA7 AA7164613344?a=d&c=hdl&d=HASH04f8de7b160860fc6d6ee1.9&sib=1&p.a=b&p. sa=&p.s=ClassifierBrowse&p.c=hdl

excluded from virtually all WTO bodies, except for the plenary sessions of the Ministerial Conferences (Steffek and Ehling 2008, 98). Even in these conferences, the General Council decided to tone down the level of NGO participation from one of "observing" to "attending." The difference became obvious in the 1996 Singapore conference when NGOs were not even allowed to make a statement at the end of the meeting (Charnovitz 2000).

The WTO allowed for some degree of NGO participation in 1998 and 1999 in several of its symposia on trade facilitation, environment, and sustainable development. However, after NGOs used their presence at one symposium to call for more WTO accountability, several governments argued that the IGO had already gone too far in allowing NGO input and requested that their access to future symposia be restricted (International Environmental Report 1999).

As one would expect, the governmental versus nongovernmental tensions increased even more after the Seattle riots of 1999. Although the WTO sought to improve its image, members nevertheless did not accept greater NGO access in the aftermath of the riots. Director-General Mike Moore stated on multiple occasions that the WTO was an intergovernmental organization and not a supranational one. He, like other critics of NGO access to the organization, emphasized the strong link between sovereignty (that was set in contrast to the supranational role NGOs played) and democracy. He argued: "What could be more democratic than sovereign governments instructing Ambassadors to reach agreements that are then accepted by cabinets and parliaments? Our job is to advance the sovereignty of States by giving rules within which our ever more inter-dependent world can manage itself better" (Moore 1999). Similar arguments, linking sovereignty to democracy, were made by governments and even academics who opposed NGO involvement in the WTO (Charnovitz 2000, 198–199).

In April 2000 the Joint Economic Committee of the U.S. Congress offered a set of recommendations for the reform of the WTO, based on six "core principles." The first among these was the one of "sovereignty" defined as "the desire to ensure that democratic processes and sovereign authority are respected in both borrowing and lending countries" (Meltzer 2000, 41). Although the United States joined (and even led) other states in emphasizing the tension between NGO participation and sovereignty, compared to others, it nevertheless became a strong supporter of greater NGO involvement in the WTO, even as it remained one of the greatest opponents of such involvement in the UN (Williams 2011, 125).

Another argument used by those opposing greater NGO involvement in the WTO (and in other IGOs) in the post-Seattle period is that such nongovernmental organizations lacked legitimacy. NGOs, according to many such critics, were even less accountable to the public or other actors than IGOs (Williams 2011, 124). Also, it was argued that the NGO constituencies were never clearly defined and, therefore, their representation of civil society was at best debatable (O'Brien, Goetz, Scholte, and Williams 2000, 58). One of the harshest critics of NGO participation in the WTO argued: "If NGOs were indeed representative of the wishes and desires of the electorate, those who embrace their ideas would be in power" (Wolf 1999, 14).

All of these challenging strategies have eroded the pro-NGO normative pressures. The organization even today offers very few opportunities for NGOs to influence intergovernmental deliberations (Steffek and Ehling 2008, 110). As discussed in Chapter 5, the most important change undergone by the organization in the past decade is that it began allowing for greater access to information as a token (narrow) concession to NGO demands (Williams 2011, 114).

The European Union has also been fairly slow to open up to meaningful NGO participation. As mentioned, the ECSC and the EEC were not very supportive of collaborations with NGOs and, unlike the UN, did not even have an accreditation system in place to officially include NGOs in their work.

The literature generally suggests that 1992 was the turning point in EU-NGO relations (Friedrich 2008, 140; Greenwood 2009, 95). The problems that the European Union Treaty had during the ratification stage emphasized the need to better connect the institutions with the public. NGOs were seen as important transmission belts that would enable the EU to reduce its democratic deficit.

The Commission appears to have been the EU body most supportive of close relations with NGOs. This should not be surprising as it has always been the institution with the greatest need for resources and democratic legitimacy (Greenwood 2009, 97). In 1993 the EU's Commission drew up the "Green Paper on European Social Policy" that encouraged the establishment of a formal dialogue between the EU and NGOs. By 1995, with support from the Parliament, a Social Platform, with about forty NGO members emerged as a formal structure recognized by all EU institutions (Cullen 2009, 142). This "family structure" model of involving NGOs was later followed by similar initiatives that brought together EU institutions and NGOs from the realm of human rights, development, and health.

Following the resignation of the Santer Commission in 1999, there was an even greater emphasis on the need for consultation with civil society groups. The EU quickly formed an Ad-Hoc Task Force on Consultation. By 2003, the European Social Platform began hosting meetings of an umbrella organization of all "families" of NGOs (Greenwood 2009, 95). The Commission has presented these new pro-NGO initiatives as a way of achieving a greater degree of "participatory democracy" (European Commission 2000).

Although, in practice, the Council of the European Union has been the least supportive of NGO participation in the EU's work (Friedrich 2008, 159), on paper it has supported the efforts of the Commission in calling for such partnerships (European Commission and Council of the European Communities 1997). The European Parliament, on the other hand, has been fairly open to NGOs in practice (despite some critiques that security concerns have limited NGO access to the EP), but its rhetoric has been critical of the promotion of the concept "participatory democracy" as it eroded the importance of (and, for many, even challenged) the much touted "representative democracy" embodied by the EP (Greenwood 2009, 101). Over the past decade, as participatory democracy has become institutionalized in the Lisbon Treaty, tensions between proponents of the two "solutions" to the democratic deficit ("representative," through the EP, and "participatory," through NGOs) have increased (Saurugger 2010, 488).

The combination of half-hearted rhetorical support from the European Parliament, half-hearted support in the implementation of rhetoric from the EU Council, and half-hearted institutionalization of NGO accreditation has led to inconsistent advances in the role NGOs actually play in the EU. Most observers note that, while a small number of very large, visible, and wealthy NGOs are usually consulted on most issues in most forums, the vast majority of other organizations rarely play a significant role in policy formulation (Friedrich 2008, 160). The informal process through which the NGOs are selected to play a greater or smaller role by EU institutions raises both questions about their representative character (leading to even greater tensions in debates over participatory vs. representative democracy) and independence (Greenwood 2009, 99).

Several initiatives, such as the 2007 Commission's European Transparency Initiative (ETI), have attempted to answer such critiques by offering more information about the EU institution's consultations with outsiders.[9] However, as the well-publicized 2011 case of three members

---

[9] See http://ec.europa.eu/transparencyregister/info/homePage.do

of the European Parliament who accepted bribes to propose amendments on legislation reminds us, the increased access of NGAs in the EU is still not sufficiently regulated and can lead to un-democratic outcomes (euroenews 2011).

Although this section has emphasized the slow advancement (and even reversals) of pro-NGO measures in some of the major IGOs discussed in this book – the World Bank, UN, WTO, and EU – one should note that the post–Cold War era has nevertheless been characterized by a general trend of greater acceptance of NGOs as partners in the majority of (somewhat less visible) IGOs. Organizations as diverse as the Commonwealth (Shaw and Mbabazi 2011), Organisation of Economic Co-operation and Development (OECD) (Ougaard 2011), the Organisation of the Islamic Conference (Ameli 2011), and the Organization for Security and Co-operation in Europe (OSCE) (Mayer 2008) have all taken steps in that direction over the past two to three decades. If one considers all these reforms as connected (rather than independent developments), it can be argued that governments applied a strategy of narrowing the actions that derive from the pro-NGO norm by selecting where to maintain greater governmental control over deliberations and where to open them to NGAs. Figure 6.4 illustrates this general trend toward greater access of transnational actors in IGOs. It is based on a survey of almost 300 bodies from 50 IGOs (Tallberg et al. 2013).

The ILO: A Not-So-Unique Relationship between IGOs and Nongovernmental Actors

Perhaps the most important clashes with regard to the role of NGAs took place in the ILO. When it was established in 1919, each country was given four votes in all decisions: two for governments, one for labor representatives, and one for employer representatives. This arrangement can be interpreted as a "valve" for defusing the normative pressure involving workers' rights. After the Soviet Revolution, powerful states sought to find ways of reducing the likelihood that similar pressures would spread revolutions across the world (e.g., O'Brien, Goetz, Scholte, and Williams 2000, 102).

The ILO quickly became the poster child for involvement of NGAs in an IGO. Indeed, labor and employee representatives groups have taken part in virtually all ILO plenary, committee, and subcommittee meetings alongside government representatives. While participation for representatives of these two groups has been assured from the inception of the organization, their independence often was a matter of contention.

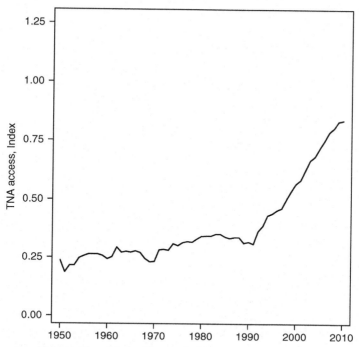

FIGURE 6.4. Transnational Actor Access Index.
Data are based on the "Transaccess" dataset. See Tallberg et al. 2013.

Authoritarian governments have imposed their will on their labor and employer representatives in the IGO. Even democratic governments have, at times, exerted pressures on such representatives, leading some to emphasize the corporatist character of the ILO (Milman-Sivan, 2009). The struggle for nongovernmental representatives' independence has therefore been at the forefront of ILO institutional debates for almost a century.

Figure 6.5 offers a possible reflection of the independence of such groups in the ILO. It represents the percentage of votes in the International Labor Conferences in which at least one nongovernmental representative voted differently than its government. The ratio is calculated for each year as an average of such percentages across all member-states.[10] This

---

[10] Of course, there are many different reasons (besides independence) why labor and employer representatives vote differently than their governments. Moreover, most debates take place within committees where, very often, participants seek consensus. The votes in the plenary (that are used in this measure) may not reflect therefore the

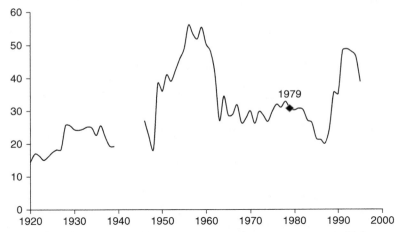

FIGURE 6.5. Independence of Nongovernmental Representatives in ILO.

measure is similar to the one used by Ernst Haas in gauging the "national cohesion" of ILO delegations and, more broadly, the "pluralism" of the ILO system (1962, 339).

Figure 6.5 shows that NGA independence experienced important variation across time, similar to the evolution of other democratic dimensions discussed in this book. Specifically, independence increased in the 1920s, the late 1940s and 1950s, and the early 1990s. It declined in the 1930s, 1960s, 1980s, and late 1990s.[11]

The most interesting developments involving nongovernmental representatives' independence unfolded during the Cold War, as ideological differences between the two superpowers led to East–West clashes, especially those involving the acceptance of employee representatives from

original disagreements. Despite these caveats, the differences in nongovernmental representatives' vs. government representatives' votes should offer an adequate reflection of the variance in NGA independence across time.

[11] A distinction needs to be made between voting before and after 1979. That year, as will be discussed, the ILO introduced voting by secret ballot on a large number of questions. Therefore, the proportion of votes in Figure 6.5 is skewed after that year by the fact that the most contentious votes (where NGAs were more likely to cast different votes than their governments) are excluded from the statistics. It is likely that the decline in the measure of independence of Figure 6.5 in the 1980s is therefore more a reflection of this change in voting procedure than in the increased voting cohesion between governmental and nongovernmental representatives. Conversely, the increase in independence reflected in the early 1990s is even more impressive considering that the most contentious (secret) votes are not counted in the figure.

the Soviet Union and its satellite countries in the ILO. Most often those debates were couched by both sides in the rhetoric of "democracy."[12]

In most cases, the debates took place simultaneously with those involving other institutional reforms in the ILO such as state participation in the Governing Body. It is therefore useful to follow nongovernmental representatives' independence while also referring to debates involving Governing Body membership, some of which were already mentioned briefly in Chapter 3.

Discussions about membership reform in the ILO's Governing Body's began almost immediately after the IGO's inception. The impetus for change came from smaller and especially non-European countries that wanted greater representation through the addition of non-permanent seats.[13] In the first two years of the ILO's existence, the pressures to increase the number of non-permanent members in the Governing Body increased rapidly. Already, by 1922, a resolution was adopted increasing the number of non-permanent members from four to eight (International Labor Office 1922, 500–508). However, because of the slow ratification processes, the changes adopted in the resolution did not go into effect until 1935.

The arguments for reform, whether based on (1) fair participation of both small and large states, (2) fair participation of all world regions, or (3) fair selection of the countries of chief industrial importance, were often framed in the early 1920s in the language of "democracy" (International Labor Office 1922, 262, 279). Of course, officials would embrace the most useful interpretation of democracy to promote their particular national interests.[14]

As suggested in Chapter 5, at the time of such membership debates in the League of Nations, powerful states were able to reduce normative pressure for state representation reform by calling for improvements in the application of other democratic principles, such as transparency. This was not possible in the ILO as the IGO was considered far more transparent than other organizations (Sweetser 1920, 196).

---

[12] See, e.g., International Labor Organization 1953, 64; International Labor Organization 1960, 40.

[13] The term "non-permanent members" is used to draw an analogy with developments in the other IGOs. Technically, this term is not accurate because there are no "permanent" members in the Governing Body. The states of "chief industrial importance" are selected periodically on the basis of economic power, a measure that has changed significantly over the ILO's existence. This has, implicitly, led to changes in the designation of such states.

[14] See, e.g., M. Hedebol, Statement in International Labor Office (1922) October 28, Appendix, p. 297.

In the ILO, opponents of membership reform therefore could not reduce normative pressures by using broadening strategies linking state participation and transparency. Yet, by the late 1920s, there were serious concerns for the erosion of nongovernmental representatives' independence, especially in the cases of Italy and Japan. Therefore, when in the late 1920s and early 1930s states that were not of chief industrial importance applied normative pressures, often using the language of democracy, to bring about change in Governing Body membership (by speeding up the ratification processes allowing for the 1922 resolution to go into effect and, if possible, to bring about even greater changes to the Governing Body membership), powerful states responded by introducing questions related to another form of IGO democracy – those of ILO nongovernmental representative independence (e.g., International Labor Office 1922, 534). The nongovernmental independence norm was sufficiently strong to lead even autocratic states, such as Japan, to accept it. For example, when in 1924 the ILO's Credentials Committee did not accept the Japanese workers' delegate because of the process through which the Japanese government had selected the representative, the Japanese representative argued that the selection had in fact been "the fairest, the most appropriate and the most democratic" (International Labor Organization 1924, 367). The tightening of the rules to keep the less representative labor and employer delegates out of the ILO, therefore, took place at the same time that pressures for increasing membership in the Governing Body were unfolding. The 1922 resolution to increase the number of seats eventually entered into force in 1935. No other reforms of Governing Body membership took place before World War II. This may be a result of the success of the broadening strategy linking membership of governmental and nongovernmental representatives.

With the imminent admission of Germany and Japan to the ILO in the early 1950s, the issue of Governing Body membership was once more placed on the organization's agenda. As the two countries clearly needed to join in capacities of states of chief industrial importance, members began jostling for position in what appeared to be a new round of seat reallocation. To alleviate the minor normative pressures in the 1950s membership reform efforts, the United States and its West European allies (which together represented the clear majority of states of chief industrial importance) argued that, to improve the democratic character of the Governing Body, it was more important to give nongovernmental representatives a greater role rather than tinker with the distribution of seats among states (International Labor Organization 1953, 247). Indeed, in 1953, the Governing Body expanded the number of non-permanent seats, altering the standing orders of the organization (therefore avoiding the processes of ratification that slowed down the changes in the Governing Body in the interwar era), and allowed for a larger number of worker and employer deputy members in the Governing Body, rather than additional seats for government representatives.

Although this action may have defused some of the normative pressures, it did not have long-term effects. Just one year later, in 1954, small states introduced a proposal to increase the Governing Body with two non-permanent seats for states. Powerful Western states (of chief industrial importance) tried once more to shift attention from small countries' proposals by introducing an amendment to the ILO Constitution that would ensure that "Workers' and Employers' representatives could only be appointed after nomination by organizations of workers and employers which are free and independent of their governments" (International Labor Organization 1954, 125). This strategy was not successful as the latter proposal was defeated while the one to add two more non-permanent seats to the Governing Body was accepted.

In the 1960s, as a result of decolonization, membership in the ILO grew rapidly. The pressure to add seats to the Governing Body became even greater as increases in membership were taking place at that time in the UNSC and ECOSOC, two highly visible UN bodies.

The rhetoric of the 1960s debates surrounding changes in the Governing Body emphasized once more norms of fair participation. And, once more, such debates reflected a clash between the various interpretations of democracy as applied to IGOs, each representing the multiple interests involved (International Labor Organization 1961, 36–40). Some of these were mentioned in Chapter 3.

Virtually all great powers in the Governing Body privately opposed any increases in the organ's membership. The United States and its Western allies, which at that time still dominated the organization, were initially able to reduce some of the pressures for this reform by emphasizing what Western powers considered now to be the real democratic problem of the ILO: the lack of Soviet Bloc's workers' and employers' independence from their governments. However, three years after such debates unfolded, and after the United States had won the battle leading to the practice of keeping Soviet Bloc employers' delegates out of most committees, there was little else left to do but support the very large majority of small countries in their quest to include more seats in the

Governing Body as the broadening strategy was not possible any more. In 1964, the Governing Body added four non-permanent seats.

By 1970 the number of ILO members had increased by another 20 percent compared to 1960, and small states again began promoting the addition of even more seats to the Governing Body. Once more, the United States and its allies tried to shift the discussion of membership reform to the one of independence of nongovernmental representatives. In 1971, a group primarily composed of Western employer delegates put together a draft resolution calling for a strengthening of tripartism and, implicitly, for greater independence of nongovernmental representatives (Ghèbali, Ago, and Valticos 1989, 133). The resolution was adopted, giving a great degree of support to the employers' groups that continued to use their independence to keep Soviet Bloc representatives out of their committees.

For a while, this strategy of shifting attention away from state membership reform in the Governing Body appeared to work. Yet, by 1976 the pressures for membership increases appear to have been too great to defuse with other changes and, therefore, the number of non-permanent members was raised again by four. In fact, the heated debates of the early 1970s had involved increasingly strong calls for the complete elimination from the Governing Body of permanent seats for the states of chief industrial importance (International Labor Organization 1971, 39, 140; International Labor Organization 1973, 1, 2, 20, 28, 136–139). The increase in the number of non-permanent seats may therefore be viewed as a relatively minor reform compared to the even more significant one that would have led great powers to lose their permanent seats.

Even before the formal increase in the Governing Body took place in 1976, the pressures to completely eliminate permanent seats led to the establishment of committees both in the ILO Assembly and in the Governing Body to study the feasibility of this proposal. The late 1970s represent the peak of clashes between (1) small (usually developing) countries supporting the "democratic" elimination of permanent seats in the Governing Body, (2) Western states of chief industrial importance promoting the "democratic" independence of nongovernmental representatives in the ILO, and (3) Soviet Bloc countries pushing for the "democratic" representation of all forms of employers in the ILO.

These tensions (and losing battles) were an important cause for U.S. withdrawal from the ILO in 1977 (Beigbeder 1979, 223–240). The U.S. absence from the organization led to a flurry of activity on the part of employers, workers, and even government groups to entice it to return. Perhaps the most important change to take place in the two years when the United States was not part of the ILO was the adoption in 1979 of an amendment to Article 19 of the Conference Standing Orders allowing voting by secret ballot. This enabled worker and employer delegates to vote, when necessary, independent of their governments, consequently strengthening the tripartite character of the IGO. In 1980, when the United States returned to the ILO, it declared that it did so because there had been sufficient improvement in this area (Shultz 1985).

Yet, after the changes allowing for greater independence of nongovernmental representatives ended, the debates in the early 1980s surrounding the membership reform of the Governing Body continued. It quickly became clear that such reforms could not be delayed any longer. In 1986 they eventually led to the adoption of a major amendment to the ILO Constitution involving simultaneous changes to the composition and governance of the Governing Body, the procedure for appointment of the director-general, and the voting procedures, as well as to the rules governing how the Constitution may be amended (International Labor Organization 1986). For the purposes of this study it is especially relevant to note that, although the amendment stipulated that the number of countries in the Governing Body remain the same, all states were to be elected and, implicitly, the permanent seats of states of chief industrial importance were to be eliminated.

Once more, the debates preceding these changes were strewn with various interpretations of what constitutes a truly democratic body (International Labor Organization 1974, 600, 770; ibid. 1975a, 24, 26, 29, and 33; ibid. 1975b, 24, 26; ibid. 1980, 4; ibid. 1981, 3–4). The Soviet Union once more laid out its version of democratic reforms and unsuccessfully pushed for equal status for its employer representatives in all committees and subcommittees (International Labor Organization 1980, 12). In the end, only Soviet Bloc countries voted against the 1986 amendment. Almost three decades after the amendment passed, it has not yet entered into force because of the lack of sufficient ratifications. Yet, the changes to voting procedures that allowed for greater nongovernmental representatives' independence did not need to go through such a complex ratification process and have been in place for several decades.

The previous examples of the linkages between nongovernmental representatives' independence and Governing Body membership rules in the ILO offer an obvious example of the broadening strategy used by actors opposing the latter reforms. The United States and other powerful Western states tried to defuse normative pressures by making such linkages. Although, in theory, the broadening strategy was not successful because the majority of small states were able to adopt the change in membership rules, in practice, the complex process of ratification of the reforms has nevertheless been able to maintain the status quo. It is also worth noting that the Soviet Bloc countries unsuccessfully tried using broadening strategies that would allow for reforms giving their nongovernmental representatives access to ILO committees to piggyback on the other "democratic" reforms.

Answering the Questions of the Study

What Types of Decision-Making Rules Were Being Established or Changed?

Virtually all IGOs discussed in this chapter included some nongovernmental actors in their work at some point in their history. The League, UN, World Bank, EU, and WTO all considered rules establishing the degree to which NGOs could participate (1) in deliberative processes and (2) in the implementation of IGO decisions. In the ILO, the rules focused more on the number of seats nongovernmental representatives of labor and employers were given in the Governing Body and, more importantly, on their independence from their government representatives. Specifically, the rules debated in this context involved the selection of nongovernmental representatives and procedures that would allow representatives to vote independently of their governments. The rules were often discussed in a broader context to defuse the normative pressures for changes to state participation in the ILO Governing Body.

Did Actors Invoke Democratic Norms to Pressure Others in Accepting New Decision-Making Rules?

None of the original documents or secondary sources consulted on the establishment of the League of Nations, UN, World Bank, or ECSC referred to the rules involving participation of NGOs in their work as "democratic." At the founding of the League and UN there were some normative pressures for giving NGOs significant roles, but these derived from a common understanding that they "deserved" to be partners because of the work they had done prior to or during the establishment of the IGOs.

Democratic norms were invoked in the World Bank beginning in the late 1980s and in the UN and EU starting in the early 1990s. Democratic pro-NGO norms also have been invoked in the context of the WTO,

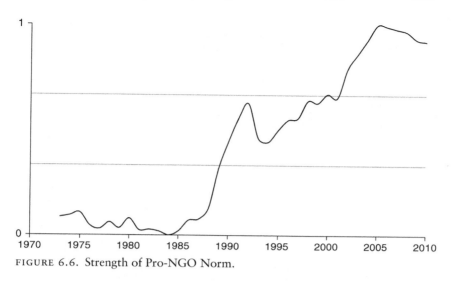

FIGURE 6.6. Strength of Pro-NGO Norm.

even before the IGO was formally established. The debates surrounding NGAs' independence in the ILO referred to democratic norms as far back as the 1920s. They were also invoked in the 1930s and throughout the Cold War.

How Powerful Were Such Pressures?

Figure 6.6 reflects the same evolution of the pro-NGO norm depicted in Figure 6.1 but scaled from 0 (least free) to 1 (most free) as other similar measures of norm strength from the previous chapters. I consider the global pro-NGO norm, in its democratic interpretation that emphasizes the important role of an independent civil society, as weak until the late 1980s, moderate in the 1990s, and strong starting around 2000. One needs to point out that even though for a long time NGO participation was not perceived as democratic, it was nevertheless seen as useful. The nineteenth-century nongovernmental traditions in the international realm led many in the League and ILO to accept NGAs in their work. There was indeed a sense of appropriateness in this decision, but not one based on domestic analogies but, rather, on habit (Kratochwil 1984, 686).

When the League and ILO were established after World War I, there were no real debates about the role of NGAs because the nongovernmental tradition was so strong that it was obvious to all that such organizations would need to be included in the work of IGOs. This was reflected

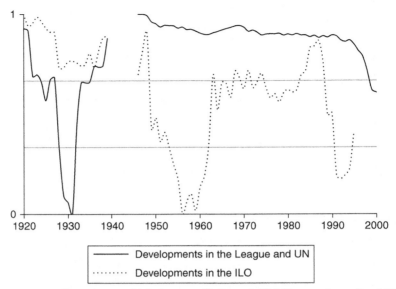

FIGURE 6.7. Degree to which League, ILO, and UN Depart from Pro-NGO Norm Prescription.

in the originally confusing term "international bureaux" used in the League Covenant, which initially referred both to intergovernmental and nongovernmental organizations. The actual debates emerged later, when the rules needed to be put in practice.

Figure 6.7 assesses such practices. It represents the degree to which the League, ILO, and UN departed from the pro-NGO norm prescriptions. For the League and UN it uses the aforementioned measures of NGO participation. It scales the measures from 0 (when the proportion of NGOs included in an IGO was at the all-time high and therefore the departure from norm prescription was the smallest) and 1 (when the proportion of NGOs included in an IGO was at the all-time low and therefore the departure from norm prescription the greatest). For the ILO it uses the measure of independence of nongovernmental representatives based on their voting records across time, represented in Figure 6.5, also scaled from 0 (most independent) to 1 (least independent and therefore greatest departure from norm prescription). The measures reflect the understanding of norm prescriptions as promoted by those who wanted to bring about change to the IGOs.

Figure 6.7 shows that throughout the 1920s the League increasingly accepted NGOs as partners. By 1930 the status quo reached a point where it departed only slightly from norm prescriptions. Yet, throughout the 1930s the role of NGOs in the League quickly eroded. The UN has almost continuously improved its relations with NGOs although such relations never reached the very high levels of cooperation of the League in the late 1920s. Only starting in the late 1990s has the UN moved from high to moderate levels of departure from norm prescriptions.

The measure of nongovernmental representatives' independence in the ILO also shows important fluctuations in the IGO's departure from norm prescriptions. Although the independence improved in the 1920s and was eroded in the 1930s, overall, in the interwar era the IGO experienced high levels of departure from the norm prescription compared to those in the post–World War II era. Independence of the nongovernmental representatives improved substantially in the first decade after World War II. Yet, as decolonization brought in a large number of countries that lacked tradition of nongovernmental independence and as Soviet Bloc countries with strong control over their workers and employer representatives became members of the ILO, the status quo quickly moved in the 1960s away from what the norm prescriptions dictated. They improved slightly in the 1970s. Although Figure 6.7 shows that the ILO moved even further from norm prescriptions in the late 1980s, as mentioned, it is difficult to interpret voting patterns after 1979 when the most contentious votes could be cast in secret.

The World Bank, WTO, and European institutions have not had (until recently) clear systems of NGO accreditation in place. Therefore, in the cases discussed here, I consider them as departing substantially from norm prescriptions.

Table 6.1 includes the values of the norm strength and departure from norm prescription previously discussed. In addition, it includes the values of the composite index of normative pressures calculated in the same way as in previous chapters.

Figure 6.8 offers another possible measure of normative pressures. I include it because it offers greater confidence in the assessment of the strength of such pressures. It reflects the press coverage of anti-IGO protests and is based on the Transaccess dataset (Tallberg et al. 2013). One can see that the anti-IGO movements (primarily organized by NGAs protesting their lack of influence in the IGOs) have increased substantially in the 1990s and, especially, in the 2000s. While the protests against the UN have been fairly constant starting with the mid-1990s, the ones against the World Bank and WTO are more sporadic but tend to attract more media coverage. Figure 6.8 suggests that the post–Cold War era indeed

TABLE 6.1 *Normative Pressures Involving NGA Participation and Reactions to Pressures*

IGO/Moment	League/early 1920s	ILO/1920s		League/early 1930s	ILO/early 1930s		UN/1945
Rule involves	NGO participation	–Independence of nongovernmental representatives	–State participation in Governing Body	NGO participation	–Independence of nongovernmental representatives	–State participation in Governing Body	NGO participation
Norm strength	L	L		L	L		L
Departure from norm prescription	H	H		L	H		H
Normative pressure	M	M		VL	M		M
Strategy	NA; BA	BN*		W	BN*		NA
Outcome	PC	C		NC	C		PC

Note: CN = challenging norm; NN = narrowing norm; BN = broadening norm; CA = challenging application of norm; NA = narrowing application of norm; BA = Broadening application of norm; W = withstanding; C = originally promoted change; NC = no change; PC = partial change; AC = alternative change.

* Strategy used to defuse normative pressure from other norms.

	ILO/1950s	ILO/1960s	ILO/1970s	World Bank/1980s–1990s	UN/1990s	WTO/late 1990s–2000s	EU/2000s
Description	–Participation of nongovernmental representatives in Governing Body; –Independence of nongovernmental representatives; –State participation in Governing Body	–Independence of nongovernmental representatives; –State participation in Governing Body	–Independence of nongovernmental representatives; –State participation in Governing Body	–NGO participation in implementation and oversight; –Access to IGO information	NGO participation in GA	NGO participation	NGO involvement in deliberations
	L	L	L	M	M	H	H
	L	M	H	H	H	H	H
	VL	L	M	H	H	VH	VH
	BN*	BN*	BN*	BA; NA	NA; CN; BA	CA; CN	CN; NA
	PC; AC	C; AC	C; AC	AC	PC	PC	PC

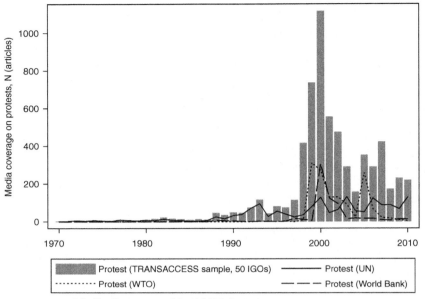

FIGURE 6.8. Media Coverage of Anti-IGO Protests.
Data are based on the "Transaccess" dataset. See Tallberg et al. 2013.

has seen a substantial growth in the normative pressures for NGO access to IGOs.

What Actions Did Actors Opposing the New Rules Take under Normative Pressure?

In the first few years of the League, officials who wanted to defuse the normative pressures generated by the pro-NGO norm used a strategy of narrowing the application of the norm by accepting only informal (and later reversible) rules for NGO participation in the IGO. Also, by giving NGOs alternative advantages for collaboration (such as using the League building for their meetings or financial support for some of their actions), they applied a strategy of broadening the actions derived from the pro-NGO norm – that is, one through which the more important actions of formalizing NGO participation in deliberations was set side by side with the less important material incentives offered to such organizations (in "package deals"). The very weak normative pressures in the 1930s did not lead to any actions for reducing such pressures or to any changes in rules (an outcome consistent with expectations based on H_1).

While the UN formalized the role of NGOs in the Charter, it also applied a strategy of narrowing by shifting their role from one of participation to consultation. Moreover, it only allowed ECOSOC to have formal relations with such organizations. Similar narrowing strategies were applied later, in the UN (and in other IGOs) by distinguishing between NGO participation in the implementation of policies and in IGO decision-making processes.

As the normative pressures to give NGOs a greater role increased considerably in the post–Cold War era, multiple strategies were indeed needed for defusing normative pressures, as H_2 posits. These strategies differed in the UN, World Bank, EU, and WTO.

In the World Bank, in the 1980s and 1990s the developed states were the first to promote the pro-NGO norm because they saw such organizations as useful for the IGO's work. Yet, as NGOs became increasingly vocal in their demand for reforms of the organization, some great powers as well as top Bank officials applied a strategy of narrowing the actions deriving from the norm by limiting the role of NGOs to the implementation of decisions and excluding them from any decision-making processes and bodies. They also adopted a strategy of broadening by discussing transparency toward NGOs simultaneously with the broader issue of NGO participation in the organization.

In the UN, in the 1990s, similar normative pressures for greater NGO involvement were met with a strategy of narrowing the application of the norm. While major states accepted a greater role for NGOs in many UN agencies and at UN conferences, they steadfastly opposed its application to the UNGA and, especially, the UNSC. Their initial decision to maintain informal rules for NGO participation in UN conferences for some time is also an example of a narrowing strategy.

In addition, the call of the ECOSOC 1996 resolution to have the UN secretariat offer secretarial support for NGOs (similar to the support offered by the League to NGOs in the early 1920s) is an example of the broadening strategy as applied to actions. One could also interpret the decision to discuss the expansion of the types of NGOs eligible for consultative status in the UN at the same time with the more important questions of where such NGOs actually had access as another example of broadening the actions deriving from the norm. The broadening strategy is often used to make negotiations more complex in the hope of a stale mate and in preserving the status quo. In most cases, as in the ones of the negotiations of 1996 in ECOSOC, such negotiations may lead, at most, to the acceptance of only minor changes. Indeed, as the UNGA president mentioned after the failed negotiations of the late 1990s, those who did not want any changes "won."

Lastly, the UN member-states also challenged the pro-NGO norm by emphasizing that many NGOs were not representative entities and, therefore, their presence in an IGO was not reflective of democracy. This strategy was reflected in the conditions that were placed on NGO participation through the 1996 ECOSOC resolution as well as, much earlier, through the resolution from 1967, which had introduced the periodic review of NGOs holding consultative status.

The challenging of the pro-NGO norm was used much more directly in the WTO in the late 1990s and early 2000s by invoking the sovereignty norm. Critics of NGOs have presented their access to the WTO as "unfair" as it gives them "two bites of the same apple" by allowing them to influence policies both at the domestic level (where they may not have been successful) and at the intergovernmental one. One U.S. official in fact argued that NGO access to the WTO raised "profoundly troubling questions of democratic theory" (Bolton 2000).

In the EU, the norm was also challenged, but in a different way. There, some saw the empowerment of NGOs (and the norm of participatory democracy) as a threat to the norm of representative democracy embodied by the European Parliament. Perhaps more important, the EU (and its predecessors) has constantly applied a narrowing strategy by only adopting informal rules for NGO access to its institutions. This has led to charges that the NGOs having access to such institutions were not truly independent.

In the cases of the EU and WTO over the past two decades, the strength of the pro-NGO norm and the departure from the norm prescriptions were equally great. In such cases, as mentioned in Chapter 2, those attempting to defuse normative pressures have a difficult choice when deciding whether they would attempt to alter the interpretation of the norm or of its application to the IGO. In the EU and WTO, as expected based on H_2, they eventually used multiple strategies, both at the norm and at the implementation levels.

Developments in the ILO offer a powerful example of the strategy of broadening the norm (that, as H_3 and H_5 together suggest, is expected when norm strength is relatively low). When normative pressure to alter state representation in the Governing Body was applied, powerful states added the independence of NGAs to the debate, arguing that the norm of fair representation should be understood broadly as referring both to states and non-state representatives. This strategy was applied in many instances throughout the history of the organization but became most visible in the 1970s.

What Were the Outcomes of the Attempts to Adopt or Change Rules?

The normative pressures did have an impact on NGO participation in IGOs. This is reflected both in long-term developments across all IGOs (see Figure 6.4) and in the ones in the most prominent IGOs, such as the League of Nations and the UN.

Interestingly, the pro-NGO norm and its implications were only challenged when the norm was actually strong (or moderate), contrary to what we would expect based on H_3. In these cases reform attempts were either not successful (in the WTO in the 2000s) or partially successful (in the UN in the 1990s and the EU in the 2000s).

In the instances when the narrowing strategy was applied, those promoting the norm were only partially successful in bringing about change, as H_7 would suggest. The informal stipulations regarding NGO participation in the early years of the League led to an erosion of their role in the 1930s. The narrowing strategy in 1945 and the 1990s in the UN led the IGO to only give NGOs a role in some of the UN organs and in conferences.

When a broadening approach to defuse normative pressures was used, the efforts to reform NGO participation rules had very little success, as in the 1990s in the UN, or were short-lived ones as in the 1920s in the League. As mentioned, the broadening strategy in the ILO was a reaction to the fair state representation normative pressures, not those of NGA independence. Therefore, if one would not consider both developments simultaneously, it would be difficult to understand how the strong fair state representation pressures discussed in Chapter 3 led to relatively small changes in ILO membership.

Would Outcomes Have Been the Same in Absence of Normative Pressures and Reactions to Pressures?

The pro-NGO norm was not very strong at the establishment of the League of Nations and UN. The "appropriateness" of their initial inclusion in the two global IGOs was based more on recognition of their past efforts in the international realm and their potential usefulness than on a domestic democratic analogy. The initial role they were given therefore could easily be accounted for without turning to norm-based explanations. This is especially true in the League, where the rules stipulating

NGO involvement in the IGO were informal ones that allowed states to later alter the actual degree to which the governmental and nongovernmental entities would work together.

However, without invoking the emergence of a strong pro-NGO norm soon after the end of the Cold War, it would be difficult to account for the increased number of such organizations involved in IGO work and the degree to which they became involved in such work.[15] Explanations based simply on NGO expertise would lead to expectations for similar informal arrangements allowing IGOs to work only with the NGOs they wanted, whenever they wanted to (much as in the case of the European institutions). Such explanations have difficulties accounting for the emergence and spread across IGOs of "liaison offices" with NGOs, of institutions where such NGOs were formally given a role (as in the World Commission on Dams), or of a formalization of NGO participation in intergovernmental forums, such as the UN conferences. Explanations based on understandings of NGOs simply as useful implementers and/or "fire-alarms" (McCubbins and Schwartz 1984), making IGOs more effective, could not account for the institutionalization of IGO-NGO relations (Tallberg et al. 2013) when informal rules would have been more beneficial for those who wanted to maintain control over such relations.

If one considers only the outcome of the 1970s–1980s attempts to reform rules for state participation in the ILO Governing Body and the ones for greater nongovernmental representatives' independence, it could indeed be argued that they would have been the same in the presence or absence of normative pressures. Powerful states have been able to keep their permanent seats in the Governing Body by delaying the ratification of the 1986 reforms. Instead, the rules for maintaining NGA independence – an important aspect of the Cold War ideological battles – were altered when the United States flexed its muscles by walking out of the IGO. What such explanations cannot account for, however, is the process through which such reform attempts took place and, implicitly, their timing. Without the growing pressures deriving from the fair participation norm and the strong normative pressure to maintain the independence of NGAs in the ILO, it would be difficult to explain the presence on the reform agenda of two such different proposals for changes in rules.

---

[15] This differentiation between the nature of the pro-NGO norm before and after the 1990s (initially based on habit rather than democratic analogies) reminds us that the temporal domain of any study of norms may affect our conclusions (see, e.g., Tallberg et al. 2013, 246–247).

Last, but not least, the focus on a small sample of important IGOs may hide the fact that, in the vast majority of such organizations, states and IGO officials did not feel that they needed to "fight" the promotion of the pro-NGO norm. In fact, the UN, World Bank, and WTO are often seen as exceptions to the general inclusive trends in IGOs starting in the 1990s. If we were to view the fairly unsuccessful (or partially successful) reform efforts in these prominent IGOs, we would perhaps be tempted to argue that they simply reflected their lack of support by powerful states. As long as powerful countries such as the United States or China do not want NGOs to be involved in the UNSC or even the UNGA, meaningful reforms will not take place. Yet, by expanding our focus toward other IGOs and IGO bodies where, partly because of a broadening strategy such changes have taken place, and even toward other changes in rules in these important IGOs (such as the ones involving transparency), it becomes apparent that the normative pressures have led to partial and/or alternative changes that other explanations could not fully account for.

7

Transnational Parliamentary Oversight

The Norm

Among the most important democratic norms to have developed at the state level is the one prescribing checks and balances between branches of government. The slow evolution of institutions within intergovernmental organizations for a long time allowed for only one analogous "branch": the executive. However, as this chapter shows, in time, international parliamentary bodies began emerging in some IGOs soon after World War II. Since then dozens more have been established, especially after the end of the Cold War. This chapter argues that a democratic parliamentary oversight norm has influenced such developments in IGOs.

There are other systems of checks and balances in IGOs besides those provided by interparliamentary bodies. Most importantly, perhaps, in a handful of organizations judicial organs have developed as checks on the power of the major IGO bodies. The European Court of Justice has played a very strong role, as one example in this chapter reminds us. The International Court of Justice has also adopted advisory opinions that influenced the relative power of UN institutions, including those of the UNSC and UNGA (e.g., Higgins 1996).

Another set of such checks and balances in IGOs are the specialized internal oversight institutions such as the Office for Internal Oversight in the UN, the Ombudsman in the European Union, or the Ethics Office in the IMF. They are all examples of "horizontal" mechanisms (O'Donnell 1999), which hold major IGO institutions accountable by independent experts working inside rather than outside the organization. Although these bodies are important for holding IGOs accountable, their link to

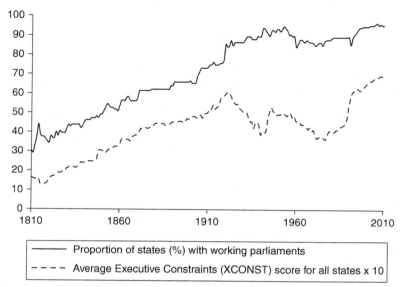

Proportion of states (%) with working parliaments

- - - - Average Executive Constraints (XCONST) score for all states x 10

FIGURE 7.1. Strength of the Parliamentary Oversight Norm Across Time.

democratic norms, the main focus of this study, is a weak one (Grigorescu 2010). They are more likely connected to the (recent) export of the anti-corruption norm from the domestic to the international realm.

While acknowledging such additional IGO accountability mechanisms, the rest of this chapter limits itself only to a discussion of international parliamentary assemblies. It does so because of the important influence that such assemblies have had on the promotion of democratic domestic norms to IGOs and on the way such norms have shaped decision-making rules in the European Union and, to some degree, in other organizations.

The Domestic Norm

The democratic norm of parliamentary oversight emerged at the domestic level hundreds of years ago, when the first parliamentary bodies were established in countries such as Britain and the United States. The norm evolved parallel to (but not entirely at the same time as) other democratic norms such as those of equal voting, fair representation, civil society representation, or transparency. Figure 7.1 uses two different gauges of the average strength of the norm across states. One is simply based on the proportion of countries with legislative bodies (based on data from Fish and Kroenig 2009). The second is based on the XCONST component of the Polity score. XCONST gauges the extent of institutionalized constraints (especially legislatures) on the decision-making powers of the executive (Marshall et al. 2010, 24).

Figure 7.1 shows that by 1850 more than half of the states in the world had some form of parliament, and by 1990 about 95 percent did. The actual degree to which such legislative branches of governments established constraints on the executive branches (represented by the measure XCONST) varied across time – increasing up through the 1920s, declining in the 1930s and 1940s, increasing once more in the late 1940s, and declining again in the 1960s and 1970s only to increase again, fairly dramatically, since the late 1980s.

The discrepancies between the two lines in Figure 7.1 can be explained in great part by the many cases (especially in autocratic or semi-autocratic states) where even though legislative bodies were formally in place, (1) their lack of representativeness (and independence) and (2) their lack of power did not allow them to act as true checks on the executive. These two problems have plagued parliaments for centuries.

Moreover, advances in the representative character of many parliaments have not always gone together with the expansion of parliamentary prerogatives. This was most visible in the first democracies, where the fight to have powerful legislatures generally preceded the one for their democratic representativeness and independence. The latter process took place slowly, primarily through the enfranchisement of large groups originally left out of the political process. As the following discussions suggest, in the international realm, it appears that the first important steps toward true parliamentary oversight over IGOs resulted from advances in the independence of such bodies and only later from an expansion of their prerogatives.

The International Norm

The European Parliament's successful struggle for influence within the European institutions, as well as the spread of the term "democratic deficit" that was coined to reflect the problem that such struggles were intended to resolve (Meny 2003; Featherstone 1994), have led to a great degree of visibility for this international body. This visibility, in turn, has led most of the scholarly work on the application of the parliamentary oversight norm to IGOs to focus solely on the EP.

Yet, as the following section shows, the EP was certainly not the first international parliamentary body of this kind. Additionally, recent

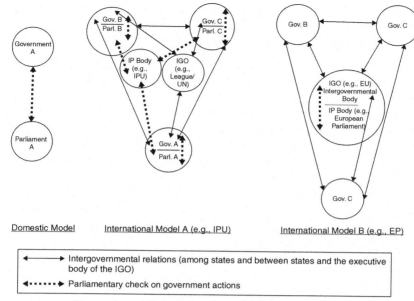

Domestic Model   International Model A (e.g., IPU)   International Model B (e.g., EP)

⟷ Intergovernmental relations (among states and between states and the executive body of the IGO)

◀·······▶ Parliamentary check on government actions

FIGURE 7.2. Domestic and International Models of Parliamentary Oversight.

literature has pointed out that international parliamentary bodies are becoming the best possible "correctives" to the democratic deficit of all IGOs, not just of the EU (Nye et al. 2003; Slaughter 2004a, 122; Kraft-Kasack 2008; Habegger 2010, 190). Therefore, although this chapter emphasizes the evolution of the EP, it will also discuss the broader evolution of the norm of parliamentary oversight across other intergovernmental organizations (IGOs) and across time.

As in the case of the other democratic norms discussed in previous chapters, there are some important differences in the application of the parliamentary oversight norm in the domestic and international realms. In the domestic realm, the relationship between the legislative and executive branch is a fairly direct one in which each one can keep the other in check. This simple relationship is represented in the first model of Figure 7.2.

In the international realm, transnational parliamentary assemblies are faced with multiple governments, multiple domestic parliamentary assemblies, and one IGO. This implies that there are two possible ways through which such parliamentary assemblies can influence IGOs. In Model A they can act outside the IGO, through national parliaments that pressure national governments that, in turn, shape IGO decisions.

Alternatively, in Model B they can act directly on the IGO institutions, as part of the international body itself.[1]

I show that the first struggles to promote the parliamentary oversight norm in the international realm, in the nineteenth century and early twentieth century, embraced Model A, through the Inter-Parliamentary Union. In the post–World War II era, Model B was preferred, most notably in the European institutions. The model that was chosen was important for the dynamics of the processes that led democratic normative pressures to alter IGO rules. Model A allowed for a great degree of independence of the interparliamentary body but, because of the indirect channels of influencing IGOs, was not very successful in establishing any real oversight. Model B, on the other hand, allowed initially for some direct influence over the IGO but struggled with gaining greater independence from governments and, implicitly, from the IGO that it was supposed to keep in check. I show that the ability to bring the two separate norms (of parliamentary independence and of parliamentary oversight) together, or to use them against each other, shaped the rules driving the work of such bodies.

A History of the Application of the Norm to IGOs

Developments before World War II

The idea of having some form of transnational parliamentary body involved in international relations has been espoused by individual authors as far back as the seventeenth century (e.g., Penn 1912), when only a handful of states actually had national parliaments. Yet the collective promotion of this idea only began taking place in the late nineteenth century with the establishment of the IPU. Not surprising, this initiative emerged in the second half of the nineteenth century, a few decades after the majority of states had already adopted some form of working national parliamentary systems (as Figure 7.1 suggests). By 1889, when the IPU was formally established, two-thirds of states in the world had parliaments.

The IPU was born out of the same tumultuous international networking that produced most other international unions of the mid-1800s. Its roots can be traced to a number of organizations associated with the peace movement of those times (Douglas 1975, 2). These networks

---

[1] While such transnational parliamentary assemblies also have relations with national parliaments, these are not represented in Figure 7.2 because their main relationship is with the IGO bodies.

were composed primarily of individuals who were members of national parliaments and who had decided to take their domestic fights for broader voting rights and workers' rights from the national level to the international one. As in the cases of other "international unions" formed in the nineteenth century, the founders of the IPU sought visible individuals (rather than governments) to fund their efforts. A great deal of the IPU's initial financial support came from Andrew Carnegie, a strong supporter of the organization's cause. In 1886 he had written the ode "Triumphant Democracy" calling for a "Parliament of Man" that would bring peace in a future "Federation of the World" (Zarjevski 1989, 37).

The ideals of these individual parliamentarians and philanthropists converged toward a common goal: the creation of a global democratic parliamentary system that would work as a collective check on the action of executive branches of their respective governments. This idea was made clear in the first conferences, where speakers agreed that their main objective was to reduce the role of governments in international relations and increase the influence of parliaments, the symbols of democracy at the national level (Gobat 1895, 266). The main instruments through which they initially saw themselves achieving their goals were supranational mechanisms of arbitration between states. In fact, the title of the first official conference (1889) of what later became the IPU was the Parliamentary Arbitration Conference. The second conference (1892) went under the name of the Inter-Parliamentary Conference for Arbitration. It was only in 1908, when the conferences broadened their focus beyond questions of arbitration that the organization took on the name of Inter-Parliamentary Union (Douglas 1975, 7).

Like other international organizations of the nineteenth century, the IPU emerged as a hybrid between an intergovernmental and nongovernmental body. While representation in the IPU was on the basis of national delegations (rather than individuals or civil society groups as in typical international nongovernmental organizations), the character of the organization was, nevertheless, greatly nongovernmental. Prominent individual parliamentarians (rather than states or national parliaments), such as William Randall Cremer of Britain or Frederic Passy of France, were behind the actual establishment of the organization. As mentioned, the funding for the organization was also primarily from wealthy individuals rather than government contributions. Most importantly, the delegations to the IPU included members of parliament from both parties in power and those in opposition from the respective states. Sometimes these delegations included former, soon-to-be, or, in a few cases, even sitting individual members of cabinets. This practice offers perhaps the best reflection of the mixed intergovernmental/nongovernmental character of the IPU.

Throughout its formative years, the IPU continuously emphasized the relevance of international parliamentary institutions as an alternative and check to the traditional intergovernmental character of international relations. Reflective of this character is the title of a memoire that was launched at the Brussels Conference of 1895 as a first official call for an International Court for Arbitration. The "Memoire to the Powers," adopted by the conference, implied that even though the authors and supporters of the memoire were members of parliament of "the powers," they did not identify themselves with the policies of the executive branches of their respective governments. This document initiated the broader movement that eventually led the 1899 Hague Conference to establish the Permanent Court of Arbitration. While the formal decision to establish the Court was, of course, that of governments, the blueprint for the organization was virtually identical to the one offered by the IPU (Sabic 2008, 263; Kissling 2011, 4, 44).

The international parliamentary model that the IPU envisioned for itself was one in which it would work outside of any governmental structures. IPU founders saw the new organization functioning as an independent intermediary between governments, allowing it to play at the international level the similar role of a check on executive power played by legislatures at the national level. Figure 7.3 offers an illustration of this model (which differs from those in Figure 7.2 as it does not include a role for IGOs).

From the beginning, the IPU struggled, on the one hand, with its purely parliamentary character based on broadly accepted understandings of democratic ideals of the times and, on the other hand, on the pragmatic need to broaden its ranks so as to include representatives of important states that were not democratic. After all, if the organization wanted to be a truly effective promoter of arbitration among governments, it needed to have relations with all states. This was especially obvious in the IPU's dealings with Russia, a country lacking democratic credentials and any form of parliamentary structure. An 1896 amendment to the organization's statutes (referred to as the "Russian article") allowed representatives of "facultative councils, or other similar institutions of non-constitutional countries," to take part in its conferences (Kissling 2011, 5). While the amendment only had a short life, it appears to have had an important impact on later developments. One of the few

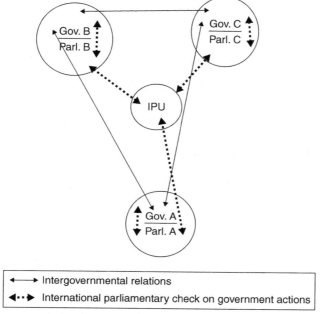

FIGURE 7.3. Original IPU Model of Parliamentary Oversight (before Emergence of IGOs).

Russian delegates to the 1896 Conference convinced Tsar Nicholas II to promote to other heads of state a Convention for the Pacific Settlement of International Disputes that eventually led to the establishment of the Permanent Court of Arbitration. Members of parliaments who were active in the organization brought the first arbitration proceedings before the court in 1902. The organization was also successful in convening the Second Hague Conference of 1907, which, as mentioned in Chapter 3, did not accomplish as much as the one of 1899 because of the clashes between great powers and small states.

Once the Permanent Court was established, the IPU did not seek to develop a formal relationship with the new IGO. This approach illustrated, even at such an early stage of the IPU's existence, its struggles with the broader (sometimes ambiguous) role it envisioned for itself. Although it wanted to influence the major decisions of the IGOs that were just emerging, it also appeared to remain content with its nongovernmental character, understanding itself as a clear alternative to the intergovernmental nature of international relations.

Its struggles with this ambiguous position became even more visible in relations with the League of Nations. Indeed, the IPU had long advocated the establishment of a League-like organization; individuals active in the IPU took part in establishing the League. In fact, one of the main drafts of the Covenant was written by the IPU's president, Lord Robert Cecil. The draft, not surprisingly, stipulated a direct role for the IPU in the League as a "friendly commentator and councilor of the Assembly of the League of Nations" (Miller 1928, 61–64). The idea behind the IPU's active role was in part a result of the realization that the organization needed now to compete in the nongovernmental realm with other emerging institutions, such as the Socialist International. Therefore, it felt that it had an obligation to be more active within the League (Kissling 2011, 7). In its first post–World War I conference, in Stockholm, as the League's Covenant was still being negotiated, the IPU was seriously considering a direct official role in the work of the new organization. In the opening of the conference, Philip Stanhope, replacing Cecil (who at the time was working on drafting the League Covenant) as president of the IPU, made a strong case for the need to include some form of parliamentary representation in the League. When he did so, he invoked, perhaps for the first time, the democratic deficit ("deficiency," as he called it) of an IGO when declaring: "It will scarcely be denied that the principle of popular representation in the Assembly of the League must necessarily be conceded. Meanwhile, what body can more reasonably claim to supply that admitted deficiency than the Union, voicing, as it does, the concerted opinions of Parliaments?" (Inter-Parliamentary Union 1921b).

At that meeting, the IPU decided to move from Brussels, where it had functioned for more than two decades, to Geneva, where the League was headquartered. Just one year later, the IPU's decision to seek closer relations with the League was codified in a 1922 amendment that stipulated that the IPU's work would now move beyond simple issues of arbitration and international law and seek "the democratic development of the work of international peace and co-operation between nations *by means of a universal organization of nations*" (Zarjevski 1989, 71; emphasis added). This qualified the IPU to deal with any problems that the new IGO did. Yet, even though some prominent IPU officials would have liked to see a more direct and inside role for the IPU in the League, the majority of the organization's members preferred maintaining their independence by keeping the organization outside any IGO.

Perhaps the greatest success of the IPU in shaping the League was the adoption in 1920 of a draft treaty that was used by governments as the basis for negotiations and the eventual establishment of the Permanent Court of International Justice (PCIJ) (Kissling 2011, 5). Although the PCIJ never developed as a check on the major organs of the League, it did offer several important advisory opinions regarding the competencies of the International Labor Organization and on the Commission of the Danube that were both under the League's institutional umbrella. Despite this significant success and the strong rhetorical support between the League and IPU, the two organizations never truly worked together as the first draft of the Covenant had anticipated. The IPU remained strictly outside of the new organization offering no more than advice (that only rarely was taken).

This IPU approach to relations with IGOs was represented in Figure 7.2 as Model A of international parliamentary oversight. It was set side by side with Model B that is discussed in the following section as characterizing the Council of Europe, European Union, and virtually all other IGOs that adopted parliamentary bodies after World War II. The main distinctions between the two models are that in Model A interparliamentary bodies function outside of the IGO. Their members can be from states that are not members of the IGO. Most important, they do not have any formal obligations to oversee the work of the IGO and the IGO has no formal obligation to consult/collaborate with the interparliamentary organization. In Model B interparliamentary oversight bodies are formally part of IGOs. Only IGO member states can have representatives in such bodies. The IGO and parliamentary body both have formal obligations to consult/collaborate with each other.[2]

The IPU's model reflected its ambiguous position in relation to IGOs. While, on the one hand, it had contributed to the formation of IGOs such as the League, on the other hand, its long-term goals required that it protect its nongovernmental character, maintaining only weak relations with governmental and intergovernmental bodies. Starting with the 1904 discussion of an American proposal to establish a "world parliament" with the same powers that national parliaments had, the IPU has continued to see itself as the embryo of an independent organization on its way toward something much greater, not as a secondary partner of the emerging global IGOs. This was, in part, because of the strong nongovernmental nature of its approach to international relations inherited from other institutions emerging in the nineteenth century. In addition, it felt

---

[2] For a more complete typology of international interparliamentary systems, see, e.g., Cofelice 2012.

that its broad goals of democratizing international relations (not states) were incongruent with a strong role in an IGO. Last, but not least, the IPU did not feel the need to establish a more formal relationship with the League in most of the interwar era because many of its members present in Geneva were also members of the national delegations to the League. Therefore, the IPU was not left out of most governmental conversations and had access to the important information it needed (Kissling 2011, 8). All of these factors led the organization to prefer trying to influence IGO work indirectly, through its contacts with national parliaments that in turn were expected to pressure their governments to alter IGO decisions. This approach stood in contrast to the models used by later IGOs in which the same national parliamentarians could act through their colleagues in the IGO parliamentary assemblies, influencing the work of such organizations in a more direct fashion.

The two models each had their supporters within the IPU. The decision to embrace the first model and not the second can be understood as the result of debates between two groups challenging each other's emphasis of one norm over another. The group that emphasized the independence of a parliamentary body over actual parliamentary oversight was successful. It is not clear why the majority of IPU members promoted Model A. Most likely, their decision was based both on their belief in the appropriateness of this solution and, perhaps, on their personal preferences for maintaining greater independence. After all, if the League would have established a transnational parliamentary body, most IPU members could not be sure whether they would be selected to be part of that body.

Regardless of the reasons behind the choice for Model A, we should note that the existence of the IPU and the modicum of parliamentary oversight that it achieved through such a model was likely responsible for the relatively low normative pressures to establish parliamentary oversight bodies within the IGOs of the interwar era, through Model B. In other words, the work of the IPU was deemed sufficient for the parliamentary oversight purposes of the times.

Developments after World War II and during the Cold War

The IPU's desire to remain independent of major IGOs became even stronger in the aftermath of World War II. There were some IPU delegates who wanted to have their organization play a more important part in the UN than it had in the League. One British representative proposed that the IPU become a UN "consultative specialized agency" similar to UNESCO, WHO, and FAO (Douglas 1975, 50). Yet, the majority of the

IPU's members were wary about such direct ties with the new global organization. Therefore, once more, although there were normative pressures to establish some form of parliamentary oversight institutions in a major global IGO, the existence of the IPU as an alternative to a strong internal intergovernmental parliamentary assembly led to a defusing of these pressures without any changes to the status quo.

The erosion of the practice of having members of parliament as representatives of their states in the UN and its affiliated agencies and, more importantly, the IPU's decision to remain in Geneva and not follow the UN to New York made the organization even more disconnected from the global IGO. In fact, many of the first discussions of the UN system within the IPU were very critical of the design of the new organization, emphasizing, among other things, that too much power was given to the UNSC and not enough to the UNGA (with which the IPU felt a strong affinity) (Zarjevski 1989, 94). It took more than a quarter century for the IPU to even offer official support for the UN in its statutes. Conversely, the UN did not take the IPU too seriously, only giving it consultative status with ECOSOC in 1950, thus bestowing on it the status of NGO, rather than observer status, as important IGOs held. Throughout the 1950s and 1960s the IPU sought multiple times to gain access to other UN organs and agencies, most notably the Trusteeship Council and the UNGA. Such efforts were only moderately successful, suggesting a narrowing strategy on the part of those opposing any transnational parliamentary oversight over the UN.

The UN's relative indifference to the IPU was because of the Union's decision to present itself as a fairly apolitical forum in which both sides of the Cold War would feel comfortable talking to each other. To achieve this goal the IPU played down its democratic ideals. With the emergence of many new states in the decolonization period of the 1950s and 1960s, the IPU was even more careful how it promoted democratic parliamentary systems for fear that it would not be able to accommodate such new states as members. In fact, in 1971 the organization chose to replace the condition that the parliaments represented in its conferences be "democratic" in nature, allowing for states to simply have "representative" bodies.[3] This erosion of democratic principles is not surprising considering the decline in the strength of democratic pro-parliamentary norms across states (as measured and represented in Figure 7.1) during the era

---

[3] Even today, about one-third of the countries that are represented in the IPU are not considered to be democratic by most standards.

of decolonization and at the peak of the Cold War. However, because of this bland approach to international issues, the UN and other major IGOs began perceiving the IPU, even more than before, as a fairly insignificant organization.

The IPU's reduced relevance in international relations during the Cold War era also resulted from the emergence of other similar organizations, such as the Parliamentarians for World Order, that were more willing to work directly with IGOs. It especially resulted from the advent of formal parliamentary bodies within many IGOs such as the Council of Europe and European Coal and Steel Community. Such IGOs did not face the same problems as the global organization because their member-states already had functioning democratic parliaments. The IPU was left to maintain relations with the official parliamentary bodies of such IGOs, rather than with the IGOs themselves (Kissling 2011, 12). While many of the post–World War II IGO parliamentary assemblies have acquired meaningful powers, the IPU – the first organization to promote the establishment of such forms of international parliamentary oversight – has barely maintained a degree of relevance in international relations, becoming better known for its efforts in domestic parliamentary issues.

The first interparliamentary institution to take shape within an intergovernmental body was the Empire Parliamentary Association (EPA). When founded in 1911, it was intended to contribute to maintaining relations between the various parts of the British Empire that was at that time beginning to break apart (Grey 1986, 3). In 1949, as the British Commonwealth was established, the EPA was transformed into a more significant institution, named the Commonwealth Parliamentary Council (CPC). The CPC was given a secretariat and began holding yearly meetings in which each parliament from the British Commonwealth sent two representatives. These meetings led to resolutions that took the form of recommendations for intergovernmental relations within the Commonwealth (Grey 1986, 42–49; Webb 1950). Nevertheless, the EPA/CPC remained throughout its history a weak institution.[4]

---

[4] When the Council of Europe established its own parliamentary assembly (to which the EPA actually gained observer status), a journalist who was familiar with both of these international parliamentary bodies explained the difference in the following way: "The European Assembly is ... a parliament and not a conference. The delegates meet not to emphasize national differences, but to abolish them. Commonwealth Parliamentary Association Conferences, on the other hand, perpetuate national differences" (Webb 1950, 7).

In 1949, the same year that the CPC emerged, the Council of Europe established the Parliamentary Assembly of the Council of Europe (PACE). The founding of the Council of Europe and its Parliamentary Assembly has been traditionally associated with the efforts of Winston Churchill. By losing the 1945 elections, Churchill found himself having to work with individuals outside of government circles, rather than directly through intergovernmental channels. As he remained a prominent member of Parliament, he wanted to continue shaping major European policies, even through nongovernmental means. This may explain his drift toward the federalist movement that advocated not just a unified Europe, but one that would be based on deep integration, at the societal and, somewhat related to this, the interparliamentary level. In fact, his status as an "outsider" to intergovernmental European relations advocating for the CoE appears to have sparked even greater negative sentiments toward the organization among British officials. In particular, Ernest Bevin, then British foreign secretary, detested the federalist movement that Churchill had, purposefully or not, come to represent (Young 1999, 41). This tension between Churchill and the Labourist government reached a peak in 1948, when the former led a march through London supporting the establishment of a parliamentary assembly in the emerging CoE. It is noteworthy that, around the same time, Bevin proposed that a study should be made of the possibility of establishing a form of global parliament directly elected by the people of the world (Walker 2003, 136). This could be interpreted as an example of the broadening strategy in the application of the parliamentary oversight norm to the international realm, used by an individual (or government) that did not truly want such interparliamentary bodies gaining ground in IGOs. Specifically, when Bevin was under normative pressure to accept a functioning parliamentary assembly in a European IGO, he called for the establishment of a global one, presenting it as an even broader and better application of the norm, yet one that he likely knew was destined at that time for failure.

The British government emerged as the greatest opponent of PACE (Hawtrey 1949, 26). It drafted a counterproposal to the blueprint for the CoE offered by the French and Benelux countries. The original British proposal only included a council of ministers, eliminating any form of a parliamentary assembly. At a later stage in the negotiations they conceded to including an assembly but only one that met once a year and that remained simply consultative in nature (similar to the weak Commonwealth Parliamentary Council model).

Throughout the debates, the British government had to work against the strong democratic rhetoric used by those supporting a powerful PACE. Therefore, to defuse some of the normative pressure that had been building, they eventually conceded on the establishment of PACE in a compromise providing for one-week meetings, four times a year. In Bevin's words, he finally acquiesced and "gave them this talking shop" (Young 1999, 42). However, the British did all they could to erode the body's power by using a narrowing strategy. Perhaps more important, to gain greater government control over PACE, the United Kingdom only accepted PACE after wording in the CoE statute stipulated clearly that the delegations to PACE would be appointed by governments, not parliaments (something that most other delegations were supporting), and certainly not through direct elections, as only very few of those involved in negotiations were advocating (Robertson 1956, 5). In addition, they made sure that the rules only allowed for the CoE to take up issues that did not fall within the functions of other IGOs, such as the UN or the Organization for European Economic Co-operation (the precursor of the OECD). Moreover, they only gave very little relative power to PACE within the organization (Young 1999, 43). Of course, these decisions led the new PACE to be a weak institution within the broader post–World War II international arrangements. It was only after the CoE and PACE were stripped of much of the originally proposed powers that the British accepted this novel IGO structure.

The fight for a more powerful PACE was primarily weakened by the realization that any attempt for a supranational institution governing European affairs needed to be developed without the United Kingdom (and even without the Scandinavian countries), which opposed such a solution. What the members of the CoE were able to agree on was an endorsement of the "functionalist" approach to a greater European union through intergovernmental accords and "specialized authorities in the field." This formal acceptance of functionalism was seen by many as a mere consolation prize to those who did not succeed in making the CoE into an international body with a powerful interparliamentary and federal character (Schuman 1951, 736–737). To use the terminology of this book, this action is an example of the broadening strategy used for defusing pressure for the application of the parliamentary oversight norm to the CoE. Specifically, the opponents of a more independent PACE added the loosely connected issue of functionalism to debates involving future European institutions. When both issues were placed on the agenda, only the endorsement of functionalism was accepted, whereas PACE remained unchanged. However, this consolation prize was not a trivial one. In the long run it contributed to the establishment of the European Coal and Steel Community and, ultimately, to shaping the supranational entity that the European Union has become. The CoE's Committee of Ministers accepted this endorsement of functionalism at the same time that it turned down a last attempt to give PACE any additional power through the so-called Mackay Plan (Council of Europe 1950, 7–21). It became evident by 1951 that any parliamentary efforts, if they were to be successful, needed to take place in the new ECSC, made up of a smaller, yet more like-minded, group of European states, rather than in the larger CoE.

The decision to offer a stronger role to the Common Assembly of the ECSC than to PACE can be interpreted as yet another example of the broadening strategy in applying democratic norms. Indeed, as the CoE and ECSC were established around the same time, the opponents of strong interparliamentary bodies were able to defuse the normative pressure for instituting a meaningful parliamentary assembly in the CoE precisely because they could signal that they were willing to give the assembly in the new ECSC greater power. Just as Chapter 4 suggests, for example, that the acceptance of the veto in the UNSC was "packaged" with egalitarian voting procedures in the other UN institutions, it is suggested here that the strong intergovernmental component of the CoE led those opposing a strong parliamentary body in this IGO to be more accepting of one in the ECSC. When faced with the institutional design of two European IGOs, member-states chose to allow for a greater role of the parliamentary assembly in the IGO that was more technical (and less political) at the time: the ECSC (Robertson 1956).

When the ECSC was founded in 1951, the Treaty of Paris established a common assembly composed of seventy-eight representatives selected by parliaments. The treaty provided for the possibility of having the representatives elected directly by the public, something that was never truly acceptable to the founders of the CoE.

In its first few years the assembly simply played a deliberative role as member-states gave the ECSC's supervisory role almost entirely to the ECSC Council, where governments were represented. One reason they avoided giving too much power to the ECSC Common Assembly was because they did not want to transfer even more sovereignty to the supranational level after they had already given unprecedented power to the supranational ECSC High Authority (Westlake 1994, 34).

It should be noted that Jean Monnet's original plan for the ECSC did not include an assembly. He considered it simply a "representation of the west's spiritual superiority" (in other words, he saw it simply as a token recognition of the parliamentary oversight norm), rather than a necessary institution in the ECSC. Yet, when the first proposals for a special council emerged (an institution that he tried to block outright), he came to prefer the Common Assembly as it did not seem to interfere with the power of the supranational ECSC High Authority and, moreover, was seen by him as a competitor to the more "dangerous" ECSC Council (Featherstone 1994, 160).

As soon as the Common Assembly was established, its members began seeking ways to increase their institution's relevance. One of their first major initiatives toward this goal was to create supranational (and more relevant) political parties in the Common Assembly (e.g., European Coal and Steel Community 1955).

Early on, those who sought to empower the Common Assembly considered two different paths. On the one hand, they fought to increase their independence and authority through legitimizing direct elections of the members of the Common Assembly, an option left open through Article 21 of the Treaty of Paris establishing the ECSC. On the other hand, and more important, they pushed for the broadening of the Common Assembly's responsibilities. The arguments for both goals often referred to their relevance for achieving greater European integration, but, more often, they were simply explained by their supporters as necessary steps for making the ECSC more democratic (e.g., European Coal and Steel Community 1952). The distinction between the two goals was often blurred and, therefore, virtually all of those supporting greater power for the Common Assembly also appeared to want deeper integration. Such individuals were labeled "federalists."

Those who opposed deeper European integration and the empowerment of the Common Assembly, referred to as the "confederalists," took advantage of the original two-pronged approach of the federalists and used an argument that was often described as "devious" (e.g., European Community 1960). On the one hand, they posited that giving too much power to an unelected parliament was not appropriate (e.g., Constitutional Assembly of the Ad Hoc Assembly 1953, 4). On the other hand, they argued that it was wrong to elect a parliament that was just a powerless talking shop. For example, one supporter of such a view complained that "elections in which people have no interest will be used to form assemblies which are not representative" (Constitutional Assembly of the Ad Hoc Assembly 1953, 142).

Even though this circular argument appears to have been somewhat stronger in the ECSC than in the later European Economic Community because of the greater technical character of the former compared to the latter, it was used by confederalists well throughout the 1970s. For the strategy to be effective, both types of reforms (direct elections and greater powers) needed to be simultaneously on the agenda to maintain a strong link between them. Confederalists hoped that through concomitant discussions of both types of reform it would be difficult to bring about any change to the institutional status quo (European Coal and Steel Community 1953).

This broadening strategy brought together under one umbrella the two aforementioned prescriptions derived from equally important democratic norms. The first emphasized the need for a truly representative and independent parliamentary body, whereas the second emphasized the need for such a body to act as an effective check on the power of the executive. As mentioned earlier, the two norms did not necessarily go hand in hand with each other in the first domestic democratic systems. Many national parliaments had first been able to become effective checks on executive power and only later developed into truly representative bodies. The EP, on the other hand, first became a representative forum (after direct elections were introduced) and only later gained its role as a check on the other institutions in the EEC and, later, on those in the EU. Interestingly, the opponents of a greater role for the EP publicly promoted the simultaneous application of the two norms because they felt that their circular arguments would delay any type of reform for a long time.

As in all cases of broadening discussed in this book, the promoters of this strategy had a clear preference between the two types of reforms. Indeed, confederalists were much more interested in maintaining unfettered Council control (and, implicitly, government control) over all affairs in the European institutions. Therefore, they were particularly keen on maintaining an institutionally weak parliament with very few and narrow prerogatives. While they also did not want the EP to gain greater independence and legitimacy through direct elections, they viewed this as only a secondary issue. The fact that governments first conceded to such elections and only later to giving real powers to the EP reflects such preferences. Overall, it can be argued that the main reason they opposed direct elections was because they wanted to continue applying the broadening strategy and defuse pressures for real empowerment for as long as possible.

One of the most explicit descriptions of this strategy was offered by Alain Peyrefitte, De Gaulle's information minister, in a 1960 confidential memo to his colleagues in the French cabinet. In the memo that was eventually leaked to the press, Peyrefitte argued: "Nevertheless, there does not seem to be any advantage in opposing [direct elections] in the abstract, whilst we could use it as a negotiating lever. It would be sufficient to make these elections into the last stage in the gradual progress towards confederalism" (Peyrefitte 1962, 6).

The proponents of a greater role for the EP, on the other hand, took great care to separate the two issues (e.g., European Parliament Political Committee 1961). For example, during the struggle for direct elections in the early 1960s, they did not simultaneously call for an expansion of the institution's supervisory role. Conversely, when seeking to gain greater budgetary powers in the late 1960s, they dropped any references to the issue of direct elections. They turned once more to promote such elections in the 1970s, only after some budgetary powers were acquired by the EP.

The task before the federalists appeared to become even more daunting after the Rome (EEC) Treaty of 1957 dropped the provision from the ECSC Treaty that allowed members to select their representatives to the ECSC Common Assembly through direct elections. It only provided for the designation of EP members by national parliaments. Article 138(3) of the Treaty nevertheless stated that the EP should draw up proposals for direct elections. The debates surrounding the two paths toward empowering the European parliamentary body therefore became even more contentious after 1957.

To mark a break with its previous status, after the Rome Treaty the ECSC Common Assembly was renamed the "European Parliamentary Assembly," later simply called the "European Parliament." As soon as it was established, the EP formed thirteen committees. The largest of these was on political affairs and Institutional questions, with twenty-four members. Within this committee, a subcommittee of thirteen members was to deal with direct elections. The relevance of this issue is reflected in the fact that most other EP committees had fewer members than this subcommittee (European Community 1958, 4).

The arguments used by the federalists in their fight for direct elections continued to be based primarily on the need for making the European institutions more democratic as well as on the importance of this change for deeper European integration. They emphasized the importance of such elections by drawing an analogy to the strong relationship that unity and democratic elections had brought to many European states several centuries earlier and argued that the Council had mistakenly taken on the task of overseeing the Commission (e.g., European Community 1960, 9).

The parliamentary debates within the EEC continued for several decades to be strewn with such domestic-international democratic analogies.

Throughout the late 1950s and the 1960s, the main opposition to direct elections of the EP came from France. De Gaulle and his government argued on numerous occasions that an indirectly elected parliament would embody democratic principles more efficiently because of the general public's lack of familiarity and interest with the European institutions (Peyrefitte 1960). Proponents of reform unsuccessfully tried shaming strategies, for example, reminding the French government that in 1950, when de Gaulle had temporarily withdrawn from politics, even he had supported the idea of a stronger and directly elected EP (Schuijt 1959, 8). The French nevertheless did not budge.

The opponents of direct elections also learned to use the language of democracy to support their positions. In fact, they often suggested that their proposals were even more democratic than those of the federalists because they considered multiple democratic mechanisms (as they simultaneously supported greater parliamentary powers and the legitimacy that came along with direct elections), albeit, as they presented it, over a much longer time frame.

The confederalist approach was purposeful and well thought out, as the aforementioned memo written by Alain Peyrefitte suggests. The information minister explained in his memo, point by point, the tactics that high ranking French officials needed to use in making the other countries "feel morally obliged" to follow them. Moreover, the memo began by emphasizing that such tactics were necessary to alleviate the "psychological difficulties" (perhaps a different name for the term "normative pressures" used in this book) that France faced in "government circles and public opinion" (Peyrefitte 1962, 2). He argued that the French needed to continue opposing efforts for increased integration and more powers for the EP, while seeming to promote greater institutional democracy.

Peyrefitte also offered an example of such democratic rhetoric when making the case against direct elections in a four-part essay published in 1960 in Le Monde. He concluded that article by asking: "Why should the man on the street and the man in the field bother to elect an Assembly to which specialists barely pay attention" (author's translation; Peyrefitte, 1960, 5).

During the debates surrounding direct elections, some of the confederalists also tried challenging the norm of parliamentary oversight directly. They emphasized the communitarian model of democracy, arguing that government representatives in the Council of Ministers were likely to be more accountable to the public than directly elected MEPs (that represented the cosmopolitan model). Implicitly, they considered the EEC Council's oversight over the Commission as even more democratic than the Parliament's (European Community 1972, 11).[5] Federalists argued that an independent (directly elected) EP was needed as a check on the EEC Council, not only on the Commission, just as parliaments had traditionally checked executive power in the domestic realm (European Parliament 1965; European Community 1968, 51–54).

In 1960 the EP formally proposed a system of universal suffrage. The Council sat on the proposal for the next decade. By repeatedly vetoing this proposal, the French defeated all efforts for direct suffrage.

Confederalists also continued to use the strategy of linking direct elections to increased parliamentary powers (European Community 1970, 102). Most of their declarations during the struggles for direct elections would open (or at least mention in the text) how such elections need to be viewed in a "broader context" of the EP's role and power within the European institutions (e.g., European Community 1972, 4). Conversely, those supporting the reforms made every possible effort to de-link the two issues. As mentioned, this had been especially evident in the late 1960s, when the push toward increased budgetary powers left the question of direct elections almost unspoken by the federalists.

After a struggle of about five years, in 1970, the Treaty of Luxembourg finally gave some budgetary powers to the EP by allowing it to fix its own budget and propose modifications to the EEC's draft budget. This success was primarily a result of the fact that the Commission had now acquired for the first time its own budget with very little institutional oversight. It was therefore the ensuing increase in normative pressure (resulting from the understanding that the lack of budgetary oversight had made the EEC drift even further from prescriptions of the parliamentary oversight norm) that led to the change.

Nevertheless, we should note that this was just a small step because any budgetary modification made by the EP could be rejected by a majority of the EEC Council (Scalingi 1980, 114). Although the Luxembourg Treaty only constituted a token increase in the EP's power, it was nevertheless viewed as an important step.

As soon as the EP acquired these budgetary powers, its members reignited the fight for direct elections. The 1970s saw a concerted effort among

---

[5] For a more complete discussion of the two models as applied to the European institutions, see Bellamy and Castiglione 1998.

all supporters of direct elections, from within the EP, the governments, and even the EEC Commission. In 1970, in an attempt to add urgency to its request, the EP invoked Article 175 of the EEC Treaty, in which inaction by an organ of the institution can be referred to the European Court of Justice. Indeed, by then, a decade had gone by from its 1960 proposal to organize direct elections.

Similar debates as the older ones mentioned earlier, between the promoters of a greater role for the EP and those opposing it, resurfaced. One of the few differences in such debates was that in the 1970s, the usual references to "democracy" were accompanied by many more that used the new "democratic deficit" catchphrase.

By the 1970s the use of the democratic analogy appears to have long been accepted by all those discussing the direct elections. One speaker in the EP debates on direct elections even went so far as to argue that "democracy is the primary objective of the new Europe" (European Community 1975, 39). Even government officials who opposed the further empowerment of the EP now had to defend themselves by arguing that they were misunderstood and that "of course" they supported democratic principles and the idea of direct elections, as was the case of Gaston Thorn, then president of the Council of the EEC, in a 1972 speech in EP (European Parliament Political Committee 1972, 3–4).

In the 1970s, confederalists had to rely on more subtle methods for postponing the direct elections. Most often, they presented their opposition by pointing to additional factors that needed to be considered before direct elections could be held. Among the concerns they raised were the fears that the public may oppose the European project once it had a voice in such elections, apprehensions that some of the extremist parties would gain access to the EP, problems in finding a fair representation of states in a directly elected Parliament, questions of whether to allow members of national parliaments to simultaneously hold seats in the European Parliament, and difficulties in holding elections when the political parties were not yet organized across European lines (e.g., European Parliament 1971, 7; European Community 1976a; European Community 1976b, 45, 62–63). Some of these arguments can be interpreted to reflect a narrowing strategy as they implied that, even if direct elections were to be organized, they needed to be somehow restricted through a set of additional rules.

The promoters of direct elections patiently dealt with each individual concern and slowly pushed the reform proposals forward (e.g., European Parliament Political Affairs Committee 1974, 4). Despite such developments, until 1974 there was still great skepticism that the Council was actually going to allow for elections. Even before joining the EEC in 1973, the United Kingdom appeared to replace France as the main opponent of direct elections and EP empowerment. Many therefore thought at the time that the fight was going to be a long one. Yet, in 1974 the EEC Council somewhat surprisingly agreed to hold elections for the EP (European Community 1974, 84).

The decision came at the same summit meeting that formalized the establishment of the European Council (European Parliament General Directorate for Research and Documentation 1976, 1). This initially informal forum, embodying the intergovernmental character of the European institutions, was seen as a necessary addition to the EEC (European Parliament 1971, 59; European Parliament Political Committee 1972). In fact, confederalists saw such summit meetings as the supreme authority for solving European problems (Bulmer and Wessels 1986, 39) and welcomed the added intergovernmental dimension that the new institution offered the EEC. Critiques of this forum mounted, primarily because it functioned completely outside of the other European institutional arrangements. To counter such critiques, governments of the major states first moved to make the European Council a formal part of the institutional arrangements. Moreover, as a response to the increasing democratic normative pressures to enhance the oversight of an IGO that now had an even greater intergovernmental character, they finally allowed for direct elections of MEPs in exchange for the more important formalization of the European Council. Therefore, in the end, such opponents of direct elections gave in to the normative pressures after they felt assured that, with the new European Council, they could remain in charge of virtually all EEC decisions, even with the added legitimacy of the EP (and the power that such legitimacy brought).

The trade-off leading to the final decision for direct elections took place between the British, French, and Germans who were strong supporters of institutionalizing the European Council and the smaller countries that requested direct elections (Moravcsik 1998, 310). The link between direct elections and the formal establishment of the European Council was provided by the argument that the EP now truly needed to play a greater role to balance the increased intergovernmental character of the system (European Community 1975, 41; French Embassy in Washington 1979). The first direct elections of the EP were held in June 1979.

Soon after the 1979 elections gave the EP its long sought legitimacy it became clear how effective the broadening strategy linking direct elections and parliamentary power had actually been. Some staunch confederalists vowed to fight the increase of EP prerogatives to maintain governments' abilities to protect national economies (Agence Internationale D'Information Pour La Presse 1979). Yet, the majority of opponents of direct elections conceded the defeat and realized that the EP was now going to acquire much greater powers. For example, Luxembourg's prime minister (and former EEC Council president), Gaston Thorn, stated:

> It seems to me absolutely normal especially after a twenty-year fight, that once one has finally resolved to allow this Assembly to be elected by direct universal suffrage, one should allow a change of dimension and practically a qualitative leap.... I therefore believe that it would be a good idea to transfer these powers to [the European Parliament] rather than conduct war of attrition which would cost us all too much. (Agence Internationale D'Information Pour La Presse 1978)

After 1979, members of parliament turned their attention, once more, to finding ways of enhancing the institution's prerogatives. They applied the same normative pressure, based on the need to enhance the democratic character of the system. Yet, after 1979, it appears that the speed with which they were able to advance was much greater than before.

In 1983, member-states adopted the "Solemn Declaration on European Union." Through this the Council of the EEC took on the responsibility to answer all questions addressed by the Parliament.

In the next few years, major powers acquiesced to proposals for qualified majority voting (QMV). In great part this was because of the need to make decision-making in the EEC Council more effective after its membership had recently increased by three (and had doubled since the founding of the ECSC). With the prospect of QMV, the federalists made the argument that a more intrusive EEC with a swifter decision-making process would create a legitimacy gap that needed to be filled (McCormick 2011, 57; Rittberger 2005, 149). Therefore, when the Single European Act (SEA) of 1986 allowed QMV to replace the previous unanimous voting procedures on many issues, it simultaneously provided for a check to the now increased power of the EEC Council by adding the cooperation procedure to the "tools" that the Parliament could use. The procedure was seen at the time as a supranational institutional balance that was now necessary because of the "creeping deparliamentarisation" of national political systems in European decision-making (Rittberger 2005, 128). The cooperation procedure allowed the EP to truly enter the legislative process by offering amendments that would need a unanimous EEC Council vote to be rejected (although the amendments needed also to be supported by the EEC Commission). The SEA is considered the third key moment in the evolution of the EP during the Cold War era, after the granting of budgetary powers of 1970 and the direct elections of 1979 (Westlake 1994, 102).

Developments in the Post-Cold War Era

Just five years after the SEA entered into force, the 1992 Treaty on the European Union added the co-decision legislative procedure for the EP in fifteen policy areas; this gave the EP an absolute right to veto and placed its signature alongside the Council's on European legislation. Furthermore, the EP could now initiate legislation by requesting the European Commission to bring forward proposals. The Treaty of Maastricht established a formal relationship between EP and the president of the Central Bank. It also allowed the Parliament to elect an ombudsman and to bring other EU organs before the European Court (Corbett 1994, 31–34).

Nevertheless, this empowerment of the EP was real only for the "European Community" pillar of the new EU, generally seen as the continuation of the European Economic Community. The EP (as well as the European Commission and the European Court of Justice – ECJ) hardly had any power over the two other pillars that had been added to the organization: Common Foreign and Security Policy and Justice and Home Affairs. This was the result of the narrowing strategy used in the negotiations leading to the Maastricht Treaty by the United Kingdom and a few other countries opposing institutional changes. Despite its limitations, the adoption of the Maastricht Treaty is generally considered the moment when the Parliament became a genuine legislature with real policy-making prerogatives (Judge and Earnshaw 2003, 13, 52, 65).

Five years after Maastricht, the 1997 Amsterdam Treaty expanded the Parliament's co-decision procedure to twenty-three new policy areas (European Parliament Directorate-General for Committees and Delegations, Committee on Institutional Affairs 1997). Perhaps most reflective of the great power and perceived legitimacy that the EP has acquired was the important role it played in 1999, when the Santer Commission was forced to resign because of serious corruption allegations in a very visible scandal. Before the resignation took place, the Commission narrowly escaped a no-confidence vote in the EP.

In 2000, another intergovernmental conference was held in which the EP made the case that it deserved further institutional power. The debates, once more, revolved around the now ubiquitous democratic deficit of the EU and the democratic legitimacy that the EP could offer. The Parliament emphasized the differences between two models of democratic representation discussed earlier. It argued that the EU should be understood as both a "union of the states" and a "union of the peoples" (analogous to the "communitarian" and "cosmopolitan" models of democracy, respectively). The former would be represented by the Council and the latter represented by the EP (European Union 2000).

By 2001 the Treaty of Nice added thirty-five new policy areas to the ones in which the Parliament stood on equal footing with the ministers. The EP also began approving nominations by the EU Council for European Commission president.

In 2004 the Treaty Establishing a Constitution for Europe proposed making co-decision the "ordinary legislation procedure" and finally extending the EP's influence to all policy areas (Rittberger 2003, 179). Although the treaty was not ratified, in 2007, the less radical Treaty of Lisbon gave Parliament co-decision on 75 percent of policy areas and control over the totality of the Union's budget. After Lisbon, the EP was considered to have "equal treatment" in the legislative process. The European Commission needed now to include the EP in legislative preparation as it did the Council of the EU (Dosenrode-Lynge 2012, 166).

The Parliamentary Oversight Norm Beyond the EU

Even though the European Parliament was not the first international parliamentary assembly, it did evolve into the most powerful and visible one and, implicitly, into a model for other parliamentary IGO bodies. The changes that took place in the EU toward the end of the Cold War and in the decades that followed it appear to have been accompanied by a spread of such bodies across other IGOs as Table 7.1 indicates. Indeed, in the first two decades of the post–Cold War era (from 1989 to 2009) twenty-five IGOs established some form of parliamentary bodies. This rapid growth is illustrated in Figure 7.4. A previous increase in the number of such bodies (yet not as substantial as the recent one) took place in the immediate post–World War II era, especially among European IGOs.

The pressure to establish international parliamentary bodies by now has reached major global IGOs such as the UN, World Bank, and WTO. Calls to establish a UN Parliamentary Assembly that would function in a similar way as the EP and as other parliamentary assemblies in IGOs emerged soon after the end of the Cold War. In 1992 the World Federalists advocated for such a UN organ (Dieter 1992). Over the past two decades, several other organizations such as the Campaign for a Democratic United Nations, the International Network for a United

TABLE 7.1. *International Parliamentary Assemblies in IGOs*

Intergovernmental Organization	International Parliamentary Assembly	Year Established
Commonwealth	Empire Parliamentary Association	1911
Nordic Council of Ministers	Nordic Council	1912
Council of Europe	Parliamentary Assembly	1949
European Union	European Parliament	1951
Western European Union (WEU)	Assembly of the WEU	1954
Benelux	Benelux Parliament	1955
North Atlantic Treaty Organization (NATO)	NATO Parliamentary Assembly	1955
International Organization of La Francophonie	Parliamentary Assembly of La Francophonie	1966
Association of South-East Asian Nations (ASEAN)	ASEAN Inter-Parliamentary Assembly	1967
European Free Trade Association (EFTA)	EFTA Parliamentary Committee	1977
Andean Community of Nations	Andean Parliament	1979
Pacific Island Forum	Association of Pacific Island Legislatures	1981
Arab Maghreb Union	Consultative Parliamentary Council	1989
Central America Integration System	Central American Parliament	1991
Organization for Security and Cooperation in Europe (OSCE)	OSCE Parliamentary Assembly	1991
Commonwealth of Independent States (CIS)	The Inter-Parliamentary Assembly of the CIS	1992
Asia-Pacific Economic Cooperation	Asia Pacific Parliamentary Forum	1993
Black Sea Economic Cooperation Organization (BSEC)	Parliamentary Assembly of BSEC	1993
Arctic Council	Conference of Arctic Parliamentarians	1994
Council of Baltic Sea States	Baltic Sea Parliamentary Conference	1994
Caribbean Community	Assembly of Caribbean Community Parliamentarians	1996
Southern African Development Community (SADC)	SADC Parliamentary Forum	1997

Intergovernmental Organization	International Parliamentary Assembly	Year Established
West Africa Economic and Monetary Union	Inter-Parliamentary Committee	1998
Central European Initiative	Parliamentary Assembly	1999
Organization of the Islamic Conference (OIC)	Parliamentary Union of OIC members	1999
EurAsian Economic Community	Inter-Parliamentary Assembly	2000
Organization of the American States	Inter-Parliamentary Forum of the Americas	2000
East African Community	East African Legislative Assembly	2001
Economic Community of Central African States	Network of Central African Parliamentarians	2002
Economic Community of West African States	ECOWAS Parliament	2002
Euro-Mediterranean Partnership	Euro-Mediterranean Parliamentary Assembly	2003
African Union	Pan-African Parliament	2004
GUAM – Organization for Democracy and Economic Development	Guam Parliamentary Assembly	2004
Union for the Mediterranean	UfM Parliamentary Assembly	2004
Mercosur	Parliament of Mercosur	2005
Organization of the Collective Security Treaty (OCST)	Parliamentary Assembly of the OCST	2006
Community of Portuguese Language Countries (CPLC)	Parliamentary Assembly of the CPLC	2007
Economic and Monetary Community of Central Africa	Communitarian Parliament	2010
League of Arab States	Arab Parliament	2010

Table builds on Cofelice 2012.

Nations Second Assembly, One World Trust, and the Global People's Assembly Movement also made the establishment of such an assembly one of their main goals. More importantly, several national parliaments (starting with the Canadian House of Commons in 1993) offered their support for a UN parliamentary body. Even more significant, in 2005, the European Parliament adopted a resolution calling for the establishment of a UN Parliamentary Assembly, "which would increase the democratic profile and internal democratic process of the organisation and

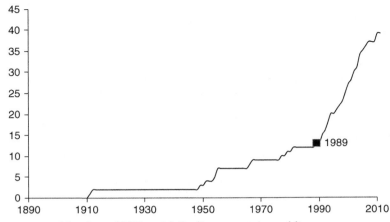

FIGURE 7.4. Number of IGOs with Parliamentary Assemblies.

allow world civil society to be directly associated in the decision-making process" (European Parliament 2005).

Such pressures have not yet led to any serious proposals within the UN itself. The exception may be Kofi Annan's 1999 call to establish a so-called People's Assembly within the organization. In fact, the Pilot Peoples' Assembly organized in 2000 in San Francisco was in part the result of this call (Alger 2003). However, this timid attempt has not been followed by any meaningful initiatives. For now, the UN seems content simply to improve collaboration with national parliaments and with transnational parliamentary organizations (including the IPU) that act outside the organization (Habegger 2010, 198).

The World Federalist Movement has also been at the forefront of efforts to promote a World Trade Organization Parliamentary Assembly (Levi 2003). The topic was raised, for example, in 2002 at a WTO Symposium by Caroline Lucas, a member of the European Parliament. WTO Director-General, Mike Moore, who participated in the symposium, did not address the topic directly but rather responded by encouraging greater involvement of national parliaments in the WTO's work.[6]

The World Bank, an IGO in which, as Chapters 5 and 6 show, the U.S. Congress and other legislatures have played important roles in the struggles for reforms, has also been under pressure to develop a parliamentary institution. Perhaps because of its experience in dealing with national legislatures, it appears to have moved faster than some of the

[6] See www.revistainterforum.com/english/articles/050602artprin_en3.html.

aforementioned global IGOs. In 2000 it established a partnership with the Parliamentary Network on the World Bank (PNoWB) as well as with several regional and global parliamentary organizations, including the IPU.[7] The PNoWB, the most influential of these organizations, defines itself "as an informal network of individual parliamentarians, to strengthen accountability and transparency in international financial institutions in general and in the Bank, in particular" (Parliamentary Network on the World Bank 2008, 4). Also starting in 2004, the World Bank began organizing training programs for members of parliament through its World Bank Institute. So far, more than 10,000 parliamentarians have received such training.[8] To enhance its work with parliamentarians, it has established a World Bank Parliamentary Relations Team that, notably, is based in the Bank's Paris office, not at its Washington headquarters. Overall, the World Bank's approach to such international parliamentary influences can be understood as a narrowing strategy emphasizing only informal institutions (unlike the formal ones in Table 7.1). If the Bank intended to defuse normative pressures for adopting of a formal parliamentary assembly, it appears to have been successful. Indeed, since the establishment of the PNoWB, there have hardly been any direct calls to establish a parliamentary body within the World Bank.

Interestingly, of the six IGOs emphasized in this book, the ILO is the one that appears to have been the least active in establishing a formal or even informal interparliamentary body. This is somewhat surprising considering that all major ILO decisions come into force only after legislative bodies ratify them. One would have expected, therefore, a closer relationship between the IGO and national parliamentarians. For now, the only step the ILO has taken toward establishing such a relationship has been to grant observer status in 1999 to the IPU, its longtime neighbor in Geneva.[9]

Answering the Questions of the Study

What Types of Decision-Making Rules Were Being Established or Changed?
Although, as mentioned, there are multiple possible types of checks on IGO executive bodies, this chapter emphasizes the role of transnational

---

[7] See http://go.worldbank.org/EFCWNL3WP0
[8] See http://web.worldbank.org/WBSITE/EXTERNAL/NEWS/0,,contentMDK:20261636~menuPK:34480~pagePK:34370~piPK:34424~theSitePK:4607,00.html.
[9] See www.ilo.org/pardev/civil-society/parliamentarians/lang--en/index.htm.

parliamentary assemblies. All IGOs establishing such bodies need to answer at least three important questions: On what issues does the parliamentary body have oversight prerogatives? How much power does the body have to influence decisions made by the IGO? How are the members of such parliamentary assemblies selected (in other words, how independent and representative is the parliamentary body)? With the exception of the European Parliament, IGO parliamentary bodies have narrow prerogatives, are fairly weak, and/or are strongly dependent on governments because of the process through which their members are selected.

In the case of the EU, the European Parliament has first advanced in terms of its independence, by holding direct elections in 1979. It later became more powerful through the acceptance of the cooperation and co-decision procedures in 1986 and 1992. The co-decision procedure has expanded in 1997, 2001, and 2007 to increasingly more policy areas. None of the other major IGOs discussed in this study (the League of Nations, ILO, UN, World Bank, and WTO) have established similar parliamentary bodies. Although the IPU played a small role in the League, its role declined substantially in the UN. The World Bank has developed a very loose and informal relationship with parliamentarians through the PNoWB. There have been discussions of introducing parliamentary assemblies in the UN and WTO, but not in the ILO.

Did Actors Invoke Democratic Norms to Pressure Others in Accepting New Decision-Making Rules?

Democratic norms based on the domestic analogies involving parliamentary assemblies were used intensely in debates within the European institutions. They were invoked in earlier debates in the IPU and CoE, involving the need for effective and representative international parliamentary bodies. Democratic norms were also used in the promotion of UN and WTO parliamentary bodies.

It is perhaps not surprising that the European Union has become the IGO with the most powerful international parliamentary body as its members are all democratic states that, in most cases, have long-standing parliamentary traditions. Therefore the strength of democratic norms in member-states (and, implicitly, in the IGO) was consistently high. However, as this study has repeatedly emphasized, it is not sufficient for such norms to be strong for them to have an impact. For a long time, the EP was not given a great degree of power, despite the high level of norm strength.

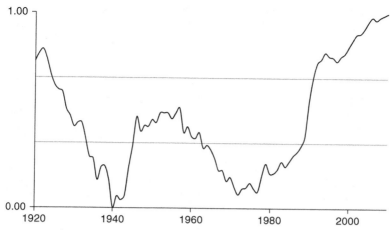

FIGURE 7.5. Average Strength of the Parliamentary Oversight Norm Across All States.

How Powerful Were Such Pressures?

Figure 7.5 gauges the relative strength of the global parliamentary oversight norm between 1920 and 2010. It is based on the measure "executive constraints" from the Polity dataset, used in Figure 7.1. As discussed in the first section of this chapter, the measure is closely related to the emergence of parliamentary bodies at the national level and to the strength of such bodies. Figure 7.5 is scaled, like all other representations of norm strength in the previous chapters, from 0 (the weakest level of the norm in the period under consideration) to 1 (the strongest level). It shows that norm strength was high in the early 1920s and post–Cold War era. Not surprisingly, these are also the periods when global IGOs experienced the most important debates on the establishment of parliamentary bodies. The norm strength was moderate in the late 1920s, the early 1930s, and the first two decades after World War II. It was low throughout the other periods under consideration.

In contrast, the strength of the norm was consistently high in the European institutions. It is important, for example, to note that the average executive constraints score in the six original members of the ECSC in 1951 was a perfect 7, at a time when the global average was only 4.4. The score has remained near perfect in the European institutions since then, and, therefore, the norm strength will be considered high for the EU and its precursors throughout all periods discussed here.

As the issues that have been raised by those promoting the parliamentary oversight norm in IGOs have varied, I assess in several different ways the degree to which the status quo has departed from norm prescriptions. In the UN, World Bank, and WTO, the main change promoted by those supporting greater parliamentary oversight has been simply the establishment of an interparliamentary body. As none of these IGOs have established such a body, I consider that throughout their history, in all these cases the status quo has departed substantially from the norm prescription. In the League of Nations, the IPU played an indirect role as some of the national representatives in the League were also members of the IPU at a time when both organizations were headquartered in Geneva. As a result of the informal role played by the IPU, I consider that the League departed moderately from norm prescriptions.

The same issue of establishing a parliamentary assembly was relevant at the founding of the CoE[10] and of the ECSC. In the debates that took place before PACE and Common Assembly were formally established, I also consider the status quo to depart substantially from norm prescription.

In the European institutions I consider that the status quo departed moderately from what the parliamentary oversight norm prescribed from 1951 (when the ECSC was established) to 1979 (with the first direct elections). This is because the issues that were raised by those promoting a greater role for the parliament (selection of MEPs and prerogatives of the EP) were partially resolved:

1. MEPs were selected by their national parliaments (not by governments).
2. The EP had, since its establishment, a modicum of power because, at minimum, it could influence decisions through the consultation procedure.
3. Starting in 1970 it also gained some control over the budget.

Compared to developments in the ECSC and EEC prior to the first direct elections (and to those in other IGOs), the status quo in the European institutions starting in the 1980s is considered to have only strayed "slightly" from norm prescriptions.

Table 7.2 includes the values for the strength of the parliamentary oversight norm and for the degree to which the status quo departed from

---

[10] The CoE is the only IGO discussed in the five comprehensive tables summarizing Chapters 3–7 that is not one of the six major IGOs discussed in this book. I include it in Table 7.2 because of its very important relationship (through the broadening strategy) to the establishment of a parliamentary assembly in the ECSC. The case is not included, however, in the assessment of the seven hypotheses in Chapter 8.

norm prescriptions. It also includes the overall measure of normative pressure, assessed as the interaction between the two aforementioned gauges.

While democratic pressures have been defined as the interaction between the strength of a norm and the degree to which the status quo is perceived to depart from the norm prescription, the focus on the European institutions also allows us to utilize a more direct gauge of such pressures, the one of public opinion. This is possible because of the wealth of opinion polls that have been collected through the Eurobarometer over the years.

Figure 7.6 uses such polls conducted in 1973, 1975, 1976, 1977, and 1978 to assess support for direct elections. It indicates that such pressures indeed grew substantially over that five-year span, while the European Council was being established and when one would expect perceptions that the organization was straying away from the parliamentary oversight norm prescription increased.

This alternative gauge of normative pressure is more refined than the one included in Table 7.2 and allows us to differentiate between the years immediately preceding the direct elections. Overall, while in 1973 barely half of respondents said that they supported direct elections, by 1978, right before they were held, support increased to more than 70 percent. The public support (or pressure) for such elections in each EEC member-state is actually even more relevant than the aggregate numbers for all countries might suggest. Indeed, in 1973, in the three new EEC members (Denmark, Ireland, and United Kingdom) less than half of respondents (36%, 45%, and 33%, respectively) had supported the elections. In France, even in the post–De Gaulle era, barely half (51%) were in favor of direct elections. By 1978, support increased substantially in all four countries (54% in Denmark, 67% in Ireland, 63% in the United Kingdom, and 67% in France).[11] These changes were particularly important considering that all states had to support direct elections for the decision to be passed by the Council.

Figure 7.6 also includes a measure of the strength of the parliamentary oversight norm (based on the measure XCONST). This score is very high and remains constant throughout the 1970s. This suggests that the simple strength of democratic norms is not sufficient to explain developments

---

[11] See Eurobarometer 10 (published January 1979) and Eurobarometer 12 (published December 1979).

TABLE 7.2. *Normative Pressures Involving Parliamentary Bodies and Reactions to Pressures*

Rule involves	League of Nations /1919	UN/1945	Council of Europe/1949–1951	ECSC/1951	ECSC/mid-1950s	EEC/1960s
	Establish parliamentary body	Establish parliamentary body	–Establish parliamentary body –Selection of PACE members –Frequency of PACE meetings –Prerogatives of PACE	Establish parliamentary body	–Selection of members of parliamentary Assembly –Prerogatives of Assembly	–Selection of members of EP –Prerogatives of Assembly
Norm strength	H	L	H	H	H	H
Departure from norm prescription	M	H	H	H	M	M
Normative pressure	H	M	VH	VH	H	H
Strategy	CN	CN	NA; BA	Y	BN; CA	BN; CA; CN
Outcome	NC	NC	PC; AC	C	NC	C

Note: CN = challenging norm; NN = narrowing norm; BN = broadening norm; CA = challenging application of norm; NA = narrowing application of norm; BA = broadening application of norm; W = withstanding; C = originally promoted change; NC = no change; PC = partial change; AC = alternative change.

* Strategy used to defuse normative pressure from other norm.

EEC/1970s	EEC/mid-1980s	EU/early 1990s	World Bank/1990s	EU/late 1990s and 2000s	UN/1990s and 2000s	WTO/1990s and 2000s
–Direct elections of EP –EP prerogatives	–Cooperation procedure –Use of QMV in Council	–Co-decision procedure –Use of QMV in Council	Establish parliamentary body	–Co-decision procedure –Use of QMV in Council	Establish parliamentary body	Establish parliamentary body
H	H	H	H	H	H	H
M	L	L	H	L	H	H
H	M	M	VH	M	VH	VH
BN; BA*; CA; CN	BA*	NA; BA*	NA	NA; BA*	NA	W
C; AC	C; AC	PC	PC	C	PC	NC

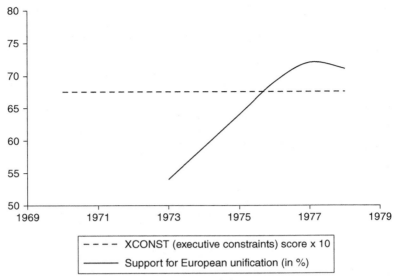

FIGURE 7.6. Support for Direct Elections of the EP.

surrounding the changes in the EP.[12] The increase in normative pressures and subsequent changes in the IGO rules were because of perceptions that the EEC was straying further from the prescriptions of the very strong parliamentary oversight norm.

What Actions Did Actors Opposing the New Rules Take under Normative Pressure?

When the League of Nations was established a number of officials called for the IPU to play an important role to resolve the "democratic deficiency" of the new IGO. The promoters of the parliamentary oversight norm applied considerable pressure to transform the IPU into an important institution within the League. However, these pressures were defused by those challenging the parliamentary oversight norm by setting it against the parliamentary independence one. Many IPU members believed that their organization could not maintain its independence if it were to become part of an intergovernmental structure. Therefore they

---

[12] Similar Eurobarometer polls conducted in the years preceding the Single European Act and the Maastricht Treaty also offer support for this argument. Public support for a greater role for the EP increased in the years immediately preceding both important developments, even though the strength of democratic norms was consistently high and hardly changed from 1979 to 1992. See Eurobarometer 38 (published December 1992).

preferred the external and weaker model of parliamentary oversight (Model A) over the internal and stronger one (Model B).

When the UN was established the normative pressures were smaller yet the question of parliamentary oversight was once more discussed in the IPU. Yet again, the IPU members promoting independence from the new global IGO were more numerous than those pushing for their organization to become an internal "consultative specialized agency." The moderate pressures were therefore quickly defused by those challenging the parliamentary oversight norm with the more powerful parliamentary independence one. To varying degrees, such pressures continued to exist throughout the history of the UN but were withstood by virtually all member-governments. Only in the 1990s, when they became very high, there appear to have been some vague attempts to defuse them by narrowing the application of the norm, as was the case of the informal and temporary Pilot Peoples' Assembly in 2000.

Other IGOs appear to have adopted a similar strategy of narrowing the application of norm by accepting weak and often informal interparliamentary bodies as their partners. One such example of the application of the narrowing strategy is the case of the World Bank that helped establish the Parliamentary Network on the World Bank. The WTO, on the other hand, offers an example of an IGO withstanding the parliamentary oversight normative pressures.

When very strong normative pressures for the establishment of a powerful PACE in the CoE were being applied, the opponents of such rules (primarily the United Kingdom) adopted multiple strategies for defusing them (as H_2 would suggest). They took several actions that can be interpreted as a strategy of narrowing the application of the parliamentary oversight norm. They accepted the establishment of PACE but only after they stripped it of any real power by limiting the prerogatives and the ability to select parliamentarians through direct elections and even by limiting the number of meetings of the new organ.

Opponents of PACE also used a strategy of broadening the application of the norm. First, they suggested the establishment of a world parliament alongside the European one that was being proposed in the CoE. Second, and more important, they included in the negotiations for PACE questions involving the emerging ECSC. In the end, such opponents were willing to offer somewhat greater power to the ECSC to defuse the normative pressures for a greater role for PACE. One can argue that the emergence of a relatively powerful assembly in the ECSC is partly because of the broadening strategy used in the CoE negotiations. Therefore, when negotiations for the Assembly's role in the ECSC came up, there was little that its opponents could do to alleviate the normative pressure, and they yielded to them.

The main strategy used by opponents of an increased role for the ECSC Assembly and later the EP, throughout the 1950s, 1960s, and 1970s, was the broadening of the norm. As discussed earlier, the confederalists made strong efforts to link parliamentary independence (and direct elections) with parliamentary oversight (and prerogatives of the parliamentary body). This strategy was different than the one of challenging the norm of parliamentary oversight used at the establishment of the League and UN, when only one norm and model was accepted. In the European institutions both norms were discussed purposefully at the same time, allowing for a circular argument that was effective in reducing the pressures.

Of course, the federalists fought to de-link the two issues (implicitly, countering the broadening strategy). They were successful in doing so in 1970 when they were able to gain budgetary powers for the EP. They were also successful in the late 1970s when they focused entirely on direct elections and were able to have them accepted by the confederalists.

Yet, by focusing almost entirely on the norm of democratic representation, the federalists encouraged their opponents to adopt arguments challenging this norm by offering an alternative communitarian model of representation (which emphasized the role of democratically elected governments) to the cosmopolitan one (emphasizing the role of all European citizens and their direct votes for MEPs). The confederalists argued that direct elections were not more democratic than the indirect system of selecting MEPs already in place. Moreover, as the public did not pay sufficient attention to the work of the parliamentary body, the indirect selection of MEPs that was in place led to a more effective organization than the one of direct elections. This latter argument reflects a strategy of challenging the application of the norm.

The eventual acceptance of direct elections can be considered as another example of the broadening strategy, but one focusing on the actions that derived from the norm rather than on the norm itself. Indeed, in 1975 the confederalists (who were trying to defuse the parliamentary oversight normative pressures) included the founding of the European Council on the same agenda with direct elections. For them the link between the two was not based on normative arguments at that point. It was essentially seen as a bargain that was beneficial to both sides, just as Peyrefitte had suggested as far back as 1960.

After direct elections were held and the departure from the norm prescription declined, as expected on the basis of H_4, the broadening strategy was used only at the action level (rather than at the norm level) when a deal appeared to be made through the acceptance of more qualified majority voting at the same time as the cooperation procedure was introduced. The gradual shifts toward more co-decision voting (giving power to the EP) have also taken place as part of deals placing increasingly more emphasis on QMV. These too can be seen as examples of the strategy of broadening the application of the norm.

Virtually all reform proposals involving the EP over the past two decades that have focused on introducing the co-decision procedure in more policy areas were met with narrowing strategies from those opposing a greater role for the Parliament. This was reflected in the Maastricht Treaty's narrowing of the EP role to only one of the three pillars. It is also reflected in the decision to give it prerogatives over only some (not all) policy areas, successively, in 1997, 2001, 2004, and 2007.

What Was the Outcome?

Throughout most of the history of the global IGOs discussed here, normative pressures did not lead to the establishment of transnational parliamentary bodies. The challenging strategies adopted at the founding of the League and UN and the narrowing ones of the post–Cold War have led to only token changes.

Developments in the European institutions stand in contrast with those in the global IGOs. A long-term view suggests that the normative pressures did have an impact on the empowerment of the EP. However, in most cases, the use of strategies of challenging, broadening, and narrowing led to many instances in which there were only partial or alternative changes. The most effective strategy for the confederalists appears to have been the one of broadening of norms that linked direct elections to broadening of EP prerogatives. This was fairly successful for delaying changes in the 1960s and 1970s. Once the broadening strategy at the norm level could not be used, starting in the 1980s, most reform attempts went through quickly, even if each time narrowing strategies made them only partially successful (as expected on the basis of H_7), giving the EP a role in only some policy areas and not in others. Also, some of the broadening strategies at the level of norm application led to bargains between the federalists and confederalists – ones that not only gave the EP greater power but also introduced important changes to the intergovernmental decision-making bodies.

Would Outcomes Have Been the Same in Absence of Normative Pressures and Reactions to Pressures?

The parliamentary oversight norm was very strong among members at the establishment of the CoE and the ECSC. This led to the inclusion of transnational parliamentary bodies in the two IGOs. Although the idea of establishing such bodies had been discussed for almost a century prior to their emergence in European institutions, the creation of parliamentary assemblies in the two organizations was viewed as a revolutionary idea. This outcome is difficult to comprehend in the absence of strong democratic norms and pressures. The fact that parliamentary bodies have spread to other IGOs, in other regions of the world, once their member states became more democratic further supports the argument that norms have played an essential part in this particular institutional development.

The different trajectories of PACE and the EP also suggest that, despite the equally strong democratic norms among a similar set of member-states, the strategies used to defuse normative pressures indeed have an important effect on the institutional balance within IGOs. Moreover, arguments based on power politics would have great difficulties in explaining the variance in the degree of success of the multiple attempts to empower the EP.

Overall, the norm of parliamentary oversight appears to be the most recent of the five main democratic norms discussed in this book to truly influence IGO rules. Perhaps this is because of the complexity of the norm and its linkages to the norm of parliamentary independence. However, over the past six decades it has become just as pervasive as the other four ("older") ones) discussed in this book.

8

Conclusions: Summarizing and Interpreting the Main Trends

Summing Up the Answers to the Questions

This study began from one main question: How have democratic norms shaped IGO decision-making rules? In Chapter 2 I posited that norms are more likely to affect rules when normative pressures for change are high. I also argued that, even when under normative pressure to change such rules, international actors rarely yield to them, accepting the exact changes that are proposed. More often they will adopt strategies of challenging, narrowing, and broadening the interpretation of the norm itself or of its application. I developed a set of seven hypotheses based on these arguments.

To assess the plausibility of these hypotheses, I considered attempts to change decision-making rules in six major IGOs across time. The cases were organized across five democratic norms: fair representation of states, fair voting, transparency, nongovernmental actor participation, and transnational parliamentary oversight. In Chapters 3 to 7 I sought answers to the same set of six questions for the evolution of rules related to each of the five norms. In this chapter, I sum up the answers to these six questions from the five empirical chapters.

What Types of Decision-Making Rules Were Being Established or Changed?

By taking a long-term view of IGOs over the past century rather than a short one, covering only a few years or decades (as many studies do), I found that there was considerable variance across IGO rules. If one were to focus only on the six major IGOs included in this study, there have been, on average, more than a dozen attempts to alter such rules throughout each one of their histories. There were attempts to alter the number of permanent and non-permanent members in executive bodies, the relative weight of votes, the existence and use of vetoes, the ways in which nongovernmental actors can participate in implementing and shaping IGO decisions, the independence of NGAs included in the work of intergovernmental organizations (IGOs), public access to information rules for various IGO bodies, the existence of IGO parliamentary bodies, their prerogatives, and the selection processes of representatives in these bodies, as well as other decision-making rules. Overall, Tables 3.1, 4.1, 5.1, 6.1, and 7.2 include seventy-two distinct instances when there were attempts to adopt new rules or alter existing ones.

Did Actors Invoke Democratic Norms to Pressure Others in Accepting New Decision-Making Rules?

The empirical chapters showed that, indeed, in most of these cases, those who were trying to alter the status quo presented the new rules as democratic. They felt that by drawing on domestic democratic analogies, and by framing their arguments as deriving from generally accepted democratic norms, they would be more successful in bringing about the changes they desired than if they had not referred to the norms. Of course, there are some important exceptions. Immediately after World War I, even though fair participation was presented as an important norm (as it was presented even at the founding of the Concert of Europe), its democratic character was not emphasized as strongly as its relationship to the sovereignty norm. Similarly, attempts to include more NGOs in IGO work before the 1990s were not presented as necessary democratic changes but, rather, as a way to improve the efficiency of IGOs. Only the pro-NGO movements of the past few decades resorted to democratic norms to promote changes to IGO policies on NGO participation. Yet, throughout most IGO histories discussed in this study, the changes to these rules were promoted by being described as democratic, with various actors invoking different domestic analogies to increase the normative pressures for reforms or, in some cases, to defuse such pressures.

How Powerful Were Such Pressures?

The cases discussed in the empirical sections of the study showed that normative pressures experienced both ups and downs across time in virtually all IGOs and all norms. In part, their variance can be explained by the fluctuations in the strength of the democratic norms. By taking a

TABLE 8.1. *Distribution of Normative Pressure Across Cases*

Normative pressure	Very low	Low	Moderate	High	Very high
Proportion of cases	8.1%	12.7%	41.6%	21.1%	16.5%

long-term perspective, the study was able to discern between periods when domestic democratic norms (that in turn shaped the ones in IGOs) were becoming stronger, weaker, or stayed at about the same levels. However, the pressures also varied as a result of changes in the degree to which the rules departed from what democratic norms prescribed. This sometimes happened gradually, as in the cases when decolonization slowly raised pressures to increase the number of non-permanent members in the UNSC or when the domestic intrusiveness of the European institutions led to a greater need to keep them in check through a strong European Parliament. Other times legitimacy crises sparked by various scandals surrounding IGOs led to rapid changes in the normative pressures.

The various gauges that were used to assess the level of such normative pressures led me to characterize about 40 percent as "very high" or "high," 40 percent as "moderate," and 20 percent as "low" or "very low" (see Table 8.1). It is somewhat expected that there are fewer instances of low and very low pressures in the cases where there were attempts to alter rules. It is less expected, however, that there were very many cases when actors did not wait for pressures to be high (and acted when they were moderate or even low and very low) before attempting to change the rules in IGOs. Overall, there was considerable variance across time and IGOs with regard to such pressures.

What Actions Did Actors Opposing the New Rules Take under Normative Pressure?

As I explain in greater detail later in this chapter, in the vast majority of cases when normative pressures were applied, those opposing changes in rules sought to defuse them by using at least one strategy (and often multiple strategies) of narrowing, broadening, or challenging. They attempted to alter proposals both at the norm level and at the level of implementation. In only about 5 percent of cases actors accepted the proposed changes without using any of these strategies, yielding to the pressures. Tables 3.1, 4.1, 5.1, 6.1, and 7.2 suggest that in yet another approximately 6 percent of cases they simply withstood the pressures. This latter statistic needs to be interpreted with great care. It is quite likely that in

TABLE 8.2. *Distribution of Outcomes Across Cases*

Outcome	Originally promoted change	Partial change	Alternative change	No change
Proportion of cases	23.8%	40.5%	22.6%	13.1%

many instances actors did not even try to alter existing rules through normative pressures, knowing that those supporting the status quo were going to withstand such pressures. Therefore, the research design may lead to a built-in bias toward cases in which withstanding was unlikely to take place. Nevertheless, the fact that in the vast majority of cases actors adopted the more subtle strategies of challenging, narrowing, and broadening, rather than the more straightforward ones of yielding or withstanding (that the literature tends to emphasize), supports one of the most important arguments of this study.

What Were the Outcomes of the Attempts to Adopt or Change Rules?

The seventy-two cases had eighty-four outcomes. That is because in twelve cases there were multiple outcomes (the originally promoted change and an alternative change or a partial change and an alternative change). Table 8.2 illustrates the variance across all cases. It shows that the outcomes that have been less discussed in the norms literature, of partial change and alternative change, are together almost twice as common as the traditional ones of the originally promoted change and of no change.

Would Outcomes Have Been the Same in Absence of Normative Pressures and Reactions to Pressures?

Together, the two previous observations regarding strategies and outcomes suggest that, indeed, by focusing only on the straightforward processes through which a norm and its prescriptions are completely accepted or not accepted at all, we may miss a great deal of the actual dynamics and the subtle changes taking place in IGOs. Perhaps more important, the chapters have shown that by only considering arguments related to power and effectiveness of IGOs, we would not be able to fully understand many of the changes that took place across IGO rules over the past century. Normative pressures have indeed led to changes in IGO rules, even if in most cases such changes were not the exact ones that those seeking to alter the status quo had originally promoted.

Plausibility of Hypotheses

In Chapter 2 I offered a set of seven hypotheses. I referred to many of these hypotheses throughout Chapters 3 to 7, especially in their concluding sections. Nevertheless, as mentioned earlier, by focusing on individual cases, or even the relatively small number of cases for each individual norm, it is difficult to assess the plausibility of the hypotheses. This section therefore uses all seventy-two cases to offer a more complete evaluation of each of the seven hypotheses.

H_1: *Changes to IGO rules are more likely to take place when normative pressures are high.*

Table 8.3 offers some support for this baseline argument. One reason for the fairly weak support is that the study considers cases when actors attempted to alter IGO rules. It is very likely that, when norms and the departure from norm prescriptions were weak, there were simply fewer such attempts. Even taking into account this possible bias, the results nevertheless show that, when normative pressure is very low, it is highly unlikely for the originally promoted change to take place. As pressures increase, the likelihood of achieving the originally promoted changes increases considerably. For example, when pressure levels are high or very high, the likelihood that the originally promoted change will take place is about five times as high as in cases in which the normative pressures are low or very low. Just as important, Table 8.3 shows that, when normative pressures are very high, it becomes very likely (in more than 90% of cases) for the IGO to experience at least some change in rules.

Despite such observations, overall, there is only lukewarm support for this first hypothesis. This encourages us, as the theoretical arguments originally suggested, to "open up the black box" of the negotiations among states and consider the various actions actors took when confronted with normative pressures. In other words, we should expect that the final outcomes are not solely the result of the normative pressures but also the result of the strategies that were used to defuse them.

H_2: *The stronger the normative pressure for change, the more likely it is that actors will seek multiple strategies to defuse them.*

Table 8.4 offers support for this argument. It shows that when normative pressures are moderate, low, or very low it is unlikely that actors will apply multiple strategies for defusing them.[1] When they are high or very

---

[1] Cases of yielding or withstanding pressures are not counted here among such strategies.

TABLE 8.3. *Relationship between Strength of Normative Pressures and Outcomes*

Pressures	No change	Partial change	Alternative change	Originally promoted change
Very low	25%	50%	25%	0%
Low	8.33%	50%	33.3%	8.33%
Moderate	12.1%	45.5%	12.1%	30.3%
High	15%	20%	35%	30%
Very high	9.1%	45.5%	18.2%	27.3%

TABLE 8.4. *Relationship between Normative Pressures and Number of Strategies Used*

Strength of normative pressure	One strategy	Two or more strategies
Very low	80%	20%
Low	66.7%	33.3%
Moderate	65.4%	34.6%
High	26.7%	73.3%
Very high	44.4%	55.6%

high, they apply multiple strategies in the majority of cases. These findings offer direct support for the arguments linking normative pressures to actors actions and, implicitly, to outcomes. As normative pressures increase, actors who want to defuse them are more likely to seek multiple strategies in the hope that one or more of them will work. These strategies, in turn, will increase the likelihood that some changes (partial or alternative ones) will take place. In other words, strong norms and pressures do not automatically translate into significant changes (as Table 8.3 indicated). Rather, they lead to significant reactions to defuse such pressures that, in turn, are likely to bring about some changes to IGO rules. I consider this to be one of the most important findings of this study.

H_3: *When under normative pressure, actors who want to avoid changing IGO rules are more likely to attempt altering the interpretation of the norm when the norm is weak than when it is strong.*

Table 8.5 offers support for this argument. The likelihood that actors will use strategies to alter the interpretation of the norm (rather than the interpretation of their implementation) is one and a half times higher when norms are weak than when they are strong.

TABLE 8.5. *Relationship between Norm
Strength and Strategy Choice*

Norm strength	Alter interpretation of norm
Low	35.7%
Moderate	25.9%
High	23.9%

TABLE 8.6. *Relationship between Departure from
Norm Prescription and Strategy Choice*

Departure from norm prescription	Alter interpretation of actions deriving from norm
Low	86.7%
Moderate	63.3%
High	57.1%

H_4: *When under normative pressure, actors who want to avoid changing IGO
rules are more likely to attempt altering the interpretation of how to apply
the norm to the IGO when the status quo does not depart much from the
norm prescription than when it departs substantially from such prescription.*

Table 8.6 shows that, indeed, the smaller the degree to which the rules of
an IGO depart from norm prescriptions, the more likely it is that an actor
seeking to defuse normative pressures will attempt to offer an alternative
interpretation to what it means to apply that norm. Yet, interestingly, even
when it is very clear that the IGO rules are departing considerably from
norm prescriptions, it is still likely (in the majority of cases) that some
actors will still attempt to challenge, broaden, or narrow the understanding of how to apply the norm to IGO rules. Taken together with the findings reflected in Table 8.5, the ones of Table 8.6 indicate that actors are
overall more likely to attempt altering the interpretation of how to apply
a democratic norm to IGOs (in about two-thirds of all cases) than the
interpretation of the norms themselves. This finding reminds us of the difficulties in exporting democratic mechanisms "vertically," from states to
IGOs, compared to similar processes of "horizontal export," across states.

H_5: *When under normative pressure to change IGO rules that they do not
want to change, actors who attempt to alter the interpretation of a norm
will prefer the broadening strategy to the narrowing and to the challenging
strategy.*

TABLE 8.7. *Distribution of Strategies Used at the Norm Level*

Strategy	Proportion of cases
Broadening the norm	58.6%
Narrowing the norm	7.0%
Challenging the norm	34.5%

TABLE 8.8. *Distribution of Strategies Used at the Implementation Level*

Strategy	Proportion of cases
Broadening the understanding of the application of the norm	30.9%
Narrowing the understanding of the application of the norm	49.6%
Challenging the understanding of the application of the norm	19.7%

Table 8.7 supports the previous argument. It shows that in the majority of cases when actors applied a strategy intended to alter the understanding of a norm so as to defuse normative pressures, they preferred one of broadening.

H_6: *When under normative pressure to change IGO rules that they do not want to change, actors who attempt to alter the interpretation of the application of the norm will prefer the narrowing strategy to the broadening strategy and to the challenging strategy.*

This argument is also supported by the findings. Table 8.8 shows that in about half of the cases in which actors used a strategy intended to alter the understanding of the norm's application to IGO rules, they preferred the narrowing strategy.

H_7: *Challenging strategies are likely to lead to no changes in IGO rules; narrowing strategies are likely to lead to partial changes; broadening strategies are likely to lead to additional or alternative changes to such rules.*

Table 8.9 shows that for two of the three types of strategies (narrowing and broadening), the dominant outcome was the expected one. In almost two-thirds of all cases when the narrowing strategy was used, the outcome was one of partial change. Similarly, in 40 percent of cases when the broadening strategy was used, there were alternative changes to the rules.

TABLE 8.9. *Relationship between Strategies and Outcomes*

	Originally proposed change	Alternative change	Partial change	No change
Challenging	15.4%	19%	38.1%	29.8%
Narrowing	15%	17.5%	65%	2.5%
Broadening	24%	40%	30%	6%

The challenging strategy does not appear to be as "effective." Only in a little more than one-quarter of cases does it lead to the expected outcome of no change. In more than one-third of cases when the strategy was applied, states eventually accepted partial changes to the rules.

More broadly, Table 8.9 shows that the eventual outcomes are not entirely determined by the strategy that was used. There were many other cases in which the strategies did not lead to the dominant expected outcomes. There are multiple possible explanations for this finding. First, actors often used multiple strategies, hoping that at least one of them would defuse the pressures. Indeed, Table 8.9 shows that not all such strategies work equally well.

Additionally, it is likely that when actors challenge a norm or its application, they may do so simply as a bargaining tactic, hoping to reach a deal in which only partial or alternative changes to the rules actually take place. The fact that such actors often use multiple strategies of defusing normative pressures suggests that they may indeed be open to multiple outcomes, just as in the case of regular (material) bargaining processes. In fact, in some cases, they may seek multiple possible changes (for example, through the broadening strategy) simply to make negotiations more complex in the hope that this will delay or even completely stop the reform process.

Yet another explanation for the instances of "unsuccessful" use of such strategies for defusing normative pressures (that is, of cases when the originally proposed changes actually took place or when the outcome was not the dominant one expected for such a strategy) may simply be based on the weakness of the arguments that were used by those attempting to defuse the normative pressures. After all, not all situations allow for challenging, broadening, or narrowing strategies. There need to be strong arguments that allow those opposing the changes to the rules to be sufficiently convincing. To rephrase this statement in wording from existing literature, not all arguments can maneuver opponents "into a corner" from which they cannot find a "socially sustainable rebuttal" (Krebs and Jackson 2007, 36). One example of an argument that was used with some degree of success at one point in time but that could not be used later was the one challenging the equal voting norm in the UN in 1945. As a reminder, the British delegation in San Francisco argued that, because the P5 at that time represented more than half of the world's population, it was only appropriate that they have an advantage in the voting system. The fact that those supporting the veto in the UNSC adopted multiple strategies in 1945 may be a reflection of the relative weakness of this argument as well as of the importance of the rule that was at stake. As decolonization led to the decline in the French and British empires' population and as the split of China led to almost one billion people not being represented in the UN, the argument was not used again by the P5 after 1950. Ironically, the argument connecting countries' population to democratic voting in the UNSC was only brought up after 1992 by India, as it was claiming a permanent seat for itself in that UN body.

These observations and examples suggest that the relationship between strategies and outcomes is a complex one. More research is needed to explain the results of clashes between the various normative arguments used by actors in IGOs. This will allow us to understand better additional factors that affect outcomes of normative bargaining, such as the strength and specificity of norms, the power of those promoting the arguments, or the deals that are made by states outside the visible IGO debates. Such factors may be different or similar to the ones accounting for outcomes in material bargaining situations.

Before moving on to the broader conclusions that one can draw from this study, we need to emphasize two important aspects of the previous results. First, the tests of the arguments and expectations are based on operationalizations (such as the one of norm strength, departure from norm prescription, and strategy) that allow us to compare developments across (1) time, (2) different IGOs, and (3) different norms. This, inevitably, leads to gauges that are less precise than those one would develop for single cases across short periods of time. Examples of such gauges (such as public support for reforms in the European institutions or the number and press coverage of NGO protests) were offered in several chapters. Future research on such narrower cases, using more specific measures of normative pressure, can complement this broader survey and further assess the degree of support for the present study's arguments.

Second, while the findings of this book are expected to be of use for understanding developments involving other issues, beyond the narrow ones of changes to rules in IGOs, it is also important to be aware of the potential differences between this study and others. For example, the proportion of cases when actors tried shaping norms rather than their application is likely to be determined by the relative strength of such norms. Many studies in the literature have been interested in the emergence and empowerment of weak norms, especially related to human rights, rather than the export of already powerful norms from one realm to another. It is therefore likely that the patterns in the use of strategies discussed here, in which powerful and long-standing domestic democratic norms were involved, will differ from those in cases involving newer (and weaker) norms. In the latter cases, as the understanding of norms is still being shaped, status quo actors may be more inclined to try shaping the norms themselves, rather than the actions deriving from the norms.

Moreover, one should note that the five norms discussed here all fall under the broad "democratic umbrella." Indeed, there is a general agreement that without disaggregating democracy one cannot truly tackle the democratic deficit of IGOs (Barton et al. 2006, 193) and, implicitly, that various norms need to (or at least can) be discussed simultaneously. This makes such norms more conducive to the broadening strategy because their democratic character offers the glue allowing them (and their application to IGO rules) to be discussed simultaneously on the same reform agenda. It is possible that other norms, relevant for other cases, may not fit as easily under a broader normative umbrella and, therefore, the strategies used to defuse normative pressures may follow different patterns.

Theoretical and Practical Implications of the Findings

Despite the aforementioned caveats, the preceding findings nevertheless lead to important and fairly generalizable conclusions of theoretical and practical significance. Some of these were suggested briefly throughout Chapters 2 and 1, respectively. Here I discuss the implications of the findings in greater detail.

Normative Pressures

A first important implication for international relations theories is that the processes through which norms shape outcomes are more complex than the literature has so far suggested. Norm strength and the departure of the status quo from norm prescription determine together the likelihood that change will actually occur. This allows us to understand many cases in which strong norms did not have an impact on events.

Indeed, norms are seen as useful concepts in the social sciences because they allow for linkages between human behaviors in different social environments. They travel across space (for example, from one country to another) and across levels of social interaction (for example, from the domestic to the international realm). Yet, in many cases, even though the strength of a norm in one state, or at one level, may be equal to its strength in another, we may observe changes only in one locus, not in all. The study suggests that the departure from the norm prescription is just as important for understanding norm-induced change as the strength of the norm. One important implication of this conclusion is that the study of de-legitimizing scandals in international relations (the ultimate type of departure from norm prescriptions) needs to move beyond the spectacular yet simplistic case studies and engage in more comprehensive comparative and even large N research, just as it has in studies of the domestic realm (e.g., Thompson 2000).

There is an additional reason why we should pay attention more closely to the departure from norm prescription (this second component of normative pressure). Whereas norm strength appears to change slowly, the application of norm prescriptions seems to be altered faster. The adoption of new rules and laws may reduce or increase the perceived departure of the status quo from the norm's prescription. Scandals, mentioned earlier, may lead to rapid changes in the perceived departure from the norm's prescriptions. As change in the social realm is often a result of both slow, incremental shifts in structural factors and events that quickly alter existing conditions, it is important that we analyze both types of factors triggering changes.

Strategies of Defusing the Normative Pressures

An even more important theoretical implication of this study is that norms should not be viewed simply as "magic wands" that, once in existence and empowered, can change events and institutions virtually automatically. There are important battles for shaping the normative environment and for determining the actions that need to be taken based on norms. Actors rarely accept norms and the actions supposedly deriving from such norms without putting up a fight. They attempt to alter the understandings of norms and their application to the cases at hand through strategies of challenging, narrowing, and broadening.

At a broader level, the study offers an additional way of understanding the continuous interactions between agency and structure that the IR literature has been emphasizing for almost three decades (Wendt

1987). Indeed, the changes to normative pressures discussed in this book are often the result of structural changes (that lead to slow shifts in democratic norms or slow changes in material capabilities).[2] Yet, actors react to such pressures. Their strategy choices, and, ultimately, the outcomes of their negotiations, are partially based on the arguments that are available to them. These, in turn, are dictated by structural factors (shifts in countries' populations, changes in countries' economic wealth, or increases in the number of states in the international system). Conversely, the new rules that emerge from such interactions between agents also contribute to shaping the normative environment. For example, once smaller states were accepted in the League Council, the expectations that any IGO body will include at least some small powers increased. In other words, many of the empirical sections of this book can be understood as examples of the mutual constitution between agency and structure.

In seeking to develop a more complete understanding of the interactions between agency and structure and of the normative battles that take place, this research has also generated a series of additional important questions that need to be pursued beyond this study: When and how can actors more effectively challenge a norm or its implementation? When and how can they limit the understanding of a norm or of its implications? What happens when two norms clash? Which one is more likely to win out? Perhaps more importantly, based on the results of this study, what happens when multiple norms come together under a broader normative umbrella? Do they mutually strengthen each other or do they lead to the erosion of one norm and the empowerment of the other? Such questions are important beyond the study of IGOs and deserve further consideration.

The Strategy of Broadening Norms and Application of Norms
Future research should, in particular, seek to understand better the use of broadening strategies. As this study has shown, it is a strategy that has been used many times by actors trying to avoid taking certain actions promoted through normative pressures. It is surprising that the strategy has not received more attention because it is analogous to the very common one of issue-linkage in regular (material) bargaining processes.

---

[2] Of course, they are also shaped by discrete unexpected events involving individuals, such as those surrounding the scandal that led Paul Wolfowitz to step down from the presidency of the World Bank or the death of Roosevelt only a few months before the UN was established.

The previous discussions emphasized that the broadening strategy was, in fact, more common for actors trying to alter the understanding of democratic norms than those of narrowing or challenging. It was also used often in altering the interpretation of norm application.

This finding should not surprise us. There are two main reasons why the broadening strategy should be preferred to other strategies. First, the norms literature has suggested that the narrower norms are, the less likely they will be challenged or altered. Conversely, when the normative argument is loose, there are multiple "rhetorical strands" that ensure that those who want to reshape the argument can indeed do so (Krebs and Jackson 2007, 48). If an actor opposes a norm and is only taking action to reduce the pressure that results from it, we would expect that it prefers a normative framework that allows for ambiguity rather than specificity. States that intend to violate the anti-torture norm, for example, would prefer having loose definitions, which can later be reinterpreted so as to match their interests, rather than very specific ones that they will be pressured to follow more closely. This logic is behind the ambiguous wording of international treaties seeking broad state acceptance rather than strong actions.

The second reason the strategy of broadening is expected to be preferred by actors is that it brings other norms and/or actions into the debate. As mentioned earlier, the actor may see this strategy as developing into a package deal that involves not only costs (as the original norm and its implementation alone would) but also benefits. In addition, like any package deal, its acceptance by multiple actors involves time-consuming, convoluted, and uncertain processes. In fact, it may not be accepted at all by a majority of actors. In such cases, the actor that initiated the broadening may be seen as very successful because the strategy reduced the normative pressure without triggering any real change. Moreover, there are important cases (such as the one in which the United States and its allies promoted NGA independence in the ILO in addition to fair state representation) in which the acceptance of such package deals was followed solely by actions derived from the additional norms that had been tacked on and not by the ones the actors had been originally pressured to take. The interest in broadening strategies is therefore practical in nature, and not just theoretical.

The Use of Analogies
Another important implication of this research is that domestic analogies play an important role in shaping international outcomes. This

observation runs counter to a long tradition in IR that discarded the usefulness of such analogies (e.g., Waltz 1979). Yet, as the empirical sections of this book emphasized, practitioners often used domestic democratic mechanisms and norms both when seeking changes to IGO rules and when opposing such changes. They often sought examples for the usefulness of specific democratic mechanisms from the state level. For example, when seeking to establish oversight bodies and transparency rules for IGOs, officials sometimes requested advice from experts on similar domestic mechanisms (Grigorescu 2008). Of course, in all such cases actors used the interpretations of analogies that best suited their purposes. Yet, overall, the domestic models have come to influence IGO rules considerably, from the ones determining voting rules to those governing the functioning of transnational parliaments.

The Trend Toward more Democratic Rules in IGOs

Perhaps the most important practical observation derived from this study is that there have been important, albeit often slow, continuous changes in IGOs over more than a century that have led IGO decision-making rules to move closer to domestic democratic models. These changes have been in great part the result of democratic normative pressures.

The empirical sections showed that in most cases status quo states seeking to alleviate democratic normative pressures avoided directly challenging a norm and its application or withstanding the normative pressures. Most often they accepted partial changes (especially when they decided to alter the interpretation of the norm's application) or sought alternative ones (especially when they attempted to alter the norm's understanding). Usually, the latter concessions led to changes in rules of other IGOs or changes to different rules within the IGO. Yet, overall, in one instance or another, they all eventually led to rules that were closer to domestic democratic models.

These changes to rules often appear to be small ones. Moreover, in some cases, such as the advances in transparency in the League or the UN, the changes that took place were reversible. Yet, even such a "two steps forward one back" dynamic has led to a consistent advancement over the past century toward IGO rules and practices that are closer to the ones of democratic domestic systems. Moreover, one should note that the number of narrowing and broadening strategies available at one point is limited. Once some narrowing or broadening strategies are adopted (and partial and alternative changes take place), it becomes more difficult to find yet other ways to defuse pressures. When normative pressures are later applied, the originally promoted changes are even more likely to occur in the future. An example of this process is the one on the EEC in which, as soon as direct elections for MEPs were accepted, and the broadening strategy could not be applied as before, many more reforms followed that truly allowed the European Parliament to play an oversight role over the other European institutions.

Overall, it is difficult to imagine IGOs ever reverting to the exclusionary practices of the Concert of Europe. It is just as difficult to imagine them reverting to the secretive practices prior to World War I or even to the ones of the Cold War. Even though the first parliamentary assemblies in the immediate World War II era seemed at best symbolic yet useless institutions, now it is increasingly common to hear that yet another IGO has established such a body or that an existing parliamentary assembly has acquired new powers. Such trends appear, at least for now, to be unidirectional toward "more democracy." In other words, just as the number of democratic countries and institutions has continued to grow across time, despite the existence of counter-waves of democracy (Huntington 1991), IGOs have moved toward adopting and applying decision-making rules more closely related to the ones characterizing democratic polities despite fluctuations in the strength of democratic norms and democratic pressures.

The study needs to offer yet another note of caution. While democratic advances are generally viewed as positive developments (hence their normative character), the messy processes that lead to such advances can have, at least in the short-term, negative implications. One such important implication is the tendency to develop informal mechanisms either to narrow the application of a norm or to broaden its application by complementing some formal rules with informal ones. For example, when IGOs adopted policies allowing for greater public access to information, states have tended to replace some of their formal meetings (in the League, UN, or WTO) with informal (and secretive) ones. Such meetings have now become closed not just to outsiders of the organization but also to many state-members, thus leading to a status quo that is, de facto, less transparent than the original one, before the formal reforms took place.

Despite the similarities between democratic developments in the domestic realm and those in the international realm, this book has shown that there are also important differences in the applicability of democratic models at the two levels. Such differences also need to be taken into account in understanding the general direction in which IGOs are headed.

A first observation is that, because democracy emerged in domestic systems much earlier than in the international realm, virtually all attempts to apply democratic norms to IGOs have used domestic models. Moreover, the domestic models that were applied to IGOs have generally been well-developed ones, which had already been tried at the state level. Because of that, we may not experience in IGOs quite the same types of "growing pains" associated with democratic trends as we saw in domestic ones. For example, when IGOs began adopting public information policies, they could already use the experiences of the dozens of states that had accepted freedom of information laws. The battles over the type of information that should be made available, the procedures for requesting it, the procedures for challenging refusals to grant it, and the time frames in which such requests must receive answers had already been fought at the state level. IGOs simply copied many of the same procedures that were present in national FOI laws, altering them only slightly. This suggests that, once IGOs accept a new democratic norm, they may move more swiftly than states to apply it.

This optimistic conclusion should be balanced with another argument. Precisely because the debates surrounding democracy in IGOs are taking place after the battles have already been fought at the domestic level and because IGOs now need to catch up and apply multiple democratic norms, the clashes in the international realm appear to be more about which democratic norm is more important and should be applied first. The intense use of the broadening strategy at the norm level illustrates this trend. As powerful states continue to have the greatest influence in IGOs, when multiple democratic rules are set on the agenda, the rules that are more likely to be altered are those that lead to benefits for this group of states or that are at least less costly for them. It is not surprising therefore that IGOs have made greater strides in improving transparency and NGO participation than in altering representation and voting rules to make them more "fair" (whether fairness derives from a communitarian or cosmopolitan model).

This trend is especially interesting when comparing it to domestic ones. In the domestic realm, when strong leaders want to maintain as much control over domestic politics as possible and simultaneously show their support for democratic norms, they are likely to accept the more direct and formal aspects of democracy, such as those surrounding elections and the functioning of parliamentary assemblies. However, they are unlikely to allow for less visible and often informal changes, such as the empowerment of civil society or increased free flow of information that broaden the spectrum of actors involved in the political process. In the post–Cold War era such incomplete processes of democratization, favoring some democratic norms over others, have led to the emergence of many "illiberal democracies," in which fairly correct elections produce governments that are not kept in check by other domestic actors and that have encroached on the rights of various societal groups (Zakaria 2003, 89–118).

This domestic trend appears to be the opposite of the one in the international realm, in which the emphasis has been on encouraging transparency and NGO participation rather than on more egalitarian voting and representation rules. The more visible changes in IGO transparency, NGO participation, internal oversight mechanisms, and, more broadly, the development of IGO accountability systems have, not surprisingly, led to a strong emphasis in the literature on this type of IGO democratization (see, e.g., Woods 1999; Kahler 2004; Grigorescu 2007; Tallberg et al. 2013) and a relative neglect of the other facets of democratic processes.

Power Relations in IGOs and in the International Realm

Yet another important long-term implication of the findings of this book is that the application of democratic norms to IGOs will affect power relations among states as well as between state and non-state actors. Such shifts in power may take place both in IGOs and outside of them. The IR literature has emphasized that IGO rules are shaped by power (e.g., Mearsheimer 1994). At the same time, power relations are shaped by IGO rules (e.g., Gruber 2005). Indeed, decision-making rules involving participation, voting, and access to information affect the ability of actors to get others to do what they would not otherwise do (Dahl 1957). If, for instance, Brazil were to be accepted as a permanent member of the UNSC as a result of the normative pressures for reform, its influence in Latin America, and even in the world, would increase considerably. If India were to be admitted as a permanent member of the UNSC, the dynamics of its relations with its neighbors (especially Pakistan) are also likely to be affected. As NGOs acquire greater access to information and to the decision-making process of the World Bank, the NGOs headquartered in the developed world, with greater material resources and know-how, are more likely to benefit from such changes and become even more powerful than the ones from the developing world.

Of course, as some actors will gain power through such processes, others will have their power eroded. Most obvious, if democratic rules become more widespread, the traditional great powers of IGOs, such as the United States, Russia, France, the United Kingdom, and China will find themselves "more equal" to all other member-states (at least within IGOs), similar to the process that led power-wielding individuals at the state-level to lose some of their political and economic influence as domestic democratic rules were being established. Not surprisingly, in almost all cases discussed in this book, great powers were the ones that were most likely to oppose the democratic normative pressures for reform, even though some of them were long-standing democracies.

As the battles over IGO democracy will continue to unfold, it is possible that other actors, such as NGOs, national parliaments, transnational parliamentary assemblies, and even the general public, will become more involved than before. Yet, as the empirical chapters of this book have shown, great powers are likely to remain the main players deciding on IGO rules for a long time to come.

Because of such great power opposition, the democratic trends have led to very slow changes in IGO rules and, in some cases, have been followed by reversals. Yet, looking back over the past two centuries, as global democratic norms have become more powerful, the general direction of the messy trends in IGOs appears to be the same one as in the domestic realm and in all other levels of human interaction.

Works Cited

Acharya, Amitav. 2004. "How Ideas Spread: Whose Norms Matter? Norm Localization and Institutional Change in Asian Regionalism." *International Organization*, 58: 239–275.

African Union. 2000. "Constitutive Act of the African Union," at http://www.au.int/en/sites/default/files/ConstitutiveAct_0.pdf

Agence Internationale D'Information Pour La Presse. 1978. "European Elections," 579: 5.

1979. "France: Gaullist Memorandum," 590: 3.

Alger, Chadwick. 2003. "Searching for Democratic Potential in Emerging Global Governance." In *Transnational Democracy in Critical and Comparative Perspective: Democracy's Range Reconsidered.* Bruce Morrison ed. London: Ashgate, 87–106.

Almond, Gabriel, and Sidney Verba. 1963. *The Civic Culture.* Princeton: Princeton University Press.

Ameli, Saied Reza. 2011. "The Organisation of the Islamic Conference, Accountability and Civil Society." In *Building Global Democracy: Civil Society and Accountable Global Governance.* Jan Aart Scholte ed. Cambridge, UK: Cambridge University Press, 146–162.

Annan, Kofi. 1998. Address to the World Economic Forum Davos, Switzerland, 31 January 1998. UN SG/SM/6448

Archibugi, Daniele. 1993. "The Reform of the UN and Cosmopolitan Democracy: A Critical Review." *Journal of Peace Research,* 30(3): 301–315.

Archibugi, Daniele, Mathias Koenig-Archibugi, and Raffaele Marchetti. 2012. *Global Democracy: Normative and Empirical Perspectives.* Cambridge: Cambridge University Press.

Audley, John, and Ann Florini. 2001. "Overhauling the WTO: Opportunity at Doha and Beyond." *Carnegie Endowment for International Peace Policy Brief,* 6: 1–7.

Augustyn, Maja, and Cosimo Monda. 2011. "Transparency and Access to Documents in the EU: Ten Years on from the Adoption of Regulation

1049." *EIPAscope*, 1: 17–20, at http://www.eipa.eu/files/repository/eipa-scope/20110912103927_EipascopeSpecialIssue_Art2.pdf.

Axelrod, Robert. 1986. "An Evolutionary Approach to Norms." *American Political Science Review*, 80(4): 1095–1111.

Bailey, Sydney Dawson, and Sam Daws. 2005. *The Procedure of the UN Security Council*. Oxford: Clarendon Press.

Bank for International Settlements. 1930. "Statutes of the Bank for International Settlements," at http://www.bis.org/about/statutes-en.pdf.

Bank Information Center. 2013. "Access to Information at the World Bank," at http://www.bicusa.org/issues/wbtransparency.

Barfield, Claude. 1994, June 26. "Will the World Trade Organization Work? – Sure It Will – If We Resist Protectionist Pressures." *Washington Post*, p. C3.

Barkin, Samuel J. 2003. "Realist Constructivism." *International Studies Review*, 5(3): 325–342.

Barton, John H., Judith L. Goldstein, Timothy E. Josling, and Richard H. Steinberg. 2006. *The Evolution of the Trade Regime: Politics, Law, and Economics of the GATT and the WTO*. Princeton: Princeton University Press.

BBC. 2005, April 15. "World Bank and IMF 'Undemocratic,'" at http://news.bbc.co.uk/go/pr/fr/-/2/hi/business/4450749.stm.

Beattie, Alan. 2010, April 26. "Reform of Voting Rights Secures Capital Boost for World Bank." *Financial Times*, at http://www.ft.com/intl/cms/s/0/cb0e63e8-5ocb-11df-bc86-00144feab49a.html.

Beckmann, David. 1991. "Recent Experiences and Emerging Trends." In *Nongovernmental Organizations and the World Bank: Cooperation for Development*. Samuel Paul and Arturo Israel eds. Washington, DC: World Bank, 134–154.

Beigbeder, Yves. 1979. "The United States' Withdrawal from the International Labor Organization." *Relations industrielles / Industrial Relations*, 34(2): 223–240.

Bellamy, Richard, and Dario Castiglione. 1998. "Between Cosmopolis and Community: Three Models of Rights and Democracy within the European Union." In *Re-imagining Political Community: Studies in Cosmopolitan Democracy*. Daniele Archibugi, David Held, and Martin Köhler eds. Stanford, CA: Stanford University Press, 152–178.

Bengtsson, R., O. Elgström, and Jonas Tallberg. 2004. "Silencer or Amplifier? The European Union Presidency and the Nordic Countries." *Scandinavian Political Studies*, 27(3): 311–334.

Benner, Thorsten, Wolfgang H. Reinicke, and Jan M. Witte. 2004. "Multisectoral Networks in Global Governance: Towards a Pluralistic System of Accountability." *Government and Opposition*, 39 (2): 191–210.

Bienen, Derk, Volker Rittberger, and Wolfgang Wagner. 1998. "Democracy in the United Nations System: Cosmopolitan and Communitarian Principles." In *Re-imagining Political Community: Studies in Cosmopolitan Democracy*. Daniele Archibugi, David Held, and Martin Köhler eds. Stanford, CA: Stanford University Press, 287–308.

Blackhurst, Richard. 1998. "The Capacity of the WTO to Fulfill Its Mandate." In *The WTO as an International Organization*. A. O. Krueger ed., with C. Aturupane, Chicago: University of Chicago Press, 31–58.

Blanton, Thomas. 2002, March. "The International Movement for Freedom of Information." Paper presented at International Studies Association annual meeting. New Orleans, LA.

Bloom, Sol. 1948. *The Autobiography of Sol Bloom*. New York: G.P. Putnam's Sons.

Bob, Clifford. 2009. "Introduction: Fighting for New Rights." In *The International Struggle for New Human Rights*. Clifford Bob ed. Philadelphia: University of Pennsylvania Press.

Bohman, James, and William Rehg. 1997. *Deliberative Democracy: Essays on Reason and Politics*. Cambridge, MA: MIT Press.

Bohne, Eberhard. 2010. *The World Trade Organization: Institutional Development and Reform*. New York: Palgrave MacMillan.

Boli, John, and George M. Thomas. 1999. *Constructing World Culture: International Nongovernmental Organizations since 1875*. Stanford, CA: Stanford University Press.

Bolton, John R. 2000. "Should We Take Global Governance Seriously?" *Chicago Journal of International Law*, 1(2): 205–221.

Bonsal, Stephen. 1944. *Unfinished Business*. Garden City, NY: Doubleday, Doran and Company.

Bourantonis, Dimitris. 2005. *The History and Politics of UN Security Council Reform*. Abingdon, UK: Routledge.

Bourgeouis, Leon, and Lord Balfour. 1922, November. Letter to the President of the Council. Submitted to the Council on September, 1922, League of Nations Official Journal, Annex 423, C. 685.

Boutros-Ghali, Boutros. 1992. "An Agenda for Peace Preventive Diplomacy, Peacemaking and Peace-Keeping." A/47/277 – S/24111, at http://www.un.org/Docs/SG/agpeace.html.

Bowles, Ian A., and Cyril F. Kormos. 1995. "Environmental Reform at the World Bank: The Role of the U.S. Congress." *Virginia Journal of International Law*, 35: 777–839.

Brademas, John, and Fritz Heimann. 1998. "Tackling International Corruption: No Longer Taboo." *Foreign Affairs*, 77:5: 17–22.

Bretton Woods Project. 2010. "Analysis of World Bank Voting Reforms Governance Remains Illegitimate and Outdated," at http://www.bretton-woodsproject.org/art-566281.

Brierly, James Leslie. 1942. *The Law of Nations: An Introduction to the International Law of Peace*. 3rd Edition. Oxford: Oxford University Press.

Brinkhorst, Laurens Ian. 1999. "Transparency in the European Union." *Fordham International Law Journal*, 22: S128–S135.

Broms, Bengt. 1959. *The Doctrine of Equality of States as Applied in International Organizations*. Helsinki: University of Helsinki Press.

Brown, David L., and David C. Korten. 1991. "Working More Effectively with Nongovernmental Organizations" in *Nongovernmental Organizations and the World Bank: Cooperation for Development*. S. Paul and A. Israel eds. Washington, DC: World Bank.

Bulmer, Simon, and Wolfgang Wessels. 1986. *The European Council: Decision-Making in European Politics*. Basingstoke: Macmillan.

Bunyan, Tony. 1999. *Secrecy and Openness in the EU*. London: Kogan Page.

Burley, Anne-Marie. 1993. "Regulating the World: Multilateralism, International Law, and the Projection of the New Deal Regulatory State." In *Multilateralism Matters*. John Ruggie ed. New York: Columbia University Press, 125–156.

Butterworths, Sir Edward Hertslet. 1891.*The Map of Europe by Treaty: Showing the Various Political and Territorial Changes Which Have Taken Place since the General Peace of 1814*. Volume 4. Farnborough: Gregg.

Caliari, Aldo, and Frank Schroeder. 2002. *Reform Proposals for the Governance Structures of the International Financial Institutions*. Washington, DC: New Rules for Global Finance.

Cambon, Jules Martin, and Christopher Rede Turner. 1931. *The Diplomatist*. London: P. Allan.

Canadian House of Commons. 1993. *Eighth Report of the Standing Committee on External Affairs and International Trade*. Ottawa: Canadian House of Commons.

Caporaso, James A. 2003. "Democracy, Accountability, and Rights in Supranational Governance." In *Governance in a Global Economy: Political Authority in Transition*. M. Kahler and D. A. Lake eds. Princeton, NJ: Princeton University Press, 361–385.

Cardenas, Sonia. 2004. "Norm Collision: Explaining the Effects of International Human Rights Pressure on State Behavior." *International Studies Review*, 6: 213–232.

Center for UN Reform. 2009. "Second Meeting on Security Council Reform Addresses the Veto," at http://www.centerforunreform.org/node/394.

Cernea, Michael. 1988. "Non-governmental Organisations and Local Development." World Bank Discussion. Paper 40. Washington DC.

Charnovitz, Steve. 1997."Two Centuries of Participation: NGOs and International Governance." *Michigan Journal of International Law*, 18 (2): 183–286.

2000. "Opening the WTO to Nongovernmental Interests." *Fordham International Law Journal*, 24: 173–216.

Chase-Dunn, Christopher, Ellen Reese, Mark Herkenrath, Rebecca Giem, Erika Gutierrez, Linda Kim, and Christine Petit. 2008. "North-South Contradictions and Bridges at the World Social Forum." In *North and South in the World Political Economy*. Rafael Reuveny and William R. Thompson eds. Oxford: Blackwell, 341–366.

Checkel, Jeffrey T. 1997. "International Norms and Domestic Politics: Bridging the Rationalist-Constructivist Divide." *European Journal of International Relations*, 3(4): 473–496.

1998. "The Constructivist Turn in International Relations Theory." *World Politics*, 50 (2): 324–348.

2012. "Norm Entrepreneurship: Theoretical and Methodological Challenges." Paper prepared for the Evolution of International Norms and "Norm Entrepreneurship": The Council of Europe in Comparative Perspective, Wolfson College, Oxford University.

Chiang, Pei-heng. 1981. *Non-Governmental Organizations at the United Nations*. New York: Praeger.

Clark, John D. 2002. "The World Bank and Civil Society: An Evolving Experience." In *Civil Society and Global Finance*. Scholte, Jan Aart, and Albrecht Schnabel eds. London: Routledge.

Claude, Inis L., Jr. 1964. *Swords into Plowshares.* 3rd Edition, revised. New York: Random House.

Cleary, Seamus. 1996. "The World Bank and NGOs." In *"The Conscience of the World": The Influence of Non-governmental Organisations in the UN System*. Peter Willetts ed. Washington, DC: Brookings Institution, 63–97.

Codding, George A., Jr. 1964. *The Universal Postal Union: Coordinator of International Mails*. New York: New York University Press.

Cofelice, Andrea. 2012. "International Parliamentary Institutions: Some Preliminary Findings and Setting a Research Agenda." United Nations University Comparative Regional Integration Studies Paper W-2012-3, at http://www.cris.unu.edu/fileadmin/workingpapers/W-2012-3bis.pdf.

Commission of the European Communities. 2003. "Communication from the Commission to the Council, the European Parliament and the European Economic and Social Committee on a Comprehensive EU Policy against Corruption."

Connelly, Joel. 1999, December 2. "Clinton Implores WTO to Open Itself Up." *Seattle Post-Intelligencer*.

Constitutional Assembly of the Ad Hoc Assembly. 1953. "Analyze de Principaux Arguments presentees dans la Commission et l'assemblee a l'appui des dispositions institutionnelles du projet de traite." AA/CC/GT (5) 42.

Constitutional Court of South Africa. 1997. Soobramoney v. Minister of Health (Kwazulu-Natal), Case CCT 32/97.

Cooper, Duff. 1967. *Talleyrand*. Stanford: Stanford University Press.

Corbett, Richard. 1994. "Governance and Institutional Development." *Journal of Common Market Studies* 31: 27–50.

Cortell, Andrew, and James Davis. 2000. "Understanding the Domestic Impact of International Norms: A Research Agenda." *International Studies Review*, 2(1): 65–87.

2005. "When Norms Clash: International Norms, Domestic Practices, and Japan's Internalisation of the GATT/WTO." *Review of International Studies*, 31(1): 3–25.

Council of Europe. 1950. *Agendas and Minutes of Proceedings, Official Reports, Working Papers, and Compilation of Recommendations and Resolutions of the Consultative Assembly*. New York: Columbia University Press.

1993. *Statutory Resolution (93)27 on Majorities Required for Decisions of the Committee of Ministers* (adopted by the Committee of Ministers on 14 May 1993 at its 92nd Session).

Craig, Gordon A., and Alexander L. George. 1995. *Force and Statescraft: Diplomatic Problems of our Time*. New York: Oxford University Press.

Crider, John. 1944, July 2. "Delegates Search for Warm Clothes." *New York Times*, p. 14.

Cullen, Pauline P. 2009. "Pan-European NGOs and Social Rights: Participatory Democracy and Civil Dialogue." In *Transnational Activism in the UN and EU: A Comparative Study*. Jutta Joachim and Birgit Locher eds. London: Routledge, 140–153.

Curtin, Deirdre. 1999. "'Civil Society' and the European Union: Opening Spaces for Deliberative Democracy?" In *Collected Courses of the Academy of European Law*. Academy of European Law ed. Florence: Martinus Nijhoff Publishers, 185–280.

Dahl, Robert A. 1957. "The Concept of Power." *Behavioral Science*, 2(3): 201–215.

2001. "Can International Organizations Be Democratic? A Skeptic's View." In *Democracy's Edges*. Ian Shapiro and Casiano Hacker-Cordón eds. London: Cambridge University Press, 19–35.

Dawson, Thomas C., and Gita Bhatt. 2002. "The IMF and Civil Society Striking a Balance." In *Civil Society and Global Finance*. Jan Aart Scholte and Albrecht Schnabel eds. London: Routledge, 144–161.

De Franch, Ramon. 1926, February 12. Letter to Mr. Pierre Comert, Head of Information Section of League of Nations. League of Nations Archives.

de Vera y Figueroa, Juan Antonio. 2004. "The Perfect Ambassador." In *Diplomatic Classics: Selected Texts from Commynes to Vattel*. Geoff Berridge ed. Hampshire: Palgrave Macmillan, 88–97.

De Vries, Margaret Garritsen. 1986. *The IMF in a Changing World, 1945–85*. Washington DC: International Monetary Fund.

Denniston, Lyle. 1994, September 11. "When It Comes to Trade, Is the U.S. Ready for Democracy?" *Seattle Times*, p. A3.

Dieter, Heinrich. 1992. *The Case for a United Nations Parliamentary Assembly*. World Federalist Movement: Toronto.

Doerflinger, Robert. 1987. "La Commission Centrale pour la navigation du Rhin: 170 ans d'évolution du statut international du Rhin; Strasbourg: Central Commission for the Navigation of the Rhine," at http://www.ccr-zkr.org/files/histoireCCNR/07_ccnr-170-ans-evolution-statut-international-du-rhin.pdf

Donnelly, Jack. 2005. *Universal Human Rights in Theory and Practice*. New Delhi: Manas Publications.

2006. *International Human Rights*. Boulder, CO: Westview Press.

Doornbos, Martin. 2003. "Good Governance": The Metamorphosis of a Policy Metaphor. *Journal of International Affairs*, 57(1): 3–17.

Dosenrode-Lynge, Sören Zibrandt Von. 2012. *The European Union after Lisbon: Polity, Politics, Policy*. Farnham, Surrey: Ashgate.

Douglas, James. 1975. *Parliaments across Frontiers: A Short History of the Inter-Parliamentary Union*. London: Her Majesty's Stationary Office.

Driessen, Bart. 2012. *Transparency in EU Institutional Law: A Practitioner's Handbook*. Alphen aan den Rijn: Wolters Kluwer Law & Business.

Ebrahim, Alnoor, and Steven Herz. 2011. "The World Bank and Democratic Accountability: The Role of Civil Society." In *Building Global Democracy?: Civil Society and Accountable Global Governance*. Jan Aart Scholte ed. Cambridge: Cambridge University Press, 58–77.

Eckstein, Harry. 1992. *Regarding Politics: Essays on Political Theory, Stability and Change*. Berkeley: University of California Press.

Economic and Social Council. 1996. "Consultative Relationship between the United Nations and Non-Governmental Organizations," Resolution 1996/31, at http://habitat.igc.org/ngo-rev/1996-31.htm

Economist. 1999. "The Non-Governmental Order." *Economist,* 353(8149): 20–21.

Elrod, Richard B. 1976. "The Concert of Europe: A Fresh Look at an International System." *World Politics,* 28 (2): 159–174.

Erler, Jochen. 1970. "Review of *Law-Making in the International Civil Aviation* Organization by Thomas Buergenthal." *American Journal of Comparative Law,* 18(3): 647–650.

euroenews. 2011. European Parliament probes corruption claims, at http://www .euronews.com/2011/03/21/european-parliament-probes-corruption-claims/

European Coal and Steel Community. 1952. Memorandum sur L'articulation des Taches Initiales de la Haute Autorite. XI.075.350.

    1953. Common Assembly. Report Presented on Behalf of the Committee on Political Affairs on the Powers of Scrutiny of the Common Assembly and Their Use. CARDOC AC AP RP/RELA. AC-0005/540010.

    1953, January 9. Ad Hoc Assembly. Minutes in Extenso.

    1955, May 10–14. Common Assembly Debates.

European Commission. 2000. "The Commission and Non-Governmental Organisations: Building a Stronger Partnership," at http://ec.europa.eu/ transparency/civil_society/ngo/docs/communication_en.pdf

European Commission and Council of the European Communities. 1997. "Communication from the Commission on Promoting the Role of Voluntary Organisations and Foundations in Europe." COM 97 241 final.

European Community. 1958, March 20. *Official Journal.* General Debates of the European Parliament. Session constitutive.

    1960, June 27. *Official Journal.* General Debates of the European Parliament.

    1968, May. *Official Journal.* General Debates of the European Parliament.

    1970, February. *Official Journal.* General Debates of the European Parliament – Annex.

    1972, May. *Official Journal.* General Debates of the European Parliament.

    1974. *Bulletin,* 5: 72.

    1975, January 14. *Official Journal.* General Debates of the European Parliament.

    1976a, January 15. *Official Journal.* General Debates of the European Parliament.

    1976b, June 16. *Official Journal.* General Debates of the European Parliament.

    1976c, September 15. *Official Journal.* General Debates of the European Parliament.

European Parliament. 1960. Minutes of European Parliamentary Assembly Debates. Sitting of May 10.

    1965, July. Monthly Bulletin of European Documentation.

    1968. *European Parliament: The First Ten Years, 1958–1968.* Luxembourg: General Secretariat of the European Parliament.

    1971, May 26. Press Release.

    2005. "European Parliament Resolution on the Reform of the United Nations," P6_TA(2005)0237, at http://www.europarl.europa.eu/sides/getDoc.do?type =TA&reference=P6-TA-2005-0237&language=EN.

European Parliament Directorate-General for Committees and Delegations, Committee on Institutional Affairs. 1997. *The European Parliament as It Would Be Affected by the Draft Treaty of Amsterdam of 19 June 1997.* Brussels: European Parliament.

European Parliament – Directorate-General for Research and Documentation. 1976. Note to Georges Spenale, President of European Parliament.

European Parliament Political Affairs Committee. 1974, June 9. Draft Report on the Submission of a new Convention on Direct Elections to the European Parliament, PE 37.881/II.

European Parliament Political Committee. 1961. Working Papers on the Community's Objectives during the Second Stage of the Transitional Period of the Common Market. CARDOC PEO AP RP /POLI. 1961 A00100/62.

1972, March 2. Minutes of Political Commission of the European Parliament. PE/I/PV/72–6.

European Union. 2000. Minutes from Intergovernmental Conference, A5-0086/2000.

Fassbender, Brando. 2003. "All Illusions Shattered? Looking Back on a Decade of Failed Attempts to Reform the UN Security Council." In *Max Planck Year Book of United Nations Law*. The Hague: Kluwer Law International, 138-218.

Fearon, James D. 1995. "Rationalist Explanations for War." *International Organization*, 49 (3):379–414.

Featherstone, Kevin. 1994. "Jean Monnet and the 'Democratic Deficit' in the European Union." *Journal of Common Market Studies*, 32(2): 149–170.

Fenwick, Charles G. 1948. *International Law*. New York: Appleton-Century-Crofts.

Feuerle, Loie 1985. "Informal Consultations: A Mechanism in Security Council Decision-Making." *New York University Journal of International Law and Politics*, 18(1): 267–308.

Finel, Bernard, and Kristin Lord eds. 2000. *Power and Conflict in the Age of Transparency*. New York: St. Martin's Press.

Finnemore, Martha.1996. *National Interests in International Society*. Ithaca, NY: Cornell University Press.

1996. "Norms, Culture, and World Politics: Insights from Sociology's Institutionalism." *International Organization*, 50: 325–347.

Finnemore, Martha, and Kathryn Sikkink. 1998. "International Norm Dynamics and Political Change." *International Organization*, 52(4): 887–917.

Fish, M. Steven, and Matthew Kroenig. 2009. *The Handbook of National Legislatures: A Global Survey*. Cambridge: Cambridge University Press.

Florini, Ann. 1996. "The Evolution of International Norms." *International Studies Quarterly*, 40(3): 363–381.

2000. "The Politics of Transparency." Paper presented at the International Studies Association Annual Meeting, Los Angeles, CA.

2002. "Increasing Transparency in Government." *International Journal on World Peace*, 19(3): 3–34.

2003. *The Coming Democracy: New Rules for Running a New World*. Washington, DC: Island Press.

Fosdick, Raymond B. 1919. Letter to Eric Drummond, July 20, 1919. League of Nations Archives. File 22/133.

Fox, Jonathan A., and L. David Brown eds. 1998. *The Struggle for Accountability: The World Bank, NGOs, and Grassroots Movements*. Cambridge, MA: MIT Press.

Franck, Thomas M. 1992. "The Emerging Right to Democratic Governance." *American Journal of International Law*, 86(1): 46–91.

Friedman, Elisabeth J., Kathryn Hochstetler, and Ann Marie Clark. 2005. *Sovereignty, Democracy, and Global Civil Society State-Society Relations at UN World Conferences*. Albany: State University of New York Press.

French Embassy in Washington. 1979. *European Elections*. Washington DC: French Embassy.

Friedrich, Dawid. 2008. "Democratic Aspiration Meets Political Reality: Participation of Organized Civil Society in Selected European Processes." In *Civil Society Participation in European and Global Governance: A Cure for the Democratic Deficit?* Jens Steffek, Claudia Kissling, and Patricia Nanz eds. Basingstoke: Palgrave Macmillan, 140–165.

Gargarella, Roberto. 2000. "Demanding Public Deliberation: The Council of Ministers: Some Lessons from the Anglo-American History." In *Democracy in the European Union: Integration through Deliberation*. Erik Oddvar Eriksen and John Erik Fossum eds. London: Routledge, 189–201.

General Agreement on Tariffs and Trade. 1947. "The Text of the General Agreement on Tariffs and Trade." Article XXIV: 10, Article XXV: 1, Article XXVIII: 1, and Article XXX: 1, at http://www.wto.org/english/docs_e/legal_e/gatt47_02_e.htm.

George, Alexander L., and Andrew Bennett. 2005. *Case Studies and Theory Development in the Social Sciences*. Cambridge, MA: MIT Press.

Ghèbali, Victor-Yves, Roberto Ago, and Nicolas Valticos. 1989. *The International Labor Organisation: A Case Study on the Evolution of U.N. Specialised Agencies*. Dordrecht: Nijhoff.

Gianaris, William N. 1990. "Weighted Voting in the International Monetary Fund and the World Bank." *Fordham International Law Journal*, 14(4): 910–945.

Global Policy Forum. 1996. "ECOSOC Concludes NGO Review," at http://www.globalpolicy.org/social-and-economic-policy/social-and-economic-policy-at-the-un/ngos-and-ecosoc/31786.html.

   1997, December 22. Cover Letter to the President of the Security Council Signed by all ten non-permanent members, at http://www.globalpolicy.org/security-council/security-council-reform/transparency- including-working-methods-and-decisionmaking- process/32868.html

   2006. "European CSO Open Statement," at http://www.globalpolicy.org/component/content/article/209/43095.html.

   2011. "NGOs in Consultative Status with ECOSOC by Category," at http://www.globalpolicy.org/component/content/article/176-general/32119-ngos-in-consultative-status-with-ecosoc-by-category.html.

Gobat, Albert. 1895. "Organisons-nous!" *La Conférence Interparlementaire*, 2(17): 264–266.

Goertz, Gary, and Paul F. Diehl. 1992. "Toward a Theory of International Norms: Some Conceptual and Measurement Issues." *Journal of Conflict Resolution*, 36(4): 634–664.

Gold, Joseph. 1972. "*Voting and Decisions in the International Monetary Fund*." Washington DC: International Monetary Fund.

Goodrich, Leland. 1947. "From League of Nations to United Nations." *International Organization*, 1(1): 3–21.

Gordon, Joy. 2006. "Accountability and Global Governance: The Case of Iraq." *Ethics & International Affairs*, 20(1): 79–98.

Government Accountability Project. 2007. *Review of the Department of Institutional Integrity at the World Bank*. Washington DC: Government Accountability Project.

Grant, Ruth W., and Robert O. Keohane. 2005. "Accountability and Abuses of Power in World Politics." *American Political Science Review*, 99(1): 29–43.

Greenwood, Justin. 2009. "Institutions and Civil Society Organizations in the EU's Multi-Level System." In *Transnational Activism in the UN and EU*. Jutta Joaquim and Birgit Locher eds. London: Routledge, 93–104.

Grey, Ian. 1986. *The Parliamentarians: The History of the Commonwealth Parliamentary Association, 1911–1985*. Aldershot, Hants, England: Gower.

Grigorescu, Alexandru. 2002. "European Institutions and Unsuccessful Norm Transmission: The Case of Transparency." *International Politics*, 39(4): 467–489.

2003. "International Organizations and Government Transparency: Linking the International and Domestic Realms." *International Studies Quarterly*, 47: 643–667.

2005. "Mapping the UN – League of Nations Analogy: Are There Still Lessons to Be Learned from the League?" *Global Governance*, 11(1): 25–42.

2007. "Transparency of Intergovernmental Organizations: The Roles of Member-States, International Bureaucracies and Non-Governmental Organizations." *International Studies Quarterly*, 51(3): 625–648.

2008. "Horizontal Accountability in Intergovernmental Organizations." *Ethics & International Affairs*, 22(3): 285–308.

2010. "The Spread of Bureaucratic Oversight Mechanisms across Intergovernmental Organizations." *International Studies Quarterly*, 54(3): 871–886.

Gruber, Lloyd. 2005. "Power Politics and the Institutionalization of International Relations." In *Power in Global Governance*. Michael N. Barnett and Raymond Duvall eds. Cambridge: Cambridge University Press, 102–129.

Haas, Ernst B. 1962. "System and Process in the International Labor Organization: A Statistical Afterthought." *World Politics*, 14(02): 322–352.

1990. *When Knowledge Is Power: Three Models of Change in International Organizations*. Berkeley: University of California Press.

Habegger Beat. 2010. "Democratic accountability of international organizations: Parliamentary control within the Council of Europe and the OSCE and the prospects for the United Nations." *Cooperation and Conflict*, 45 (2): 186–204.

Habermas, Jürgen. 1974. "The Public Sphere: An Encyclopedia Article." *New German Critique*, 3: 49–55.

Hampton, Mark. 2004. *Visions of the Press in Britain, 1850-1950*. Urbana: University of Illinois Press.

Hankey, Maurice. 1919. Letter to Eric Drummond, July 23, 1919. League of Nations Archives. File 22/133.

Hansen, Mie. 2011, May 5. "S5 Presents Draft Resolution on Improving Working Methods of the Security Council." Center for UN Reform Education, at http://www.centerforunreform.org/node/436.

Hardy, Jeff. 1994. "Heflin, Shelby Dismayed by passage of Gatt." *Mobile Register*, December 2, p. 4A.

Hawtrey, R. G. 1949. *Western European Union: Implications for the United Kingdom*. London: Royal Institute of International Affairs.

Held, David. 1995. *Democracy and the Global Order: From the Modern State to Cosmopolitan Governance*. Stanford, CA: Stanford University Press.

1996. *Models of Democracy*. Stanford, CA: Stanford University Press.

2000. "The Changing Contours of Political Community: Rethinking Democracy in the Context of Globalization." In *Global Democracy: Key Debates*. Barry Holden ed. London: Routledge, 17–31.

2001. "The Transformation of Political Community: Rethinking Democracy in the Context of Globalization." In *Democracy's Edges*. Ian Shapiro and Casiano Hacker-Cordón eds. London: Cambridge University Press, 84–111.

2004. "Democratic Accountability and Political Effectiveness from a Cosmopolitan Perspective." *Government and Opposition*, 39(2): 364–391.

Held, David, and Mathias Koenig-Archibugi. 2004. "Introduction." *Government and Opposition*, 39(2): 125–131.

Herrmann, Richard K., and Vaughn P. Shannon. 2001. "Defending International Norms: The Role of Obligation, Material Interest, and Perception in Decision Making." *International Organization*, 55(3): 621–654.

Higgins, Rosalyn. 1996. "A Comment on the Current Health of Advisory Opinions." In *Fifty Years of the International Court of Justice: Essays in Honour of Sir Robert Jennings*. R. Y. Jennings, A. V. Lowe, and M. Fitzmaurice eds. Cambridge: Grotius Publications, 567–581.

Hiscocks, Richard. 1974. *"The Security Council: A Study in Adolescence."* New York: Free Press

Holden, Barry. 2000. *Global Democracy: Key Debates*. London: Routledge.

Holsti, K. J. 1992. "Governance without Government: Polyarchy in Nineteenth-Century European International Politics." In *Governance without Government: Order and Change in World Politics*. James N. Rosenau and Ernst-Otto Czempiel eds. Cambridge: Cambridge University Press, 30–57.

Hosli, Madeleine O. 2000. "Smaller States and the New Voting Weights in the Council." Netherlands Institute of International Relations, at http://www.clingendael.nl/publications/2000/20000700_cli_ess_hosli.pdf

House of Representatives. 1998. House of Representatives Bill 3331. 105th Congress: IMF Transparency and Efficiency Act of 1998, at http://www.govtrack.us/congress/bills/105/hr3331/text

Hudson, Manley. 1943. *The Permanent Court of International Justice 1920–1942: A Treatise*. New York: Macmillan.

Human Rights Watch. 2011, February 28. US: Ban All Antipersonnel Landmines, at http://www.hrw.org/news/2011/02/28/us-ban-all-antipersonnel-landmines

Humphrey, John P. 1984. *Human Rights & the United Nations: A Great Adventure*. Dobbs Ferry, NY: Transnational Publishers.

Huntington, S. P. 1991. *The Third Wave: Democratization in the Late Twentieth Century*. Norman: University of Oklahoma Press.

Hurd, Ian. 1997. "Security Council Reform: Informal Membership and Practice." In *The Once and Future Security Council*. Bruce Russett ed. New York: St. Martin's Press, 135–152.

2005. "The Strategic Use of Liberal Internationalism: Libya and the UN Sanctions, 1992–2003." *International Organization*, 59: 495–526.

2007. *After Anarchy: Legitimacy and Power at the UN Security Council*. Princeton: Princeton University Press.

Ikenberry, John. 2001. *After Victory: Institutions, Strategic Restraint, and the Rebuilding of Order after Major Wars*. Princeton: Princeton University Press.

International Environmental Report. 1999, March 17 and 22. "Developing Countries Resist Expansion Role for World Trade Body."

International Labor Office. 1922. Minutes of the 9th Session of the Governing Body.

International Labor Organization. 1924. Record of Proceedings of the International Labor Conference. Sixth session.

1948. Record of Proceedings of the International Labor Conference. Thirty-third session.

1953. Minutes of the 125th Session of the Governing Body.

1954. Minutes of the 127th Session of the Governing Body.

1960. Minutes of the 145th Session of the Governing Body.

1961. Minutes of the 148th Session of the Governing Body.

1971. Minutes of the 182nd Session of the Governing Body.

1973. Minutes of the 190th Session of the Governing Body.

1974. Record of Proceedings of the International Labor Conference. Fifty-ninth session.

1975a. Record of Proceedings of the International Labor Conference. Sixtieth session.

1975b. Report of the Third Meeting of the Working Party on Structure.

1980. Record of Proceedings of the International Labor Conference. Sixty-sixth session.

1981. Record of Proceedings of the International Labor Conference. Sixty-seventh session.

1986. "Instrument for the Amendment of the Constitution of the International Labour Organisation," at http://www.ilo.org/public/english/bureau/leg/download/amend/1986e.pdf.

2013. "Non-governmental International Organizations Having General Consultative Status with the ILO," at http://www.ilo.org/pardev/civil-society/ngos/WCMS_201411/lang--en/index.htm.

International Monetary Fund. 2000. "Transparency at the IMF Factsheet." Washington: IMF.

2003. "Guide for Staff Relations with Civil Society Organizations," at https://www.imf.org/external/np/cso/eng/2003/101003.htm.

2009. "Reforming the International Financial System," at http://www.imf.org/external/np/exr/key/quotav.htm.

International Union of League of Nations Associations. 1921. "Report for Year 1921." Geneva: International Union of League of Nations Associations.

Inter-Parliamentary Union. 1921a, February 18. Letter from Christian Lange, Secretary General of Inter-parliamentary Union to Eric Drummond, Secretary General of the League of Nations. League of Nations Archive. Document no 11009. File no 299.

1921b. Conference Interparliamentaire. Geneva: Inter-parliamentary Union.

Jacobs, Didier. 2002. "Democratizing Global Economic Governance." Paper presented at the Alternatives to Neoliberalism Conference sponsored by the New Rules for Global Finance Coalition, May 23-24, 2002 at http://www .new-rules.org/storage/documents/afterneolib/jacobs.pdf

Johnston, Alastair I. 2001. "Treating International Institutions as Social Environments." *International Studies Quarterly*, 45(3): 487–515.

Jones, Kent Albert. 2010. *The Doha Blues: Institutional Crisis and Reform in the WTO*. Oxford: Oxford University Press.

Judge, David, and David Earnshaw. 2003. *The European Parliament*. Houndmills, Basingstoke, Hampshire: Palgrave Macmillan.

Kahler, Miles. 2004. "Defining Accountability Up: The Global Economic Multilaterals." *Government and Opposition*, 39(2): 132–158.

Kant, Immanuel. 2005. *Perpetual Peace*. New York: Cosimo.

Karl, Wolfram. 2006. "Article 69." In *The Statute of the International Court of Justice: A Commentary*. Andreas Zimmermann, Karin Oellers-Frahm, and Christian Tomuschat eds. New York: Oxford University Press, 1481–1486.

Katzenstein, Peter, ed. 1996. *The Culture of National Security*. New York: Columbia University Press.

Kelsen, Hans. 1944. "The Principle of Sovereign Equality of States as a Basis for International Organization." *Yale Law Journal*, 53(2): 207–220.

Kennedy, P. M. 2006. *The Parliament of Man: The Past, Present, and Future of the United Nations*. New York: Random House.

Keohane, Robert O. 1984. *After Hegemony: Cooperation and Discord in the World Political Economy*. Princeton, NJ: Princeton University Press.

2001. "Governance in a Partially Globalized World." *American Political Science Review*, 95(1): 1–13.

2003. "Global Governance and Democratic Accountability." In *Taming Globalization – Frontiers of Governance*. D. Held and M. Koenig-Archibugi eds. Cambridge, UK: Polity, 130–159.

2005. "Abuse of Power." *Harvard International Review*, 27(2): 48–58.

Keohane, Robert O., and Joseph S. Nye. 2000a. *Power and Interdependence*. London: Longman.

2000b. "Introduction." In *Governance in a Globalizing World*. J. Nye and J. Donahue eds. Washington, DC: Brookings Institution Press, 1–41.

2002. "The Club Model of Multilateral Cooperation and Problems of Democratic Legitimacy." In *Power and Governance in a Partially Globalized World*. R. Keohane ed. New York: Routledge, 219–244.

Kingsbury, Benedict. 1998. "Sovereignty and Inequality." *European Journal of International Law*, 9(4): 599–625.

Kissling, Claudia. 2011. "The Inter-Parliamentary Union: Its Development and Its Contribution to Global Democracy." Moncalieri, Italy: International

Democracy Watch, at http://www.internationaldemocracywatch.org/attachments/453_IPU-kissling.pdf.

Klein, Robert A. 1974. *Sovereign Equality among States: The History of an Idea.* Toronto: University of Toronto Press.

Koenig-Archibugi, Mathias. 2011. "Is Global Democracy Possible?" *European Journal of International Relations,* 17(3): 519–542.

2012. "Global democracy and domestic analogies." In *Global Democracy: Normative and Empirical Perspectives.* D. Archibugi et al. eds. Cambridge: Cambridge University Press.

Koremenos, Barbara, Charles Lipson, and Duncan Snidal. 2004. *The Rational Design of International Institutions.* Cambridge, UK: Cambridge University Press.

Kraft-Kasack, Christiane. 2008. "Transnational Parliamentary Assemblies: A Remedy for the Democratic Deficit of International Governance?" *West European Politics,* 31(3): 534–557.

Krasner, Stephen. 1983. "Structural Causes and Regime Consequences: Regimes as Intervening Variables." In *International Regimes.* Stephen Krasner ed. Ithaca, NY: Cornell University Press, 1–21.

Kratochwil, Friedrich. 1984. "The Force of Prescriptions." *International Organization,* 38(4):685–708.

Krebs, Ronald R., and Patrick Thaddeus Jackson. 2007. "Twisting Tongues and Twisting Arms: The Power of Political Rhetoric." *European Journal of International Relations,* 13(1): 35–66.

Krock, Arthur. 1943. "Covenants that Are Not Openly Arrived at." *New York Times,* April 12, p. 1.

Kuyper, Jonathan W. 2013. "Designing Institutions for Global Democracy: Flexibility through Escape Clauses and Sunset Provisions." *Ethics & Global Politics,* 6(4): 195–215.

Kyodo News Service. 1999. "Japan to Seek Reform of WTO Decision-Making Process." December 28 at http://www.thefreelibrary.com/Japan+to+seek+reform+of+WTO+decision-making+process.-a058533846

Lador-Lederer, J. J. 1962. *International Non-Governmental Organizations and Economic Entities.* Leyden: Sythoff.

Lansing, Robert. 1921. *The Peace Negotiations: A Personal Narrative.* Boston: Houghton Mifflin Co.

Lauren, Paul Gordon. 1983. "Crisis Prevention in Nineteenth Century Diplomacy." In *Managing U.S.-Soviet Rivalry: Problems of Crisis Prevention.* Alexander L. George ed. Boulder, CO: Westview Press, 31–57.

League of Nations. 1919. "Covenant of the League of Nations," at http://avalon.law.yale.edu/20th_century/leagcov.asp

1920, July–August. Official Journal.

1921a. Council Meetings Minutes.

1921b, February 16. Relations of the League of Nations to International Bureaux. Memo from Inazo Nitobe, Director of Section of International Bureaux to League Legal Section. Document 10946. File 299.

1922a, August. *Official Journal.*

1922b, September 25. Minutes of League Assembly: Statement on Behalf of Netherlands, League Assembly, 16th Plenary meeting.

1922c. Bulletin of Information on the Work of International Organisations.

1923. Handbook of International Organisations.

1925, October 10. "Collaboration de la Presse a L'Organization de la Paix: Resolutions de la Sixieme Assemblee." Geneva. League of Nations Archives. C 611 M 196 1925.

1926, September. Official Journal.

1927. Council Meeting Minutes.

1931, September 16. Minutes of League Assembly. Ninth Plenary meeting.

League of Nations Archives of Section of International Bureaux and Intellectual Cooperation. Various years. Section 13: 198–442.

League of Nations Information Section. 1928. *The League of Nations and the Press*. Geneva: League of Nations Information Center.

League of Nations Information Section. 1935. *Essential Facts about the League of Nations*. Geneva: League of Nations.

League of Nations Legal Section. 1921. "Commentary on Article 24 of the Covenant." Geneva: League of Nations. League of Nations Archives. Document 10948. File no 299.

League of Nations Secretariat. 1922. Section of International Bureaux. Bulletin of Information on the Work of International Organisations.

Lee, Dwight E. 1947. The Genesis of the Veto. *International Organization*, 1(1): 33–42.

Legro, Jeffrey. 1997. "Which Norms Matter? Revisiting the "Failure" of Internationalism." *International Organization*, 51(1): 31–63.

Levi, Lucio. 2003. "Globalization, International Democracy and a World Parliament." In *A Reader on Second Assembly and Parliamentary Proposals*. Saul H. Mendlovitz and Barbara Walker eds. Wayne, NJ: Center for UN Reform, 54–67.

Liese, Andrea. 2010. "Explaining Various Degrees of Openness in the Food and Agriculture Organization of the United Nations." In *Transnational Actors in Global Governance: Patterns, Explanations, and Implications*. Christer Jönsson, and Jonas Tallberg eds. Basingstoke, Hampshire [England]: Palgrave Macmillan, 88–108.

Lorimer, James. 1884. *The Institutes of the Law of Nations: A Treatise of the Jural Relations of Separate Political Communities*. Volume II. The Institutes of the Law of Nations. Edinburgh: Blackwood.

Los Angeles Times. 1943, April 11. "Senators Assail Banning Newsmen at Food Parley," p. 8.

Luard, Evan. 1982. *A History of the UN. Volume 1*. New York: St. Martin's Press.

Luck, Edward C. 2003. "Reforming the United Nations: Lessons from a History in Progress." International Relations Studies and the United Nations Occasional Papers, No. 1, at http://www.reformwatch.net/fitxers/58.pdf p. 50.

Lupovic, Amir. 2009. "Constructivist Methods: A Plea and Manifesto for Pluralism." *Review of International Studies*, 35: 195–218.

Lyons, F. S. L. 1963. *Internationalism in Europe: 1815–1914*. Leyden: Sythoff.

MacDonald, Nina. 1934, February 19. Letter to Adrian Pelt, Director of Information Section. League of Nations. League of Nations Archives 10943. File 299.

Manger, W. 1961. *Pan America in Crisis: The Future of the OAS.* Washington: Public Affairs Press.

March, James, and Johan Olsen. 1994. *Democratic Governance.* New York: Free Press.

   1998. "The Institutional Dynamics of International Political Order." *International Organization,* 52: 943–970.

Marks, Sally. 1995. "The Small States at Geneva." *World Affairs,* 157(4): 191–196.

Martens, Kerstin. 2011. "Civil Society and Accountability in the United Nations." In *Building Global Democracy?: Civil Society and Accountable Global Governance.* Jan Aart Scholte ed. Cambridge, UK: Cambridge University Press, 42–57.

Marshall, Monty G., Keith Jaggers, and Ted Robert Gurr. 2010. POLITY IV PROJECT, Political Regime Characteristics and Transitions, 1800–2010, Dataset Users' Manual, Center for Systemic Peace.

Martin, Robert, and Estelle Feldman. 1998. *Access to Information in Developing Countries.* Berlin: Transparency International.

Mason, Edward S., and Robert A. Asher. 1973. *The World Bank since Bretton Woods: The Origins, Policies, Operations, and Impact of the International Bank for Reconstruction and Development and the Other Members of the World Bank Group: The International Finance Corporation, the International Development Association [and] the International Centre for Settlement of Investment Disputes.* Washington: Brookings Institution.

Mater, Andre. 1920. "Another French Point of View." In *The Nations and the League.* G. Paris ed. London: T.F. Unwin, 69–134.

Mayer, Peter. 2008: "Civil Society Participation in International Security Organizations: The Cases of NATO and the OSCE." In *Civil Society Participation in European and Global Governance. A Cure for the Democratic Deficit?* Jan Steffek, Claudia Kissling, and Patricia Nanz eds. Basingstoke: Palgrave Macmillan, 116–237.

McCormick, John. 2011. *Understanding the European Union. A Concise Introduction.* New York: Palgrave Macmillan.

McCoy, Jennifer L. 2001. "The Emergence of a Global Anti-Corruption Norm." *International Politics,* 38: 65–90.

McCubbins, Matthew and Thomas Schwartz. 1984. "Congressional Oversight Overlooked: Police Patrols Versus Fire Alarms." *American Journal of Political Science,* 28: 16–79.

McGrew Anthony. 2002. "Transnational Democracy: Theories and Prospects." In *Democratic Theory Today.* G. Stokes and A. Carter eds. Cambridge: Polity Press, 269–294.

Mearsheimer, John. 1994. "The False Promise of International Institutions." *International Security,* 19(3): 5–49.

Meltzer, Allan H. 2000. *Report of the International Financial Institution Advisory Commission.* Washington, D.C.: International Financial Institution Advisory Commission.

Mendel, Toby. 1999. "Freedom of Information as an Internationally Protected Human Right," at http://www.article19.org/data/files/pdfs/publications/foi-as-an-international-right.pdf

Mény, Y. 2003. "De La Démocratie en Europe: Old Concepts and New Challenges." *Journal of Common Market Studies*, 41(1): 1–13.

Micossi, Stefano. 2008. "Democracy in the European Union." Centre for European Policy Studies CEPS Working Document No. 286.

Miller, David H. 1928. *The Drafting of the Covenant*. Volumes I and II. New York: G. P. Putnam's Sons.

Miller, Judith. 2005, February 9. "Theft and Mismanagement Charged at U.N. Weather Agency." *New York Times*, p. A14.

Milman-Sivan, Faina. 2009. "Representativity, Civil Society, and the EU Social Dialogue: Lessons from the International Labor Organization." *Indiana Journal of Global Legal Studies*, 16(1): 311–337.

Mitchell, Ronald. 1998. "Sources of Transparency: Information Systems in International Regimes." *International Studies Quarterly*, 42: 109–130.

Mock, William. 1999. "On the Centrality of Information Law: A Rational Choice Discussion of Information Law and Transparency." *John Marshall Journal of Computer and International Law*, 17(4): 1069–1100.

Monbiot, George. 2004. *The Age of Consent. A Manifesto for a New World Order*. London: Flamingo.

Moore, Mike. 1999. "Challenges for the Global Trading System in the New Millennium," at http://www.wto.org/english/news_e/spmm_e/spmm08_e.htm.

Moravcsik, Andrew. 1998. *The Choice for Europe: Social Purpose and State Power from Messina to Maastricht*. Ithaca, NY: Cornell University Press.

2004. "Is There a 'Democratic Deficit' in World Politics? A Framework for Analysis." *Government and Opposition*, 39(2): 336–363.

2008. "The Myth of Europe's 'Democratic Deficit.'" *Intereconomics: Journal of European Economic Policy*, 43(6): 331–340.

Motta, Giuseppe. 1926, September 8. Statement on Behalf of the Swiss Delegation, League Assembly, 4th Plenary Meeting, Minutes of League Assembly.

Müller, Harald. 2004. "Arguing, Bargaining and All That: Communicative Action, Rationalist Theory and the Logic of Appropriateness in International Relations." *European Journal of International Relations*, 10(3): 395–435.

Murphy, C. 1994. *International Organization and Industrial Change: Global Governance since 1850*. New York: Oxford University Press.

Nader, Ralph. 1994, November 28. "US Should Say No to WTO's Antidemocratic Procedures – Proposed Trade Pact Ignores Human Rights and Labor Protections." *Christian Science Monitor*, p. 18.

Nelson, Paul J. 1995. *The World Bank and Non-Governmental Organizations: The Limits of Apolitical Development*. New York: Palgrave Macmillan.

2000, "Transparency in International Organizations: Testing the Strength of the Norm in Regional and Global Multilateral Development Banks." Paper presented at the International Studies Association Annual Meeting, Los Angeles, CA, 14–18 March, 2000.

2001. "Transparency Mechanisms in the Multilateral Development Banks." *World Development*, 19: 1835–1847.

New York Times. 1943, April 15. "Newsmen Protest Food Parley Curb," p. 1.

New York Times. 1944, June 10. "Two Congress Republicans to Get Places in Monetary Delegation," p. 1.

Neyer, Jürgen. 2000. "Justifying Comitology: The Promise of Deliberation." In *European Integration after Amsterdam: Institutional Dynamics and Prospects for Democracy*. K. Neunreither and A. Wiener eds. Oxford: Oxford University Press, 112–128.

Nicolson, Harold. 1946. *The Congress of Vienna; A Study in Allied Unity, 1812–1822*. London: Constable & Co.

Nielson, Daniel, Michael Tierney, and Catherine Weaver. 2006. "Bridging the Rationalist-Constructivist Divide: Engineering Change at the World Bank." *Journal of International Relations and Development*, 9(2): 107–139.

Ninčić, Djura. 1970. *The Problem of Sovereignty in the Charter and in the Practice of the United Nations*. The Hague: M. Nijhoff.

Nye, Joseph. 2001. "Globalization's Democratic Deficit: How to Make International Institutions More Accountable." *Foreign Affairs*, 80: 2–6.

2004a. *Power in the Global information Age from Realism to Globalization*. London: Routledge.

2004b. *Soft Power: The Means to Success in World Politics*. New York: Public Affairs.

Nye, Joseph S., J. P. Einhorn, B. Kadar, H. Owada, L. Rubio, and S. Young. 2003. *The "Democracy Deficit" in the Global Economy Enhancing the Legitimacy and Accountability of Global Institutions*. Washington, DC: Trilateral Commission.

O'Brien, Robert, A. M. Goetz, J. A. Scholte, and M. Williams. 2000. *Contesting Global Governance Multilateral Economic Institutions and Global Social Movements*. Cambridge: Cambridge University Press.

O'Donnell, Guillermo. 1999. "Horizontal Accountability in New Democracies." In *The Self-Restraining State: Power and Accountability in New Democracies*. A. Schedler, et. al. eds. Boulder CO: Lynne Rienner, 29–51.

Official Journal. 1992. C191 of 29/07/1992. Treaty on European Union.

1993. L 340, 31/12/1993. Code of Conduct Concerning Public Access to Council and Commission Documents.

1997. C 340, 10/11/1997. Treaty of Amsterdam Amending the Treaty on European Union.

Opoku-Mensah, Paul. 2001. "The Rise and Rise of NGOs: Implications for Research, Journal of the Institute of Sociology and Political Science," at http://www.svt.ntnu.no/iss/issa/0101/010109.shtml.

Organization of African Unity. 1994, September 2. "Reformes des Nationes Unies: Position Africane Commune." OAU Doc. NY/OAU/POL/84/94/Rev. 2.

Osterhammel, J., and N. P. Petersson. 2005. *Globalization: A Short History*. Princeton, NJ: Princeton University Press.

Ottaway, Marina. 2001. "Corporatism Goes Global: International Organizations, Nongovernmental Organization Networks, and Transnational Business." *Global Governance*, 7(3): 265–292.

Ougaard, Morten. 2011. "Civil Society and Patterns of Accountability in the OECD." In *Building Global Democracy?: Civil Society and Accountable Global Governance*. Jan Aart Scholte ed. Cambridge, UK: Cambridge University Press, 163–181.

Page, Clarence. 1999, December 7. "WTO Makes Its Own Problems." *Chicago Tribune*, 6.

Paloni, A., and M. Zanardi. 2006. *The IMF, World Bank and Policy Reform*. London: Routledge.

Parliamentary Network on the World Bank. 2008. "Paris 2008- Annual Conference" at http://www.parlnet.org/admindb/docs/Conference_Report_April_8_2009_WEB_version.pdf

2010. "New World Bank Voting Structure, Bank Watchgroups Question Reforms," at http://www.pnowb.org/admindb/docs/New%20World%20Bank%20voting%20structure_190510.pdf.

Payne, Rodger A. 2001. "Persuasion, Frames and Norm Construction." *European Journal of International Relations*, 7: 37–62.

Pelt, Adrian. 1944. "Suggestions by A. Pelt for the Organization of a Secretariat Information Center." In *The International Secretariat of the Future: Lessons from Experience by a Group of Former Officials of the League of Nations*. London: Royal Institute of International Affairs, 61–64.

Peet, Richard. 2009. *Unholy Trinity*. London: Zed Books.

Pevehouse, Jon C. 2005. *Democracy from Above: Regional Organizations and Democratization*. Cambridge, UK: Cambridge University Press.

Pew, Marlen. 1925, December 19. Letter to Arthur Sweetser. League of Nations Archives for Press Conference. File 24/103.

Penn, William. 1912. *An Essay Towards the Present and Future Peace of Europe: By the Establishment of an European Dyet, Parliament or Estates*. Boston: Directors of the Old South Work.

Peyrefitte, Alain. 1960, September 11. "L'Avenir de L'Europe." *Le Monde, 1 and 5*.

1962. "The Negotiations for Political Europe – A Document Outlining a Tactic." *Agence Internationale D'Information Pour La Presse*, 142: 1–8.

Pickard, Bertram. 1956. *The Greater United Nations; An Essay Concerning the Place and Significance of International Non-Governmental Organizations*. New York: Carnegie Endowment for International Peace.

Pincus, Jonathan, and Jeffrey A. Winters. 2002. *Reinventing the World Bank*. Ithaca: Cornell University Press.

Price, Richard. 2003. "Transnational Civil Society and Advocacy in World Politics." *World Politics*, 55: 579–606.

Przeworski, Adam. 1991. *Democracy and the Market: Political and Economic Reforms in Eastern Europe and Latin America*. New York: Cambridge University Press.

Przeworski, Adam et al. 2013. Political Institutions and Political Events (PIPE) Data Set. Department of Politics, New York University.

Putnam, Robert D. 1988. "Diplomacy and Domestic Politics: The Logic of Two-Level Games." *International Organization*, 42(3): 427–460.

2000. *Bowling Alone: The Collapse and Revival of American Community*. New York: Simon & Schuster.

Raghavan, Chakravarthi. 2000, March 2. *Continuing Conceptual Divides at the WTO.* Penang, Malaysia: Third World Network.

Ranshofen-Wertheimer, Egon. 1945. *The International Secretariat: An Experiment in International Administration.* Washington, DC: Carnegie Endowment for International Peace.

Rawls, John. 1971. *A Theory of Justice.* Cambridge, MA: Belknap Press of Harvard University Press.

Red Cross. 1989. *The League of Red Cross and Red Crescent Societies 1919–1989.* Geneva: League of Red Cross and Red Crescent Societies.

Reinalda, Bob. 2009. *Routledge History of International Organizations: From 1815 to the Present Day.* London: Routledge.

Reimann, Kim D. 2006. "A View from the Top: International Politics, Norms and the Worldwide Growth of NGOs." *International Studies Quarterly,* 50(1): 45–67.

Reinsch, Paul. 1911. *Samuel, Public International Unions.* Boston: World Peace Foundation.

Replogle, Sherri. 2013. "*The Civilian and the War on Terror: Do Norms Shape Strategy?*" Dissertation, Loyola University Chicago.

Reus-Smit, Christian. 1997. "The Constitutional Structure of International Society and the Nature of Fundamental Institutions." *International Organization,* 51(Autumn): 555–589.

Rich, Bruce. 1994. *Mortgaging the Earth: The World Bank, Environmental Empoverishment, and the Crisis of Development.* Boston: Beacon Press.

Richardson, Louise. 1999. "The Concert of Europe and Security Management in the Nineteenth Century." In *Imperfect Unions: Security Institutions over Time and Space.* Helga Haftendorn, Robert O. Keohane, and Celeste A. Wallander eds. Oxford: Oxford University Press, 48–79.

Riches, Cromwell A. 1940. *Majority Rule in International Organization: A Study of the Trend from Unanimity to Majority Decision.* Baltimore: Johns Hopkins Press.

Right2INFO.org. 2012. "Access to Information Laws: Overview and Statutory Goals," at http://www.right2info.org/access-to-information-laws

Risse, Thomas. 2000. "Let's Argue!: Communicative Action in World Politics." *International Organization,* 54(1): 1–39.

Risse-Kappen, Thomas. 1994. "Ideas Do Not Float Freely: Transnational Coalitions, Domestic Structures, and the End of the Cold War." *International Organization,* 48(2): 185–214.

Risse-Kappen, Thomas, Stephen C. Ropp, and Kathryn Sikkink. 1999. *The Power of Human Rights: International Norms and Domestic Change.* New York: Cambridge University Press.

Rittberger, Berthold. 2003. "The Creation and Empowerment of the European Parliament." *Journal of Common Market Studies,* 41(2): 203–225.

2004. "The Politics of Democratic Legitimation." Nuffield College Working Papers in Politics, 2004-W4, at http://www.nuffield.ox.ac.uk/Politics/papers/2004/Rittberger%20Politics%20of%20Democratic%20Legitimation.pdf

2005. *Building Europe's Parliament: Democratic Representation Beyond the Nation State.* Oxford: Oxford University Press.

Roberts, Alasdair. 2003. "NATO, Secrecy, and the Right to Information." *East European Constitutional Review*, 12: 86–94.

2006. *Blacked Out: Government Secrecy in the Information Age.* Cambridge: Cambridge University Press.

Robertson, Arthur H. 1956. *The Council of Europe: Its Structure, Functions and Achievements.* New York: Praeger.

Rodan, Garry. 2004. *Transparency and Authoritarian Rule in Southeast Asia: Singapore and Malaysia.* London: Routledge.

Sabic, Zlatko. 2008. "Building Democratic and Responsible Global Governance: The Role of International Parliamentary Institutions." *Parliamentary Affairs*, 61(2): 255–271.

Salamon, Lester M. 1994. "The Rise of the Nonprofit Sector." *Foreign Affairs*, 73(4): 109–122.

ed. 1999. *Global Civil Society: Dimensions of the Nonprofit Sector.* Bloomfield, CT: Kumarian Press.

Sandberg, Eve. 1994. *The Changing Politics of Non-Governmental Organizations and African States.* Wesport, CT: Praeger.

Sandholtz, Wayne. 2007. *Prohibiting Plunder: How Norms Change.* Oxford: Oxford University Press.

Sandholtz, Wayne, and Kendall W. Stiles. 2009. *International Norms and Cycles of Change.* Oxford: Oxford University Press.

Saul, Graham. 2002. "Transparency and Accountability in International Financial Institutions." In *The Right to Know, the Right to Live: Access to Information and Socio-Economic Justice.* R. Calland and A. Tilley eds. Cape Town: Open Democracy Advice Center, 127–137.

Saurugger, Sabine. 2010. "The Social Construction of the Participatory Turn: The Emergence of a Norm in the European Union." *European Journal of Political Research*, 49(4):471–495.

Scalingi, Paula. 1980. *The European Parliament: The Three Decade Search for a United Europe.* Westport, CT: Greenwood Press.

Scharpf, Fritz W. 1997. "`Economic Integration, Democracy, and the Welfare State." *Journal of European Public Policy*, 4(1): 18–36.

Schimmelfennig, Frank. 2003. *The EU, NATO and the Integration of Europe: Rules and Rhetoric.* Cambridge, UK: Cambridge University Press.

Schlesinger, Stephen C. 2003. *Act of Creation: The Founding of the United Nations: A Story of Superpowers, Secret Agents, Wartime Allies and Enemies, and Their Quest for a Peaceful World.* Boulder, CO: Westview Press.

Scholte, Jan Aart. 2004. "Civil Society and Democratically Accountable Global Governance." *Government and Opposition*, 39(2): 211–233.

Schuijt, W. J. 1959, February/March. "L'Election D'un Parlement au Suffrage Direct: Fondement de L'Edification Europeenne," Nieuw Europa. Translation in French in the Altiero Spinelli Collection of the EU Historical Archives. AS/APE 1639.

Schultz, Kenneth. 1999. "Do Democratic Institutions Constrain or Inform: Contrasting Two Institutional Perspectives on Democracy and War." *International Organization*, 52: 233–266.

Schuman, Frederick L. 1951. "The Council of Europe." *American Political Science Review*, 45(3): 724–740.

Seary, Bill. 1996. "The Early History: From the Congress of Vienna to the San Francisco Conference." In *"The Conscience of the World": The Influence of Non-Governmental Organisations in the UN System*. Peter Willetts ed. Washington, DC: Brookings Institution, 15–30.

Sédouy, J.-A. 2009. *Le concert européen: Aux origines de l'Europe (1814–1914)*. Paris: Fayard.

Sending, Ole Jacob. 2002. "Constitution, Choice and Change: Problems with the 'Logic of Appropriateness' and Its Use in Constructivist Theory." *European Journal of International Relations*, 8(4): 443–470.

Shannon, Vaughn P. 2000. "Norms Are What States Make of Them" *International Studies Quarterly*, 44(2): 293–316.

Shaw, Timothy M., and Pamela K. Mbabazi. 2011. "Civil Society and Accountability in the Commonwealth." In *Building Global Democracy?: Civil Society and Accountable Global Governance*. Jan Aart Scholte ed. Cambridge, UK: Cambridge University Press, 128–145.

Shihata, Ibrahim F. I., Margrete Stevens, and Sabine Schlemmer-Schulte. 1991. *The World Bank in a Changing World: Selected Essays and Lectures*. Volume 2. Brussels: Martinus Nijhoff.

Shultz, George. 1985, November. "U.S. Role in the ILO – International Labor Organization." U.S. Department of State Bulletin, 85: 8–15.

Simmons, Beth A. 2009. *Mobilizing for Human Rights: International Law in Domestic Politics*. Cambridge, UK: Cambridge University Press.

Singer, J. David, Stuart Bremer, and John Stuckey. 1972. "Capability Distribution, Uncertainty, and Major Power War, 1820–1965." In *Peace, War, and Numbers*. Bruce Russett ed. Beverly Hills, CA: Sage, 19–48.

Slaughter, Anne-Marie. 2004a. *A New World Order*. Princeton: Princeton University Press.

2004b. "Disaggregated Sovereignty: Towards the Public Accountability of Global Government Networks." *Government and Opposition*, 39(2): 159–190.

Smith, Brian H. 1990. *More than Altruism: The Politics of Private Foreign Aid*. Princeton, NJ: Princeton University Press.

Steffek, Jens, and Ulrike Ehling. 2008. "Civil Society Participation at the Margins: The Case of the WTO." In *Civil Society Participation in European and Global Governance: A Cure for the Democratic Deficit?* Jens Steffek, Claudia Kissling, and Patrizia Nanz eds. Basingstoke England: Palgrave Macmillan, 95–115.

Steger, Debra, and Natalia Shpilkovskaya. 2010. "Internal Management of the WTO: Room for Improvement." In *Redesigning the World Trade Organization for the Twenty-first Century*. Ottawa, Canada: International Development Research Center, 129–164.

Stein, Arthur. 1999. "Constrained Sovereignty: The Growth of International Intrusiveness." Paper presented at the annual meeting of the American Political Science Association, Atlanta, GA, 4 September, 1999.

Steinberg, Richard H. 2002. "In the Shadow of Law or Power? Consensus-based Bargaining and Outcomes in the GATT/WTO." *International Organization*, 56(2): 339–374.

Stiglitz, Joseph. 2006. *Making Globalization Work*. New York: Norton.

Stoetzer, O. C. 1965. *The Organization of American States: An introduction*. New York: Praeger.

Struycken, M. 1922, September 25. Statement on behalf of Netherlands, League Assembly, 16th Plenary meeting, Minutes of League Assembly.

Suganami, Hidemi. 1989. *The Domestic Analogy and World Order Proposals*. Cambridge: Cambridge University Press.

Sunstein, Cass R. 1996. "Social Norms and Social Roles." *Columbia Law Review*, 96(4): 903–968.

Sweetser, Arthur. 1919, September 2. Memorandum to Eric Drummond. League of Nations Archives. File 22/133.

1920. *The League of Nations at Work*. New York: Macmillan.

Sweetser, Arthur, and W. R. Sharp. 1944. *The Differential Participation of States in International Organization*. New York: Council on Foreign Relations.

Tallberg, Jonas, and Anders Uhlin. 2012. "Civil Society and Global Democracy: An Assessment." In *Global Democracy: Normative and Empirical Perspectives*. Daniele Archibugi, Mathias Koenig-Archibugi, and Raffaele Marchetti eds. Cambridge: Cambridge University Press, 210–232.

Tallberg, Jonas, Thomas Sommerer, Theresa Squatrito, and Christer Jonsson. 2013. *The Opening Up of International Organizations: Transnational Access in Global Governance*. Cambridge, UK: Cambridge University Press.

Temperley, L. H., and Penson, L. M. 1966. *A Century of Diplomatic Blue Books, 1814–1914*. London: Frack Cass.

Third World Network et al. 2003. *Memorandum on the Need to Improve Internal Transparency and participation in the WTO*, at http://www.ecolomics-international.org/n_san_ngo_memo_wto_transp_particip.pdf

Thomann, Lars. 2008. "The ILO, Tripartism, and NGOs: Do Too Many Cooks Really Spoil the Broth." In *Civil Society Participation in European and Global Governance: A Cure for the Democratic Deficit?* Jens Steffek, Claudia Kissling, and Patrizia Nanz eds. Basingstoke, UK: Palgrave Macmillan, 71–94.

Thompson, John B. 2000. *Political Scandal: Power and Visibility in the Media Age*. Malden, MA: Blackwell Publishers.

Time. 1926. "*Double Affront*" 7(25): 13.

Tobin, James. 1999. "A Comment on Dahl's Skepticism." In *Democracy's Edges*. Ian Shapiro and Casiano Hacker-Cordón eds. London: Cambridge University Press, 37–40.

Udall, Lori. 1998. "The World Bank and Public Accountability: Has Anything Changed?" In *The Struggle for Accountability: The World Bank, NGOs, and Grassroots Movement*. Jonathan Fox and L.D. Brown eds. Cambridge: MIT Press, 391–427.

Union of International Associations. Various years. *Yearbook of International Organizations*. Brussels: Union of International Associations.

United Nations. 1946a. Report of the First Session of the Preparatory Committee of the United Nations Conference on Trade and Employment. UN Doc E/PC/T/33.

1946b. *Official Journal*.

1993a. General Assembly. "Question of Equitable Representation on and Increase in the Membership of the Security Council." A/48/264.

1993b, November 23. General Assembly Provisional Verbatim Record of the 69th Meeting. A/47/PV.69.

1994. General Assembly Resolution. A/49/231.

2009, September. General Debate of the 64th Session 23–26 & 28–29, at http://www.un.org/en/ga/64/generaldebate/.

2013. *Democracy and the United Nations*, at http://www.un.org/en/globalissues/democracy/democracy_and_un.shtml.

United Nations Conference on International Organization. 1945. Documents, Volume XI, Commission III, Security Council, Washington, DC, Library of Congress.

United Nations General Assembly. 2005, July 12. Fifty-ninth Session, 112nd Plenary Meeting, A/59/PV.112.

United States Department of Justice. 2002. Memorandum from Jay Bybee, Assistant Attorney General, to Alberto Gonzales, Counsel to the President.

United States Department of State. 1945. *Postwar Foreign Policy Preparations, 1939–45*. Washington, DC: Government Printing Office.

1998. Saudi Arabia Country Report on Human Rights Practices for 1997, at http://www.state.gov/www/global/human_rights/1997_hrp_reports/saudi-ara.htm.

United States Senate. 1955, April 9. Hearing before a Subcommittee of the Committee on Foreign Relations, Eighty-Fourth Congress, Proposals to Amend or Otherwise Modify Existing International Peace and Security Organizations, Including the United Nations, Part 10.

1965, April 28, 29. Hearings before the Committee on Foreign Relations, Eighty-ninth Congress.

Van Belle, D. 2000. *Press Freedom and Global Politics*. Westport, CT: Praeger Publishers.

Van Den Bossche, Peter. 2010. "NGOs and WTO: Limits to Involvement?" In *Redesigning the World Trade Organization for the Twenty-First Century*. Debra P. Steger ed. Waterloo, Ontario: Wilfrid Laurier University Press, 248–289.

Van Eysinga, W. J. M. 1935. *La Commission centrale pour la navigation du Rhin: Historique*. Leyde: Société d'éditions A.W. Sijthoff.

Vattel, Emer de. 1916. *Le Droit des gens, ou principes de la loi naturelle appliqués à la conduite et aux affaires des nations et des souverains*. Washington, DC: Carnegie Institution of Washington.

Vincent, David. 1998. *The Culture of Secrecy: Britain, 1842–1998*. Oxford: Oxford University Press.

Vleugles, Roger. 2012, September 30. "Overview of all FOI Laws." *Fringe Special*, at http://freedominfo.org/documents/Fringe%20Special%20-%20Vleugels2012oct.pdf

von Freiesleben, Jonas. 2008. "Security Council Reform." In *Managing Change at the United Nations*. Estelle Perry ed. New York: Center for UN Reform, 1–20.

Wade, Robert H. 2011. "Boulevard of Broken Dreams: The Inside Story of the World Bank's Polonoroeste Road Project in Brazil's Amazon." Grantham Research Institute on Climate Change and the Environment Working

Paper No. 55, at http://www.lse.ac.uk/GranthamInstitute/wp-content/uploads/2014/02/WP55_world-bank-road-project-brazil.pdf

Walker, Barbara. 2003. "Selected Timeline – Events, Efforts and Ideas to Create Global Assemblies." In *A Reader on Second Assembly and Parliamentary Proposals*. Barbara Walker and Saul H. Mendlovitz eds. Wayne, NJ: Center for UN Reform Education, 136–144.

Walther, Henri. 1965. "Revision de la Convention de Mannheim Pour la Navigation du Rhin." *Annuaire Français de Droit International*, 11(1): 810–822.

Waltz, Kenneth. 1979. *Theory of International Politics*. Reading MA: Addison Wesley.

Webb, Richard E. 1950. "Commonwealth Parliamentary Council." *World Affairs*, 113(1): 6–8.

Webster, C. K., and Sydney Herbert. 1933. *The League of Nations in Theory and in Practice*. Boston, MA: Horton Mifflin.

Weiss, Thomas. 2003. "The Illusion of UN Security Council Reform." *Washington Quarterly*, 26(4):147–161.

Wells, S. B. 2007. *Pioneers of European Integration and Peace, 1945–1963: A Brief History with Documents*. Boston, MA: Bedford/St. Martin's.

Wendt, Alexander. 1987. "The Agent Structure Problem in International Relations." *International Organization*, 41(3): 335–370.

1995. "Constructing International Politics." *International Security*, 20(1): 71–81.

2001a. "Driving with the Rearview Mirror: On the Rational Science of Institutional Design." *International Organization*, 55(4): 1019–1049.

2001b. "A Comment on Held's Cosmopolitanism." In *Democracy's Edges*. Ian Shapiro and Casiano Hacker-Cordón eds. London: Cambridge University Press, 127–133.

West, Darrell. 2005. *Digital Government*. Princeton, NJ: Princeton University Press.

Westlake, Martin. 1994. *A Modern Guide to the European Parliament*. London: St. Martin's Press.

1998. "Maastricht, Edinburgh, Amsterdam: The End of the Beginning." In *Openness and Transparency in the European Union*. Veerle Deckmyn and Ian Thomson eds. Maastricht, the Netherlands: European Institute of Public Administration, 127–146.

Whelan, Daniel J., and Jack Donnelly. 2007. "The West, Economic and Social Rights, and the Global Human Rights Regime: Setting the Record Straight." *Human Rights Quarterly*, 29(4): 908–949.

White, Lyman Cromwell. 1951. *International Non-Governmental Organisations*. New Brunswick: Rutgers University Press.

Wiener, Antje. 2004. "Contested Compliance: Interventions on the Normative Structure of World Politics." *European Journal of International Relations*, 10(2): 189–234.

Wiener, Myron. 1998. "The Clash of Norms: Dilemmas in Refugee Policies." *Journal of Refugee Studies*, 11(4): 433–453.

Wight, Martin. 1960. "Why Is There No International Theory?" *International Relations*, 2: 35–48.

Wilcox, Francis O. 1945. "The Yalta Voting Formula." *American Political Science Review*, 39(5): 943–956.

Willetts, Peter. 2000. "From 'Consultative Arrangements' to 'Partnership': The Changing Status of NGOs in Diplomacy at the UN." *Global Governance*, 6 (2): 191–212.

2006. "The Cardoso Report on the UN and Civil Society: Functionalism, Global Corporatism, or Global Democracy." *Global Governance*, 12: 305–324.

2013. "What is a Non-Governmental Organization," at http://www.staff.city .ac.uk/p.willetts/NGOS/NGO-HOME.HTM#What

Williams, Marc. 2011. "Civil Society and the WTO: Contesting Accountability." In *Building Global Democracy: Civil Society and Accountable Global Governance*. Jan Aart Scholte ed. Cambridge, UK: Cambridge University Press, 105-127.

Winkelmann, Ingo. 1997. "Bringing the Security Council into a New Era." In *Max Planck Year Book of United Nations Law*. Volume I. Armin von Bogdandy and Rüdiger Wolfrum eds., at http://www.mpil.de/en/pub/research/details/ publications/institute/mpyunl/volume_1.cfm

Wolf, Martin. 1999, January 9. "Uncivil Society." *Financial Times*, p. 14.

Wood, Henry. 1926, February 26. Letter to Pierre Comert. League of Nations Archives. File 22/185.

Woods, Ngaire. 1999. "Good Governance in International Organizations." *Global Governance*, 5(1): 39–61.

2003. "Holding Intergovernmental Institutions to Account." *Ethics and International Affairs*, 17(1): 69–80.

Woods, Ngaire, and Amrita Narlikar. 2001. "Governance and the Limits of Accountability: The WTO, the IMF and the World Bank." *International Social Science Journal*, 170: 537–550.

World Bank. 1981. Central Projects Note 10.05 Involving Non-Governmental Organizations (NGOs) in the Preparation and Implementation of Bank-Financed Projects.

1994. *The World Bank Policy on Disclosure of Information*. Washington, DC: World Bank.

1998a. *The Bank's Relationship with NGOs*. Washington, DC: World Bank.

1998b. *Operational Manual: GP 14–70 – Involving Non-governmental Organizations in Bank-Supported Activities*. Washington, DC: World Bank.

2001. *World Bank & Civil Society Collaboration: Progress Report for Fiscal Years 2000 and 2001*. Washington, DC: World Bank.

2010. "Latin America Gets Greater Voice at World Bank after Voting Rights Increase" at http://go.worldbank.org/6RU60OUX40.

World Economic Forum. 2005, December 15. "Trust in Governments and Global Institutions Continues to Decline." Press Release, at http://www.weforum .org.

World Trade Organization. 1994. "Marrakesh Agreement Establishing the World Trade Organization," at http://www.wto.org/english/docs_e/legal_e/04-wto .pdf

1996, July 23. Guidelines for Arrangements on Relations with Non-Governmental Organizations. WTO Doc WT/L/162, at http://www .wto.org/english/forums_e/ngo_e/guide_e.htm.

1999. "10 Common Misunderstandings about the WTO," at http://depts.washington.edu/wtohist/Research/documents/WTOmisunderstandings.pdf.

2012. "Understanding the WTO: The Organization – Membership, Alliances and Bureaucracy," at http://wto.org/english/thewto_e/whatis_e/tif_e/org3_e .htm.

Young, Hugo. 1999. *This Blessed Plot: Britain and Europe from Churchill to Blair*. Woodstock, NY: Overlook Press.

Zakaria, Fareed. 1997. "The Rise of Illiberal Democracy." *Foreign Affairs*, 76(6): 22–43.

2003. *The Future of Freedom: Illiberal Democracy at Home and Abroad*. New York: W.W. Norton & Co.

Zarjevski, Yefime. 1989. *The People Have the Floor: A History of the Inter-parliamentary Union*. Dartmouth: Aldershot, Hants.

Zimmern, Alfred. 1936. *The League of Nations and the Rule of Law: 1918–1935*. London: MacMillan.

Zürn, Michael. 2000. "Democratic Governance beyond the Nation-State: The EU and Other International Institutions." *European Journal of International Relations*, 6: 183–221.

2004. "Global Governance and Legitimacy Problems." *Government and Opposition*, 39(2): 260–287.

Index

access to information legislation, 131–133, 149–150, 156, 165–168
accountability, 6–7, 10–11, 131, 135, 172, 179, 199–200, 222–223, 242, 280
  horizontal, 6–7, 222
  types of 6–7, 10–11
African Development Bank, 110, 113, 156
African Union, 117, 249
  Organization of African Unity, 150
analogies, domestic-international, 3, 6, 14, 14n5, 49–50, 55, 57, 62–63, 65, 68, 73, 76, 90–91, 97–98, 102, 107, 114, 118–119, 138, 157, 172, 175, 222, 240–241, 243, 252
Annan, Kofi, 250
Asian Development Bank, 155–156

Bank for International Settlements, 66, 101, 120
Barbosa, Ruy, 57
Belgium, 4, 54, 56, 60, 61, 66, 99, 109, 110n5, 127
Bevin, Ernest, 235–236
Boutros-Ghali, Boutros, 73
Brazil, 4, 57, 64, 73, 75, 100, 140, 153, 280
Bretton Woods Conference, 101, 103, 110, 145, 192
broadening strategy, 2, 31, 33–34, 39–40, 63, 64, 69, 70–71, 75, 76, 82, 83, 84, 109, 275–276
  of norm, 2, 31, 33–34, 70–71, 83, 84, 143, 148, 148, 206–210, 239, 244, 260, 276

of norm application 2, 31, 33–34, 37–38, 63, 64, 69, 82, 83, 84, 113, 114, 125, 126, 127, 197–198, 235, 236, 237, 259, 260, 261, 270, 273, 276

Canada, 66, 75, 196, 249
Caribbean Development Bank, 156
case selection, 17, 43–44
Cecil, Robert, 60, 230
Central Commission for the Navigation of the Rhine (CCNR), 58, 95–96, 98–99, 101
challenging strategy, 2, 31–32, 40, 269–272
  of norm, 2, 31, 62, 70, 83, 102, 107–108, 125–126, 180–181, 201, 218, 232, 241–242, 258–259
  of norm application 2, 35–36, 61, 67–68, 154, 200–201, 260
Checkel, Jeffrey, 19, 20, 29, 33, 46, 196
China, 68, 85–86, 87, 104, 105, 272, 281
civil society, 10, 151, 153, 160, 177–179, 194–195, 200, 201–211, 250
Commission of the Danube, 231
Commonwealth, 202, 234
  Commonwealth Parliamentary Council, 234, 235, 248
Concert of Europe, 28, 50, 51–56, 60, 75, 86, 92–95, 117, 128, 136–137, 174, 264, 278
  Congress of Vienna, 50, 51–54, 58, 93, 95
  French participation in, 52–53
  principle, great power, 52–53

Concert of Europe (*cont.*)
  rules compared to other international
    institutions, 52
  and Spain, 53
  state participation, 52–54
  and Talleyrand, 52–53
constructivism, 19–22, 33
corruption, 27, 34, 114, 193n5, 246
  norm of anti-corruption, 34, 158, 223
Council of Europe, 72, 109, 231, 234,
    235–237, 248–256, 259, 262
  and Churchill's role, 235
  Parliamentary Assembly, of the Council
    of Europe, 235–237

Dahl, Robert, 5, 7, 130, 280
decolonization, 70, 72, 207, 213, 233–234,
    265, 272
De Gaulle, Charles, 239, 241
democracy, global, 7–10, 277–280
  cosmopolitan model of, 8–9, 70, 83, 150
  vs. communitarian model, 8–9, 70, 93,
    107, 126, 150, 241, 247, 260
  and practitioners, 12–15
democracy, waves of, 16, 48, 61, 73, 278
democratic deficit, 4, 149, 201–202, 224,
    225, 243, 246, 273
  in the context of the IPU, 230
democratic density, 24
development, 34, 192–193
Drummond, Eric, 138–139
Dumbarton Oaks Conference, 104, 146

European Bank for Reconstruction and
    Development, 156
European Coal and Steel Community
    (ECSC)
  Common Assembly, 237–240
  NGO access, 191
  participation rules, 72
  transparency, 148
  voting rules, 109–110
European Economic Community
  Luxembourg Treaty, 242
  NGO access, 191
  parliamentary oversight, 238–246
  participation rules, 72
  Single European Act, 245, 258n12
  transparency, 148–150
  voting rules, 110
European Union (EU)
  Copenhagen criteria, 72

and corruption, 201–202, 246
Council of, 149, 161–163, 201, 246–247
  elections, direct 163, 238–245
European Commission, 149, 161–163,
    246–247
European Council, 244, 255, 260
European Court of Justice, 162, 176,
    191, 222, 243, 246
European Parliament, 149, 162,
    200–202, 246–247
European Transparency Initiative, 201
NGOs, relations with, 200–202
Ombudsman, 162, 176, 222, 246
qualified majority voting, 110, 119, 124,
    127, 128, 245, 261
Social Platform, 200–201
transparency, 161–163
Treaty of Amsterdam, 163
Treaty of Lisbon, 110, 124, 201, 247
Treaty of Maastricht, 161, 246,
    258n12, 261
Treaty of Nice, 110, 124, 247
exit strategy, 109, 128, 208–209

Finnemore, Martha, 1n1
Finnemore, Martha and Kathryn Sikkink,
    20, 21, 27, 46
Florini, Ann, 20, 20n1, 130, 131, 132,
    133, 134
Food and Agriculture Organization (FAO),
    156, 191, 232
Fosdick, Raymond B., 138–139
France, 52–53, 58, 59, 60, 68, 94, 95, 99,
    101, 104, 105, 106, 109, 127, 139,
    161, 235, 255
  and European Parliament, 239–240,
    241, 242, 244
Freedom House dataset, 132n2,
    178–179, 179n1

Germany, 61, 63–65, 69, 73, 99, 106, 109,
    127, 150, 206, 244
great power primacy, 49–50, 53, 62–63,
    65–66, 70, 82, 86, 102, 104, 108,
    109–110, 117, 126

Haas, Ernst, 130, 204
Hankey, Maurice, 137–139
Held, David, 7–9, 91
human rights
  and democracy, 6, 9, 11
  NGOs, 187–190

and strategies of defusing normative
    pressures, 32–33
hypotheses, 38–42

illiberal democracy, 10, 280
India, 14, 73, 75, 150, 153–154, 196,
    272, 280
Institute of Agriculture, 97, 99
Inter-American Development Bank, 110,
    113, 155
intergovernmental organizations
    and power, 3, 11, 19, 85–88, 280–281
    trends, democratic, 277–280
International Commission for Air
    Navigation, 66, 101
International Commission of the Elbe, 99
International Committee of the Red Cross,
    181, 186, 194–195
international conferences,
    Hague 50, 57, 181, 228, 229
    of nineteenth century, 56–57
    in UN system, 195, 197
International Court for Arbitration,
    57, 228
International Labor Organization (ILO)
    "employers' and workers' groups"
        independence, 202–209
        and Soviet position, 208–210
        and U.S. position, 207–210
        voting, 202, 203–204
    founding, 63, 144, 202
    Governing Body, 63–64, 65–66, 69–70,
        144–145, 205–210
    states of Chief Industrial Importance,
        63, 65–66, 69–70, 208–209
    state participation, 63–64, 65–66,
        68–71, 205–209
    transparency, 144–145, 168
    NGO access, 189–195
International Monetary Fund (IMF),
    44, 113
    and voting, 101–103, 110, 190, 192, 222
International Office of Chemistry, 101
International Renewable Energy
    Agency, 117
International Sugar Regime, 101, 181
International Telegraph Union, 58, 97
International Trade Organization, 198
International Wine Office, 101
Inter-parliamentary Union, 226–234
    and League of Nations, 230–232
    non-governmental character, 227, 233

origins, 226–228
and UN, 232–234
Interpol, 56, 156
Italy, 54, 59, 60, 65, 66, 70, 99, 100, 101,
    109, 127, 206

Japan, 60, 65, 66, 69, 73, 75, 101, 154,
    157, 160

Keohane, Robert O., 5, 6, 19
Keohane, Robert O. and Joseph S. Nye, 6,
    7, 130, 135, 159
Keynes, John Maynard, 102
Koenig-Archibugi, Mathias, 9
Krebs, Ronald R. and Patrick T. Jackson,
    21, 35, 272, 276

Lansing, Robert, 62
League of Nations
    and Abyssinia, 100
    Council
        state participation, 59–63, 76–77,
            143–144
        transparency, 137–144
        voting rules, 99–101
    Covenant, 59–63, 101, 182–184, 186,
        188, 230–231
    Information Section, 140–142
    International Bureaux Section, 182–184
    and IPU, 230–232
    NGO access, 182–187
    Permanent Court of International
        Justice, 141, 144n7, 230–231
legitimacy, 3, 30, 53, 115, 200, 239, 244–246
    crises of, 3, 157, 265, 274
    of NGOs, 200
Legro, Jeffrey, 20, 25
logics of action
    of appropriateness, 21, 32
    of communicative action, 35, 38
    of consequences, 21, 32, 38, 174

Miller, David Hunter, 60, 60n7
Moore, Mike, 199, 250

narrowing strategy, 2, 31, 270–271
    of norm, 2, 32, 33, 159–160
    of norm application, 2, 32, 36–38, 54,
        61, 63, 64, 74, 83, 84–85, 103–104,
        111, 114, 126–127, 155, 159, 161,
        196, 200, 202, 233, 236, 243, 246,
        251, 259, 261

NATO, 50, 72, 248
Nicolson, Harold, 53n3
non-governmental organizations
    access to IGOs, 180–202
    in European institutions, 191, 200–202
    in ILO, 189, 195
    independence, 179–181, 189–191
    in League, 182–187
    measurement of participation, 187,
        190, 204
    trends, domestic, 178–179
    in UN, 187–191, 194–198
    in World Bank, 191–194
    in WTO, 198–200, 218
normative pressure
    analogy to physics, 23
    changes to, 26–29
    definition, 22
    measurement, 24–26, 77–82, 119, 124,
        165–171, 214–215, 253–258,
        264–265
    strategies for defusing, 2, 38–39, 78–79,
        82–85, 122–123, 166–167, 171–
        173, 214–215, 216–219, 256–261,
        265–266
    withstanding, 22, 27–28, 29–30, 84,
        126, 127, 259, 265–266, 277
    yielding to, 30, 260, 263, 265–266
norms
    definition, 1n1
    interactions among, 32–33, 272, 275
    resonance, 20n1, 20–21, 33–34
    specificity of, 20, 21, 272, 276
    strength of, 25, 26, 77, 119–120,
        165–168, 211–212, 253
Nye, Joseph S., 4, 6, 30, 130, 135, 225

Organization of American States (OAS),
    59n6, 109, 156, 249
Organization for Economic Cooperation
    and Development (OECD),
    202, 236
Organization of Petroleum Exporting
    Countries, 90, 106n4

parliaments
    independence, 224, 238–244,
        258–260, 262
    oversight role, 222–223, 224–226,
        232–234, 242
    transnational, 226–251
    trends, national, 223–224

participation, 47–88
    of NGOs in IGOs, 177–202, 210–221
    states in European institutions, 72
    states in ILO, 63–64, 65–66, 69–71
    states in League, 59–63, 76–77,
        143–144
    states in UN, 67–69, 73–74, 84, 148,
        150–152
    states in World Bank, 71–72, 74–75
    states in WTO, 75
    trends, national, 48
persuasion, 21, 35, 35n4
Peyrefitte, Alain, 239–240, 241, 260
Political Institutions and Political Events
    dataset, 91
Polity dataset, 24, 48–49, 224, 253
power
    and IGO design, 3, 11, 19, 85–88,
        97–98, 99–100, 101–102, 104–108,
        120–121, 280
    and information, 130
    measure of, 11–112, 55–56, 85–87,
        120–121
    soft, 30
press, 102, 135–137, 140–141, 145
    correspondents, 140–141, 149
    freedom of, 131–132, 165
    role in League, 140–141
Prussia, 52, 58, 86, 98
public international unions, 58, 97, 137

realism, 19, 29, 85–88
Rittberger, Berthold, 20n1, 245, 247
rules in IGOs
    formal vs. informal, 28, 37, 74, 75,
        147–148, 151, 159, 164, 171, 219,
        278–279
Rusk, Dean, 68
Russia, 52, 56, 86, 136, 228–229, 281

Sardar Sarovar Dam project, 14, 153–154
scandals, 189–191, 201–202
    domestic, 157
    in IGOs 14, 27, 153–154, 157–158, 163,
        170–171, 246
sovereign equality norm, 49–50, 53, 55,
    66, 73, 76, 97, 104, 109, 126
sovereignty
    and democracy, 199, 218
    norm, 24, 32–33, 48–49, 92–93, 96, 125,
        181, 218
    and unanimity rules, 92–93, 95, 100

Soviet Union, 28n3, 61, 65, 66, 68, 71, 72,
    75, 87, 202, 205, 207, 210
Spain, 94
    and Concert of Europe, 52–53, 95
    and League of Nations, 4, 64
Sweden, 52, 95, 131, 150, 168n15
    and EU transparency, 162, 163, 176
Sweetser, Arthur, 104, 136, 138, 144

Tallberg, Jonas, Thomas Sommerer,
    Theresa Squatrito and Christer
    Jonsson, 6, 11, 30, 202, 203, 213,
    216, 220, 280
Transaccess dataset, 203, 213, 216
transparency
    definition, 130
    in European institutions, 148–150,
        161–163
    in ILO, 144–145, 168
    internal, 133–134, 159–160
    kinds of, 133–135
    in League, 137–144
    measure of, 142, 152
    trends, domestic, 131–133
        vs. international, 156–157
    in UN, 145–148, 150–153
    in World Bank, 145, 153–155, 164
    in WTO, 148, 158–161

UN Conference on International
    Organization, 13, 67, 106–108,
    146–147, 187–188
UNESCO, 44, 109, 109, 153, 185, 189
UNICEF, 189
Union for the Protection of Industrial
    and Literary and Artistic
    Property, 56, 97
United Kingdom, 51, 58n5, 86, 94–95, 99,
    101, 102, 105, 106, 107, 109,
    129, 137–139, 150, 161, 172,
    234, 244
    and Council of Europe, 235–236
United Nations (UN)
    Charter, 50, 66, 68, 101, 104–108,
        187–188, 196, 217
    Economic and Social Council, 69, 109,
        188–190, 195–197, 217–218
        and NGO status, 187–191, 194–198
    Food Conference, 145
    General Assembly, 67–68, 69, 73–74,
        109, 112, 115, 146, 233
        Budget Committee, 115

International Court of Justice, 68–69,
    109, 222
    reform proposals of, 74
    and IPU, 232–234
    NGO participation, 187–191, 194–198
    Oil-for-food Program, 14, 27, 158
    Pilot Peoples' Assembly, 250, 259
    and Roosevelt, 108, 145, 275n2
    Security Council
        Arria formula, 74, 151, 164, 171
        Open-Ended Working Group on
            reform, 151, 196–198
        P5, 67–68, 75, 87–88, 105–109, 113,
            126, 150–152
        participation of states, 67–69, 73–74,
            84, 148, 150–152
        transparency, 146–147, 150–153
        veto, 105–108, 118–119
    Trusteeship Council, 68, 109, 233
United States, 59–61, 87, 101, 102,
        103–104, 105, 107, 109, 111–112,
        113, 116, 121, 126, 138–139, 144,
        145, 154, 157, 168, 175–176,
        187–188, 196, 199, 206–209,
        220, 281
    Congress, 68, 116, 153–158, 176, 199
    and founding of League, 59–61
    and founding of World Bank, 101–102
    and Mine Ban Treaty, 37–38
    and UN Charter, 13, 14
    votes in World Bank, 111–112,
        120–121
Universal Postal Union, 58, 97, 99,
    109, 182
UN Population Fund, 189

Vattel, Emer de, 49, 50
voting
    in European institutions, 109–110,
        118, 127
    in ILO, 127
    in League, 99–101
    majority, 91–92, 97–98, 100, 106
    rules, informal, 96, 98, 115–116, 118,
        126–128
    trends, national, 90–92
    in UN, 104–109, 111–112, 115
    unanimity, 91–92, 93–100, 115–117
    weighted, 98–99, 101–103,
        101–110, 111
    in World Bank, 101–103, 110–116
    in WTO, 115–117

Wendt, Alexander, 3, 20, 22, 274
Wilson, Woodrow, 59–62, 70, 135, 137, 137n3
Wolfowitz, Paul, 27, 158
World Bank
    Board of Directors, 37, 71–72, 81, 84,
        154–155, 164, 174, 194
    Board of Governors, 71, 194
    International Development Association,
        110–111
    Multilateral Investment Guarantee
        Agency, 111
    and NGO participation, 191–194
    Parliamentary Network on the, 251,
        252, 259
    participation of states, 71–72, 74–75
    transparency, 145, 153–155, 164
    and US Congress, 153–155
    and US vote, 111–112, 120–121
    voting, 101–103, 110–116

World Commission on Dams, 193, 220
World Federalist Movement, 250
World Health Organization (WHO),
        44–45, 109
World Meteorological Organization,
        157–158
World Trade Organization (WTO)
    Green Room, 75, 80, 85, 133, 159
    NGO access, 198–200, 218
    and parliamentary assembly, 250
    Quad, 75
    and Seattle Riots, 158, 160, 171, 199
    state participation, 75
    transparency, 148, 158–161
    and US Congress, 116–117, 158, 199
    voting, 115–117
Württemberg, King of, 55

Zürn, Michael, 3